POLITICS IN THE NEW HARD TIMES

A volume in the series
Cornell Studies in Political Economy
Edited by Peter J. Katzenstein

A list of titles in this series is available at
www.cornellpress.cornell.edu.

POLITICS IN THE NEW HARD TIMES

The Great Recession in Comparative Perspective

Edited by Miles Kahler and David A. Lake

CORNELL UNIVERSITY PRESS ITHACA AND LONDON

First published 2013 by Cornell University Press

First printing, Cornell Paperbacks, 2013
Printed in the United States of America

Library of Congress Cataloging-in-Publication Data

Politics in the new hard times : the great recession in comparative perspective / edited by Miles Kahler and David A. Lake.
p. cm. — (Cornell studies in political economy)
Includes bibliographical references and index.
ISBN 978-0-8014-5151-5 (cloth : alk. paper)
ISBN 978-0-8014-7827-7 (pbk. : alk. paper)
1. Global Financial Crisis, 2008–2009—Political aspects. 2. World politics—2005–2015. 3. International economic relations—Political aspects. I. Kahler, Miles, 1949– II. Lake, David A., 1956– III. Series: Cornell studies in political economy.

HB37172008 .P65 2013
330.9'0511—dc23 2012033983

Cornell University Press strives to use environmentally responsible suppliers and materials to the fullest extent possible in the publishing of its books. Such materials include vegetable-based, low-VOC inks and acid-free papers that are recycled, totally chlorine-free, or partly composed of nonwood fibers. For further information, visit our website at www.cornellpress.cornell.edu.

Cloth printing 10 9 8 7 6 5 4 3 2 1
Paperback printing 10 9 8 7 6 5 4 3 2 1

To Peter Gourevitch
Scholar, Colleague, Friend

Contents

Illustrations

Figures

Tables

Preface

Politics in the New Hard Times is the result of both misfortune and good fortune. The misfortune—a very large and collective misfortune—was the Great Recession, a global economic crisis that has upended lives, erased vast amounts of wealth, and called into question many assumptions of the previous era of globalization, deregulation, and macroeconomic stability. The great good fortune is personal: our long-standing friendship with our colleague Peter Gourevitch. When we asked Peter if we might honor his career, he responded with his characteristic modesty and intellectual curiosity. Rather than a standard Festschrift, full of panegyrics and recycled scholarship, he asked for a research conference on the economic downturn that was affecting our university, our country, and our world.

We set out to satisfy Peter's request, and we quickly discovered that assembling a world-class group of scholars to investigate the political causes and consequences of the Great Recession was remarkably easy, given Peter's academic reputation and collegiality. When we issued invitations for the first conference in the project in early 2010, every invited participant responded positively; the only exceptions were those with unavoidable and unbreakable prior commitments. We wish to thank not only the authors who appear in this volume but also the other participants in the project, whose written contributions and commentary on earlier drafts of these papers have improved the final publication immeasurably: Gordon Hanson, G. Mark Hendrickson, Takeo Hoshi, Robert O. Keohane, Stephen D. Krasner, Ronald Rogowski, Sebastian Saiegh, Beth Simmons, David Soskice, and David Victor.

We are particularly grateful to Peter Cowhey, dean of the Graduate School of International Relations and Pacific Studies (IR/PS), who not only took time from his busy schedule to craft a chapter for this volume but also contributed the financial resources that made the project possible. We also wish to acknowledge the Institute for International, Comparative, and Area Studies, the Rohr Chair for Pacific International Relations, and the Jerri-Ann and Gary E. Jacobs Chair of Social Sciences for additional funding in support of the project. Derek Brendel, of the Center on Pacific Economies at IR/PS, provided superb staff support for both of the conferences that produced this volume. Lynne Bush of the University of California Institute on Global Conflict and Cooperation contributed her excellent editorial skills, as she has to so many other publications in the past.

With the publication of this book, we wish that we could also bid farewell to the Great Recession and the economic hardship that it brought to so many citizens of so many countries. Unfortunately, as we write this preface, the latest European and International Monetary Fund program for Greece still hangs in the balance, and economic recovery in United States remains under threat. The economic and political consequences of the Great Recession will remain with us for years to come; this volume is our contribution to understanding that event.

Miles Kahler and David A. Lake
La Jolla, California

Introduction

ANATOMY OF CRISIS

The Great Recession and Political Change

Miles Kahler and David A. Lake

The Great Recession that began in December 2007 is the worst economic crisis to beset the world economy since the Great Depression of the 1930s.[1] In contrast with most financial crises since 1945, the Great Recession began at the developed center of the world economy, and the industrialized countries were both the most seriously affected and slowest to recover. Although parts of the developing world that were dependent on trade with the industrialized countries experienced sharp recessions, the largest emerging markets—China, India, Indonesia, and Brazil—experienced only brief inflections in their high rates of growth. This variation persisted into a shaky global economic recovery. On a measure of real gross domestic product (GDP) per capita, by mid-2011 only a handful of industrialized economies, including Germany and resource-rich Australia, had surpassed their pre-recession levels. The United States, the United Kingdom, and Japan lagged well behind. Those European economies that were entangled in sovereign debt crises—Greece, Ireland, and Portugal—remained mired in deep economic downturns.[2] Fear remains that the crisis of the Eurozone, the largest aftershock of the economic earthquake of 2008–9, could produce another global recession deeper

1. Reinhart and Rogoff (2009, 208), who label the crisis "the Second Great Contraction," offer a typical assessment: this crisis "stands as the most serious global financial crisis since the Great Depression."

2. "Checking the Depth Gauge," *Economist*, August 20, 2011, http://www.economist.com/node/21526392.

than the last.[3] At the same time, emerging economies, such as Argentina, Indonesia, and Poland, had rapidly returned to growth, and GDP per capita now surpasses pre-crisis figures by more than 10 percent. Variation in how the Great Recession was experienced around the world is as important substantively and analytically as the recession itself.

Economic explanations for the Great Recession have proliferated, divided between microeconomic accounts that focus on deregulation and macroeconomic perspectives that attribute the crisis to fiscal and current account deficits in the United States and other indebted industrialized countries. The political causes and consequences of the economic crisis have received less systematic attention. This volume aims to correct that deficit in political analysis and explanation. The political consequences of the Great Recession remain uncertain. Some early predictions—a permanent expansion of the regulatory role of the state, an eruption in international economic conflict—now seem seriously overdrawn. Despite its negative effects on incumbent governments, the economic crisis has provided few signs of fundamental political realignment, policy experimentation (apart from central banks), or mobilization by new political actors in any of the most seriously affected economies. In the global economic order, rampant economic nationalism or serious erosion of international collaboration have not emerged. Although backlash against increased government spending and rising levels of debt is real in the United States and the United Kingdom, this severe economic crisis has to date failed to produce political change on the scale of the New Deal or the collapse of the Weimar Republic. The most striking contemporary example of political contagion—the Arab Spring and its demands for democratization—cannot be linked directly to the Great Recession.

In investigating the Great Recession as a political crisis, we are able to draw on both a rich literature in economics on the crisis and also a line of research in political economy begun by Peter Gourevitch (1986). At the same time, we revisit and revise earlier accounts in two key respects. First, we reconstruct crisis as a variable rather than as an undifferentiated and exogenous shock. Variations in the causes and consequences of crises have political significance. That the Great Recession was centered in the United States and Europe, for instance, has undermined the so-called Washington consensus supporting neoliberalism and may propel future policies toward the financial sector. Second, we do not assume that economic and political interests are fixed. Instead, we explore the definition and redefinition of interests in conditions of crisis. Variation occurs here as well: not all crises produce such redefinition, and the mechanisms by which interests are

3. IMF Economic Counsellor Olivier Blanchard warned in January 2012 that if the European crisis intensified, "the world could be plunged into another recession." http://www.imf.org/external/pubs/ft/survey/so/2012/NEW012412A.htm.

redefined in the context of crisis have not been adequately explored. Together, we develop a view of crises as endogenous events both caused and mediated by past political decisions that reshape how political actors understand and pursue their interests and, thus, how their political consequences unfold.

We begin with an account of the Great Recession as an economic crisis, highlighting the implicit political arguments that are embedded in explanations offered by economists. Next, using Gourevitch (1986) as a benchmark, we consider the Great Recession as a political crisis, one that originates in political dynamics and may yet produce definable political effects. Two central concepts, crisis and interests, are then reexamined in light of periods of past economic turmoil and the experience of the Great Recession. Finally, we introduce the authors' contributions, which use a comparative perspective to investigate the linked issues of the political sources of crisis and interest redefinition during these seismic economic events.

The Great Recession: A Crisis Unfolds and Persists

Economic and journalistic accounts of the Great Recession have reached broad agreement on its essential contours. A major real estate bubble in the United States and several European economies (United Kingdom, Ireland, Spain) began to deflate in 2006–7, creating stress on the financial systems of those countries and sending the U.S. economy into recession. At this point, the crisis might have remained an unusually widespread but sectorally isolated event with financial consequences comparable to the U.S. savings and loan crisis of the late 1980s. In the intervening decades, however, financial innovation and globalization meant that large and tightly linked financial institutions were placed at risk by their holdings of mortgage-backed securities and derivatives based on those securities. In March 2008, the forced sale of Bear Stearns, an investment bank heavily involved in subprime mortgage-backed securities, signaled the wider financial implications of the real estate downturn. The financial crisis had become a transatlantic one, in which major financial institutions in both the United States and Europe were threatened.

The bankruptcy of Lehman Brothers, one of the oldest investment banks on Wall Street, on September 15, 2008, signaled the onset of a global financial crisis. Preceded by the nationalization of Fannie Mae and Freddie Mac, a sign of deepening distress in U.S. mortgage markets, and succeeded by the takeover, by government or other financial institutions, of the American International Group (AIG), Merrill Lynch, Washington Mutual, and Wachovia, as well as government assistance to major European banks, a financial panic ensued. Many shadow banking markets, inflated during the boom, essentially froze. This heightening of the crisis—with the risk of worldwide financial collapse—produced dramatic government responses, first by central banks and finance ministries (the U.S. Troubled Assets Relief Program was a prime example), and later in the form of large-scale fiscal support by national governments. Those responses could not prevent a deepening of the recession and its spread, with unemployment sharply increasing in many of the major industrialized economies. Finally, the crisis, through its effects on global demand and trade finance, produced a rapid decline in the volume of world trade, amplified by the new organization of trade through networks centered on Asia. Even economies, such as China, that were not deeply integrated into the global financial system, were affected through the trade link (Baldwin 2009).

The acute phase of the crisis appeared to end in mid-2009, as global production began to recover and financial systems stabilized. Although the world economy had been headed on a downward path that was steeper than the start of the Great Depression, government countermeasures had averted an outcome as severe as the prolonged slump of the 1930s (Eichengreen and O'Rourke 2010). By 2011, world output and trade had exceeded pre-recession levels, but divergent patterns of recovery from the recession characterized both the industrialized and emerging economies. Germany and northern Europe returned to relatively high levels of export-led growth. In the United States, Japan, and other European economies, slow growth has made the economic recovery barely perceptible to many. Unemployment, which crested at 10.1 percent in the United States in October 2009, had fallen only to 8.3 percent in early 2012; job growth remains sluggish for a post-recession economy.[4] Household wealth in the United States, which peaked in the second quarter of 2007 at $64.4 trillion, had, by the first quarter of 2009, fallen by $14 trillion to $50.4 trillion—a startling 21.7 percent decline.[5] Some now predict a "lost decade" or more for the United States, similar to Japan's experience since the 1990s (Chinn and Frieden 2011).

Among the emerging economies, as described by Stephan Haggard (chapter 2, this volume), the largest Asian emerging economies did not experience a recession and quickly returned to robust economic growth; Latin America, in contrast to its record in recent crises, recovered quickly from a brief economic downturn. With some exceptions, eastern Europe, more financially connected to the industrialized world, suffered a sharper decline in growth and a weaker recovery.

4. http://data.bls.gov/cgi-bin/surveymost.

5. http://money.cnn.com/2009/06/11/news/economy/Americans_wealth_drops/?postversion=2009061113.

This uneven global economic recovery was threatened by a major aftershock from the Great Recession's earthquake: a crisis centered on sovereign debt in the Eurozone that began in 2010. The indebtedness of Greece touched off the crisis: as it became clear that sovereign debt issued by countries in the Eurozone might be subject to restructuring or default, financial contagion spread to other, much larger economies, such as Italy and Spain. The crisis was marked by efforts on the part of the European Union and the International Monetary Fund (IMF) to shore up finances in Greece and other counties at risk, but those efforts were uniformly perceived by the financial markets as too little and too late. The crisis revealed a design flaw in the Economic and Monetary Union, weak European control over fiscal policy in member states, a flaw that the EU moved to correct in late 2011. A second weakness was the gap in competitiveness between northern Europe and Mediterranean Europe, a gap that could be corrected in a currency union only through harsh measures to restrain wages and curb government spending. Most worrying, however, was a link to the earlier global financial crisis: the exposure of European banks to the sovereign debt of their governments.[6] That exposure threatened to produce a replay of the earlier financial panic in 2008, a threat temporarily reduced by measures taken by the European Central Bank in December 2011. At the same time, pressures for fiscal consolidation—driven by domestic politics and financial markets—threatened to tip Europe, the largest region in the world economy, back into recession. Involvement by the IMF symbolized global interest in a resolution of the European debt crisis, but actors outside the region had neither the levers nor the resources to influence Europe's choices. In a technical sense, the Great Recession was over, but its lingering effects continued to place global economic prosperity at risk.

The Great Recession as an Economic Crisis

Economists have provided two contrasting explanations of the Great Recession. The macroeconomic view embeds the Great Recession in a long series of debt-induced financial crises that have occurred with increasing regularity as financial liberalization has advanced. Despite the scale of the crisis that began with the U.S. mortgage meltdown, "this time is not different."[7] From this perspective, a major culprit in the financial crisis is the current account deficit of the United

6. Jacob Funk Kirkegaard, "The Euro Area Crisis: Origin, Current Status, and European and US Responses," Testimony before the U.S. House Committee on Foreign Affairs Subcommittee on Europe and Eurasia, October 27, 2011, http://www.iie.com/publications/interstitial.cfm?ResearchID=1969.

7. Reinhart and Rogoff (2009) are the best representatives of this view. Chinn and Frieden (2011) place the United States in the company of previous debtors in the developing world.

States and other heavily indebted developed countries, financed by capital inflows. Those inflows in turn fuel speculative bubbles in nontradable assets, such as real estate, and encourage buildup of consumer debt. As the bubbles deflate, the risk of financial crisis soars.

A second view, with resonance in the media and public debate, emphasizes the unique microeconomic characteristics of this crisis. Although the industrialized world has had financial and currency crises since 1970, none have had repercussions as widespread as the Great Recession, the first crisis since the Great Depression to originate at the core of the world economy in the financial systems in the United States and Europe. These analysts have concentrated on the United States and its policy and political failings in their explanations for the crisis and their recommendations for crisis prevention.[8] In these models of the crisis, growing political influence on the part of an expanding financial sector leads to financial deregulation and increasingly risky behavior by banks and shadow banking institutions in global financial centers. Iceland was the most extreme case of a failed financial center that rose rapidly through reliance on deregulated global financial markets and then crashed.

A counterpart microeconomic account explains the surprising resilience of the developing world during the crisis. Open economies that were integrated into global manufacturing supply chains faced sharp drops in economic activity (Taiwan, South Korea) and speedy recoveries; others, particularly in east and central Europe, suffered from the withdrawal of international credit. The large emerging economies, however—China, India, Brazil, and Indonesia—experienced few financial costs and no financial crises because of their better-regulated financial systems (the product of earlier crises) and capital controls that limited their links to global finance.

These explanations of the Great Recession have competed for scholarly and public attention. Surprisingly little effort has been made to evaluate necessary and sufficient causes by examining counterfactuals rigorously: why did the U.S. real estate boom result in a crisis of this severity rather than a replay of the savings and loan crisis? Why did economies in Europe that lacked the American array of exotic financial instruments still experience their own bubbles and subsequent financial crashes? Too often, every possible variable is given a role, if not a starring role.[9] Even within accepted narratives of the crisis, the relative roles of government policies (or absence of same, in the case of regulation), financial

8. Rajan (2010) emphasizes the United States and the sources of its financial fragility to the exclusion of other affected countries. As Krugman and Wells (2010) note, many of the explanations derived from the American experience do not travel well to other cases of "bubble and bust" economies in Europe.

9. An example of this approach is Roubini and Mihm (2010).

innovation, and macroeconomic imbalances are assessed differently. For example, relative culpability for the U.S. housing boom and bust has been vigorously contested, with Rajan's (2010) emphasis on U.S. government policies to support home ownership by low-income buyers pitted against claims that private mortgage lenders were most responsible (Krugman and Wells 2010).

Despite ongoing disagreements, however, two explanatory threads link these accounts of the Great Recession as an economic crisis. One, which we use as well, is a geological metaphor, the crisis as earthquake. Rajan (2010) titles his book *Fault Lines*; Roubini and Mihm (2010) label one chapter, "Plate Tectonics." The earthquake metaphor captures structural features in the world economy that increased the risk of debt-driven crisis and a sudden shock triggered by a decline in asset prices or loss of confidence by market participants. Although this metaphor is useful in considering the meaning of crisis and its implications, it is rarely exploited for that purpose in these accounts. Which "fault lines" are most likely to result in financial crises? Are there many structural roads to crisis or only a few? Can preventive measures that deal with the short-term causes of crisis, such as regulatory reform, be swamped by structural features, such as a "global savings glut"?

A second link among these accounts is their reference to political variables in explanations of the Great Recession. Underlying descriptions of plate tectonics in the global economy are political dynamics, at times clearly specified, at times not. In the years before the Great Recession, persistent global macroeconomic imbalances were deeply rooted in the export orientation of Asian economies and lessons learned from the Asian financial crisis (self-insurance through reserves rather than reliance on the IMF). Persistent deficit countries—not limited to the United States—display their own political syndromes. Explanations at this level are often closely connected to the rich literature on varieties of capitalism. Rajan (2010), for example, links the U.S. tendency to use fiscal and monetary policies that produce one bubble after another to the peculiarities of American capitalism, particularly its limited social safety net.

Politics also enters prominently in any explanation of cycles of regulation and deregulation. Roubini and Mihm (2010) note the development of an underregulated shadow banking system as a key element in the U.S. financial crisis. The underregulation of this sector and the weakening of other financial regulations often appear to be an inevitable consequence of the bubble environment in his account. Johnson and Kwak (2010), on the other hand, attribute deregulation to the hegemonic political influence of the financial sector in the United States. The political power of entrenched ideas, such as a belief in the stability of financial markets, is also mobilized to explain the now-obvious gaps in regulatory oversight. Although united by a focus on the political economy of the crisis, each approach implies different strategies for reform. In all of these accounts of the Great

Recession as economic crisis, however, the role of politics—and the political consequences of the crisis—remains largely in the background.

The Great Recession as a Political Crisis

The point of departure for any systematic examination of the political dimensions of economic crises is Peter Gourevitch's *Politics in Hard Times* (1986). In this landmark study, Gourevitch treats crises as a common exogenous shock with three properties: a major downturn in the business cycle, a major change in the geographic distribution of production, and a significant growth in new products and production processes (1986, 20). He then explains variations in the choices made by political leaders in response to crises by five factors: the policy preferences of societal actors as determined by their respective positions in the international economy (their "production profile"), intermediate associations that link societal actors to the state, the structure of the state that governs decision making in government, economic ideology or models of the political economy that guide actors, and finally, the international system of political-military rivalries. For Gourevitch, crises are both causal, with "lean years" being "times when old relationships crumble and new ones have to be constructed" (9), and laboratories in which politics are more fluid and the effects of other factors are more easily observed (22). In all cases, the economic interests of various societal actors are fundamental, although economic interests became muted over time as politics were institutionalized.

As suggested by the title of this volume, *Politics in Hard Times* remains central to an analysis of the politics of economic crises. The years since its publication, however, and the experience of the Great Recession have led to reconsideration and revision of two of its central premises. First, for Gourevitch, crises are exogenous; the Great Recession, however, makes clear that crises are at least partly endogenous, the product of past political coalitions and policies. As Gourevitch recognizes in the final chapter, one consequence of neoliberalism in the 1980s and 1990s was rapid growth in the financial services sector in most developed countries and a concomitant increase in its political influence over policies of liberalization and deregulation. Those policies, in turn, exacerbated the bubble created by government fiscal and current account deficits by permitting banks and other financial institutions to assume greater risk. The financial crash of 2008 that turned ordinary recession into near-disaster was not independent of these earlier policy choices. The neoliberalism of preceding decades set the stage for the current crisis.

Second, the policy preferences of political actors are often more complex and less predictable than their economic positions would predict, particularly during crises. For Gourevitch, intermediate associations, state structure, and ideology mediate the translation of sectorally defined policy preferences into politics and policy. As politics becomes more institutionalized, the independent effects of these policy drivers become harder to distinguish, rendering generalizations and predictions contingent and difficult. Suzanne Berger argues in chapter 6 that even in earlier financial crises, economic interest cannot be identified separately from prior mediating institutions and ideologies. Megumi Naoi and Ikuo Kume (chapter 8) show in a contemporary setting that economic interests are influenced by self-identification of individuals as producers or consumers. Peter Cowhey (chapter 9) demonstrates that structural change in the U.S. economy has made old readings of trade policy interests, rooted in simple sectoral analysis, increasingly obsolete. The indeterminate nature of economic interests, moreover, is likely to be magnified during crises, which are associated with higher degrees of uncertainty. Less able to identify future coalitions and policies, actors are more likely to define their preferences and formulate their strategies in terms of broader, socially constructed ideologies and ideas (Katzenstein and Nelson, chapter 10). In contrast to older maps of economic interests, a more complex and contingent theory of interest formation during crises is required.

Treating crises as undifferentiated and exogenous shocks is unlikely to lead to a clearer understanding of either their political causes or their political consequences. Regarding political and policy preferences as easily predicted on the basis of clearly defined economic interests may also be misleading. We turn to each of these critical concepts in turn, in an effort to build a political theory of economic crises and their outcomes.

Crisis and Political Change

For social scientists, crisis has too often served as an undifferentiated deus ex machina, a convenient explanation for otherwise unexplained changes. The concept of crisis, though frequently invoked in discussions of the Great Recession (see Rajan 2010; Roubini and Mihm 2010), is undertheorized. Most important, although often treated as a homogenous class, crises themselves vary in important ways that may condition their effects. We begin with a review of the concept of crisis and how it is used to draw out possible dimensions of variation. We then turn to the ways in which crises can influence the definition and redefinition of interests.

Crisis as Concept

A crisis is typically defined in one of two ways. In one meaning, a crisis is an unstable situation of extreme danger or difficulty. This conception is applied most often to international security crises, such as the Cuban missile crisis, and to severe financial crises, such as bank runs or the freezing of credit markets that occurred in late 2008. Crisis instability has three characteristics.[10] First, crisis begins in a triggering event, a surprising outcome that, for a defined group of actors, lies outside normal expectations. The failure of Lehman Brothers, a venerable Wall Street institution, was the trigger for the financial crisis. Second, crisis entails a significant threat to core values, the prospect of a catastrophically negative outcome.[11] Following the bankruptcy of Lehman Brothers, for instance, government policymakers and other analysts believed that a meltdown of the global financial system was possible and that such an event would likely produce a major depression. Third, actors perceive that the time for remedial action to avoid the threat is highly compressed. In March 2008, the Federal Reserve was informed that Bear Stearns was on the brink of bankruptcy and responded overnight with a $14 billion loan; when even this loan proved insufficient, Timothy Geithner, then president of the Federal Reserve Bank of New York, and Secretary of the Treasury Henry Paulson concluded that they had only the weekend to devise a solution to the investment bank's imminent failure (Wessel 2009, 157–58, 164).

These characteristics of crises produce greater than usual uncertainty about the causes and consequences of action.[12] During a crisis, the existing model of cause and effect used by actors is called into question by the occurrence of events that "should not have happened." Encountering a flock of "black swans"—in the case of the Great Recession, a series of extreme financial events occurring in 2007–8 with a frequency that was not predicted by analysts or their models—causes actors to suddenly doubt their prior understanding of how the world works.[13] In turn, the significant threat to core values and the need for quick action preclude the development of a new understanding of the world or even a studied and considered response. The pace of events forces the hands of key decision makers who must rely on their "gut" reactions and intuitions. They may also turn to novel courses of action that were, prior to the crisis, not part of the accepted politi-

10. The standard characteristics of a crisis were originally defined by Hermann (1963) in the context of international security disputes. His criteria are refined and generalized by Billings et al. (1980). See also Phillips and Rimkunas (1978).

11. The magnitude of the threat is a combination of the value itself and the probability of its loss.

12. On uncertainty as a defining characteristic of crises, see Katzenstein and Nelson (chapter 10, this volume). See also Frieden et al. (2011).

13. Of course, a key argument of Reinhart and Rogoff (2009) is that financial crises have been very likely in the wake of debt-driven expansions: not black swans at all. The events of 2007–8 were also predicted by a number of economists, as detailed by Roubini and Mihm (2010) and others.

cal repertoire. The Troubled Assets Relief Program would have been unthinkable for a Republican administration in circumstances other than those of September to October 2008; the Federal Reserve's innovations throughout the crisis were also dependent on the heightened sense of risk attached to inaction or conventional prescriptions.

A second, alternative definition of crisis is a turning point. In politics, crises in this sense might be major political realignments spurred by the collapse of an ancien regime (Capoccia and Keleman 2007). The collapse can be the product of challenges to the existing order, as in the structural-functional approach (Binder 1971; Almond, Flanagan, and Mundt 1973), new party configurations (Key 1955; Nardulli 1995), or changes in the international division of labor driven by new technologies and geographies of production, as for Gourevitch (1986). Analytically, these turning points are most often defined by the political outcome and are recognized and appreciated only in retrospect. Crisis in this second sense is defined by the significance of the outcome, not the risk of an unexpected, negative change. A turning point may entail a widening of policy options, induced by the triggering event. Redefinition of interests may occur, and subsequently, a realignment of political coalitions. Viewed through a longer-term lens, new institutional "fixes" may have important long-run consequences: the Reciprocal Trade Agreements Act, a relatively minor element of the New Deal, provided the basis for unwinding the initial protectionist response to the Great Depression in the United States. Crisis may imply ideational innovation, although typically the helter-skelter grasping at solutions during the peak of a crisis is only rationalized after the fact, if at all. Finally, crisis may occur at the level of regime: the Great Depression is generally related directly to the failure of the Weimar Republic, and its economic effects undermined the legitimacy of many other apparently ineffectual regimes.

Crisis in this second sense of a turning point is often *not* compressed in time. Two notable examples, in addition to Gourevitch (1986), give decades-long time spans to their crises: Arthur M. Schlesinger Jr.'s classic history of the New Deal (*The Crisis of the Old Order, 1919–1933*) and E. H. Carr's equally influential meditation on the interwar international order (*The Twenty Years' Crisis, 1919–1939*). The Great Recession was certainly a crisis in the first sense. It may or may not be a crisis in this second sense, a question that recurs throughout this volume.

Although typically distinct in the literature, most crises carry both meanings: a situation in which decisions are forced in the face of extreme danger and short time horizons and a turning point in politics or policy. On this point, the geological metaphor of earthquakes, already deployed by economists, is useful. Physical damage and some loss of life occurs as a result of the temblor—the shaking that occurs as tension is released along a fault line—and additional lives are lost in the aftermath as societies are often poorly equipped to deal with the ensuing humanitarian crisis. But the quake itself—the trigger event—cannot be separated from the slow, incremental movements of the earth's tectonic plates that produce built-up energy that must eventually be released. The earthquake—the triggering event in a crisis—is not entirely predictable, but its likelihood and location may be estimated. Yet, over time, the underlying movements of the tectonic plates that comprise the earth's crust can create mountains, move continents, and even alter the rotation of the earth. In this sense, earthquakes are only the manifestation of these underlying movements and the process through which major shifts occur.

Political crises typically share the qualities of both decision-forcing events and inflections in longer-term trajectories. In the Cuban missile crisis—the exemplar of an international crisis—most analysts focus on the thirteen days between the discovery of Soviet missiles sites being built in Cuba and the turnaround of the Soviet freighters carrying the missiles to be installed (Allison 1971). Yet, this event—the trigger—carries meaning only in the larger context of the superpower competition between the United States and Soviet Union, the stepped-up efforts by the Kennedy administration to respond to the nonexistent "missile gap" with Moscow, and the Soviet Union's fear of falling behind in a renewed arms race. Although the placement of missiles on Cuba was indeed a surprise, it had been preceded by a series of disputes between the two superpowers, in Berlin and elsewhere. Another crisis was hardly unlikely, but its level of danger and its location could not be predicted accurately. The Cuban missile crisis is also recalled, however, for its injection of caution and even collaboration into a dangerous rivalry. The Nuclear Test Ban Treaty succeeded a crisis fraught with peril. In similar fashion, the bankruptcy of Lehman Brothers and subsequent bailout of the U.S. banking system—trigger events for the most dangerous phase of the Great Recession—are intimately and inextricably tied to the macroeconomic imbalances that had accumulated over decades and the long-standing current account deficits (Chinn and Frieden 2011). Triggers assume meaning only as a result of underlying changes, but in the absence of such shocks to a system we observe only the incremental change of normal politics.

Crisis as Explanation

How are these contending views of crisis related as explanations for political change? Does an economic crisis in the first sense merely illuminate more profound changes in politics and society, or do financial and economic crises trigger those changes? Is it possible to identify crises (under either definition) that are more or less likely to have identifiable political consequences? These relations are further complicated by the controversial character of the key fault lines at any point in time: did the Great Recession reveal the inadequacies of a cycle of deregulation stretching back decades or the perils of government-produced moral hazard (the "Greenspan put")? Did politicians and their response to electoral demands drive the macroeconomics of the boom or were central bankers blind to the dangers of asset and property bubbles?

As explanatory devices, crises are used in three ways, which may be complementary. Crises may be treated as *exogenous shocks*—whether periodic or not—from which societies recover. This view of the Great Recession was pushed by financial executives themselves, as witnessed in the testimony of Wall Street chief executive officers before Congress; the financial crisis was portrayed as a "tsunami" or freak of nature that could not be predicted and was not the responsibility of any agent or agents. As an explanation, crises as exogenous shocks are usually understood to ignite a process of reaction and possibly political change but do little to explain the direction or type of change.

A long-standing line of research in the political economy of development has investigated the effects of exogenous international shocks—declines or surges in commodity prices, interest rate increases on international debt, abrupt stops to capital flows—that plunge economies into economic turmoil.[14] As for Gourevitch (1986), the political and policy consequences of such shocks were necessarily mediated through domestic variables that could produce differences in the timing and content of responses. The Latin American debt crisis of the 1980s, for example, uniformly produced initial stabilization programs; no governments chose the default and delinking strategies that were characteristic of the 1930s. On the other hand, market-oriented structural reforms were often delayed and at times followed attempts at heterodox economic policy packages. An economic shock may undermine the old policy regime, but precisely because it is exogenous and outside of normal political processes, it may have no predictable effect on the outcome of the ensuing political struggle. A purely exogenous treatment of crisis therefore begs the question of explanation and often serves political purposes—obscuring an investigation of the causes of crisis.

For others, crises are *epiphenomenal*, especially for scholars who define them as crucial turning points. In this often-dialectical view, crises and especially trigger events are a product of internal economic and political developments, but they are not in themselves a causal force. The shaking of the earth has no independent effect beyond its manifestation of shifting tectonic plates. As epiphenomena, crises may open politics and policy to new alternatives, but they do not directly influence the direction of subsequent change. This view, for instance, is shared by

14. For one early example, see Nelson (1990).

those who locate the causes of the Great Recession not in the financial crisis itself but in the government deficits that drove the current account deficits, asset bubbles, and increased political power of the financial sector, which ultimately led to the crash (Chinn and Frieden 2011). More generally, as an endogenous outcome of other forces, crises are events to be studied—boundaries on time periods that structure a particular historical narrative—but as a concept, the term carries little independent explanatory power.

A third and final approach treats crises—whether exogenous or endogenous—as fundamental *causes* of political change. This approach is most often adopted by analysts who recognize the dual nature of crises as both situations of danger and turning points. In this view, how the crisis unfolds and how it molds coalitions influences the direction of future change. Here, the trigger event and how it is interpreted may matter beyond its manifestation of the underlying changes in society. That the Great Recession began with the collapse of the subprime mortgage market and spread through the shadow banking system via complex derivatives based on these risky assets, for instance, may affect how credit markets subsequently function, how these markets are regulated in the future, who wins and who loses from different policy choices, and ultimately, the balance of political power between consumers and financial institutions. In this way, the crisis itself exerts an independent effect on the play of politics.

Whether a crisis is defined as exogenous or endogenous is not a purely analytic judgment. Political and economic actors will have important interests in portraying a crisis as one or the other. Those who might be held accountable for negative economic results have a strong interest in constructing an exogenous narrative of the crisis. Like Wall Street bankers pleading "tsunami," politicians in indebted developing countries are much more likely to assign blame for economic collapse to malevolent foreign financial institutions or unstoppable economic tides rather than missteps in domestic policy formation. During past financial crises in Latin America and Asia, the international financial institutions (in particular, the IMF) and private lenders were quick to assign responsibility to precisely those domestic policy choices rather than the imperfections in international capital markets. Asymmetries in bargaining power, specifically the need for additional foreign lending, forced the Northern interpretation of crisis on the Southern debtors. Fifteen years later, however, Asian governments resisted a similar attribution of their financial crash to crony capitalism and a flawed model of development. Ultimately, the IMF was forced to concede some of the Asian arguments: the crisis and its aftermath affected not only the Asian countries, but also the international financial institutions and the evolving policy consensus.

Crises are, in our view, best understood as endogenous turning points with trigger events that surprise actors in their precise timing, if not their actual arrival. Although many pointed to the underlying problems in the macroeconomy before the failure of Lehman Brothers, for example, exactly how and when the real estate bubble would burst was not clearly anticipated. As a corollary, this view of crisis implies that not all crises are the same, and not all countries are affected by or experience the crisis in the same way. As Miles Kahler discusses in chapter 1, the rules of international economic cooperation during the Great Depression deepened the global financial crisis; during the Great Recession, global institutions served to increase the latitude for national policies that sustained cooperation. As both Kahler and Stephan Haggard (chapter 2) argue, Latin America and East Asia, often at the epicenter of earlier international financial crises, were largely spared the worst effects of the Great Recession. Their changing experience of crisis led to defection from the gold standard during the Great Depression and support for international economic regimes in the latest economic crisis. The Great Recession makes clear that we need a new understanding of crisis and policy change.

Moving beyond purely economic risk factors, such as fiscal and current account deficits, Lawrence Broz (chapter 3) and Pablo Pinto (chapter 4) provide the outlines of an endogenous political model of the Great Recession and other economic crises. For Broz, a partisan cycle explains both the political genesis and consequences of financial crisis, at least in countries with current account deficits. Right-wing coalitions will satisfy their constituents through asset bubbles and financial deregulation; their left-wing opponents, returned to power in the aftermath of crisis, will reinstate tougher financial regulation. Pinto argues that countries that are politically divided and reconcile competing political demands through pro-cyclical fiscal policies, such as Argentina or the United States in its current, highly partisan era, will be prone to economic crises. Political immobilism also characterizes the European Union in the Great Recession, where individual states retain fiscal autonomy and veto power over major policy initiatives. Conversely, countries that are more open to continuous political and economic adjustments, such as the smaller European states (Katzenstein 1985), or those that have more recently been forced to adjust by outside pressure, as many developing countries were in the aftermath of the Asian financial crisis, may be less prone to crises and relatively immune to crises originating elsewhere in the global economy. As all of the chapters in part I indicate, the prior policy regime affects both the likelihood of crises and the pattern of their diffusion across countries. Obstacles to policy change help to explain the depth of the current crisis in the developed democracies, which are deeply divided politically or subject to rules of near unanimous consent, and its relatively lighter impact on many developing countries, which either suffered recent crises that realigned policy or, as in China, have less democratic regimes that permit greater political and policy flexibility—though they may not always use it wisely (MacIntyre 2001).

Although all crises have deep economic and, in turn, political roots, trigger events may also matter in important ways if they undermine the legitimacy of the prior regime and permit a new political alignment to emerge. During the Great Depression, a banking crisis and unprecedented levels of unemployment in the United States fragmented the coalition behind existing economic orthodoxy, permitting a new alignment of labor, farmers, and international business. As noted, the nature of the financial crisis of 2008, as well as the attendant bailout of the largest banks and the automobile industry in the United States, has deepened political cleavages in the United States over the role of the government in the economy, on the one hand, and economic inequality, on the other. Bracketed by the Tea Party and the Occupy Wall Street movements, the seeds of political change are certainly present in the United States. Likewise, the alternatives of deepening fiscal coordination or countenancing a breakup of the Eurozone threaten to divide both the European Union and its member countries, opening the way for major political change. Whether the financial meltdown that triggered the Great Recession is sufficient to overcome the political immobilism and partisanship that led to the crisis, or whether it simply deepens existing political divides, is a function of how groups interpret their interests during the crisis.

Interests, Coalitions, and Crisis Outcomes

With crises as both shocks to the system and turning points, the consequences of a crisis depend to a significant extent on how groups are united and potentially reshaped by shared understandings of their political interests. Crises may force interest redefinition through, first, competing retrospective assessments of the crisis and its causes; second, the effects of the crisis itself, particularly a rapid increase in uncertainty; and finally, through prospective evaluations of the effects of actions chosen to deal with the crisis. For example, the Depression of the late nineteenth century (1873–96) led to redefined interests and a shuffling of dominant coalitions in Europe, producing, among others, the German coalition of iron and rye that supported protectionism and naval rearmament. In similar fashion, the Great Depression of the 1930s increased the political power of labor throughout most of the industrialized world and offered new political allies to labor movements. These coalitions sustained new policy positions: expansion of the welfare state and more activist management of the economy. Support for the gold standard, which had occupied a hegemonic position in the constellation of economic interests, now claimed few important political supporters. The Great Recession, on the other hand, has been marked by the resilience of conservative (in the sense of sustaining existing policies) definitions of economic interest, in global governance (Kahler, chapter 1) and national policy regimes (Haggard, chapter 2; Cowhey, chapter 9).

The negative consequences of an economic crisis typically initiate a competitive political process in interpreting the causes of the crisis, assigning accountability, and deriving political and policy answers. Retrospective evaluation may produce social learning, although that concept may overstate the degree to which political actors reassess their options. Collectively, "learning" may simply mean a process of sorting through political alternatives until one that "works" is discovered. Old solutions are typically tried and discarded first; more innovative options may be introduced, if required. Redefinition of interests, if it occurs, will be based in part on a reading of the past and the lessons that it offers. The current debate over regulatory reform, at the national and global levels, offers an example of the role that retrospective assessments may produce in a redefinition of political interests—in this case, a possible swing back toward re-regulation after an era of financial deregulation.

The time pressure and elevated risk during a crisis may prevent a measured, retrospective process of learning. Instead, interests are redefined in the "fog" of crisis. Two different accounts suggest how the redefinition of interests under pressure might take place: one sociological, the other rationalist. Sociological explanations of interest redefinition begin with actors that are socially embedded or the product of their institutional environment, broadly defined. In this view, crises have two opposing effects on interests. On the one hand, crises open up social structures and allow agents to imagine their political interests in new ways. As social institutions are themselves drawn into the maelstrom of political and economic change during a crisis, the interests of agents—and even the definition of agents themselves—are contested. As politics become more plastic, new agents, interests, and political coalitions may emerge.

On the other hand, under higher levels of uncertainty associated with crises, both material constraints and social norms offer fewer predictable guideposts for action. Unable to anticipate the results of their possible actions, agents are less likely to be guided by the logic of consequences and more likely to rely on a logic of appropriateness as defined by more general social scripts or ideologies (Gourevitch 1999; Katzenstein and Nelson, chapter 10). Thus, at the same time that crises challenge existing institutions and, in turn, render problematic existing socially embedded interests, agents are forced back onto more general social constructs to navigate the new terrain. As familiar economic ground shifts during the earthquake of a crisis, political actors grasp for other indicators of their interests: ideology, norms, traditional definitions of adversaries and allies. For example, Suzanne Berger (chapter 6) argues that, under the press of globalization and international financial openness in the late nineteenth and early twentieth centuries, French workers defined their interests not in material terms but on a traditional left-right, state-church dimension. Their redefinition produced a surprising (in materialist eyes) acquiescence in capital market openness.

For rationalists, crises also have two important effects. They depreciate the value of interests "vested" in the extant order and increase uncertainty, which then creates fissures in existing political coalitions. As in the sociological view, this first effect permits new coalitions and even new institutions to form. Crises also embody long-term processes of change, however, that affect rates of return to different activities and assets. In the case of economic crises, these processes of change are often embodied in shifts in the relative prices of different commodities (Frieden et al. 2011). By altering the environment of actors, long-term changes in relative prices are likely to change the interests of actors and, in turn, create new groups and coalitions. In the rationalist account, however, interests remain "objective," predictable by an outside observer with access to underlying data (such as changes in relative prices) that will drive interest redefinition in the longer run. What remains unknown in this rationalist account, however, is how the winners and losers from political change will form new political and policy coalitions.

Finally, crises may shape a redefinition of interests through estimation of the prospective effects of offsetting measures taken during the crisis. Although a brief and shallow consensus may emerge to support crisis management measures, those measures often involve costs that will be paid in the future. That future due date allows for political conflict and interest formation over the distribution of those uncertain future costs. For example, inflation "hawks" within central bank governing boards during the Great Recession have opposed additional quantitative easing in monetary policy because of possible inflationary "taxes" in the future. The odd alliance between big business and the Tea Party during the U.S. midterm elections in 2010 can be seen as a possibly temporary redefinition of interests on the part of those groups to align against the future costs of fiscal consolidation.

Although they arrive by different routes, all three mechanisms expect crises to lead to a redefinition of interests and consequently to a regrouping of coalitions. As interests are understood in new ways, political strategies—whether driven by a logic of appropriateness or a logic of consequences—are altered and the constellation of politically active groups may change. It is this reshuffling of interests and coalitions that produces potential political change rather than the direct influence of the crisis.

Outline of the Volume

The two themes of crisis as an endogenous event produced and mediated by prior political choices and as processes of interest redefinition structure the chapters in this volume. Although individual papers often touch on both themes, those grouped in part I primarily focus on the nature of crises and those in part II on how crises shape political interests and thus produce varying consequences.

The Great Recession as Endogenous Crisis

The contributors to this volume go beyond the notion of crisis as exogenous "earthquake" and begin to develop an approach driven by politics in explaining crises, including the Great Recession, and their consequences. In comparative context, the Great Recession illustrates forcefully that the political sources of crises and their political effects vary, and that variation requires explanation. Crises are not events that "happen" but are themselves caused by the political choices of particular actors and, in turn, affect future political choices. To understand the effects of any crisis therefore requires a close analysis of its origins in and interactions with the existing political landscape.

In chapter 1, Miles Kahler examines why the Great Recession, despite its large economic effects, has not yet produced significant change in the structure of global economic governance, a key feature of international politics. Kahler argues that the effects of economic crisis were mediated by existing international institutions and by persisting patterns of exchange in the international economy. Although the origins of the 2008 financial crisis might be like preceding crises, the amplification of recession into a broader crisis of international governance is not automatic. International economic interests proved sturdier than they had been in earlier crises, particularly the Great Depression. The liberal orientation that dominated the global institutions of the second era of globalization was questioned, but not overturned. At the international level, this time may be different.

In chapter 2, Stephan Haggard develops a similar theme of political and policy persistence at the domestic level by examining the differential regional impact of the Great Recession. Although global economic integration insured that the financial crisis would spread internationally, variation in the type of economic linkage and its political beneficiaries (and victims) also insured that policy responses would vary as well. Despite a common aversion to protectionism and statism of the 1930s variety, Latin American and East Asian economies diverged from those countries that were more dependent on the European Union. Prior political experience with financial crisis—and the political changes produced by that experience—served some regions well. The magnetic pull of the

European market (and both European banks and finance) produce much harsher adjustment options for political economies that had opted for a different variety of liberalism. The much deeper crisis that has ensued on the European periphery is also more likely to induce broader political change. Elsewhere in the developing world, relative success at crisis management has reinforced regimes from China to Latin America.

In chapter 3, Lawrence Broz finds that crises in the industrialized countries after 1973 originate in partisan financial cycles. Right-wing governments cut taxes and expand fiscal deficits, deregulate the financial sector, and worsen current account deficits, thereby setting the stage for financial crises. They are then replaced with left-wing parties that reverse course. Crises reflect underlying political dynamics in a world of high capital mobility, but those dynamics have not yet produced a definitive shift in coalitions and policies that would end the political cycle. Pablo Pinto (chapter 4) points to a different political cycle in the experience of modern Argentina: in an era that witnessed a larger government role in the economy, pro-cyclical fiscal policies—ultimately unsustainable and often at the root of recurrent debt crises—appeared and reappeared. Like the right-of-center parties described by Broz, the Argentine political class found a solution to distributional conflict in policies that were prone to crises. Pinto's endogenous model of crisis also explains, paradoxically, the relative ease with which Argentina surmounted the latest global financial crisis. Its immediate past crisis—less than a decade ago—foreclosed dependence on foreign capital; its legacy of pro-cyclical fiscal policy was not the precursor to crisis in this case, but its antidote. As Haggard describes in chapter 2, other countries in Latin America and Asia learned from past crises; Argentina did not, but a new combination of constraints imposed by the past made its lack of learning less destructive.

A Crisis without Political Consequences?

As the Great Recession enters its latest phase of fragile recovery and fiscal consolidation, it presents a paradox that lies at the center of this volume: the most severe economic downturn since the 1930s has not produced dramatic political consequences within or among nations. There certainly has been an increase in political volatility—in Japan, where the recently elected Democratic Party government suffered an early setback with a prime minister's resignation and a defeat in Upper House elections; in Britain, where a coalition government was formed for the first time since 1945; in the United States, where midterm elections produced the largest swing against the incumbent party in the House of Representatives since 1948. On the other hand, the emergence or strengthening of new political groups in the industrialized countries, primarily on the far right—

the Tea Party in the United States, anti-immigration political parties in Europe—has not yet signaled a more profound set of political realignments. In the developing world, as Haggard (chapter 2) documents, the depth of attachment to neoliberal policy packages has been striking, reinforced by strong economic performance in many of those jurisdictions. More to the point, interest redefinition is difficult to discern: conventional political parties have reinforced their messages rather than groping for new combinations of political appeal and policy innovation. At the global level, modest institutional innovation (the Group of 20, the Financial Stability Board) has so far stabilized international cooperation and prevented a sharp turn toward delinking and economic nationalism.

The current lack of political change differs dramatically from past crises. Peter Hall, in chapter 5, reviews the Fordist model of industrial politics that emerged after the Great Depression and was reinforced during the Keynesian era of the 1950s and 1960s, and how that model was challenged as a result of the crisis of the 1970s. A new neoliberal model in the 1980s relied more heavily on services and international trade and deemphasized class conflict. Within the shift toward more market-oriented policies, however, variation persisted among the industrialized countries. That institutional variation continues in their responses to the Great Recession, in which governments have reached for the "building materials on hand" in the face of economic crisis. Diffuse political discontent coupled, in some cases, with tight international constraints, has failed to produce durable new policy formulas that can be matched with equally durable political coalitions. Suzanne Berger (chapter 6) turns to an earlier era of globalization (France before World War I) to consider the redefinition of interests under the impact of capital mobility. Although labor's economic interests were threatened by the integration of international capital markets, working-class representatives continued to define their political interests in opposition to older enemies, defined in terms of long-standing sectarian cleavages. Rather than redefining interests in the face of new economic realities, old political battles were recapitulated. James Shinn (chapter 7), on the other hand, sees a trend toward change in corporate governance—greater protection for minority shareholder interests—that was temporarily interrupted by the Great Recession but is likely to resume as key actors pursue interests redefined in the wake of crisis. As global capital flows increase, international investors will press for continued change in corporate governance. Structural fiscal deficits in the Organisation for Economic Co-operation and Development countries, worsened by the crisis, will also produce more powerful constituencies concerned over the fate of their private pensions.

One powerful explanation for the initial conservative effect of this crisis on political outcomes is the relative success and resilience of the institutional and policy mix that was put in place in the industrialized countries over the past half-century. Those institutions—national and global—may have served as shock absorbers during the crisis, producing rapid response policies of monetary and fiscal stimulus coupled with more dramatic interventions (nationalizations of banks and distressed corporations) that fended off a steeper economic decline and set the stage for a weak recovery. In contrast to past crises, particularly those documented by Gourevitch (1986), the Great Recession appears distinctive: the policy response was prompt and relatively uniform. As Haggard and Hall each document, governments did not search for new remedies, for the most part; they applied the old toolkit that had been shaped by prior experience with crisis, particularly the watershed of the Great Depression. Because of the effectiveness of these institutions and policies in the short run, the crisis did not fall into a vicious cycle with regard to its depth, length, or global scope.

Of equal importance was the peculiar international economic role of the United States. At the center of the crisis, the United States occupies a unique monetary and financial position. Its turn to massive liquidity injections was not hindered by concerns over a fixed exchange rate or a lack of confidence in its public debt. Its measures of fiscal and monetary expansion have been accepted—with some grumbling—by the rest of the world, which has a deep interest in the recovery of the U.S. market. The flight to safety in the face of a sharp rise in uncertainty also benefited the United States and provided further latitude for national policy. The United States (and other large economies) did not suffer from the constraints of "golden fetters," in sharp contrast to earlier international crises (and the plight of smaller economies in this crisis) (Eichengreen 1996).

Despite an apparently widespread turn toward established political formulas and policy packages in the face of the Great Recession, political entrepreneurs may have more room for political maneuver than suggested by accounts based on economic interest or institutional resilience. At the level of micropolitics, Megumi Naoi and Ikuo Kume (chapter 8) argue that voters can be swayed by alternative primings of economic policy choice, such as trade liberalization or protectionism. The dual identities of voters as consumers and producers can be mobilized in ways that undermine notions of "hard" economic interests. In his macropolitical account, Peter Cowhey (chapter 9) portrays an Obama administration that not only recognized the political constraints on an agenda of trade liberalization but also acted strategically to reshape and strengthen a political coalition in support of its favored commercial policies. Peter Katzenstein and Stephen Nelson (chapter 10) make the strongest case for the liberating effects of uncertainty that is endemic to crises. It may open politics to new possibilities while encouraging some political actors to return to older scripts based on a limited repertoire of political ideologies.

Given these possibilities for political entrepreneurs, who may orchestrate new political coalitions in the future, the surprisingly conservative—in the sense of maintaining the status quo—political outcomes in the wake of the Great Recession may not persist. Like other crises, the trigger of the Great Recession has revealed both old and new fault lines that could produce more fundamental political change. Fiscal consolidation, the next phase of the crisis in most industrialized countries, promises to be a contentious and politically explosive process. Mervyn King, governor of the Bank of England, predicted that the party winning the national election in Britain in 2010 would be out of power for a generation, given the severity of spending cuts and tax increases that would be required.[15] The 2010 midterm elections in the United States set the stage for a conflict-filled process of achieving fiscal balance in the medium and longer run, with competing views being put on the table during the 2012 presidential election. The European Union will continue to face challenges as its peripheral, heavily indebted members attempt some of the most wrenching economic policy changes in recent history.

Rebalancing internationally will also be part of the post-crisis adjustment. It has already become apparent that the "cooperation" of uncoordinated fiscal and monetary expansion frays quickly when those measures are unwound: disagreement between the United States and the European Union on the timing of fiscal consolidation; continued friction between China and the United States over exchange rate policy; and new doubts about the effectiveness of the G-20 process of collaboration that was instituted with such fanfare only a few months ago. Although globalization is hardly at risk, and the interests vested in an open international economy are formidable, anti-immigration backlash in many countries could be a harbinger, as it was in the early twentieth century, of a broader hostility toward international openness.

Japan's record over the past two decades may be the most interesting parallel case: a deep economic and financial crisis that did not produce a new political realignment for nearly two decades, despite electoral reforms and mediocre economic performance. Policy innovation was limited and belated; the old "variety of capitalism" demonstrated remarkable resilience as Japan persisted in its entrenched export orientation and its policies of propping up less-competitive sectors and firms. The Japanese example suggests the complicated relationship between our two meanings of crisis and their linkage: redefinition of politically expressed interests and long-run political change.

To paraphrase a well-known political claim, one should never waste a serious crisis. That advice applies to scholars as well as politicians. The Great Recession

---

15. http://www.guardian.co.uk/business/2010/apr/29/mervyn-king-warns-election-victor.

may have ended in formal economic terms (the trough has been passed), but its theoretical and historical effects remain. It has raised once again the meaning of crisis as an explanatory variable as well as the variation among crises over time. It also poses anew the ways in which individuals and groups have redefined their interests during a time of economic flux. Even more pointedly, it highlights the disjuncture between a deep economic crisis and its relatively slender effects to date on political realignment and ideational reorientation. Even at this early point in its history, as its severe effects on employment and economic activity linger, the Great Recession provides a ground for testing our understanding of the political genesis of economic crises and their variable political effects.

Part I

CRISES AND POLITICS

Is This Time Different?

1

ECONOMIC CRISIS AND GLOBAL GOVERNANCE

The Stability of a Globalized World

Miles Kahler

In the public imagination, economic crises seem to offer a simple lesson: economic hard times threaten international cooperation and the institutions of global governance. The cataclysm of the Great Depression has shaped our views of global governance for eight decades. Vivid memories of post-Depression international economic disorder—the demise of the gold standard, rapid descent into competitive currency depreciation, beggar-thy-neighbor trade protectionism and discrimination, and imposition of capital controls—were prominent drivers of institution-building during World War II and in the postwar decades.

The steep economic recession of the early 1980s, which succeeded two oil shocks and an inflation that was unprecedented in the post-1945 era, did not produce a collapse of international economic exchange and cooperation comparable to the Great Depression. Nevertheless, the early 1980s were a threatening period for the global trading system, as Fortress Europe raised protectionist barriers, and the United States embarked on aggressive unilateralism against its Asian trading partners. The Reagan administration in the United States and its European allies in free-market orthodoxy were deeply skeptical of international institutional collaboration, even though the International Monetary Fund (IMF) and the World Bank played a key role in managing the international debt crisis of the 1980s. Japan, although aspiring to economic preeminence, did not appear

The author thanks Peter J. Katzenstein and James Shinn, participants in a seminar at the Center for American Studies, Fudan University, and participants in two Politics in the New Hard Times conferences for comments on an earlier version of this paper. The author is also grateful for the research assistance of Joseph Giljum.

politically interested or economically equipped to play a leading role in strengthening global or regional governance. The economic downturn posed a threat to both global governance institutions and the great power collaboration that they embodied.

Economic Crisis and Its Effects on International Economic Cooperation

Apart from the easily observed consequences of crisis in both periods, a simple causal model seems to explain the detrimental effects of crisis on international cooperation: the mutual policy adjustments required for cooperation and sustained by international institutions became too costly for politicians facing unparalleled economic distress. Under the pressure of rapidly mounting economic distress—the first meaning of crisis given in the introduction to this volume—unilateral measures, based on national self-interest, promised a higher and more immediate payoff than cooperative steps with longer-run benefits. Although international institutions that sustain cooperation are not synonymous with that cooperation, institutional disruption or collapse is likely to signify that international cooperation—mutual adjustment or coordination of national policies—has eroded or ended in a particular domain. Crisis as an unstable situation of extreme economic difficulty becomes crisis as a turning point in the pattern of international cooperation, the second meaning of crisis.

This simple lesson and the model that links crisis to an undermining of cooperation are both questionable, even for these earlier economic crises. The effects of economic crisis on global economic cooperation and governance—positive or negative, short-term versus long-term—are more ambiguous than a simple equation of international economic crisis with a weakening of global governance institutions. First, that conventional model fails to incorporate possible endogeneity: institutionalized cooperation may itself deepen or prolong economic crisis. Economic historians now assign a major role to the gold standard in deepening the Great Depression, the "golden fetters" that promoted policies of deflation as a first response to an unprecedented economic crisis. As Barry Eichengreen has described, the gold standard prevented unilateral responses by national central banks that were, at the same time, unable to enact a different model of international cooperation that would have permitted them to collaborate in monetary easing to arrest the economic collapse (Eichengreen 1996a, 2002). Why this attachment to a particular modality of international cooperation that was inhibiting a politically and economically desirable reflation? Eichengreen and Temin have attributed the power of the gold standard to ideational factors: "the ideology, mentalité, and rhetoric of the gold standard led policymakers to take actions that only accentuated economic distress in the 1930s. Central bankers continued to kick the world economy while it was down until it lost consciousness" (Eichengreen and Temin 1997, 1–2).

The gold standard has also been associated with the disastrous spiral into protectionism that occurred during the Great Depression. Eichengreen and Irwin (2009) demonstrate that those countries that delayed their exit from the gold standard were most likely to implement protectionist measures. Protectionism was less a response to the clamor of domestic interests than a desperate, second-best macroeconomic choice by governments with a (self-) limited menu of policy options. In other words, the content of international cooperation and the policy guides embodied in existing institutions are critical in any assessment of the influence of international collaboration on economic outcomes. Cooperation can deepen crises, just as crises may undermine cooperation. When international monetary collaboration revived in the late 1930s and even more clearly after 1945, governments rejected a revived gold standard as the model for cooperation.

Second, establishing either the independent effects of economic crisis on international cooperation or the sign of those effects is difficult. The trigger event of an economic or financial crisis may reflect ongoing structural change, in this case international cooperation that is already in decline. The 1920s, for example, were not a golden age for economic cooperation and institution building. The gold standard was managed through a loose system of central bank cooperation, which came under increasing strain from democratic demands well before the onset of the Great Depression. In similar fashion, protectionist measures and mercantilist industrial policies multiplied following the first oil shock and recession of 1973–74. Those shocks also confirmed the end of the Bretton Woods fixed exchange rate system. The singular contribution of the 1981–82 recession to a further fraying of the General Agreement on Tariffs and Trade (GATT) and the global trade regime is difficult to estimate.

Finally, any complete calculus of the effects of crisis must also include longer-run positive consequences for international economic cooperation and institutions. Sociological accounts of crisis emphasize the importance of interpretation and learning that occur during and after crises. Because the Great Depression discredited both the old institutional rules (the gold standard) and the subsequent economic disorder, that crisis ultimately produced new global institutions that awarded national governments greater policy autonomy while curbing their impulses toward closure. The recession of the 1980s stimulated interest in a further round of trade negotiations (the Uruguay Round, begun in 1986) and in the Single European Act (also 1986). For regional governance, the effects of crisis may also be positive. When an economic shock affects all states in a regional economy in similar fashion, defensive regional responses may enhance cooperation and regional institution building. The 1930s was an era of regional blocs that were often hierarchical or imperial in design. Monetary disorder in the 1970s spurred European measures to build a regional monetary arrangement. Most notably, the Asian economic crisis—viewed by Asian governments as originating outside the region—lent crucial support to a framework for regional financial cooperation, the Chiang Mai Initiative (Henning forthcoming). The longer run effects of crisis on international cooperation are at best inferred; tracing such effects in any systematic way is even more difficult than evaluating the negative consequences of crisis.

If earlier global economic crises raise doubts about the conventional model in which economic crisis leads to an inevitable deterioration in global economic cooperation and rejection of governance institutions, the Great Recession poses a contemporary and empirical challenge. The economic and political aftershocks of the global economic crisis continue to be felt, and its ultimate effects remain difficult to estimate. Nevertheless, international cooperation during this sharp economic recession has been more sustained and stable than the course of international cooperation during two previous economic downturns that matched or exceeded its severity, the Great Depression of 1929–33 and the global recession of 1981–82. In the present crisis, concrete steps for deepening global economic cooperation have been agreed on, and discussion of such measures continues in multilateral settings, such as the Group of Twenty (G-20) summits. Existing institutions of global economic governance have, in most cases, received additional resources and authority. Only the Eurozone crisis that erupted in 2010 threatened an existing system of governance, in that case, a regional one. Despite the severity of the Great Recession in most of the core industrialized economies, this crisis did not appear to mark a turning point, even a temporary one, in the global economic governance and its existing institutions.

Economic Integration and Global Governance: The Fragility of a Globalized World

The deepest economic recession in the era of globalization might have produced a very different pattern of national policies and international collaboration. In the pre-crisis decades, economic globalization had not produced a uniform strengthening of global governance institutions that could restrain the unilateral impulses of national governments. Although the creation of the World Trade Organization (WTO) in 1995 signaled a strengthened and legalized global trade regime, other globalized sectors did not match this award of greater authority to global economic institutions.

During the 1990s, the IMF expanded its advisory role for economies transitioning from socialism to capitalism. Its role in monetary and financial surveillance, particularly with regard to the major national economies, remained minimal. Efforts at formal macroeconomic policy coordination, which had culminated in the Louvre Accords of 1987, were effectively abandoned during the 1990s. Calls for a reformed international monetary system that would constrain national choices of exchange rates and exchange rate regimes were ignored.

Cross-border financial flows outstripped regulatory and supervisory capacities that were only weakly coordinated at the global level. International oversight of national regulation was vested primarily in the Basel Committee on Banking Supervision, based at the Bank for International Settlements (BIS). Its combination of information sharing and peer pressure served to fill gaps in the oversight of internationally active financial institutions. Apart from its agreement on capital adequacy standards, however, few binding international regulatory standards were implemented. The financial turmoil of the late 1990s produced the Financial Stability Forum, a new mechanism for loose coordination among an expanded collection of national regulators. Demands from the developing countries for regulation of nonbank financial institutions, such as hedge funds, were rejected by the major financial powers (Eichengreen 2003).

In other domains of global economic integration, multilateral governance was minimal or absent. Foreign direct investment has been a major driver of economic globalization, growing more rapidly than trade since 1990. Attempts to create a global investment regime under the Organisation for Economic Cooperation and Development (OECD) failed, however. Bilateral investment treaties (BITs) remained the core instruments in international governance of foreign direct investment. Although it hardly equaled the scale of migration during the pre-1914 era of globalization, cross-border movement of labor became an important component of the new globalized economy. Remittances from migrant labor became an essential contributor to economic development in many poor economies. Yet policies governing economic migration (in contrast to refugee flows) remained subject to national authorities and, occasionally, regional and bilateral agreements. No global migration regime existed; no proposal for such a regime was on the international agenda.

Rather than the runaway, unaccountable international institutions that preoccupy critics of globalization, a more accurate observation in the new century is the limited reach of supranational institutions, given the extent of global economic integration.[1] Regional institution building presented a similar mixed picture. The Economic and Monetary Union of the European Union (EU) appeared to succeed with the adoption of the euro as a common currency by most members in 2002. At the same time, European electorates repeatedly demonstrated their skepticism regarding deeper political integration, a costly shortcoming that contributed to the onset of the Eurozone's sovereign debt crisis in 2010. In the most economically dynamic region of the global economy, Asia, modest steps were made toward greater regional collaboration, particularly in the Chiang Mai Initiative and in bilateral and subregional trade agreements. In parallel with the global trend, however, institutional development failed to match the growth and integration of the Asia-Pacific regional economy.[2]

The Great Recession and the Persistence of International Economic Cooperation

When the global economic crisis began in 2008–9, intergovernmental cooperation and the authority vested in global intergovernmental institutions had not kept up with rapid integration of the world economy. Markets were regarded as stable and market actors as stabilizing; self-regulation or limited regulation became the new norm. Given the thinness of global governance in the face of a transformed international economy, one might have predicted that a global economic and financial crisis would produce a failure of international cooperation as great as that of the early 1930s. Instead, when the crisis began in 2007 and deepened in late 2008, politicians for the most part reached for familiar solutions, encouraged by existing international institutions. Cooperative behavior dominated during a period of deep economic distress and uncertainty. In the face of crisis, existing global institutions have been strengthened, and modest institutional innovations have been promoted. Economic crisis was not transformed into a crisis or turning point in global governance.

The International Monetary Fund experienced the most significant reversal of fortunes. Only a few years before the Great Recession, many feared (or hoped) that the IMF had become obsolete in a world of expanding private capital flows. Resistance to IMF prescriptions after the Asian financial crisis explained in part

1. On trends in global governance under conditions of globalization, see Kahler (2009) and Kahler and Lake (2009).

2. Economic interdependence in the Asia-Pacific region has grown, but the institutional gap has "stubbornly refused to close, despite the recent proliferation of bilateral and minilateral PTAs [Preferential Trade Agreements] and security dialogues" (Aggarwal and Koo 2008, 288).

the rapid buildup of reserves by Asian and other developing countries. The same member countries bridled at their underrepresentation in the IMF's governance. Countries that had long been on the IMF client list, such as Argentina, hastened to end IMF programs. The loss of clients in a period of apparent financial calm produced unfamiliar budget constraints at the IMF and forced a reduction in staff.

This downturn in the IMF role in global governance was quickly reversed during the economic crisis. The IMF has resumed its familiar role of providing financial assistance to countries that have been excluded from the troubled financial markets.[3] In addition, the IMF instituted a new lending facility designed for large, credit-worthy economies beset by global financial turmoil, the Flexible Credit Line (FCL). Steps were taken for an overdue revision of IMF quotas to reflect the growing importance of developing economies, a commitment reinforced at the Pittsburgh Summit of the G-20 in September 2009. (A similar, though smaller, shift in voting power and quotas was agreed for the World Bank.) Governments of the largest emerging economies, such as China, found additional leverage in their commitments to increase the resources of the IMF by purchasing IMF-issued bonds. This prospective shift in the balance of influence within the IMF was predicted to strengthen its representative character and its global legitimacy.[4]

The IMF was also awarded new roles by the G-20: as the provider of "candid, evenhanded, and balanced analysis" for the new Framework for Strong, Sustainable, and Balanced Growth (FSSBG) agreed at the Pittsburgh Summit. Although commitments under the framework would not be binding and the principal enforcement mechanism would be peer pressure, the IMF was, for the first time, offered a process and a role that might allow it to fulfill its surveillance role for the major economies. This role was reaffirmed at the Seoul Summit in November 2010, where the IMF was designated to provide technical support to the mutual assessment process and, specifically, to develop "indicative guidelines" for identification of "persistently large imbalances."[5]

If the revival of the IMF, accompanied by remarkably little controversy, was one signal of sustained global economic cooperation, the expanded role awarded

3. In December 2010, the IMF had nineteen standby arrangements (SBAs), which were its traditional means of assisting member countries with short-term balance-of-payments support. All of these SBAs were approved during or after September 2008. In September 2007, the IMF had seven SBAs; only one, with Turkey, was larger than 500 million SDRs [Special Drawing Rights]. The IMF's lending commitments rose to over $160 billion in September 2009 (from slightly more than $1 billion two years before).

4. "A Good War," *Economist*, September 17, 2009.

5. "The G20 Seoul Summit Leaders' Declaration, November 11–12, 2010," 2. http://www.g20.utoronto.ca/2010/g20seoul.html.

to the G-20 was a sign that innovation rather than restoration would also mark the post-crisis economic order. A decade earlier, the Asian financial crisis had led to the formation of this new group of "systemically important" economies that extended beyond the industrialized country club of the Group of Seven (G-7). The G-20—nineteen large industrialized and developing economies plus the European Union—had not played a central role in global economic governance before the onset of the current global financial crisis. As the crisis deepened, however, an emergency meeting of the G-20 in November 2008 signaled a greater willingness by the industrialized countries to include key emerging economies in global economic decision making. That new role was confirmed at the Pittsburgh Summit in September 2009, in which the G-20 was proclaimed the new locus for discussions of global economic policy. Little sign was given, however, of any increased institutionalization for the G-20; even the basis for membership in the group remained imprecise. As one observer noted, "The G20 itself remains a remarkably ad hoc structure . . . no permanent secretariat, no research function, no mechanism for dispute settlement."[6]

U. S. Treasury Secretary Timothy Geithner labeled the Financial Stability Board (FSB) the "fourth pillar" of global economic governance. A strengthened version of the networked Financial Stability Forum, its elevation within the architecture of global governance signified both the perceived importance of regulatory failures in producing the global crisis and discontent with international oversight of national regulatory regimes. As Eric Helleiner (2010b) points out, the FSB was strengthened by the addition of a full-time secretary-general and an enlarged secretariat. More important, the new mandate of the FSB included a strengthened role in enforcing compliance with international financial standards, with both member jurisdictions and nonmembers. This strengthening of global governance in the domain of financial regulation along Anglo-American lines was surprising, given the damage that the Great Recession had inflicted on those models of financial regulation (Helleiner 2010b).

In the revival of existing institutions and the creation or elevation of new ones, the incumbent economic powers recognized and accepted a larger role for the emerging economies. The Pittsburgh Summit agreed that the quota shares of the emerging economies in the IMF and the World Bank would be expanded. Membership in the FSB was enlarged to include the most prominent developing economies; its role was simultaneously elevated to match the elevated importance of regulatory reform on the global agenda. Most important, the central role

6. Alan Beattie, "The G20: Ad Hoc Institution Faces Tough Struggle to Show It Has Teeth." *Financial Times*, November 10, 2010. http://www.ft.com/intl/cms/s/0/bbfe94ae-eb8a-11df-bbb5-00144feab49a.html#axzz1mntcjIZt.

awarded to the G-20 confirmed the arrival of these new economic powers in the formal structures of global economic governance.

In other areas of global economic governance, the economic crisis produced less innovation and more concerns over backsliding in national policies. Particularly in the trade regime, the economic downturn produced increased protectionism, as recessions had in the past. Those measures were largely directed against China, the powerhouse of manufactured exports in the new global economy (Bown 2009). Of particular concern, given their economic interdependence in several domains, were the tit-for-tat trade measures taken by the United States against Chinese exports of low-cost tires and steel pipe; steps countered by Chinese tariffs on U.S. exports of chicken meat and steel products. As U.S. elections approached, the Obama administration stepped up its scrutiny of China's commercial policies, beginning an investigation of Chinese solar panels exported to the United States. China countered in December 2011 with antidumping and antisubsidy tariffs imposed on selected automobile imports from the United States.

More difficult to evaluate were measures of "murky protectionism," WTO-legal national measures that are "abuses of legitimate discretion . . . used to discriminate against foreign goods, companies, workers, and investors." A review of such measures indicates that the industrialized countries tend to use subsidies for these purposes; developing countries deploy all forms of protection, concentrating on border measures such as tariffs (Baldwin and Evenett 2009, 4). "Murky protectionism" reproduced in less extensive form the "gray area" of semi-legal protectionism that was widespread in the 1980s. At the same time, the current round of trade negotiations under WTO auspices, the Doha Round, remains stalled, with little prospect of forward movement during the crisis.

Although discriminatory and protectionist trade measures taken during the Great Recession ran counter to G-20 pledges made in November 2008 and April 2009, their import should not be exaggerated. Most of the measures taken did not violate either bilateral trade agreements or the rules of the existing international trade regime. The WTO remained a secure bulwark against many forms of trade policy backsliding. Most of the sectors involved were hardly central to global trade or to national economies: these were "classic" cases of protectionism directed by import-competing sectors against their more competitive (and often state-guided) rivals. Given the depth of the recession, protectionist measures were surprising in their limited scope; they did not approach sectoral protection of such key sectors as automobiles or semiconductors during the 1980s. Equally important, most governments were willing to deal with commercial conflicts through the accepted dispute settlement procedures of the WTO.

Explaining Cooperation in the Face of Economic Crisis

Despite a thin layer of global governance—thinness that may have contributed to the onset of the financial crisis—as well as sharp declines in exports and employment in most major industrialized economies, intergovernmental cooperation and global governance institutions have not shattered in the face of the crisis. Although many questions remain regarding the commitments undertaken to rebalance global institutions and strengthen surveillance of national policies, outcomes so far suggest that this crisis will not prove to be a turning point that undermines cooperation and erodes existing institutions. Three possible explanations for this outcome should be mentioned at the outset. They distinguish this recession from the Great Depression, but they cannot account for the contrast between the 1981–82 recession and the recent economic crisis.

The length and depth of the Great Depression is one plausible explanation for the greater damage to global economic cooperation in the earlier crisis. Unemployment in several of the major economies, including the United States and Germany, peaked at much higher levels than those reached in 2007–10. Recovery from the crisis also took longer: more than three years for the United States in the Great Depression as compared to eighteen months for the Great Recession of 2007–9. Nevertheless, the severity of the Great Depression was a function of government policies, and those policies insured that an economic downturn became an unparalleled cataclysm. On certain dimensions—decline in manufacturing, fall in global stock markets, the collapse of world trade—the Great Recession demonstrated an initial severity equal to or greater than the Great Depression. Key governments, however, responded faster and more aggressively, countering the economic downturn with through changes in monetary and fiscal policies (Almunia et al. 2009). The contrast in government responses during the two episodes is most important: shocks to global economic cooperation and governance were directly related to those policy choices. Those choices may have been eased, in turn, by the maintenance of international cooperation.

Changes in the menu of countercyclical policies represent a second and more important distinction between the Great Depression and the two later episodes. International collaboration at the start of the Great Depression was undermined by conflict between the demands of the gold standard—the cooperative benchmark at that time—and domestic growth and employment. Political pressures in key economies during the slide into depression were amplified by the absence of stabilizing policies that would cushion the effects of unemployment and provide demand stimulus. As Barry Eichengreen has noted, the gold standard survived in the decades before 1914 because polities in the key economies were not fully democratic. With the advent of universal adult suffrage in most industrial economies after World War I, demands grew for government intervention to ensure economic prosperity, even at the expense of the gold standard. By the 1980s, on the other hand, countercyclical policies were firmly in place, despite considerable variation among the industrialized economies in unemployment insurance and other social safety net programs. In the early 1980s, however, those policies were not enough to prevent a shift toward an inward-looking and less cooperative orientation on the part of the major economies. Successful adoption of policies to offset economic downturns, so apparent during the Great Recession, were a necessary, but not a sufficient condition for sustaining international economic cooperation and the existing institutions of global governance.

Finally, the Great Depression can be distinguished from both the 1981–82 recession and the Great Recession of 2007–9 by the complicating effect of political and military conflict on economic collaboration. The linked issues of German reparations and the war debts of Britain and France made sustained financial cooperation difficult. Underlying these issues were the deep distrust that persisted from World War I, rendering Germany, the largest European economy, an uncertain partner and occasional spoiler in international economic governance. The two post-1945 recessions did not overlay security rifts of similar magnitude: the United States, the major European economies, and Japan were and remained allies. Although China's mixed relationship with the United States was historically less close, the security disputes between the two countries did not approach those of Europe in the 1920s and 1930s.

Although these explanations underline the distinctiveness of the Great Depression, international collaboration during the Great Recession is best explained by three features of the global political economy that had emerged during the previous two decades: the character of economic globalization, the emerging economies and their support for the existing international economic order, and the peculiar pattern of institutional development in global economic governance. The first two explanations are based on interests that were *not* redefined during the crisis; the stability of those interests, shaped in a globalized world, was essential to international cooperation during the Great Recession. Global institutional design reinforced policies based on those stable interests, rather than creating a choice between the existing global order and domestic political survival.

Globalization and the Decline of Economic Nationalism

Peter Gourevitch (1986) notes that governments adopting the most radical break with economic orthodoxy during the Great Depression did so with the support—often temporary—of a broad coalition that included some sectors of capital, labor, and agriculture. These radical cases, which included the United States and Germany among the largest economies, also adopted strategies of economic nationalism, erecting protectionist barriers, abandoning the gold standard and monetary cooperation, and instituting other controls over cross-border exchange. The Great Recession has not produced similar, broad sectoral coalitions that favor economic experimentation and delinking from the world economy. Although global economic integration may have promoted diffusion of the financial crisis, it has also shifted the incentives of national governments and their supporting coalitions toward more cooperative responses, rendering both economic nationalism and decoupling from the world economy less attractive.

Consider once again the sectors that have been the initiators and targets of protectionist measures in trade conflict between the United States and China: low-cost tires, agricultural products, paper. These are sectors in which international linkages and cross-border investments are relatively low: the "nationality" of the sector or subsector is seldom in doubt. Helen V. Milner (1988) has described the significance of "international links"—export dependence and cross-border investments—in undermining protectionist pressures during the 1970s and 1980s. Perhaps the most significant feature of globalization in the two decades since Milner's account has been the rapid growth in foreign direct investment, particularly to developing economies, and within that group, to China. As a leading Asian exporter of manufactured products, China has deviated sharply from the restrictive attitude toward foreign investment that was displayed by Japan and South Korea during their rapid industrialization. For example, state-owned firms that partner with major U.S. and European multinationals, such as General Motors and Volkswagen, play a prominent role in the Chinese automobile industry. Such cross-investment weakens potential protectionist coalitions in the industrialized countries, despite labor opposition to investments that result in re-exports to the home economy. The importance of foreign production based on cross-border investment was indicated in the U.S. measures taken against Chinese tire manufacturers: no American corporations joined the petition, which was initiated by a major labor union.

In other rapidly growing sectors, such as consumer electronics, production fragmentation or disintegration has advanced, as manufacturing processes are parceled out among different economies and their producers (Irwin 2005, 24–6). A recent analysis of the Apple iPod indicates that it contains key components manufactured by Japanese and South Korean corporations, with final assembly by Taiwanese firms using Chinese labor. The iPods are then re-exported for distribution and sale around the world (Linden, Kraemer, and Dedrick 2007). Any protectionist disruption to this global supply chain is likely to harm producers of components (often politically influential multinationals in their own countries) as much or more than the manufacturer (assembler) of the final product. Once again, potential protectionist coalitions face growing obstacles to their own assembly as a result of the new, cross-border models of manufacturing. The prospect of damaging (and self-defeating) retaliation in the event of protectionist measures serves as a barrier to increased trade barriers.

The advance of globalization has removed the support of most multinational businesses from potential protectionist coalitions: the redefinition of interests induced by internationalization, described by Milner two decades ago, had intensified and broadened as multinational investment was replaced with complex production networks. Agriculture was unlikely to support intensified trade protection, since agriculture in most industrialized countries was already cosseted with subsidies, price supports, and high tariffs. As a sector, agriculture was capable of blocking compromise at the Doha Round of trade negotiations; otherwise, it could only favor the generous status quo. Finally, labor, particularly the representatives of unskilled labor in the industrialized countries, were the likeliest proponents of trade protection before and during the Great Recession. The political weight of labor had continued to decline in key economies since the recession of the early 1980s, however. In the major Asian economies, labor had never played the same prominent political rôle that it claimed in North America or Europe. Organized labor had shrunk as a proportion of the workforce in the United States, and its membership was heavily concentrated in nontradable sectors, particularly the public sector. Although labor pressed successfully for certain protectionist measures taken by the Obama administration, these were marginal victories, not an all-out attack on trade liberalization. All of these political changes, in part the product of a globalized world economy, rendered the coalitional politics of protectionism problematic. As Peter Cowhey (chapter 8, this volume) describes for the United States, trade politics, scrambled by changes in the structure of the American economy and new political dynamics, eased the Obama administration's maintenance of a liberal trade policy. At the same time, these and similar changes in other major economies made the existing structure of global governance—and the liberalized international economy that it supported—more secure.

The Developing World: No New International Economic Order

The altered circumstances of the major developing economies have been another force for international stability during the Great Recession. During the Great Depression, the economic periphery led the world into economic crisis and bore the brunt of disruptions in world trade and financial flows. With a few exceptions, those developing economies also led the world in decoupling from the international economy and embarking on import-substituting industrialization, domestic economic expansion, and debt default. The recession of the early 1980s produced a debt crisis that lasted for a decade, a lost decade for Latin American development that produced heterodox policy experiments before a regional turn to neoliberal reforms. Once again, developing economies had suffered greater and more persistent economic distress than the industrialized economies.

In the Great Recession, early hopes that developing countries might demonstrate their decoupling from the industrialized world's financial turmoil were dashed, as steep declines in exports and financial disruption spread throughout the global economy. Nevertheless, in comparison to most industrialized countries, the largest emerging economies experienced at worst a mild crisis, if crisis is defined as "an unstable situation of extreme danger or difficulty" (Kahler and Lake, introduction to this volume). Most suffered brief declines in output or reductions in their rate of growth and recovered rapidly. As Stephan Haggard (chapter 2, this volume) describes, reforms undertaken since the Asian financial crisis of the late 1990s were a partial explanation for their superior economic performance. By correcting weaknesses in their financial systems in the aftermath of that crisis, some emerging economies, such as Brazil and Indonesia, have withstood recent financial shocks despite openness to international capital flows. In other cases, such as India and China, cautious financial opening and state oversight or ownership curbed risky behavior before the crisis and enabled a rapid restarting of growth through credit expansion. Earlier crises had also convinced many developing country governments to maintain large foreign exchange reserves, which permitted fiscal stimulus to offset the effects of the international downturn.

The large emerging market economies were not immune from the global crisis, however, and their deeper integration into the international economy over the past two decades gave them a strong interest in international collaboration designed to restore the global economy to a sustainable growth path. The enhanced role of the G-20 during the crisis was a clear sign of both their relatively strong economic performance and their willingness to participate in collaborative responses to the crisis. Their participation had required commitments to adjust the formulas of global governance, which had long been tilted toward the industrialized core of Japan, Europe, and North America. Apart from demands for greater influence within the existing international economic order, however, the developing economies, particularly the largest ones, displayed little taste for radical revisions in global governance institutions. The Great Recession did not produce a redefinition of their interests away from international economic integration. Rather than delinking, as they had in the 1930s, or demanding a new international economic order, as they had in the 1970s, the developing world remained invested in the existing order and served as a key constituency in its defense.

Institutions of Global Economic Governance: Flexibility and Constraint

A third explanation for sustained international economic cooperation during the Great Recession lies in the institutions of global economic governance. Despite the weaknesses and gaps exposed by the onset of financial crisis, the particular mix of global institutions—and the combination of flexibility and constraint on national policies that they embodied—provided a means for meeting domestic political demands without rending the fabric of collaboration. International institutions accommodated national policies adopted to meet the crisis rather than restricting the menu of choice.

The ability of the major economies to chart their own macroeconomic course under a regime of flexible exchange rates enabled a rapid response of governments to the crisis, particularly the mobilization of monetary policy. The only "fetters" in the system were the "green fetters" of dollar pegs chosen by Asian economies and the "euro fetters" imposed on the economies of the Eurozone. In China and elsewhere, the former were maintained during the Great Recession as a prop for the export sector and its labor force, creating conflict with the European Union and the United States. Critics of China's exchange rate policies were more subdued as the crisis deepened, tacitly acknowledging that preserving the Asian engine of global growth was more important than an immediate alteration in macroeconomic imbalances.

The Eurozone presented an example of regional, rule-based cooperation that both produced the conditions for the sovereign debt crisis that erupted in 2010 and hindered its resolution. Although the European Union mobilized financial support for its members at levels that would have been unimaginable during the 1930s, the Eurozone crisis elicited comparisons with the gold standard and the perverse role of international cooperation in precipitating the Great Depression. Weaknesses in Eurozone monetary cooperation had been highlighted long before the crisis: a one-size-fits-all regional monetary policy, weak restraints on national fiscal policies, and limited political integration that hindered substantial intra-European fiscal transfers. Linkage among financial institutions within Europe and outside the region risked renewed financial crisis on a scale that would match the post–Lehman Brothers debacle of 2008. At the same time, economic power outside Europe, whether an alarmed American administration or a Chinese government that pledged support for Europe's finances, had relatively little leverage over the dilatory response of European governments and the EU to the crisis. What was most remarkable about the Eurozone crisis from the vantage point of early 2012 was the unwillingness of national governments experiencing deep economic distress—Greece, Portugal, Ireland—to overturn their commitment to the euro and the tight constraints that it imposed on their policy choices. Once again, crisis had induced an initial recommitment to the existing rules of the game, even when domestic political costs were high and rising.

In the years before the Great Recession, global institutions had played a relatively minor role in monitoring macroeconomic policies among the largest national economies. In contrast to their stance during earlier financial crises in the developing world, the leading international financial institutions took a much more accommodating position in this crisis, which afflicted the core economies of the United States and Europe. IMF managing director Dominique Strauss-Kahn was widely applauded for his vigorous advocacy of expansionary national fiscal policies. The IMF's recommendations during the Great Recession stood in stark contrast to the deflationary prescriptions prescribed by central bankers at the start of the Great Depression. The mechanisms of international cooperation, for the major industrialized economies and the large emerging economies, were geared toward preventing a complete financial collapse and deploying public sectors to compensate for a sharp decline in exports, investment, and private consumption. International institutions not only supported such measures, they also provided accurate analysis of the course of economic events, which lent further intellectual support to national policy measures.

In the realm of ideas, the Great Recession seemed at first to confirm an end to the Washington consensus, under challenge since the Asian financial crisis. Such a firm consensus on rolling back the public sector, reducing government intervention, and imposing fiscal and monetary austerity may never have existed (apart from its caricature by the critics of the Bretton Woods institutions). Nevertheless, even the most stalwart of market-oriented economists, as well as their allies in the financial sector, fell into line with a new, and possibly temporary, international consensus on the necessity for government and central bank intervention that was unprecedented in scope. A further marker of the changing official consensus was the IMF's validation of the usefulness of controls on capital inflows, even though it had campaigned for the abolition of capital controls in the 1990s.[7] Despite the evolving position of the IMF, developing country governments rejected new IMF oversight of their use in April 2011, suspicious that even the proposed framework might constrain their policy options.

7. Ideational sources of the IMF's changing position on capital controls before the Great Recession are discussed in Chwieroth (2008).

The institutions and spokespersons of global governance were clearly part of that shift in the policy consensus and, in some cases, led the new thinking. Whether the expedients adopted during the crisis will result in greater willingness to countenance public oversight and intervention in financial markets over the longer term remains to be seen. Even less certain was the crisis-induced consensus on government intervention and fiscal stimulus. A rapid and vehement rejection of this expanded role for government emerged in the Tea Party movement and its Republican Party allies in the United States, sweeping the 2010 elections to the House of Representatives on a platform rejecting increased government spending and a larger government role in the economy. The Conservative-led government in the United Kingdom, which took office in May 2010, also insisted on aiming at fiscal balance rather than stimulus, an embrace of austerity that was endorsed by Germany and rapidly entered into prescriptions for Eurozone governments. Any international ideological turn away from either market solutions or government intervention appears far from sturdy or long-lasting. What Widmaier, Blyth, and Seabrooke describe as a process of crisis-induced persuasion among political agents over "who they are" and "what they want" had only begun (2007, 756). Those arguments would continue to shape the ideational environment of global institutions after the Great Recession.

If the global macroeconomic response in the early stages of the crisis centered on support for national policies of monetary ease and fiscal stimulus, another key global institution, the WTO, imposed tight constraints on national efforts to use trade policy as an instrument for fighting unemployment. As described earlier, the WTO represented a clear example of stronger international rules and greater institutional authority during the era of globalization. As a result, the dispute settlement mechanism of the WTO dealt with most protectionist or discriminatory measures that were contestable under WTO rules. Despite the Doha Round impasse, the WTO functioned as intended: deterring national policies that would undermine the liberal trade regime and providing cover for politicians who were pressed to raise protectionist barriers. Official and unofficial evaluations of trade measures taken during the crisis confirmed that "crisis-related protectionism . . . [was] remarkably restrained," given the precipitous drop in world trade produced by the Great Recession.[8] Regional agreements also lent rule-based support to the norm of trade liberalization in the wake of the economic downturn: the United States approved free trade agreements with Colombia,

8. Erixon and Sallye (2010, 9); and Report on G20 Trade and Investment Measures (November 2009 to mid-May 2010), issued under the responsibility of the director-general of the WTO, the secretary-general of the OECD, and the secretary-general of UNCTAD, June 14, 2010. Erixon and Sally caution on the risks of cumulating protectionist measures and "non-traditional, non-border protectionism," however.

Panama, and South Korea and began Trans-Pacific Partnership negotiations as a means of expanding trade and investment with nine other countries. China forged the Economic Cooperation Framework Agreement with Taiwan, an economic pact that also had important political implications.

Successful Noncooperation?

These three explanations for sustained international economic cooperation—the effects of globalization on domestic political coalitions and their demands, the transformed status of the largest developing economies, and the particular mix of flexibility and constraint within existing global economic institutions—may account for much of the difference in outcomes between the current Great Recession and past global economic crises. A final explanation for the stability of international cooperation must also be entertained, however: if international cooperation is defined as agreed policy adjustments—beyond those determined by purely domestic political considerations—the current crisis may have seen very little international cooperation. Instead of international cooperation, the crisis induced harmony among the major economic powers: a label introduced by Robert O. Keohane to describe the successful achievement of national goals without negotiated policy adjustments.[9]

The major economies, in particular, undertook policy changes that were dictated by domestic political necessity: further economic decline or financial collapse would have produced political costs that the elites of those countries were unwilling to contemplate. The large fiscal stimulus programs implemented by the United States and China may have owed little to international pressure or collaboration. Both countries had an interest in preventing fiscal free-riding by economies (such as those in Europe) that preferred less fiscal stimulus and more export recovery. Even in the absence of a coordinated policy response, however, the United States and Chinese governments were likely to implement programs very similar to those that were mandated. Central bank cooperation appears more important during the crisis: the initiation of currency swaps at the height of the crisis as well as coordinated interest rate cuts were products of networked cooperation (Wessel 2009, 139–42, 229–32). Even in this domain, however, international collaboration may have had less influence on the unprecedented activism of the Federal Reserve (in contrast to the European Central Bank) than the legal mandate of the U.S. central bank, particularly its role in maintaining financial system stability.

9. On the distinction between cooperation and harmony, see Keohane (1984).

Support for a stronger IMF and an expansion of its resources often reflected domestic political considerations. For example, the European Union's support for renewed IMF activism could be traced in part to the EU's wish to avoid sole responsibility for a bailout of central and east European economies hard hit by the crisis. A European political problem was promoted to the global level to be dealt with by the IMF. For the major economic powers, cooperation with the IMF entailed few new adjustments of policy, apart from agreement to provide additional resources for the IMF.

Each of the major economic powers had their own domestic political reasons to implement policies that warded off financial collapse or economic depression. The degree of formal (and specifically new) cooperation that was undertaken has been limited. Since the end of the Cold War, the major powers have been successful in sustaining negative order: avoiding the worst, either a great power war or, its rough equivalent in the realm of the international economy, levels of economic conflict that result in mutual closure and a much lower level of global economic welfare. During the Great Recession, they have been successful once again, when their actions are measured against this benchmark.

The true test of international cooperation may arrive when national governments attempt to construct a new positive order: substantive cooperation to achieve mutually desirable goals through joint action. This more demanding collaboration would require painful adjustments of policy in the face of potent domestic resistance as memories of the crisis fade.[10] Paradoxically, some of the same features of the international environment that produced cooperation during the Great Recession may make it more difficult to agree on a path to sustainable growth and financial stability.

Global Governance after the Crisis: Shortcomings and Obstacles to Reform

Global economic cooperation during and after the Great Recession has been sustained by a pragmatic and conservative coalition that prevented the crisis from becoming a turning point toward a future of global disorder. These agents did not redefine their pro-globalization interests during a period of heightened economic uncertainty. However, each leg of the tripod that has sustained global economic cooperation during the crisis may also impede necessary additional

10. On the distinction between negative and positive order, see Kahler (1991). A similar distinction, between dilemmas of common aversions and dilemmas of common interests is made in Stein (1991).

measures of reform in global governance. Economic globalization has eroded support for economic closure and unilateralism; it also produced a chain of policy spillovers that amplified American regulatory shortcomings into a global recession. In order to deal with those consequences of closer economic integration, the existing mix of flexibility and constraint within global institutions, a combination that permitted energetic national responses to the crisis, must be altered: more surveillance of macroeconomic and regulatory policies, jealously guarded by national authorities, will be required. At the same time, the architecture of global governance must strike a balance between centralization and the risks of an uncoordinated and fragmented structure. Finally, the developing countries, which did not defect from the existing economic order during the Great Recession, have demanded more influence over governance institutions as the price for their continuing support. Their inclusion, however, may dilute the reform program and undermine the efficacy of global institutions over the longer term. In particular, they are likely to reject more intensive international scrutiny of national policies.

Policy Spillovers in a Globalized Economy: The Need for International Surveillance

A more globalized economy has produced incentives for national elites to restrain impulses toward economic nationalism and unilateralism. Globalization has made the foundation of existing global governance institutions more secure, in the sense that there are few incentives to depart from existing international regimes. At the same time, the latest economic crisis demonstrates that a more integrated international economy increases the spillover effects from policy missteps, particularly those made by the major economic powers. Even the most pessimistic observers of the American housing bubble could not predict the global consequences of collapse in the subprime sector of the American mortgage market: transatlantic banking crises (labeled as manageable at the time), financial panic following the failure of Lehman Brothers, and a sharp decline in world trade that affected even financially sound economies. American regulatory failures and Chinese exchange rate policies exemplify domestic policy choices that have large international effects.

These negative effects on innocent bystanders reinforce proposals for closer and more intrusive international surveillance of national policies. The IMF is usually the instrument in such recommendations for expanded international oversight. For example, the Manuel Committee (2009) advocated an expansion of the IMF surveillance mandate beyond exchange rates to "macroeconomic policies, prudential issues and financial spillovers." The Pittsburgh Summit of the

G-20 also appeared to endorse an important role for both the IMF and peer pressure in the new Framework for Strong, Sustainable, and Balanced Growth (FSSBG). The IMF was tasked to build on its existing surveillance activities in order to provide "candid, even-handed, and balanced analysis" of G-20 national policies, as well as estimates of whether G-20 policies are "collectively consistent with more sustainable and balanced trajectories for the global economy."[11]

Unfortunately, little in the record of earlier surveillance, under IMF auspices or in other venues, suggests that the major economic powers are willing to submit to serious multilateral surveillance of their economic policies. The Financial Sector Assessment Plan (FSAP) was designed after the Asian financial crisis to scrutinize financial sectors and lower the risk of future financial crises. Before the Great Recession, financial powers, such as China and the United States, were able to reject financial stability assessments under the FSAP. International oversight outside the FSAP did little to warn of the financial practices and conditions that led up to the current crisis.[12] Post-crisis, governments have continued to guard their regulatory prerogatives; without substantial international prodding it is not clear that national political dynamics will produce the regulatory reforms required to secure financial stability (Crockett 2009). In the past, surveillance of macroeconomic policies has been even less successful. As Edwin Truman (2008) notes, the IMF surveillance record pre-crisis added credence to those who argued that the global institution had become irrelevant. The IMF's Executive Board and management displayed little willingness to confront the major economic powers over global economic imbalances. When the IMF managing director finally instituted a process of multilateral consultation to address this issue, its "accomplishments fell far short of what was promised because of excessive timidity, unsound analysis . . . and lack of cooperation by the participants" (Truman 2008, 3). Despite steps taken in the aftermath of the crisis to expand scrutiny of national policies by the IMF and the G-20, resistance to effective international surveillance on the part of the major economic powers is likely to persist.

Global Governance: International Constraints on National Policy Choice

The issue of surveillance to prevent negative policy spillovers is closely linked to the current mix of flexibility and constraint within global economic institutions. Institutions of global governance have not thwarted national efforts at economic

11. Leaders' Statement: The Pittsburgh Summit, September 24–25, 2009. http://ec.europa.eu/commission_2010-2014/president/pdf/statement_20090826_en_2.pdf.

12. Lombardi 2009. An IMF Executive Board decision in September 2010 made such assessments mandatory for those members with systemically important financial sectors.

revival. Apart from the issue-area of trade, however, they have also failed to constrain national policies in the interests of agreed cooperative solutions. During the economic crisis, coordination of national policies was relatively easy, since most governments had strong incentives for activism and economic expansion. Cooperation has become more difficult as governments contemplate their exit strategies from these crisis measures.

The issue of increased constraints on national policy choice is perhaps most pressing, and most politically charged, in the domain of financial regulation. Resolving the issue of subsidiarity—how governance should be divided between the global and national levels—is a controversial and demanding issue in regulatory reform. Different regulatory models have been defended on the grounds that they fit better with national political institutions and financial sectors. Diversity in national policies also allows for experimentation and eventual diffusion of best national practices. Such benefits, however, are dependent on satisfactory regulatory outcomes: prevention of excessive risk-taking and adequate attention to the safety and soundness of the financial sector.

Global institutions and norms that attempt to constrain national choices too narrowly will be overturned or ignored, just as the gold standard's "golden fetters" were dissolved in the face of domestic pressure during the Great Depression. Institutions that provide too many escape clauses and are too permissive of national policy choices will be ineffective in enforcing cooperative bargains. At the regional level, the current crisis in the Eurozone illustrates the risks of institutional arrangements with the wrong mix of rules and discretion. Many member governments flouted fiscal rules, but in the wake of the Eurozone debt crisis, the common currency has limited policy options and forced painful fiscal and labor market adjustment. Given a fragile economic recovery that has already faced unforeseen shocks, such as the Japan's triple disaster in March 2011, achieving the optimal mix of constraint and flexibility in global rules and institutions will be difficult.

Global Governance: Institutional Centralization and Fragmentation

The new mandates for global economic governance also raise a different issue of balance, between institutional fragmentation and coordination. The global economic crisis has produced limited institutional innovation: the G-20 has been elevated, along with the Financial Stability Board. The IMF has been refurbished through an award of new resources and a revival of its role in surveillance. The language of "pillars" suggests a centralization of global governance and its concentration on a handful of key intergovernmental institutions. In this regard, the rhetoric of institutional reform echoes the arguments of those who advocate concentrating more authority in fewer, more accountable institutions.[13]

This tidy vision confronts a theoretical and a practical challenge. The theoretical challenge comes from the virtues of institutional variety and competition. Formal intergovernmental institutions are only one model of international order: informal networks have also demonstrated their effectiveness, as the network of central bankers, centered on the Bank for International Settlements, has repeatedly demonstrated. In practical terms, centralization will face political resistance from those with interests in other parts of the present fragmented pattern of global governance. Centralization also requires the creation of mechanisms for coordination, between the IMF and the FSB, for example, on regulatory issues.

The Developing World as Principals in Global Governance

Perhaps the most dramatic innovation in global governance in the wake of the global economic crisis—and one likely to be the longest lasting—is expansion of the influence of key developing economies in core global institutions. The award of a central role to the G-20 in global economic discussions is one of several shifts that signal recognition of the engagement and economic weight of new players such as China, India, and Brazil. Although the contribution of greater inclusiveness to the legitimacy of global governance has carried the argument so far, the definition of inclusiveness and its costs have not been carefully evaluated. The G-20 represents a large share of world population and an even larger share of world economic product; its membership reconfigures global institutions and at the same time retains a large share of influence for an expanded group of major economies. Its formula is a broader version of existing great power clubs. Many of the strongest supporters of the international economic order among the developing countries—open economies such as Chile or Singapore—are excluded. An alternative definition of inclusiveness would award greater influence to a more numerous population of smaller sovereign units, through innovations such as a double majority system of voting (Lombardi 2009).

Even if an appropriate formula can be agreed for enhancing legitimacy through greater inclusion in decision making, wider participation and influence must be weighed against possible loss of effectiveness, another source of legitimacy. The risk that accompanies a proliferation of principals in any reform of global governance is institutional paralysis and a sharp decline in decision-making efficiency. The EU has attempted to meet the challenge of an expanded

13. See, for example, the Manuel Committee Report (2009).

membership through increased use of qualified majority voting. If global institutions rely on cumbersome decision-making processes, the resulting decline in efficiency could undermine legitimacy and encourage members to seek alternative forums for their deliberations. Exit by prominent members—tacitly if not formally—has often produced clubs of powerful countries operating outside the purview of large-membership organizations. Legitimacy through inclusion, a worthwhile goal, cannot be allowed to undermine effectiveness, another key source of legitimate action.

An award of greater influence in global governance to new actors produces a third dilemma: an award of influence to such emerging powers as India and China gives greater voice to countries that have been most resistant to international surveillance of national policies. The largest developing countries (and many smaller ones) have uniformly adopted an unyielding stance on sovereignty; noninterference in domestic affairs has been their watchword. If a globalized economy requires greater scrutiny of and constraints on national economic policies by international institutions or peer governments, these new influentials are likely to be the most resistant to such an agenda.

Conclusion: Economic Crisis and Global Governance

In contrast to earlier financial crises and steep economic downturns, the current global economic crisis has not produced a crisis in global governance. Instead, the Great Recession and its aftermath have produced modest strengthening of existing global institutions, an equally modest rebalancing of their formal allocation of influence, and pledges (and mainly pledges at present) to undertake more ambitious cooperative ventures, backed by international surveillance, in policy coordination and financial regulation. These encouraging green shoots of enhanced international economic collaboration were founded on a conservative coalition of interests, interests that were not redefined under the initial shock of financial crisis and recession. The economic crisis has not produced movement away from global economic integration on the part of major private-sector actors in the rich countries or governments in the developing world. The world economy that produced this relatively benign outcome is a world more integrated economically and also one that is integrated in ways that set it apart from earlier eras. The club of industrialized countries appears willing to concede its exclusive dominance of global economic policy, and an array of international institutions lends support to economic cooperation.

Resilient in the face of recession, the very conservatism of these supports for intergovernmental cooperation and crisis-induced initiatives, however, also call into question the introduction of a long-delayed deepening of global governance to match a more integrated and vulnerable world economy. Whether played out in governance of the Eurozone or the global economy, attaining a balance between national autonomy and international oversight that is both politically acceptable and economically effective will constitute a continuing challenge, long after the Great Recession fades into memory.

2

POLITICS IN HARD TIMES REVISITED

The 2008–9 Financial Crisis in Emerging Markets

Stephan Haggard

From the onset of the U.S. housing market difficulties in 2007 through the summer of 2008, emerging markets seemed largely "decoupled" from the unfolding U.S. recession. With a few intriguing exceptions, such as Iceland, middle-income countries did not have much exposure to the subprime market and associated derivatives. Equity markets continued to boom and emerging market spreads did not turn up significantly until the collapse of Bear Stearns in mid-2008.

The Lehman failure in September 2008 quickly put an end to the myth of decoupling. The subprime crisis had a direct effect on banks and hedge funds that had been major sources of emerging-market funding. New security issues came to a virtual stop and foreign exchange markets came under heavy pressure as investors fled to safety. Borrowers in the European periphery were particularly affected, but the pullback in lending was widespread.

The extent of transmission through the trade channel varied across countries depending on their trading partners and reliance on commodity exports. Even prior to Lehman, commodity and oil prices turned down sharply. Emerging markets in Europe experienced a larger trade shock than other regions. Outside of Europe, dependence on the U.S. market proved a disadvantage; Mexico and Taiwan fared worse than regional counterparts such as Brazil and Thailand with more diversified trade structures. But the contraction of world trade during the

In addition to the editors and other members of this project, particular thanks to Peter Katzenstein for a close reading of a draft, Robert Kaufman and Barry Naughton for insights on Latin America and China, and Don Lee for research assistance.

crisis was extraordinarily rapid and widespread. Most emerging markets saw a decline in both imports and exports of between 30 percent and 40 percent from September 2008 to January 2009.

Yet despite the apparently common nature of these shocks, their effects and national responses to them were extremely diverse. Differing economic circumstances played an important role in this divergence, but these circumstances were themselves deeply rooted in politics. Why did the effects of the crisis differ so widely across the emerging markets of Europe, Latin America, and East Asia? What accounts for variation in the way governments in three regions responded to crisis?

A first nonfinding concerns dogs that did not bark, or at least not much. As Kahler (chapter 1, this volume) and Cowhey (chapter 9, this volume) point out, protectionist responses to the crisis were relatively limited. This finding largely holds for emerging markets as well. Nor do we see reversion to the type of state-led development strategies that were common in the early postwar period. A plausible explanation for this outcome follows a coalitional logic (Gourevitch 1986). As emerging market economies have reformed and become more open, a wider array of business interests gained a stake in trade and investment. Broader publics in more labor-abundant economies are supportive of free trade too, as simple Ricardian models of trade would predict.

The central question thus has to do with the extent to which emerging markets had the room to pursue a counter-cyclical, Keynesian response to the crisis, as virtually all of the advanced industrial states did. During the debt crises of the 1980s and 1990s, debtors were constrained to pursue tough stabilization programs, typically anchored by tight monetary policies designed to limit the extent of exchange rate depreciation. Crisis and external political pressures also pushed emerging markets to adopt a menu of neoliberal reforms that John Williamson (1990) codified as the "Washington consensus."

By contrast, the fiscal stimulus option was pursued by many emerging market countries in the aftermath of the crisis of 2008–9. What determined the ability of some emerging markets to exploit this option? The answers can be found in some unremarked regional dynamics as well as the political consequences of past crises.

A surprising number of countries experiencing severe distress were in Europe or on the European periphery. These countries had exploited membership in or proximity to the European Union (EU) to pursue what Arvind Subramanian (2011) has called the "foreign finance fetish": they liberalized financial markets and capital accounts and ran large—in some cases extraordinary—current account deficits. A number also sacrificed an independent monetary and fiscal policy to monetary integration (in the form of adoption of the euro) or fixed pegs. Although market-oriented center-right governments were somewhat more likely to pursue this strategy (Broz, chapter 3, this volume), the evidence in this regard is not overwhelming. Greece, Hungary, and some of the former Soviet republics constitute oligarchic, left, or populist variants of the "foreign finance fetish" model. As Gourevitch argues in the afterword of this volume, the influence of finance was not limited to one side of the left-right political aisle.

For those on the euro or seeking to enter the Eurozone, the exchange rate commitment posed a painful Hobson's choice when the crisis struck: highly costly to break, the choice of a fixed rate also implied sacrifice of macroeconomic policy autonomy and massive fiscal adjustments.

The constraints on the fixed exchange rate countries were not only economic. The crisis was followed by an intense political debate between creditors and debtors over the terms on which additional resources would be made available.

Did coalitional factors influence the tendency for those in Europe to sustain their commitments? There is some evidence for the eastern European cases that publics favored center-right responses to the crisis, including the maintenance of exchange rate commitments. But governments of very different sorts reached broadly similar conclusions—or faced broadly similar constraints—suggesting that regional commitments and institutions played a role.

A second group of emerging markets in Latin America and East Asia had more room to pursue fiscal stimulus responses. The availability of this option was not simply economic but rooted in the political economy of past crises. Governments of both left and right had abandoned fixed pegs; pursued more cautious fiscal policies that moderated the growth of government debt, including foreign debt; and accumulated substantial reserves. Evidence of the significance of distinct political cleavages in how these countries responded to the crisis is also mixed; the fiscal stimulus option proved attractive to a wide array of interests, generating an array of cross-sector and cross-class coalitions of support.

Why No Protectionism?

As Kahler (chapter 1, this volume) and Cowhey (chapter 9, this volume) both point out, the advanced industrial states largely eschewed a protectionist response to the crisis. This finding appears to hold with respect to the major emerging markets as well and only a handful of middle-income countries pursued a hard "statist" response to the crisis.[1] Why?

---

1. Those showing evidence of a statist response to the crisis were already pursuing such strategies prior to the onset of the crisis: Iran, Venezuela, Libya, Syria, and several of the former Soviet republics such as Turkmenistan and Uzbekistan provide examples. Two features of this group are notewor-

First, the evidence: a joint report of the Organisation for Economic Co-operation and Development, the World Trade Organization, and the United Nations Conference on Trade and Development (OECD-WTO-UNCTAD 2009) compares the initiation of antidumping and safeguard measures among Group of Twenty (G-20) countries pre- and post-Lehman (the first half of 2008 with the first half of 2009) as a useful proxy of early protectionist responses to the crisis. Argentina, India, and Turkey (as well as the United States) show relatively high levels of antidumping actions in both periods, but with no trend. China (with respect to antidumping) and India (with respect to safeguards) show sharp increases in cases in the first half of 2009.

But with the exception of India, which entered the crisis with relatively high tariffs, country-by-country estimates indicate that new trade restricting measures in the first half of 2009 covered only 0.2–0.8 percent of the total pre-crisis level of imports and the incidence of such measures subsequently declined and then stabilized (OECD-WTO-UNCTAD 2010; WTO 2011).[2] Even Argentine trade policy—probably the most aggressive of the developing G20 members—limited restrictive measures to particular sectors and source countries that were combined with liberalizing ones, including with respect to financial flows and foreign direct investment (FDI). A summary assessment by the WTO (2011) of the 2006–11 period suggests that emerging market members of the G-20 were not more likely than developed country members to initiate trade restrictions; to the contrary, the United States and the EU were the biggest culprits.

The explanation for this dog that did not bark seems fairly straightforward. Most of the major emerging markets have seen quite substantial increases in their trade shares over the last two decades, spurred on in part by reforms undertaken in response to previous crises. The result is a wider spectrum of trade-related business interests, including cross-border production networks of both foreign and domestic firms.

In addition, recent research has drawn attention to the trade preferences of broader publics in newly democratic middle-income countries, including labor (Milner and Kubota 2005; Pinto and Pinto 2008). The Pew Global Attitudes Project provides some suggestive evidence in this regard, based on the answer to a simple, unframed question ("Is trade a good or bad thing?"). (See table 2-1.) The two large labor-abundant giants—China and India—both show extraordinarily high support for trade. Support for trade actually increases between the pre- and

---

thy. First, they are all authoritarian, a precondition for a strategy that entails expropriation or extensive controls on the private sector. Second, a number are oil producers, with their well-known complex of political economy problems.

2. These are overestimates of the actual impact of the restrictions because they are a measure of the entire trade affected by restrictions, not of the trade forgone as a result of the restrictions; the latter would typically be only a fraction of the affected trade.

TABLE 2-1. G-20 Emerging country public opinion on trade (percent answering "good thing" to question: "Is trade a good or bad thing?")

	PRE-CRISIS (2007, PERCENT)	POST-CRISIS (2009, PERCENT)	PERCENTAGE POINT CHANGE
Argentina	68	65	–3
Brazil	72	85	+13
China	91	93	+2
India	89	99	+10
Indonesia	71	79	+8
Korea	86	92	+6
Mexico	77	79	+2
Russia	82	81	–1
Turkey	73	64	–9
Non-G20			
Egypt	61	67	+6
Nigeria	85	90	+5
Poland	77	81	+4
Spain	82	89	+7

Source: Pew Global Attitudes Project Key Indicators Database at http://pewglobal.org/database/?indicator=16.

post-crisis surveys in all countries except those two—Argentina and Turkey—for which support for trade was already at the low end of the distribution. Both of these countries are also higher-income countries facing pressures from even lower-wage competitors such as China. Despite some interesting variance that would require further explication, the overall level of support for trade in these emerging markets is high and even seemed to rise in response to crisis.

Neoliberalism or Keynesianism?

If principled protectionism and statism have had limited appeal during the current conjuncture, Keynesianism is quite a different matter. Given the sharp contraction in trade and output, it is not surprising that governments in both developed and developing countries would seek to sustain demand, employment, and labor incomes through the well-known mechanisms of monetary policy, deficit spending, and increases in public-sector indebtedness. To what extent were they both willing and able to do so?

Before undertaking a political analysis of such choices, we need to address several problems in assessing the consequences of international shocks on do-

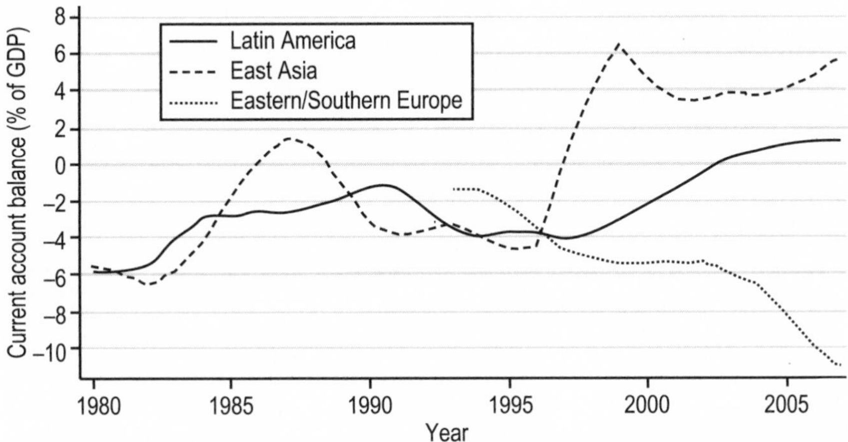

FIGURE 2-1. Current account balances in emerging markets: Latin America, East Asia, and eastern and southern Europe (percent of GDP). Note: Three-year moving average. Latin America: Argentina, Brazil, Chile, Colombia, Mexico, Peru; East Asia: Indonesia, Malaysia, Philippines, South Korea, Thailand; eastern and southern Europe: Bulgaria, Czech Republic, Estonia, Greece, Hungary, Ireland, Latvia, Lithuania, Poland, Portugal, Romania, Slovakia, Spain.

Source: World Bank (2011). http://data.worldbank.org/indicator/BN.CAB.XOKA.GD.ZS.

mestic politics (see Kahler and Lake, introduction, this volume). The first is the assumption that external shocks are largely exogenous and that they are of broadly comparable magnitude across cases. These assumptions permit a quasi-experimental design in which politics serves as the treatment that differentiates cases. These assumptions may be reasonable for large-country cases (Gourevitch 1986), but—somewhat counterintuitively—they do not necessarily hold for small open economies.

The collapse in foreign demand in 2008–9 was certainly common but countries with larger current account deficits faced more difficult economic and political adjustments. Figure 2-1 tracks the current account deficits of major emerging markets in East Asia and Latin America from 1980 and in southern and eastern Europe from 1993 (when comparable data is available for the post-socialist countries) through 2007, just prior to the onset of the crisis. The developing countries of Latin America adjusted to the crises of the mid-1980s and had moderate current account deficits going into the crisis, in part because of the commodity boom of the early 2000s. The shift in the current account positions of the major East Asian emerging markets—minus China—showed an even sharper adjustment to the crisis of 1997–98 as governments ran larger surpluses and accumulated reserves.

The European periphery, by contrast, had exploited the advantages of entry or proximity to the Eurozone to borrow, in some cases quite massively. Capital inflows fed consumption, including government consumption that would have to be adjusted or financed through increased taxes given loss of access to international capital markets. Capital inflows also financed a dramatic expansion of the nontradable goods sector, most notably real estate and finance. Bubbles in these sectors were subject not only to major corrections but to politically charged workouts. Why did some governments leave themselves exposed to extraordinary current account deficits in the first place?

A second important issue concerns the exchange rate. Emerging markets proved unable to defend fixed pegs during the debt crises of the 1980s and 1990s, but they did seek to limit the extent of depreciation through restrictive monetary policies. As Keynesian critics noted at the time, such "depression economics" would have been completely unacceptable to the advanced industrial states, a judgment that proved completely prescient (Krugman 2000; Stiglitz 2003). In line with the well-known trilemma of international finance, those countries that remained committed to a fixed exchange rate and an open capital account largely sacrificed an independent macroeconomic policy. Why did some countries find themselves vulnerable to this new cross of gold while others enjoyed greater exchange rate flexibility?

A third issue has to do with the availability of international public finance. Even the IMF acknowledges that fiscal adjustments need to balance concerns about the sustainability of deficits, debt dynamics, and market confidence with the need to sustain demand; in Nixon's famous dictum, we are all Keynesians now. But because of dependence on external public finance, the international financial institutions and major creditor governments constitute a crucial constraint on policy choices. How much credit are they willing to supply in the wake of crises and on what terms?

The underlying fiscal constraints on government can be seen in figure 2-2, which tracks the path of the primary government surplus or deficit—the overall balance excluding net interest payments—from just prior to the crisis in 2006 through 2011. Emerging markets in Asia and Latin America exhibit stronger fiscal positions going into the crisis, even running primary surpluses. They do not face the same adjustment processes in the wake of the crisis; rather, the decline in fiscal surpluses reflects their ability to exploit a Keynesian option. In eastern Europe, and particularly in Ireland, Portugal, Greece, and Spain, governments enter the crisis in a somewhat weaker fiscal position. But the collapse of external lending, and severe domestic banking crises in a number of cases, results in deep recessions and an explosion of fiscal deficits. Struggling governments are subsequently forced to undertake large fiscal adjustments, typically under strong external political as well as economic pressure.

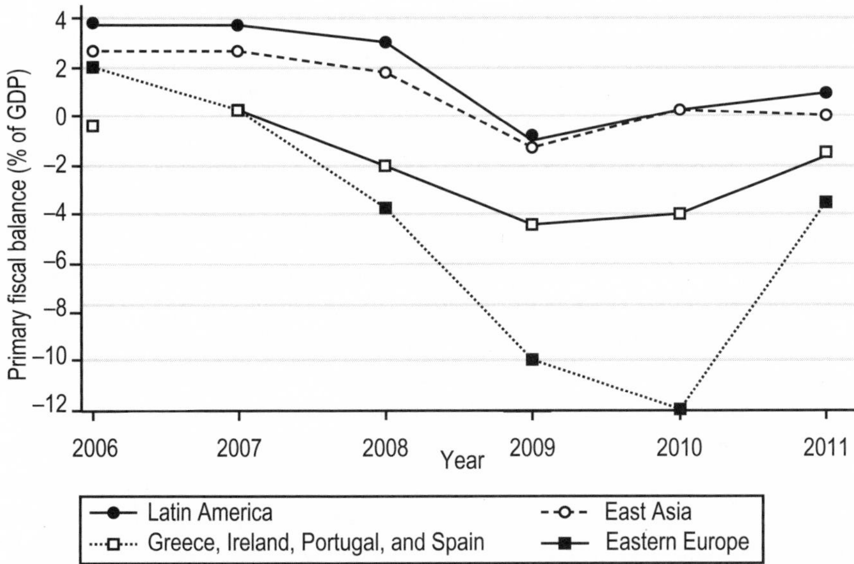

FIGURE 2-2. Primary fiscal balances in emerging markets: Latin America, East Asia, and southern and eastern Europe (percent of GDP). Note: Primary fiscal balance is the overall fiscal balance minus net interest payments. Latin America: Argentina, Brazil, Chile, Colombia, Mexico, Peru; East Asia: Indonesia, Malaysia, Philippines, Singapore, South Korea, Thailand; eastern Europe: Bulgaria, Czech Republic, Estonia, Hungary, Latvia, Lithuania, Poland, Romania, Slovakia.

Source: IMF (2011, 56). http://www.imf.org/external/pubs/ft/fm/2011/02/pdf/fm1102.pdf.

Given these considerations, what role might domestic politics play? Gourevitch's (1986) explanation for the choice of Keynesianism versus neoclassical options rested on the relative strength of "domesticist" and "internationalist" coalitions. The former is a "cross-sector, cross-class alliance of groups whose patience with market solutions had run out" (Gourevitch 1986, 131) and whose interests were more squarely rooted in the domestic market. Labor movements in the private sector constituted a key pillar of such coalitions in the past, but they would now also include government workers, private actors dependent on government contracting and procurement, and beneficiaries of government transfers and entitlements, which have grown dramatically across all of the emerging markets considered here (Haggard and Kaufman 2008).

In the internationalist camp, we might count the financial sector and those with access to foreign financing (Gourevitch, afterword, this volume) as well as export-oriented industry and agriculture. To these might also be added firms (and perhaps associated labor) embedded in international production networks through foreign investment and contracting. Whether all of these groups would necessarily support similar policies is far from clear; for example, the export sector might gain from abandoning a fixed peg or from monetary and fiscal stimulus in the face of economic slack. But the members of this internationalist coalition may nonetheless see longer-run benefits from being responsive to the concerns of creditors and the international financial institutions and may recognize the high costs in abandoning fixed exchange rates in particular; as we will see, this choice frequently drove all others.

Do we see evidence that party and major interest group cleavages correspond broadly to this coalitional logic and influenced the course of policy? The findings are mixed at best. In the European emerging markets, a variety of different types of governments exploited proximity to the EU and the capacity to borrow at dramatically reduced rates. Yet this borrowing proved costly when the crisis hit. Just as governments of very different types were attracted to the benefits of foreign borrowing, so governments of very different types were constrained to adjust to the withdrawal of credit with a tightening of fiscal policy and the initiation of a variety of structural reforms.

Outside of Europe, countries that had experienced crises in the past had converged around some macroeconomic fundamentals that permitted them to avoid the worst of the crisis and to enjoy the space to pursue countercyclical policies.[3] While coalitional differences are by no means absent, these prior adjustments were crucial in opening the space for more countercyclical policies.

Moreover, the political economy of the financial crisis was by no means purely domestic. Where governments faced severe balance of payments constraints and sought international public finance, external actors played a very important role in the adjustment process. Where countries did not face such constraints, they were capable of defining independent policy courses that did not require external ratification.

The Crisis in Europe

One way to assess the damage to emerging markets caused by the crisis of 2008–9 is to consider the list of countries that availed themselves of IMF resources from the Lehman shock of September 2008 through the end of 2011. From September 2008 through the end of 2009, sixteen countries signed regular standby agreements with the IMF (excluding facilities for low-income countries and a handful of special lines of credit and precautionary programs that were

3. On Asia, see Haggard (2000). On Latin America, see Kaufman (2011).

not subsequently drawn).[4] Ten of these programs were with countries of western and eastern Europe and the former Soviet Union, and they accounted for the overwhelming share of the fund's outstanding credit;[5] Hungary, Romania, and Ukraine alone accounted for about three-fifths of it. Eleven new programs were signed in 2010 and 2011. Again, the European countries—Greece, Kosovo, Ireland, Portugal, and new programs with Ukraine, Romania, and Serbia—accounted for the bulk of this new credit, indeed for over 95 percent of it. And this does not include the massive resources committed to the European Financial Stability Facility (EFSF) in the wake of the Greek crisis in May 2010 and subsequent additions to that facility over the course of 2011.

It is possible to distinguish three distinct groups of crisis countries in Europe. The first, represented by Greece, Ireland, and Portugal, were members of the Eurozone. The second group, including the Baltic countries, Hungary, Romania, and Bulgaria were members of the EU but had not yet adopted the euro; Iceland is a somewhat anomalous case because it was a member of the European Economic Area. A third group of countries was outside of the EU altogether, including Armenia, Belarus, Bosnia and Herzegovina, Georgia, Kosovo, Serbia, and Ukraine.

The first and most obvious point is that all of these crisis countries faced major macroeconomic and structural adjustments, aggravated in those cases where balance of payments crises overlapped with banking crises. The scope for a Keynesian response in these small open economies was very severely constrained.[6] The central question was not whether fiscal adjustments would be necessary, but how much finance would be provided by the IMF, the EU, creditor governments, and the foreign lenders in order to ease the costs of adjustment.

Europe took the lead in organizing extraordinarily large IMF programs for a number of countries outside the EU, adding additional support over time, orchestrating commitments on the part of private creditors (the European Bank Coordination Initiative), and permitting somewhat more accommodative macroeconomic policy responses than would have otherwise been necessary, at

4. The IMF also increased lending to poorer countries through its Poverty Reduction and Growth Trust (PRGT), renamed the Extended Credit Facility, and the Exogenous Shock Facility. Three Flexible Credit Line programs signed in April and May 2009 with Colombia, Mexico, and Poland had not been drawn on by the end of 2010, nor had "precautionary" standby programs with Costa Rica, Guatemala, and El Salvador.

5. Armenia, Belarus, Bosnia and Herzegovina, Georgia, Hungary, Iceland, Latvia, Romania, Serbia, and Ukraine.

6. The information provided on the European cases in this section is drawn primarily from four IMF sources: the country's letter of intent, the IMF staff report on it, subsequent reviews around each tranche release, and so-called "selected issues" papers drafted by IMF staff, all available at http://www.imf.org/external/country/index.htm.

least in the short run.[7] In virtually every one of these programs, fiscal adjustments were altered in the face of deteriorating forecasts. Difficult structural reforms of budgetary processes, including of social insurance systems, were pushed into the future. In Belarus, Georgia, and Ukraine, these adjustments were made possible by fundamental changes in exchange rate regimes, the introduction of greater exchange rate flexibility, and/or a shift to inflation targeting.

By contrast, the countries that were already in the Eurozone and those which had committed to exchange rate pegs faced tougher choices and became embroiled in very complex two-level political games with their EU creditors. On the one hand, the surplus countries, and most pivotally Germany, ultimately had little choice but to provide resources; in the absence of external support, contagion from Greece, Ireland, Portugal, Spain, and even Italy threatened to undermine the region's recovery. These actions were not merely altruistic; they were rooted in an effort to avoid default on debt held by their own banks and to prevent a more general unraveling of the euro. Of necessity, this meant accommodating a somewhat more lax—and realistic—fiscal stance on the part of borrowing countries, at least in the short run. This became particularly clear in the buildup to the fateful weekend of May 7–9, 2010, and in the subsequent management of Greece. Not only did Germany finally acquiesce to a €110 billion rescue package for the country, but it agreed to the creation of the EFSF financed by the EU budget, the euro-area governments, and the IMF. Germany was also forced to accept more aggressive intervention on the part of the European Central Bank and a partial write-down of Greek debt.

On the other hand, German resistance to bailouts has now become a leitmotif of the politics of European crisis management (Proissl 2010). Germany took the measures just outlined not only reluctantly, but slowly, and extracted a very substantial price for its grudging cooperation. The constraints on debtors were not the formal macroeconomic components of the Stability and Growth Pact; those quickly fell away in the wake of the crisis.[8] But Germany and other northern European creditors sought to attach very difficult conditions and invasive moni-

---

7. Support for third countries—those outside the EU—was extended under the Macro-Financial Assistance program; for details, see http://ec.europa.eu/economy_finance/financial_operations/market/third_countries/index_en.htm.

8. Under the Stability and Growth Pact, EU member states must submit annual macroeconomic and fiscal projections called "stability programs" for countries that have adopted the euro and "convergence programs" in the case of aspirants. The pact also requires the European Commission to prepare a report whenever the deficit of a member state exceeds 3% of GDP. Virtually all European emerging market countries fell under the excessive deficit procedures after the crisis but so did a number of the core countries in the EU, calling the entire edifice into question. For details on EDP actions, see http://ec.europa.eu/economy_finance/sgp/deficit/countries/index_en.htm.

toring on the European Community's support, backed by close coordination with the IMF. Limits on the extent of external financing ultimately constrained the scope for a Keynesian response to the crisis.[9]

Did countries that experienced crisis and subsequently chose to maintain their exchange rate commitments and/or undertake large-scale fiscal adjustments exhibit common political characteristics? Did coalitions matter? Broz (chapter 3, this volume) argues for the advanced industrial states that right-wing governments pursued policies that increased the vulnerability to crisis, leaving it to left-wing successors to clean up the mess. It is hard to find evidence of such a pattern in the southern and eastern European cases. Greece arguably fits the pattern, but Portugal was ruled by center-left coalitions before and after the crisis. In Spain a center-left coalition that had ruled during the boom years was decisively defeated by the right in the 2011 elections.

In his study of eastern Europe's response to the crisis, Aslund (2010) also finds a pattern directly at variance with the one found by Broz. Aslund shows that in the wake of the crisis publics generally supported integration with Europe and favored parties on the right that were willing to undertake the fiscal adjustments and structural reforms necessary to maintain that commitment. He cites as evidence the results of the June 2009 European parliamentary elections, which strongly favored right parties, and the fact that eight of the ten central and eastern European governments saw political shifts to the right from the onset of the crisis through August 2010.

A brief consideration of three cases—Iceland, Greece, and Latvia—suggests the diversity of political coalitions associated with both the borrowing booms and the subsequent imposition of austerity. Iceland provides a virtual textbook example of the pattern described by Broz. A right government beholden to financial interests and enamored of an extreme form of financial market liberalization set the stage for crisis, to which a left government was forced to adjust. The Greek case looks superficially similar—a right government followed by a left one. But under the nominally right-wing government, entitlements were sustained or expanded that benefited left constituencies. Partly as a result, the left-wing government was paralyzed by both parliament and strikes, proved incapable of undertaking necessary adjustments, and was ultimately forced from office in 2011. In Latvia—exemplary of the pattern described by Aslund—one right coalition was replaced by another that was similarly constrained to undertake

9. The EU's balance of payments lending was accompanied by memoranda of understanding (MOUs) that contained quite extensive conditionality complementary to the IMF letters of intent. For details on balance of payments lending, see http://ec.europa.eu/economy_finance/articles/financial_operations/index_en.htm.

major fiscal adjustments. In all three cases, politics was not solely domestic: the availability of external finance from the EU and the IMF played a substantial role in determining the scope of action available to incumbents.

Iceland is a virtual caricature of the neoliberal variant of the "foreign finance fetish" (Jonsson 2009); by the end of 2010, its external debt was 300 percent of GDP, a result of the rapid growth of three aggressively managed banking groups. Foreign borrowing also fed extraordinary leveraging on the part of Icelandic corporates, a real estate boom, and a rapid increase in private consumption.

In the aftermath of Lehman, the Icelandic banking system collapsed in spectacular fashion. Political change followed quickly; in January 2009, the conservative government fell, bringing a coalition of the Social Democratic Alliance and the Left-Green Movement to office. In addition to a particularly tough-minded bank restructuring effort, the IMF program allowed Iceland to impose capital controls and accommodated the incoming government's wish to preserve the country's Nordic welfare state.[10] When combined with exchange rate flexibility, the program permitted a somewhat more accommodative fiscal policy. But the short-run fiscal consolidation nonetheless involved policy measures totaling some 2 percent of GDP in 2009 and over 5 percent in 2010, with rationalizing reforms under debate with respect to the health and education systems, public-sector wages, and agricultural subsidies among other measures.

In Greece, creditors played an extended game of chicken with a social democratic government desperately seeking larger fiscal space through more assistance. The 2009 Greek elections constituted a virtual referendum on how the country would respond to the crisis. The conservatives under Konstantinos A. Karamanlis advocated an austerity program of freezing state salaries, pensions, and hiring, while the socialists under George Papandreou rode to a resounding victory by promising to reverse some of the conservatives' reforms (including privatization), close tax loopholes, and pursue a fiscal stimulus.

In his first three months, however, Karamanlis was immediately embroiled in a succession of controversies with both the EU and the markets over upward revisions of the budget deficit and debt numbers. The markets and ratings agencies responded accordingly, driving up the spreads on Greek debt and pulling those of Spain, Portugal, and even Italy with them.

Pressure was also coming from the EU itself, forcing a complete shift in policy emphasis through the announcement of two major fiscal adjustment programs. The EU finance ministers ultimately relented following the failure of the first bailout program in April 2010 by creating the EFSF. But the terms were stiff:

10. Another interesting feature of the adjustment process was the initial rejection in referendum of a repayment scheme to finance deposit insurance coverage of British and Dutch Internet accounts in Icelandic banks. The government ultimately relented to a repayment plan in late 2010.

the government had to commit to a massive and politically contentious fiscal adjustment. Further fiscal adjustments were unveiled in June 2011 as a condition for receipt of yet another major loan package and ultimately a partial write-down of Greek debt. Following a botched proposal to put the adjustment package to a referendum in late 2011, Karamanlis resigned in favor of a technocratic government.

The point is not to claim that Greek fiscal policy was sustainable even over the medium run; it was not. The point is that subsequent policy choices were not simply a function of domestic political coalitions. Rather the politics of the crisis must be understood in the context of a surprisingly broad commitment to remain in the Eurozone coupled with an external politics centered on the support Greece could secure from creditors and the conditions they imposed.

The Baltics demonstrate a quite different pattern, in which right governments were followed by other right governments. The neoliberal experiment in the Baltics began in Estonia in 1992–94 and was emulated in varying degrees in Latvia and Lithuania. Although Latvia was also brought down by a bank run (Parex), in other ways it represents a quite standard emerging market crisis. In the context of an exchange rate peg designed to signal its commitment to entry into the Eurozone, the country ran a truly extraordinary current account deficit (23.8% of GDP in 2007) financed by FDI, EU grants, and short-term debt to both the banking and corporate sectors. Rapid expansion of credit fueled financial-sector and real estate bubbles, but the public sector also benefitted from this process. Real expenditure grew by 80 percent between 2003 and 2007.

Although minority voices argued that the country would benefit from abandoning the peg, the crisis did not dislodge parties committed to the currency board; an oligarchic center-right coalition was replaced by a more market-oriented center-right coalition in 2009 with an overlapping composition. The decision to stay the course may have been influenced by the EU's response to Latvia's distress. In addition to the IMF program, a consortium of other EU members came to the country's support. Yet even with this important political cushion, maintaining the peg necessitated a substantial fiscal adjustment that fell heavily on government workers and pensions and a large real depreciation that affected real wages across the board.

In sum, we do see important political differences in how European countries entered and exited the crisis. Liberalizing coalitions were particularly beholden to financial interests in Iceland and had wider bases of support in Greece and Latvia. Yet we also see some common regional patterns that seem to dominate these political differences. A wide variety of different political coalitions exploited the opportunities created by access to financing from the Eurozone surplus countries (fig. 2-1). When credit dried up, governments of very different sorts were similarly constrained to adjust (fig. 2-2). Fiscal and real wage adjustments were particularly severe where exchange rates remained fixed. Moreover, politics was not simply domestic, but the outcome of contentious negotiations between surplus and debtor countries over the provision of public financing and its terms.

Latin America: More Nonbarking Dogs

As elsewhere, the crisis hit Latin America through two channels: through trade, including both the rapid fall in exports and in commodity prices; and through a financial channel. The size of the trade shock was related to dependence on the U.S. market. For Mexico—the hardest hit of the major economies in the region—fully 82 percent of exports in 2007 went to the United States. For Brazil, Chile, and Argentina, by contrast, the share of exports going to the United States was only 16 percent, 15 percent, and 8 percent, respectively. Diversification mattered.

In sharp contrast to Europe, the financial transmission mechanism proved both weaker and more transient. Spreads on Latin American debt started to rise from the middle of 2008, but the market differentiated sharply between countries carrying large political risk premiums—most notably Venezuela and Argentina—and the rest of the region. By mid-2009, yields on Latin American bonds, including sovereign debt, had come back close to pre-crisis levels and capital started to flow back into the region. Reserve loss during the crisis proved manageable, and no major countries were constrained to go to the IMF.[11] In late 2011, spreads started to widen again as a result of contagion from the Eurozone. But such contagion did not approach the magnitude of the fallout from the Mexican "tequila" crisis of 1994–95 or the Asian and Russian crises of 1997–98.

What happened—or rather, what didn't happen? The simplest explanation has to do with how governments in the region had responded to the previous two rounds of financial crises. In the wake of the crisis in the 1980s, the region undertook a range of neoliberal reforms, including the liberalization of the capital account (Williamson 1990). Capital poured in during the early 1990s—reflected in widening current account deficits (fig. 2-1)—followed by "second round" crises, most notably in Mexico (1994–95) and Argentina (1994–2001), but also in Colombia (1998), Brazil (1999), Ecuador, and Uruguay (2001).

11. Jamaica signed a standby. Precautionary standbys signed with three Central American countries (Costa Rica, El Salvador, and Guatemala) and Flexible Credit Line arrangements to Mexico and Colombia were not drawn.

In response to these second-round crises, governments of the region did not generally abandon the open capital account but undertook reforms that would make it sustainable, including a shift away from fixed exchange rate regimes. Of the seven major Latin American economies, five had flexible rates at the onset of the crisis (Argentina, Brazil, Chile, Colombia, and Mexico), Peru had an intermediate regime, and only Venezuela—exemplary of the small handful of statist responses to the crisis—had a peg. There is somewhat more debate about whether monetary and particularly fiscal policy was conservative and pro-cyclical during the subsequent boom or whether rising revenues allowed for more robust spending without an increase in public indebtedness (Inter-American Development Bank (IADB) 2008; Fernandez-Arias and Montiel 2010). But even if structural fiscal balances were not as good as the observed primary deficits shown in figure 2-2, government debt had stayed constant or fallen in most major Latin American countries, and its composition had shifted from foreign to domestic borrowing. In addition, the region accumulated substantial reserves, about $400 billion for the region as a whole in 2007.

This pattern—visible across countries of quite different political orientations—had tremendous consequences for the response to the shocks of 2008–9. First, governments could let exchange rates depreciate, which they did sharply before bouncing back in the second quarter of 2009. Exchange rate flexibility also provided the foundation for countries to pursue countercyclical monetary policies and more heterodox means of injecting liquidity; all of the countries that had flexible exchange rates and had moved toward inflation targeting did so, some such as Chile quite aggressively. With the exception of Colombia, all of the other six major Latin American countries announced significant fiscal stimulus measures in 2009 (see fig. 2-2; Cardenas and Guerreiro 2009; Jha 2009; and Zhang, Thelen, and Rao 2010).

Is there evidence that governments with different coalitional bases differed in either the decision to adopt a stimulus or its size? The short answer appears to be "no." Starting on the right of the political system, the conservative Uribe government in Colombia did not announce a separate stimulus and rather relied on already passed tax cuts and some acceleration of allocated spending. But the conservative government of Felipe Calderon in Mexico undertook a stimulus program. Although weighted toward public-private investment partnerships to be financed through the state development banks, it also included temporary employment and job retention components as well as transfers to marginalized regions.

Of particular interest is the stance taken by left governments, a major issue of interest in the study of Latin American politics at the moment (Levitsky and Roberts 2011; and particularly Kaufman 2011 and Murillo, Oliveros, and Vaishnav

2011).[12] A central observation that frames this new literature is the important variation within the Latin American left between more centrist and "responsible" variants, such as Brazil and Chile, and those that have flirted with more statist strategies, including the Kirchners in Argentina and particularly Evo Morales in Bolivia, Rafael Correa in Ecuador, and Hugo Chávez in Venezuela.

But these distinctions do not seem to be as useful as we might think in sorting out how governments responded to the crisis. Prior to the crisis, the Bachelet government in Chile had continued the disciplined and conservative approach to macroeconomic policy characteristic of the post-Pinochet left and had instituted one of the more conservative, pro-cyclical approaches to fiscal policy in the region. Nonetheless, it had one of the larger fiscal stimulus programs in the region, as well as the most aggressive monetary easing. Lulu da Silva's program in Brazil was modest by comparison despite his nominally populist orientation. The Argentine program was built on the most unorthodox foundations—a nationalization of the private component of the pension system—but it included tax incentives for investment and infrastructure and was modest when compared to the Chilean program.

The Venezuelan program was indeed decidedly populist and statist in orientation, but the shift in economic policy in that country predated the crisis, and the Chavez government was ultimately constrained to reverse some of its initial nationalizations in the wake of mounting foreign constraints. Indeed, as Murillo, Oliveros, and Vaishnav (2011) have argued more generally, the ability of the populist-left governments in the region to actually pursue their programs appears to be a function of the external economic environment: the boom of the 1990s empowered such governments to act, but the crisis of the 2008–9 period once again constrained them. Moreover, those constraints were arguably more binding precisely in the populist-left governments such as Venezuela that had increased spending most sharply during the boom.

More systematic research might well reveal partisan differences in the composition of stimulus programs. But some longer-run political factors are clearly at work. Prior crises forced reforms that gelled into bipartisan, cross-sector, and cross-class political consensus in a number of the major countries in the region. These reforms included changes in exchange rate regimes and at least relatively cautious monetary and fiscal policies, in some cases supported by important institutional changes such as more independent central banks, fiscal responsibility laws, and fiscal stabilization funds. These shifts were by no means uniform in the region; the puzzle of left-populist governments is an important one al-

12. Leftist candidates were democratically elected in Venezuela (1998), Chile (2000), Brazil (2002), Argentina (2003), Uruguay (2004), Bolivia (2005), Ecuador (2006), Peru (2006), Nicaragua (2007), and Paraguay (2008).

though it predates the crisis. But the significance of the new policy consensus should not be underestimated given the extent to which the region had been constrained to respond in a pro-cyclical fashion to past crises (Wibbels and Arce 2003).

The Noncrisis in Asia

That Latin America would see only a 2 percent decline in GDP for 2009 and would rebound so quickly from the crisis was a surprise. With even larger current account surpluses, massive reserves, low dependence on commodity exports, and a higher share of interregional trade than in Latin America, the expectation of immunity from the crisis was even stronger in East Asia. These hopes were quickly dashed post-Lehman, when emerging markets in East Asia experienced sharp contractions in the fourth quarter of 2008 and the first quarter of 2009. A number of countries ended up experiencing outright recessions for 2009 as a whole, including Taiwan, Hong Kong, Singapore, Malaysia, and Thailand; in Korea, growth was nearly flat as well (see Goldstein and Xie 2009 for an overview).

Yet as in Latin America, the response to this crisis differed quite fundamentally from the response to the Asian financial crisis of 1997–98. And as in Latin America, the reasons can be traced to a variety of reforms that were undertaken in the wake of that crisis (Haggard 2000). First, central banks quickly provided liquidity through a number of channels and pursued policies of monetary easing, a sharp contrast to the costly pro-cyclical efforts to stabilize exchange rates in 1997–98. In all cases with the exception of China and the Philippines, exchange rates depreciated; the declines were sharpest in Korea and Indonesia, the two countries that had the most vulnerable foreign debt profiles and witnessed the largest capital outflows.

Second, the emerging economies of the region pursued fiscal stimulus packages that were large by comparison with Latin America and the advanced industrial states, facilitated by generally conservative fiscal policies. Again, the range of reported estimates is wide (Jha 2009; World Bank 2009; Zhang, Thelen, and Rao 2010).[13] The composition of the fiscal programs might be called "productivist" or even "developmental." Patterns of spending could reflect not only differences

13. These differences in early estimates reflect differences in the timing of major initiatives (Thailand's second and third packages came relatively late); timeframe (lower estimates by the International Labor Organization [Jha 2009] reflect an effort to capture 2009 spending only) and the precise measures included in each estimate (for example, bank lending or credit guarantees played a large role in China and Malaysia but are not counted in some estimates).

in political coalitions but even in political regime type. In contrast to the major Latin American emerging markets, East Asia includes a higher incidence of authoritarian or semi-authoritarian governments that have historically been favorably disposed toward—if not captured by—private and semi-private interests, including China and Malaysia. The region is also home to broad, catch-all political coalitions that are difficult to differentiate along ideological grounds at all (the Philippines, Indonesia; see Dalton, Shin, and Chu 2008). Most stimulus packages were biased in favor of expenditure measures, with only a sixth of the overall regional stimulus accounted for by tax cuts; Indonesia and the Philippines were the only two countries where tax cuts dominated (World Bank 2009). The bulk of the expenditure measures focused on infrastructure spending, with social transfers accounting for a much smaller share. The cuts in taxes that did occur were dominated by cuts in corporate income taxes.

But these differences should not be exaggerated, and as in Latin America the political patterns are not obvious. Likewise, East Asian packages also included substantial new social expenditures, including targeted and untargeted social transfers; temporary consumption subsidies, including vouchers to low-income or rural households (China, Indonesia), continued reliance on price controls and food/fuel subsidies (in many countries), and support for housing (China, Indonesia, and Thailand). Tax cuts were also not limited to the corporate sector, but were supplemented by reductions in personal income tax rates (Indonesia, Thailand) and payroll contributions in more advanced countries (e.g., Singapore).

A final question that bears considering is the extent to which the Asian adjustment process had what might be called a "mercantile" component: an effort to foster exports through industrial policy and even outright subsidy. The question is important because the political economy of the Asia-Pacific region had come to look so different from that of Europe. Rather than a core of surplus countries (centered on Germany), the Asia-Pacific is characterized by the well-known imbalances and co-dependency between the United States, with its structural current account deficits, and the major East Asian surplus countries.

In a widely cited interpretation, Dooley, Folkerts-Landau, and Garber (2003) characterized the Asia-Pacific region in the post-Asian financial crisis period as a new Bretton Woods system, in which the Asian countries intervened to maintain effective exchange rate pegs. This regional system is by no means a new one, however; rather, it is a long-standing feature of the export-led growth strategies pursued by the region since the ascent—in chronological order—of Japan; the first tier of newly industrializing countries (Korea, Taiwan, Hong Kong, Singapore); the second Southeast Asian wave of newly industrializing countries; and then China and Vietnam. This model included export-oriented industrial policies; cautious import liberalization, often only under direct political duress; active exchange rate management to limit natural appreciations; and the corresponding accumulation of massive central bank reserves (totaling over $4.5 trillion by the end of 2010).

Surprisingly, political economy analysis of these models has been limited. But it is not hard to tell a plausible story in which very dynamic export-oriented firms, associated labor, and the regions in which they are located exercise undue influence vis-à-vis the nontraded goods sector and domestic consumers. Tackling this complex regional system and its domestic political foundations goes far beyond the scope of this chapter, but here I pose a more limited question: Is there evidence that countries in the region pursued such policies as a means of adjusting to the crisis? In short, was there a mercantilist response?

A brief look at the Chinese stimulus suggests some answers. As late as the summer of 2008, Chinese authorities were preoccupied with overheating. But even before the Lehman meltdown, policy shifted to address concerns about a slowdown in growth. The first line of defense was monetary, but in November the government announced its massive stimulus, with a headline 4 trillion renminbi price tag. The initial design of the stimulus was weighted overwhelmingly toward domestic investment, with transport and power infrastructure, earthquake reconstruction, rural village infrastructure, and housing taking over 80 percent of the total; each subsequent package adjusted this allocation at the margin by adding additional social components in the form of transfers and increases in social spending. But the "pure" fiscal stimulus was actually less consequential than the explosion of bank lending that occurred beginning in the first quarter of 2009; the increase in credit—mostly to investment, not consumers—exceeded in size the entire announced fiscal program.

This program had an important effect on the path of the Chinese balance of payments and the contribution of consumption, investment, and net exports to demand. The current account tells the story pretty clearly. One source of the sharp slowdown was the sudden collapse of exports in the fourth quarter of 2008; imports contracted at a roughly comparable pace. But the stimulus contributed to a much more rapid rebound of imports. In the fourth quarter of 2008, China ran a current account surplus of $114 billion; in the second quarter of 2009, this figure had shrunk to $35 billion. The country's Keynesian response to the stimulus had the effect of shifting demand away—not toward—the export sector.

But what about trade and exchange rate policy? Here the evidence is more mixed. Global Trade Alert provides detailed information on trade policy measures that discriminate against foreign commercial interests and are deemed protectionist.[14] China had instituted forty-three such measures from the onset

14. http://www.globaltradealert.org/site-statistics.

of the crisis through the end of 2010, almost half of them (twenty) in the form of antidumping, countervailing duty, and safeguards measures. China became embroiled in contentious disputes on a range of issues with the United States over the course of 2010, from rare earth exports to industrial policy in the alternative energy sector. Perhaps the most significant piece of evidence for the prosecution has to do with the exchange rate. China maintained a fixed exchange rate policy in 1997–2005 and a managed float in 2005–8 but adopted a soft peg during the crisis that effectively paused the currency's tightly managed appreciation.

China's response to the crisis mirrors in some important ways the larger issues for the political economy of the Asia-Pacific. Although the stimulus did shift demand away from exports in the short run, it by no means signaled a larger shift away from the export-oriented strategy, with the attendant trade and exchange rate conflicts that have become a staple of U.S. relations with China and the region more generally. Looking forward, the important political puzzle is whether policy will continue to be captured by export interests, reflected in ongoing central bank intervention and foreign reserve accumulation, or whether governments will gradually rebalance in favor of consumers and the nontraded goods sectors.

A Theoretical Reprise

It is possible that the Great Recession simply proved too mild an event for most emerging markets to have had an enduring impact. Recovery for many emerging-market countries was V-shaped, and the literature on both Latin America and East Asia is self-congratulatory. But this picture is misleading, and as we have seen, a number of countries in Europe experienced wrenching shocks and extremely difficult political choices that were likely to influence policymaking well into the future.

Interesting regional patterns are in evidence that suggest the political analysis of the crisis needs to look beyond contemporaneous politics to the legacy of past crises and regional political economies. In Europe, the regional political economy was anchored by a cluster of surplus countries, most centrally Germany, and a periphery that had run persistent and in some cases huge current account deficits financed by private lending. The pivotal divide in this peripheral group was between those that had also committed to a fixed exchange rate—inside or outside the Eurozone—and those that had not. The latter were no less hard hit but were more likely to opt out of their exchange rate pegs to gain some macroeconomic policy autonomy.

Major fiscal adjustments were a common feature of all countries that remained committed to a fixed exchange rate, regardless of political coalition. But the political economy of the crisis was not simply a domestic affair; it was influenced heavily by the amount of financing the creditor club and its agents in the international financial institutions (IFIs) were willing to make available. Those amounts were large, no doubt. But they were never large enough to prevent major and politically painful fiscal adjustments. Moreover, the programs provided very little room for renegotiation of external debt; outside of Greece, creditors appeared to get off scot-free, and as of this writing the saga of the restructuring of Greek debt is by no means over.

In short, some of Europe got "depression economics," implying not only short-run fiscal adjustments but structural changes that are likely to touch wide swaths of the public sector, from employment to pensions and health. The lessons of this episode, and particularly on the risks of financial integration, are likely to emerge slowly but will shape the political economy of the countries in question well into the future.

The Latin American pattern was quite different. In the 1980s and again in the 1990s after the Mexican crisis of 1994–95, the region was an epicenter of financial crises. These crises had much more profound effects than the current one, leading to reforms that cushioned the effects of the current shock. These reforms included greater exchange rate flexibility, cautious monetary and fiscal policies, and a secular decline in both government debt and foreign borrowing. Reserve accumulation was, perhaps, the ultimate insurance policy. It is certainly possible to identify countries that bucked this trend: among the major economies in the region, Venezuela stands out. But political convergence around moderate policies and rejection of fiscal populism was visible even among left governments in the region.

The Asian response to the crisis was also eased by reforms undertaken in the wake of the financial crisis of 1997–98. But the regional political economy also mattered. In Asia, the regional system also contained a core—China—but its behavior in the crisis was very much different from the conservative European creditor club. China's stimulus was massive, providing a crucial public good to the entire region and unquestionably influencing its rapid recovery. Nascent regional financing schemes, particularly the Chiang Mai initiative, played a distinct second fiddle not only to credit lines extended from outside the region but to the collective fiscal stimulus. But the longer-run issue of the rebalancing of the transpacific economy has by no means been addressed, and a deep-seated political economy appears to have kept many countries of the region locked in to export-oriented policies.

Finally, the epochal nature of the changes in the emerging markets over the last three decades is shown by two dogs that did not bark: principled protectionism and statism. The gradual transition of the developing world to more open economies remains one of the more significant story lines of the postwar period, even if that transition is by no means uniformly neoliberal. Statist responses appear at this point limited to a relatively small group of authoritarian and semi-democratic countries. However, protests in Europe to the new austerity and the resurgence of the left in Latin America are reminders that the question of how the gains from globalization will be shared remains contentious and by no means resolved.

3

PARTISAN FINANCIAL CYCLES

J. Lawrence Broz

Scholars give little attention to the partisan character of government as either a cause, or a consequence, of financial crises. Although the subprime crisis that began in 2007 has been attributed to a surge in capital inflows from abroad in the context of lax regulation, neither the policies that contributed to the capital inflow nor the level of regulatory oversight have been linked to government partisanship in the run-up to the crisis. Similarly, few scholars have analyzed government partisanship in the aftermath of financial crises or found evidence of consistent ideological shifts in the electorate in response to such crises (Bartels 2011).

I explore an endogenous argument in which the partisan character of government is both a cause and a consequence of financial crises. My hypothesis is that a "partisan-policy financial cycle" exists in which right-wing governments preside over financial booms, funding credit expansions and asset-price appreciation with large current account deficits (i.e., foreign borrowing) and deregulating financial activities in line with their pro-market ideology. When the crash occurs, voters reassess their support for right-leaning governments, making it more likely that left-wing governments will be elected after financial crashes. Once in power, left-wing governments pursue policies to unwind the financial excesses of their predecessors and oversee the broad re-regulation of financial activities. In short, the political orientation of the government is both a cause of pre-crisis policies and a consequence of financial crises.

On the basis of the small-sample comparisons I provide in this chapter, the existence of a partisan-policy financial cycle cannot be ruled out. For example, in countries that experienced a financial crisis after a foreign borrowing binge, 58 percent (seven of twelve cases) underwent a partisan shift from right to left as of three years after the onset of a crisis. By contrast, just 8 percent (1 case) moved from left to right after a crisis, and 33 percent (4 cases) experienced no change in partisan orientation. Although this evidence is far from conclusive, it is not sufficient to rule out partisanship as a *cause* of systemic banking crises, nor is it sufficient to reject the argument that government partisanship is a *consequence* of such crises.

The scope of the argument is limited to counties in the economically developed Organisation for Economic Co-operation and Development (OECD) during the post–Bretton Woods period. It is limited to the OECD because political partisanship does not hew to the left-right dimension in many developing countries, which is to say that data on the political orientation of developing-country governments is limited. It is restricted to the post–Bretton Woods period because banking crises *always* occur in an environment of financial globalization, where free capital mobility fuels asset booms (Bordo and Landon-Lane 2010). Although banking crises have been common since the early 1970s, they were nonexistent in industrialized economies during the Bretton Woods era, 1944–71 (Bordo and Landon-Lane 2010; Jordà, Schularick, and Taylor 2010). This is no coincidence. Bretton Woods was characterized by widespread capital controls and extensive financial regulations, which insulated countries from financial booms and busts. By contrast, the post–Bretton Woods period saw the removal of capital controls, the liberalization of domestic financial markets, and the return of banking crises. While crises were common during the gold standard era and the interwar period, my argument does not extend to these earlier epochs because political partisanship had not yet come to reflect the dominant left-right cleavage that it does today. Prior to the Great Depression, the role of the state in the economy was small and other issues—religion, constitutional reform, suffrage, imperialism—shaped partisan competition. Furthermore, it was only after 1973 that right-wing parties, led by the Republican Party in the United States, moved away from their traditional policy of balanced budgets and fiscal rectitude to embrace the idea that "deficits do not matter" (Bartlett 2007). I argue that international capital mobility was the enabling condition behind this partisan policy shift because large fiscal deficits would have produced much sharper declines in private investment had foreign capital not been available to finance the dissaving.

Although I evaluate the argument with evidence from all OECD countries that experienced financial crises in the recent era of large-scale, cross-border capital flows, it is most suited to deficit nations that funded external deficits with capital *inflows*. Indeed, my small sample comparisons suggest that a right-to-left partisan financial cycle is most evident in countries that run large current account deficits and experience correspondingly large capital inflows. I also give particular attention to the most severe "systemic" banking crises. Although partisan financial cycles are most likely to occur in systemic banking crises, I also consider lesser crisis, using Reinhart and Rogoff's (2009) sample of thirteen "milder" banking crises prior to 2007 and Laeven and Valencia's (2010) updated sample of eight "borderline" crises from the subprime era. Table 3-1 contains the crisis episodes employed in my comparisons.

In terms of research design, this chapter is more exploratory than explanatory. By focusing on cases where banking crises occurred, I am selecting on the dependent variable, which precludes drawing causal inferences about the relationship between partisanship and crises. Whenever possible, however, I include an "OECD baseline" to assess whether political trends observed in the crises cases are distinct from general trends among advanced countries. Even still, this research design is not suited to causal inference. But it can help rule out partisanship as a cause of whether a country experiences a financial crisis. It can also help rule out whether government partisanship is a consequence of crises. The reason is that partisanship cannot "explain" crises—or post-crisis partisanship—if it varies widely over the crises cases.

With this research design, it is crucial to select observations without regard to values of the explanatory variables. That is, the sample should be as representative of the population as possible and should never be chosen to "fit" a particular hypothesis (King, Keohane, and Verba 1994). As mentioned previously, I use the entire population of advanced-country banking crises as identified by Reinhart and Rogoff (2009) and Laeven and Valencia (2010). These authors, and the sources they reference, never mention "government partisanship" as a criterion for selecting crises observations.

Several themes set this contribution to this volume apart from my previous work. First, I treat financial crises as endogenous events originating in the policy choices of governments. Although the triggering event may vary from crisis to crisis, the preconditions are rooted in the tendency of nations to combine large fiscal and current account deficits with lax bank regulation. Second, I associate these pre-crisis policies with partisanship: in deficit countries that experience a financial crisis, right-of-center parties are more likely to be in power during the boom, overseeing policies that precipitate crises. In other words, partisanship may be a source of pre-crisis booms by way of the macroeconomic and regulatory choices of governments. I interpret the association to mean that right parties, enabled by international capital mobility, run fiscal and current account deficits to reward their high-income constituents with asset booms. Third, I argue that crises also have consequences for partisan electoral competition. I show that after a financial crisis, the electorate tends to move to the left and this

TABLE 3-1. Bank-centered financial crises in the OECD

COUNTRY	ONSET OF CRISIS
The Big Five	
Spain	1977
Norway	1987
Finland	1991
Sweden	1991
Japan	1992
Subprime Systemic Crises	
United Kingdom	2007
United States	2007
Austria	2008
Belgium	2008
Denmark	2008
Germany	2008
Iceland	2008
Ireland	2008
Luxembourg	2008
Netherlands	2008
Milder/Borderline Crises	
United Kingdom	1974
Germany	1977
Canada	1983
United States (S & L)	1984
Iceland	1985
Denmark	1987
New Zealand	1987
Australia	1989
Italy	1990
Greece	1991
United Kingdom	1991
United Kingdom	1995
France	1994
France	2008
Greece	2008
Hungary	2008
Portugal	2008
Spain	2008
Sweden	2008
Switzerland	2008

Source: Crisis cases prior to 2007 are from Reinhart and Rogoff (2009). Subprime cases are from Laeven and Valencia (2010).

leftward shift is associated with subsequent changes in government partisanship to the left. Thus, crises appear to affect the partisan orientation of electorates and governments.

In the next section, I present comparisons of partisanship across cases of financial crises. In the third section, I overlay these partisan patterns on the policies that have been associated with financial crises. I then explore two subprime cases in more detail: the United States and Germany. The cases differ in both partisanship and current account status. Before the subprime crisis, the right was in power in the United States while Germany was ruled by the left. Furthermore, the U.S. current account deficit exploded, inducing a "capital flow bonanza" in that country just as Germany's current account went into substantial surplus, indicating a large net capital outflow.[1] These cases support the argument that the effect of partisanship on crises is conditioned by the current account balance.

Partisanship and Financial Crises

Figure 3-1 compares the political orientation of government across the "Big Five" cases, the most severe financial crises prior to the subprime meltdown: Spain (1977), Norway (1987), Finland (1991), Sweden (1991), and Japan (1992). Following the convention in Reinhart and Rogoff (2009), period *T* represents the year when the banking crisis began, period *t–5* is five years prior to the onset of the crisis, and *t+5* is the period five years after the crisis began. Political orientation data is from the Database of Political Institutions (DPI), which records the left-right orientation of the party heading the executive branch (Beck et al. 2001). Governments headed by right parties are coded 0, governments headed by center parties are coded 1, and governments of the left are coded 2. As a baseline for these comparisons, the figure also includes the "OECD mean," which is the average political orientation of the chief executive for all OECD countries, minus the country in crisis, during equivalent time periods. I include the OECD baseline to assess whether partisan political patterns are specific to crisis countries or reflect more general trends.

Figure 3-1 shows that governments moved rightward before the Big Five crises, shifting from center to right-of-center orientations by the *t–4* period. A turning point in political orientation begins with the onset of the crisis, and this leftward shift continues, after a partial three-year retrenchment, with another large movement to the left. The change in government partisanship is most extreme

1. The term "capital flow bonanza" is from Reinhart and Reinhart (2009) and signifies a period of abnormally large capital inflows (i.e., above-average foreign borrowing).

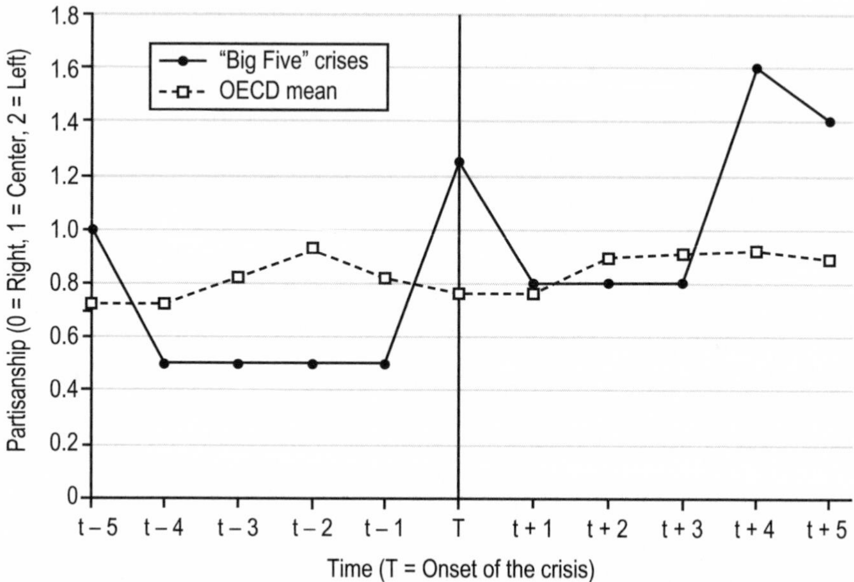

FIGURE 3-1. Government partisanship before and after a Big Five crisis. Note: Missing data: Spain 1977 (*t*–5 to *T*).

between the *t–4* and *t+4* periods, during which governments moved from right to left by 0.9 points on average—a 33 percent shift from right to left. The plot of the OECD mean indicates that this partisan pattern was not part of larger trends in other advanced countries.

Figure 3-2 displays partisan orientation in countries hit by the subprime crisis. In this graph, the data extend only to *t+2* because partisan outcomes in the DPI dataset have not been updated beyond 2010. In the systemic crisis cases, political orientation was substantially more right-wing on average than in OECD before the crisis. In the sample with borderline cases, executives were slightly more right-wing than average before the crisis. More striking is that government orientation moves sharply to the left after the crisis—an indication of a partisan turning point.

Figure 3-2 may understate the relationship between partisanship and crises because it conjoins external surplus countries, like Germany, with external deficit countries, like the United States. Unlike deficit countries that pursued macroeconomic policies that induced a capital inflow bonanza, the policy failings of surplus countries were primarily microeconomic: inadequate risk assessment on the part of the banks and their regulators leading to overinvestment in dangerous mortgage-backed securities from abroad.

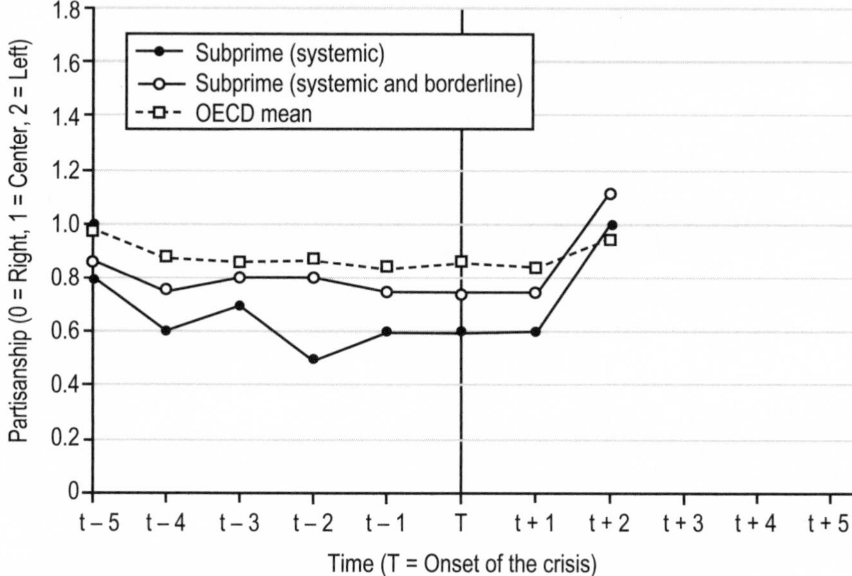

FIGURE 3-2. Government partisanship before and after a subprime crisis.
Note: Missing data: Switzerland (*t–5* to *t+2*).

If we disaggregate the subprime cases into those that were primarily home-grown with roots in macroeconomic policy ("CA deficit" countries) from those that were primarily imported and regulatory ("CA deficit" countries), as in figure 3-3, we observe a stronger partisan pattern. The CA deficit countries ran current account deficits prior to their crises; the CA surplus countries were net capital exporters. The figure reveals that, in the run-up to the crisis, the deficit countries had more centrist governments than the surplus countries or the rest of the OECD on average. But after the crisis, deficit countries moved sharply to the left while surplus countries remained steadfastly right-wing. Put another way, governments in deficit nations appear to have been punished at the polls for presiding over a crisis while governments in surplus nations avoided electoral punishment. Indeed, deficit nations experienced far greater political change, with elections bringing the left to power in all but one case—Ireland—by 2010.

This suggests that crisis politics play out very differently in deficit and surplus countries. Part of the difference may be because deficit countries experienced crises in both finance and housing whereas surplus countries avoided housing crises (Schwartz 2009). Figure 3-4 supports this intuition. It plots the percentage change in real house prices over the five years prior to a systemic crisis against the current account balance average for that period. It shows that without foreign

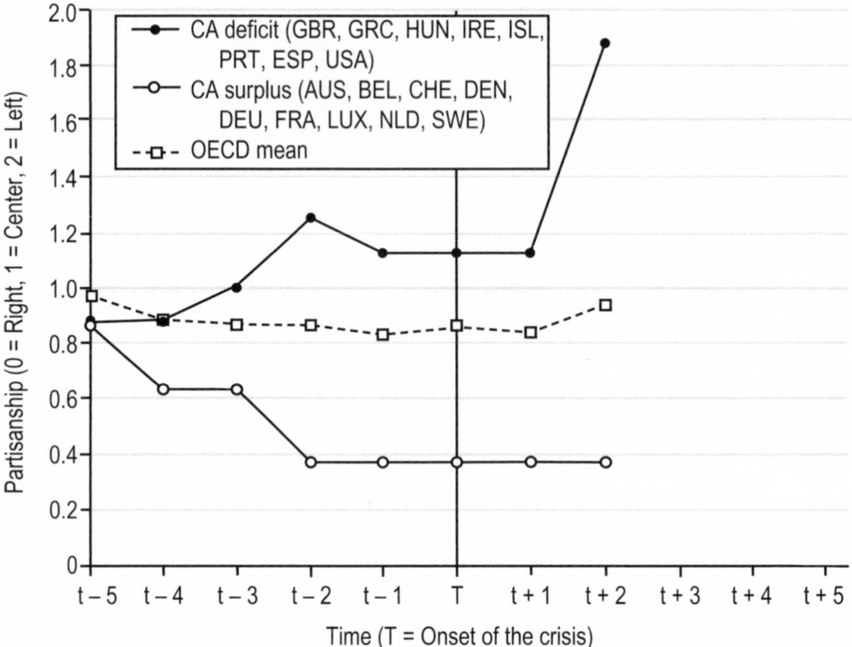

FIGURE 3-3. Partisanship before and after a subprime crisis (grouped by current account balance). Note: Missing data: Switzerland (*t*–5 to *t*+2).

capital inflows to fuel house-price appreciations, surplus countries avoided housing booms (and busts) during their financial crises.

In the case studies to follow, I explore whether the electoral fallout of a crisis tends to be smaller where voters witness only financial-sector bailouts but not collapsing house prices. I also explore the possibility that voters in surplus countries may refrain from exacting an electoral toll on the incumbent government if they viewed the crisis as originating elsewhere (i.e., in the United States) and spreading via financial linkages.

Before pursuing the deficit-surplus difference in more detail, I test to see if the partisan pattern found earlier is robust to an alternative measure of partisanship. In figure 3-5, I calculate government partisanship as the share of cabinet portfolios held by left and center parties, weighted by the number of days the government was in office in a given year. These data are from Armingeon and others (2010). Left parties are defined as labor parties, social democratic parties, and parties to the left of these mainstream left parties, while center parties include most Christian democratic parties. The figure shows that the percentage of total cabinet posts held by left and center parties declined in the run-up to the crisis in each of the three crises samples and then increased as the crisis approached.

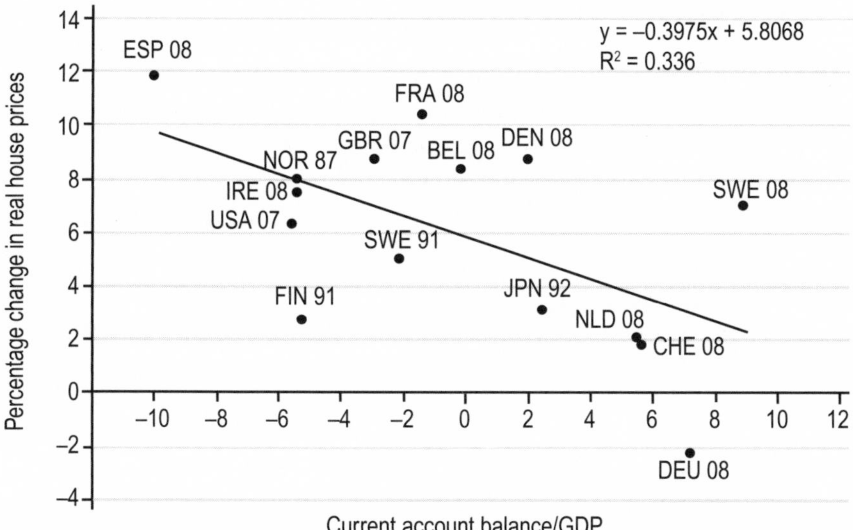

FIGURE 3-4. Real house prices and the current account balance, Big Five and subprime cases. Notes: Data are averages over the period *t–5* to *T* (crisis onset).

Sources: Current account/GDP is from the IMF's *World Economic Outlook*. The real house price index is from the BIS Property Price Statistics at http://www.bis.org/statistics/pp.htm.

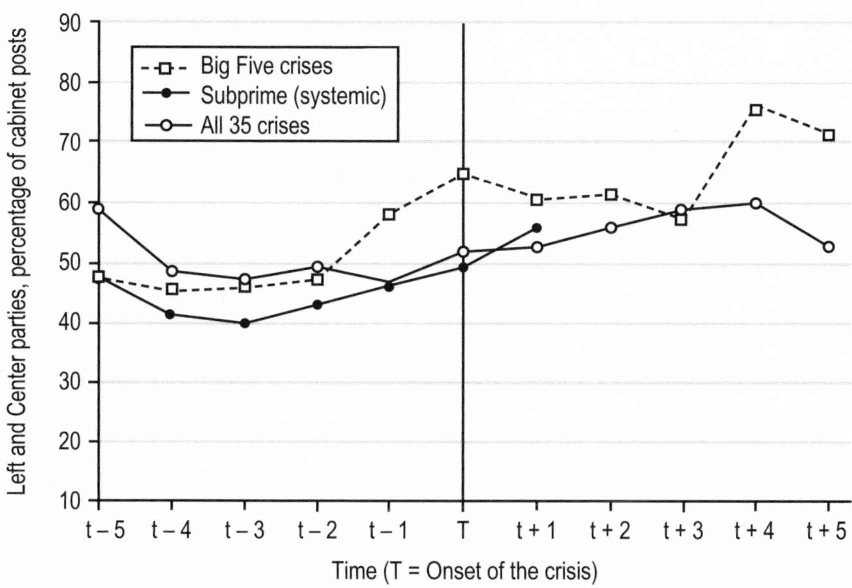

FIGURE 3-5. Partisan composition of the Cabinet before and after a banking crisis. Note: Missing data: Spain 1977 (*t–5* to *T*). See text for sources.

Left and center parties continued to increase their share of cabinet portfolios in the year of the crisis and made gains through most of the post-crisis period. This is consistent with the patterns observed in figures 3-1 to 3-3.

Figure 3-6 plots the *change* in partisanship that occurred after each systemic crisis, with the cases grouped by the current account balance. The "change in partisanship" indicates the difference in the average value of the DPI partisanship indicator between the post-crisis (T to $t+2$) and the pre-crisis ($t-3$ to $t-1$) periods. Positive values indicate a shift to the left. The figure provides evidence of a right-to-left partisan financial cycle, but only among deficit nations. Among these cases, seven of twelve cases (58%) underwent a partisan shift from right to left as of three years since the onset of crisis and only one deficit country—Sweden (1991)—moved from left to right after a crisis. Sweden's current account deficit reached 2.5 percent of GDP the year before its crisis while the left was in office. By contrast, just one surplus country—Austria (2008)—moved to the left after its crisis, and six of nine surplus nations (67%) experienced no

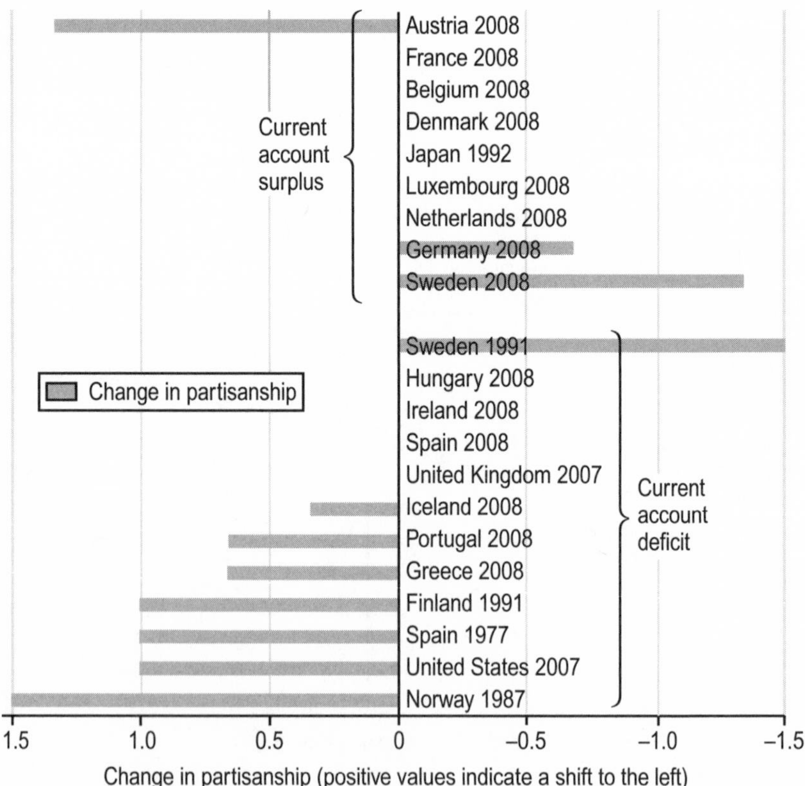

FIGURE 3-6. Change in partisanship after a crisis, Big Five and subprime.

change in political orientation. Thus, surplus countries were both more likely to be headed by right-wing governments before a crisis and to remain under right-wing rule after a crisis. Overall, the pre-crisis comparisons suggest we cannot rule out partisanship as a *cause* of major banking crises. That a slim majority of deficit countries had governments that were more left-of-center after a crisis also suggests that we cannot reject the hypothesis that partisanship is a *consequence* of crises.

We can explore this possibility further. If deficit countries have a tendency to move to the left after a crisis, then presumably changes in the electorate are driving this shift. Although election outcomes are an indirect measure of this shift, figure 3-7 provides information on the shift in mass political attitudes that follows a financial crisis. The data are from the World Values Survey (WVS), which has carried out representative national surveys of political attitudes since 1981. The series allows me to measure the change in individual attitudes that followed a banking crisis. However, no observations from the subprime era are possible since the most recent WVS was in 2007, and I can only calculate the change in mass political attitudes for ten of the eighteen crisis cases in the Rogoff and Reinhart (2009) sample of major and minor crises. In these cases, a financial crisis occurred between two consecutive WVS surveys.

The change in "mass political orientation" is the change in the country average of individual responses to the WVS query: "In political matters, people talk of 'the left' and 'the right.' How would you place your views on this scale, generally speaking?" Responses range from 1 = far left to 10 = far right. In figure 3-7,

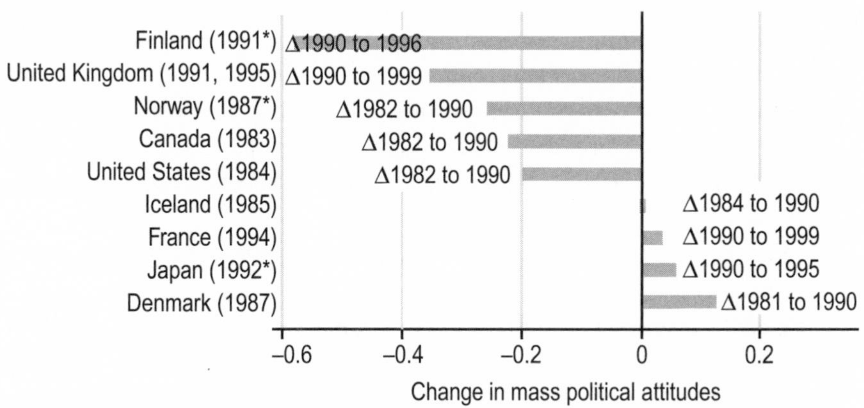

FIGURE 3-7. Change in mass political attitudes after a banking crisis.
Notes: Negative values indicate a shift to the left. Asterisk (*) indicates a Big Five crisis.

crisis countries are indicated on the left axis, with the onset year of the crisis in parenthesis. An asterisk indicates a Big Five crisis. Next to the bars are the years of the two WVS surveys used to calculate the change (delta) in national attitudes. Negative values indicate a shift to the left.

The largest change in political attitudes occurred in the deficit nation of Finland. Before its Big Five meltdown, Finland ran current account deficits that reached 5 percent of GDP; the massive capital inflow led to an uncontrolled credit expansion and rapidly rising real estate and share prices (Honkapohja 2009). Political attitudes in Finland shifted to the left by over half a point between 1990 and 1996 (the crisis occurred in 1991 but took several years to unwind). In England, where the current account deficit surpassed 4 percent of GDP in the early 1990s, two mild banking crises took place in the interval between WVS surveys. Political attitudes in England moved leftward by a third of a point during this interval. In Norway, another Big Five deficit case, attitudes shifted by almost a quarter of a point to the left. Norway's current account deficit ballooned to 6.1 percent of GDP the year before its crisis—a clear example of a capital flow bonanza.

Among the deficit cases, Denmark is the main exception to the right-to-left pattern. Like Finland and Norway, Denmark experienced a surge in capital inflows prior to its minor crisis in 1987. But unlike the other Nordic debtors, Denmark's electorate turned slightly rightward after its crisis. Perhaps by consequence, Denmark's ruling coalition remained under the leadership of the Conservative People's Party.

Japan is the only surplus country in this sample, but it appears to fit the surplus country partisan pattern. Even though Japan's financial crisis was arguably the most serious and long-lasting of the Big Five crises, the political fallout was quite minimal, with attitudes drifting only slightly to the right. Notably, Japan's crisis was a financial crisis and not a housing crisis. Although banks were heavily exposed to collapsing asset prices, the balance sheets of Japanese households were very conservative, which meant Japan did not experience widespread household bankruptcies or foreclosures (Nakagawa and Yasui 2009).

Overall, figure 3-7 suggests that political attitudes shift to the left after crises in deficit countries. Furthermore, it suggests that it is not just swing voters choosing left parties over right parties after a crisis. After a crisis, fewer people in deficit nations identify as right-wing and more identify as left-wing. Hence, we cannot rule out the possibility that mass political attitudes are affected by crises, and that a post-crises shift to the left in the electorate may be the source of the leftward shift in government orientation in deficit nations.

Partisan Policies and Banking Crisis

In the previous section, I showed that financial crises appear to have political *consequences* in deficit nations. In this section, I develop the argument that government partisanship might also be a *cause* of financial crises. I assume that political parties represent different constituencies and make policy choices that reflect the interests of their core constituents. I focus on macroeconomic policies that make boom-bust financial cycles more likely: large current account deficits driven by fiscal deficits in the context of financial deregulation. I suggest that right-of-center governments in deficit nations run these policies in order to reward their high-income constituents with sharp increases in wealth.

Current Account Deficits

Reinhart and Rogoff (2009) establish policy similarities between the U.S. subprime crisis and previous banking crisis episodes. They pay particular attention to the massive U.S. current account deficit that preceded the crisis—and the foreign borrowing binge that it precipitated—and they show that such capital flow bonanzas are a common precursor of financial crises. Likewise, Chinn and Frieden (2011) argue that the subprime crisis is but the most recent example of a capital flow cycle in which foreign capital floods a country, stimulates an economic boom, encourages financial leveraging and risk-taking, and eventually culminates in a crash.

The current account balance records the difference between a country's savings and its investment. If the current account balance is positive, it measures the portion of a country's savings invested abroad; if negative, it is the portion of domestic investment financed by foreign savings. Because any excess of national spending over income must be financed by foreigners, the current account deficit is equivalent to the net inflow of capital from abroad.

Figure 3-8 provides evidence of the association between the current account balance and financial crises. In each sample, countries amassed current account deficits in advance of a crisis, reaching 2 percent of GDP on average for the subprime cases. But averaging masks important differences between the samples. Although pre-crisis external deficits were very large for all Big Five cases save one—Japan ran a surplus—the subprime cases are more varied. Figure 3-9 displays the sharp difference between these groups. In capital inflow countries that had systemic crises (Iceland, Ireland, United Kingdom, United States), the external deficit averaged a huge 10 percent of GDP in the year of the crisis. The same holds for the deficit countries that experienced borderline subprime crises (Greece, Hungary, Portugal, Spain). In all nine deficit nations, foreign capital fueled

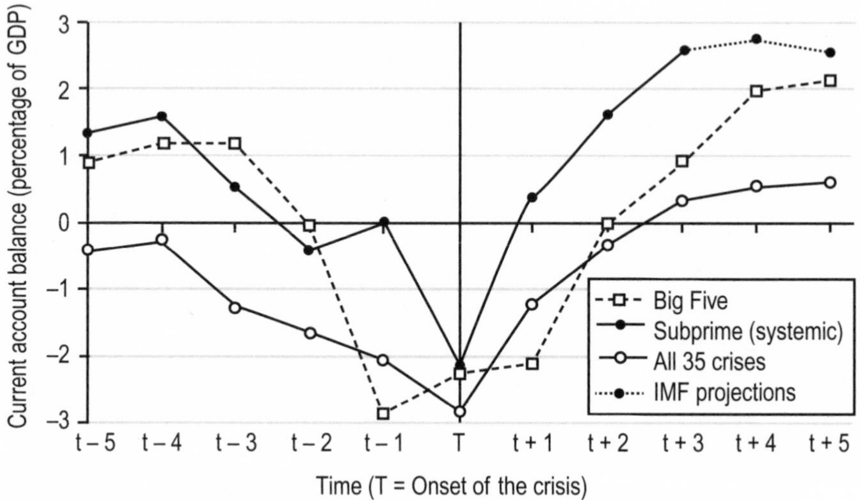

FIGURE 3-8. Current account balance before and after a systemic crisis. Notes: Missing data: Canada 1983 (*t–5* to *t-4*), Germany 1977 (*t–5* to *t+2*), Hungary 2008 (*t+4 to t+5*), United Kingdom 1974 (*t–5* to *t+5*).

Source: World Economic Outlook.

credit booms and asset-price bubbles, especially in real estate (Aizenman and Jinjarak 2009; Claessens et al. 2010). Inasmuch as macroeconomic factors determine the current account, it is fair to say that these crises were homegrown, with roots in macroeconomic policy.

Yet subprime crises also hit the surplus economies of Austria, Belgium, Denmark, France, Germany, Luxembourg, Netherlands, Sweden, and Switzerland. As export-oriented economies with high savings and low domestic demand, capital inflow bonanzas did not play a role in these nations. Rather, these surplus countries imported the subprime crisis via their banking sectors' accumulation of risky U.S. mortgage-backed securities. Their policy failures were thus microeconomic (regulatory) rather than macroeconomic—a topic I explore in the case studies.

The policy link between the current account and macroeconomic conditions is the fiscal deficit. When a government increases its fiscal deficit, domestic residents may use the additional income to boost consumption, causing total national saving to decline. Unless domestic investment decreases to offset the saving shortfall, the country must borrow from abroad (i.e., it must run a current account deficit). The connection between budget deficits and current account deficits is known as the "twin deficits" relationship. Chinn and Ito (2007) show that the budget balance is an important determinant of the current account bal-

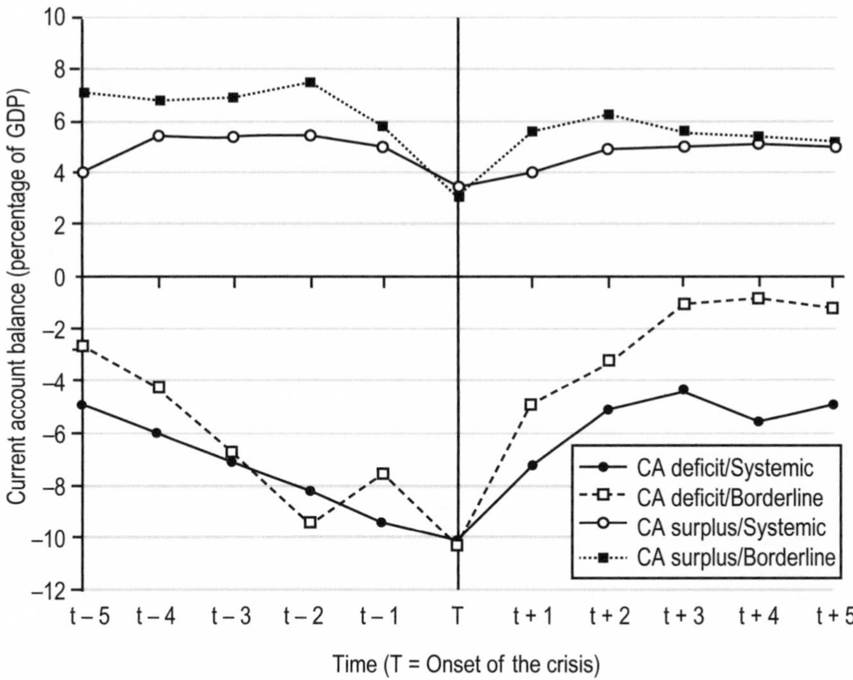

FIGURE 3-9. Current account balance in deficit and surplus countries, subprime crises. Notes: CA Deficit/Systemic: Iceland, Ireland, U.K., and U.S.; CA Deficit/Borderline: Greece, Hungary, Portugal, and Spain; CA Surplus/Systemic: Austria, Belgium, Denmark, Germany, Luxembourg, and Netherlands; CA Surplus/Borderline: France and Sweden. Missing data: Switzerland. Projections *t+3* to *t+5* are IMF estimates.

Source: World Economic Outlook.

ance for industrial countries. In the next section, I examine the fiscal accounts of deficit governments that presided over financial crises and find evidence that suggests a twin deficits policy.

Fiscal Balances

Figure 3-10 plots the average structural budget balance for the subprime crises countries, grouped by the current account balance (the structural balance is cyclically adjusted, to better capture a government's fiscal policy stance). For the cases that fit the capital inflow bonanza profile ("CA Deficit/Systemic" and "CA Deficit/Borderline"), the budget balance turned sharply negative in the pre-crisis period. These governments were running a twin deficits policy of deficit spending

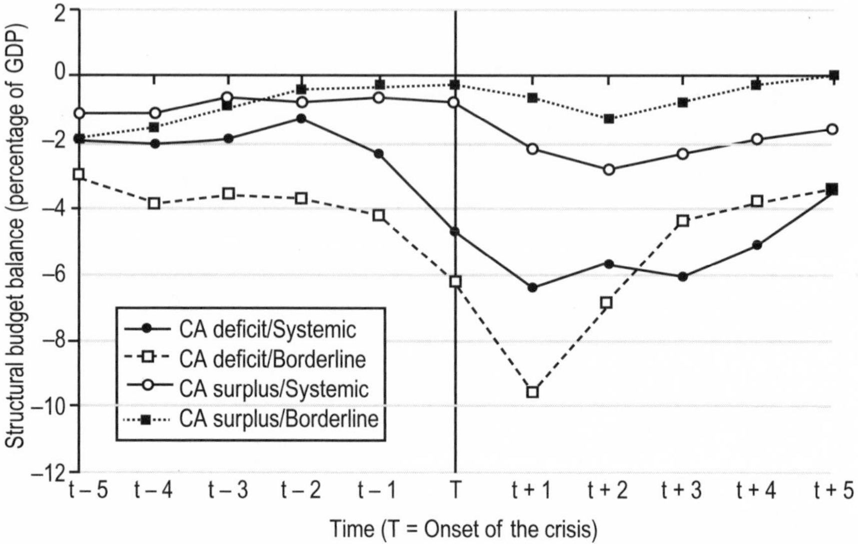

FIGURE 3-10. Central government structural budget balance before and after banking crises. Notes: Missing data: Hungary 2008 (*t–5* to *t+5)*, Luxembourg 2008 (*t–5* to *t+5*). Projections *t+3* to *t+5* are IMF estimates.

Source: World Economic Outlook.

financed by capital inflows. Typically, the fiscal balance worsens after a crisis, reflecting large stimulus spending during post-crisis recessions.

But are twin deficits preferred by the right? Connecting the fiscal component of the twin deficits relationship to the right runs counter to conventional wisdom because the right is supposed to favor balanced budgets and a low level of public consumption. However, this view finds little empirical support (Cusack 1999). In fact, a number of studies conclude that the partisan impact on fiscal policy is the opposite of the conventional wisdom. Cameron (1985) finds that left governments are usually *less* likely to incur large budget deficits than governments controlled by centrist, Christian democratic, or conservative parties. Similarly, Garrett and Lange (1991) find that OECD countries with left governments and strong labor parties tend to run smaller budget deficits than do right parties.

These findings suggest a partisan fiscal pattern in which the left is more likely to adopt a conservative stance than the right. Although unconventional, they are consistent with Persson and Svensson (1989) and Pettersson-Lidbom (2001), who theorize that right-wing governments strategically run fiscal deficits in order to force their left-wing successors to curtail public spending—a strategy known as "Starve the Beast" (Bartlett 2007). This theory echoes a similar argument by Alesina and Tabellini (1990) in the context of Reagan administration deficits. The strategy can be effective because, by lowering taxes and issuing debt, right-wing governments constrain future spending. In addition to strategically limiting the fiscal choices of successors, deficits have another attraction for the right: they favor high-income constituents by cutting taxes more than spending.

These arguments suggest an electoral mechanism for the partisan financial cycle in which right-wing governments preside over fiscal deficits. But are current account deficits that generate risky capital inflows a policy of the right? Begin with the assumption that right parties disproportionately represent homeowners and other asset owners, as in Ansell (2007, 2009). Because external deficits fuel asset booms in housing and equities markets, right-wing parties may derive short-term electoral benefits from this policy, even if the wealth effect that asset holders experience turns out to be transitory. Moreover, when capital inflows are available to finance budget deficits, right parties can generate asset-price appreciations via large fiscal deficits without crowding out private investment and thereby antagonizing their high-income business constituents. This result is because capital inflows prevent domestic interest rates from rising above the world interest rate, so that the crowding out of investment that usually takes place in a closed economy does not occur (Friedman 1992).

These arguments suggest that political parties can derive electoral benefits from pursuing macroeconomic policies that may provoke a financial crisis. When capital is internationally mobile, right parties can generate wealth gains for their constituents via a twin deficits policy without crowding out private investment. My data suggest that right-wing governments are more likely to pursue this strategy in the context of large current account deficits. In surplus nations, by contrast, the right takes a more conservative fiscal stance, discouraging excessive consumption and pre-crises asset booms.

Financial Regulation

In party manifestos, right parties champion free enterprise capitalism and the superiority of markets over government regulation and allocation (Budge et al. 2001). Did right-of-center governments act on these prior beliefs and deregulate financial markets in the run-up to crises?

Financial supervision is more than the sum of the formal rules and regulations established by law because governments can use their executive powers to interpret and implement regulations, creating a gap between de jure regulation and de facto regulation. Because I am interested in the effect of partisanship on de facto regulation, I need a measure that captures the legal rules as well as the actual implementation and enforcement of the rules. My data come from Abiad,

Tressel, and Detragiache (2010) who rely on a mix of de jure and de facto criteria to code this dimension of government financial policy. Their index of bank regulation ranges from 0 to 3, with higher values representing more (or better) regulation. I use this index to explore the argument that the right tends to deregulate the financial sector prior to crises and that their left-wing successors tend to re-regulate after the crash occurs.

Figure 3-11 plots the average value of the bank regulation index for the Big Five crises. These data do not extend beyond 2005, so comparisons of the subprime cases are not possible. The figure includes the OECD baseline and a separate plot for Japan—the only Big Five nation in external surplus before its crisis. The figure suggests that bank regulation was much weaker on average in the Big Five countries prior to a crisis. In Japan, bank regulation was even weaker. Regulation then increases sharply once a crisis has occurred. But bank regulation is improving across the OECD during the same time periods, indicating a more general trend. One reason for this upward trend is the coding of the Basel capital adequacy criterion: Abiad, Tressel, and Detragiache (2010) assigned a value of 0 to all cases prior to 1993, before Basel regulations were in place. This ensures that regulation is increasing over time in all samples. Nevertheless, the Big Five countries had weaker regulation and supervision than the OECD average before

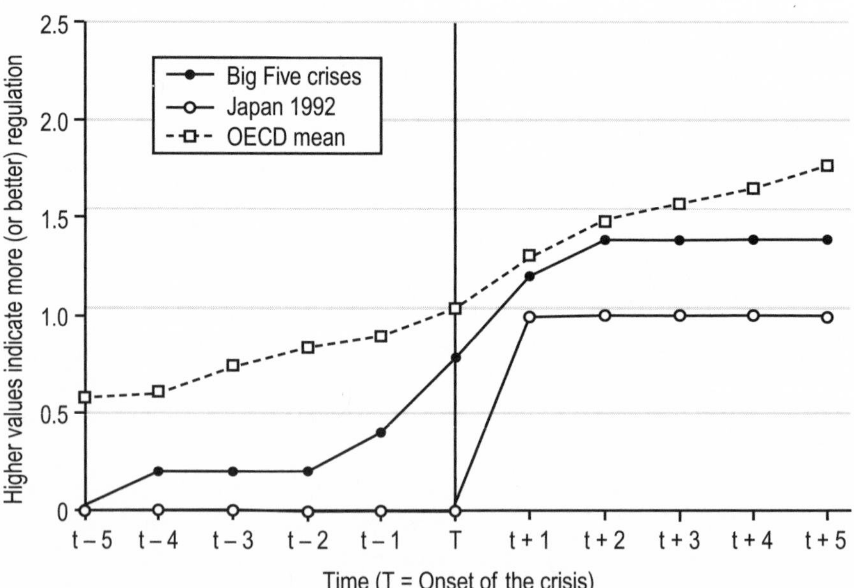

FIGURE 3-11. Bank regulation and supervision before and after the Big Five crises. See text for sources.

their crises, which is consistent with the argument that these countries made a partisan policy choice to have less regulation.

The evidence in this section is not sufficient to rule out the possibility that financial cycles have origins in partisan policy choices. The evidence is strongest with respect to macroeconomic policy in deficit countries. Prior to the onset of a major financial crisis, deficit-country governments presided over rapidly deteriorating current account deficits (capital inflow bonanzas), and these external deficits were related to a policy of government dissaving (budget deficits). The data also suggest that regulation of the financial sector was weaker than average before crises in the countries that experienced a major financial crisis. However, this finding may reflect measurement error since Abiad, Tressel, and Detragiache (2010) retrospectively code bank regulation and may have inferred that a crisis is evidence of lax regulation.

Case Studies of the United States and Germany

To provide leverage on the politics of financial cycles, this section reviews partisan patterns in the United States and Germany during the subprime episode. The cases differ in government partisanship and current account status. In the United States, the Bush administration presided over record-setting current account deficits (and thus foreign borrowing) while encouraging home ownership, private debt accumulation, and the deregulation of financial markets. These policies led to deep crises in both banking and residential real estate. In Germany, a left-wing coalition of the Social Democratic Party (SPD) and the Greens was in government between 1998 and 2005. This government ran a conservative macroeconomic policy and introduced major cutbacks in welfare programs, which encouraged saving, which led to massive current account surpluses. These conservative policies continued after the right-leaning Christian Democrats succeeded the SPD in 2005, with Angela Merkel as chancellor. There was no housing bubble and German households were not highly leveraged with debt, which may explain why the subprime crisis had different partisan consequences in Germany.

Partisanship and Crisis in the United States

The U.S. case provides partial support for the argument that right-of-center political parties are more likely to enact policies that help fuel housing booms while left-of-center parties are more likely to be elected as a consequence of financial and housing crises. Before the subprime crisis, a Republican administration was in office pursuing twin deficit policies, reducing the level of financial regulation, and actively promoting home ownership. However, deregulation began prior to Bush, under a Democratic administration, and both major parties actively promoted home ownership.

Before the crisis, the U.S. current account deficit ballooned to over 6 percent of GDP, an all-time record for the United States. Chinn and Frieden (2011) attribute the burgeoning current account deficit to Bush administration fiscal policies; the emphasis after 2001 on cutting taxes while increasing spending on national security and Medicare produced a large federal budget deficit that had to be financed. The huge pool of foreign savings available from surplus countries like China, Japan, and Germany provided the Bush administration with a way to finance its fiscal deficits. The administration had promised its right-wing constituents that it would reduce taxes while increasing spending. The globalization of financial markets allowed it to finance the resulting fiscal imbalances without crowding out domestic private investment. However, the massive foreign borrowing was not invested to increase the productive capacity of the United States. Rather, it was used to finance the rise in federal deficits and an explosion of private housing and consumer debt (Schwartz 2009; Chinn and Frieden 2011).

It may seem unconventional to argue that it is the right-wing party that lacks fiscal restraint, but this is easy to confirm in the U.S. case. Since 1973, Republican presidents have run budget deficits 2.5 times larger on average than Democratic presidents (3.2% versus 1.3% of GDP). Republican administrations also ran current account deficits that were nearly twice as large as those of Democrats (–3.0% of GDP versus –1.7% of GDP). With respect to financial regulation, however, partisan differences all but disappear.

While the Bush administration deregulated financial markets in the run-up to the subprime crisis, deregulation began in the late 1970s under a Democratic president. One of the principal deregulatory laws of the postwar era—the Depository Institutions Deregulation and Monetary Control Act of 1980 (DIDMCA)—was passed under Jimmy Carter, albeit with support of the Republican majority in Congress. The DIDMCA phased out deposit interest rate ceilings, allowed savings and loan institutions (S&Ls) and credit unions to offer checkable deposits, and permitted banks to merge. However, the Reagan administration was squarely behind the Garn-St. Germain Depository Institutions Act of 1982, which expanded the nonresidential lending powers of commercial banks and S&Ls, allowing them to move aggressively into commercial real estate lending.

The DIDMCA and Garn-St. Germain composed the "first wave" of financial deregulation (Schwartz 2009). By deregulating real estate finance, the spread between deposit rates and lending rates narrowed, encouraging banks and thrifts to sell their mortgage assets in the securities market and generate profits from fee and transaction income. By consequence, these laws expanded the supply of securitizable mortgages (Schwartz 2012). The second wave began during the Clinton administration and allowed investment banks to enter the mortgage market. The Financial Services Modernization Act of 1999 repealed the Glass–Steagall Act and reduced barriers between banks and securities firms. Investment banks were given direct access to mortgages and could securitize mortgages on their own, bypassing Fannie Mae and Freddie Mac—the government-sponsored enterprises charged with expanding the secondary market for mortgages. But since investment banks and other "private-label" issuers lacked an implicit federal guarantee, they could not compete effectively with Fannie Mae and Freddie Mac for conforming mortgages. So they concentrated on nonconforming mortgages—loans not eligible for guarantees by Fannie Mae and Freddie Mac because they were too large (jumbo mortgages) or too risky (subprime mortgages).

Although the basic features of the system were in place during the 1990s, George W. Bush accelerated the rise of subprime lending with a policy of regulatory forbearance. Among the most important changes was the 2004 decision by the Securities and Exchange Commission to relax net capital requirements on investment banks and put these firms on a regime of self-regulation (Johnson and Kwak 2010). This ruling enabled investment banks to triple their leverage ratios, fueling the growth in mortgage-backed securities and subprime lending.

Both political parties also championed home ownership as part of their electoral strategies. Since the 1970s, each party sought to engineer permanent majorities by expanding home ownership to new, largely minority, constituencies (Schwartz 2010). The strategy reached its apogee under George W. Bush's "Ownership Society," which recalls Margaret Thatcher's promotion of home ownership in the 1970s. The Bush administration's goal was to replace traditional welfare programs with an asset-based system of welfare centered on home ownership. The political mechanism behind the strategy was to remake low-income, minority voters—who traditionally aligned with the Democratic Party—into economic conservatives by removing financial barriers to home ownership. Like Thatcher, Bush strategists reasoned that rising home prices would bias the new homeowners against government welfare spending, and so motivate them to shift their allegiance to the Republican Party.

Financial deregulation and the promotion of home ownership occurred under both parties, leading some scholars to argue that the key explanation for the crisis is the excessive political influence of the financial and mortgage industries (Johnson and Kwak 2010; Mian, Sufi, and Trebbi 2010a, b). But the right deregulated while simultaneously pursuing macroeconomic policies that invited a crisis: fiscal and current account deficits twice as large as those of Democrats.

Destabilizing macroeconomic conditions brought on by such policies only tend to produce financial crises when the microeconomic rules of banking regulation are poorly designed and implemented (Calomiris 2009). It is thus fair to conclude that Republican administrations satisfied both the necessary (macroeconomic) and the sufficient (microeconomic) conditions for a homegrown financial crisis.

Partisanship and Crisis in Germany

The German case presents a mirror image of the United States in terms of partisanship, macroeconomic policy, external balance, and housing policy. Before the crisis, the left was in power pursuing restrictive fiscal policies and accumulating large external surpluses—policies that *reduced* the likelihood of a homegrown crisis. The left also reformed the welfare system, which contributed to external surpluses by causing households to ramp up their precautionary saving. Nevertheless, heavy involvement by state-owned Landesbanks in subprime assets left Germany exposed to the crisis, which cost the left dearly in subsequent elections. The German surplus-country case thus presents the partisan financial cycle in reverse: the left was in office prior to the crisis pursuing restrictive macroeconomic policies and generating external surpluses, and the right succeeded the left after the crisis occurred.

The German case also demonstrates that lax bank regulation is sufficient to induce a crisis. There was no housing bubble in Germany and therefore no easy profit opportunities in domestic real estate. Perhaps by consequence, the state-owned Landesbanks sought more attractive returns in the U.S. subprime market, as well as in the sovereign debt of peripheral Eurozone nations such as Greece. Like Fannie Mae and Freddie Mac, the German state banks operated with explicit and implicit public guarantees, and their excessive risk-taking went unchecked by regulators. With heavy exposures to off-balance sheet U.S. asset-backed securities, the Landesbanks were at the forefront of the German subprime crisis when derivatives tied to subprime mortgages in the United States were downgraded.

From 1998 to 2005, Germany was governed by a coalition of the Social Democrats and the Greens, with the SPD's Gerhard Schröder as chancellor. During this period, Schröder's "red–green" coalition practiced fiscal restraint and embarked on a major effort to reform the German welfare state. Even though collective bargaining had encouraged wage moderation in agreements between trade unions and employers' associations, German non-wage labor costs had risen steadily because employer contributions for pensions and unemployment insurance had increased (Streeck and Trampusch 2005). In the context of high unemployment and weak growth, the left initiated the "most ambitious German reform project in social insurance policy since World War II" (Kemmerling and Bruttel 2006). Known as "Agenda 2010," the reforms imposed large cuts in pension and unemployment benefits, causing an upheaval in the SPD and subsequent defeats in regional elections. The SPD losses were widely attributed to discontent with the reforms and Schröder admitted defeat and called an early election. The 2005 election produced a grand coalition between the SPD and the center-right Christian Democratic Union (CDU), with Angela Merkel as executive. The CDU had supported Schröder's reforms, making it easier for the SPD to join in coalition with the CDU rather than with traditional party allies on the left.

The welfare reforms coincided with a major shift in Germany's external balance. After a decade of external deficits in the 1990s, during which capital inflows helped finance the costs of reunification, Germany's external position moved sharply into surplus in the 2000s, reaching a record surplus of 7.5 percent of GDP in 2007. The increase in the surplus reflected several factors. Wage moderation, engendered by high unemployment, had positioned German exporters to take advantage of a cyclical surge in global demand. But low investment and high saving also contributed to the large increase in the current account surplus. While investment had slackened cyclically in the aftermath the reunification boom, household saving rose sharply as a result of SPD's welfare reforms, which reduced the generosity of pension and unemployment benefits. Falling house prices also contributed to the rise in saving.

Real house prices declined in Germany in mirror image to house price increases in the United States, with both trends reflecting the forces of global capital flows (fig. 3-4). In Germany, capital exports led to declining home values, which encouraged more saving as homeowners perceived themselves to be poorer. The antithesis occurred in the United States where capital inflows fueled house price increases, making homeowners feel wealthier and less inclined to save.

The crisis that hit Germany was thus a financial crisis but not a housing crisis. The cause was related to weak regulation in the state-owned sector of the financial system. The Landesbanks account for about a fifth of all commercial lending in Germany, more than Deutsche Bank and the other big private banks combined (Hüfner 2010). Landesbanks had a prior history of losses and public bailouts and were known to be staffed by political appointees (Hau and Thum 2009). But the key distortion was that Landesbanks operated with government guarantees on their liabilities. The guarantees helped the Landesbanks to get high credit ratings, borrow cheaply, and take big risks in international finance. With profit opportunities within Germany limited, Landesbanks turned increasingly to risky asset-backed foreign securities, where the returns were higher (Sinn 1999).

Landesbanks' assets invested in complex foreign securities more than doubled between 2005 and 2008 (Hüfner 2010). When the high-yielding assets in their portfolios were downgraded, two Landesbanks were forced to merge immediately and three others had to be bailed out by various state governments. Four months before Lehman Brothers collapsed, the Landesbanks reported write-downs of $21 billion, which accounted for 43 percent of total losses incurred by German banks—almost double the Lanesbanks' share of total banking assets. Merkel was forced to coordinate a bank bailout just five months before the September 2009 elections.

In these elections, the blame for the crisis fell squarely on the SPD, which saw its vote share drop 11.2 percent to a postwar low of 23 percent. The SPD had been in power during the crucial 2001–5 period when Landesbanks issued massive amounts of state-guaranteed debt and invested the proceeds in subprime securities from the United States. Voters did not lay blame on the right, as the CDU lost only 1.4 percent of its vote share.[2] In fact, the right made substantial gains. The biggest winner was the libertarian Free Democratic Party (FDP) which increased its vote share by 4.8 percent to 14.6 percent, an all-time record. The FDP, which formed a right-wing coalition with the CDU, had raised strong objections to use of state aid for troubled Landesbanks.

Yet caution is in order since these facts are open to alternative interpretations. For example, while I view the 2009 election outcome as consistent with my conditional argument that governments in surplus countries tend to stay right or move further to the right after an "imported" financial crisis, the election results may also be consistent with simple retrospective voting (Bartels 2011). With Germany's economy shrinking by 5.1 percent in the year prior to the election, the FDP's sharp gain may reflect the German electorate's frustration with both parties in the grand coalition. However, the electorate did not punish the coalition partners equally—the SPD's vote share declined by 11.2 percent whereas the CDU/CSU vote share fell by only 1.4 percent—a fact that is puzzling from the perspective of retrospective voting. If German voters were punishing the incumbent government for hard times, why did they penalize the SPD—the junior partner in the coalition—so much more than the CDU/CSU?

My account provides a possible answer. The SPD was held to account for the financial crisis while the CDU/CSU was not because the SPD had been in power in the crucial years before 2005, pursuing policies that contributed to Germany's huge current account surplus and the risky foreign lending that followed. During this period, the SPD sat idly by while the Landesbanks channeled enormous amounts of German savings into the U.S. subprime market. The FDP's unlikely

2. Even though the huge bailout of the Bayerische Landesbank (Bavarian State Bank) in 2008 contributed to the massive defeat of the CDU's Bavarian sister party, the Christian Social Union (CSU), in the September 2008 Bavarian state election, the SPD did not benefit. The biggest gains were made by the right-leaning Free Voters and the FDP.

electoral success in 2009 may have derived from the relevance of its anti-bailout, free-market message in the context of this regulatory failure.

The partisan-policy contrast between Germany and the United States is striking. In the United States, the right encouraged net foreign borrowing with large public deficits and then channeled the capital inflows to the housing market by deregulating the financial and mortgage industries. In Germany, the left encouraged net foreign lending with policies of fiscal consolidation and welfare state retrenchment. As a consequence of its large external surpluses, Germany experienced fewer domestic housing-related problems than the United States. But the left's structural reforms and macroeconomic conservatism helped generate large net capital outflows, which were invested unwisely in U.S. subprime securities by the underregulated Landesbanks.

Conclusion

Were the financial crises that stuck OECD economies since 1973 related to "politics" by way of the ideological orientation of government? The evidence presented in this chapter is tentative, conditional, and inconclusive. It is tentative and ultimately inconclusive because the small-sample research design precludes causal inference. It is conditional because any evidence of a right-to-left partisan financial cycle is restricted to countries that ran large current account deficits prior to a crisis. Yet when conditioned on the current account balance, the evidence suggests that partisanship may not be randomly distributed across the crisis cases. In countries that ran large external deficits, governments were slightly more likely than by chance to be right-of-center in political orientation prior to a crisis. This suggests that right-leaning governments were slightly more likely than by chance to be associated with policies that predict crises: twin deficits, capital inflow bonanzas, and financial deregulation.

Once a financial crisis happens, causing widespread distress, does the causal arrow change direction and government partisanship become a consequence of crisis? On this point, again, the evidence is tentative and inconclusive. My post-crisis comparisons confirm only the possibility that electorates move to the left in deficit countries after a financial crisis, and that this leftward shift in electorates is associated with changes in government partisanship to the left. In summary, my evidence is not conclusive one way or the other; I have merely established that it is too soon to reject the conditional partisan-policy financial cycle hypothesis.

The evidence from the surplus-country cases is somewhat more compelling because there is no evidence of a right-to-left partisan-policy financial cycle in these cases. When capital exporters experience a crisis, the right is more likely to be in office prior to the crisis, and more likely to remain in office after the crisis occurs (see figs. 3-3 and 3-6). Why major financial crises exact a smaller electoral toll on surplus-country governments is not entirely clear, but one possible explanation is that voters do not hold them as accountable when crises are of foreign origin. As net capital exporters, surplus countries are less likely to experience surges in pre-crisis asset prices than capital importers (fig. 3-4); financial crises occur because regulatory laxity permits domestic banks to invest the nations' surplus in risky foreign securities. Voters in surplus countries may thus refrain from punishing incumbents if they view the crisis as originating elsewhere and spreading via financial linkages to their countries.

Case studies of the United States and Germany are somewhat consistent with these conditional cross-country partisan patterns. In the 2000s, the Bush administration launched massive tax cuts without imposing discipline on the rate of growth of government spending. The result was record budget deficits and record current account deficits, which is to say that foreign capital financed the twin deficits and set the stage for a major run-up in asset prices. Deregulation and the promotion of home ownership channeled the foreign credit to the housing sector, where the boom continued unchecked until the crisis occurred.

From the perspective of the right's traditional association with fiscal discipline and balanced budgets, the Bush administration's macroeconomic accommodation of the boom is puzzling. At this point global capital markets enter the picture. Prior to the 1980s, fiscal restraint made sense for the right since, in the absence of large-scale capital flows, budget deficits crowded out domestic investment to the detriment of the party's business constituents. But with the free flow of international capital, the right obtained greater scope to run fiscal deficits without generating increases in domestic interest rates.

Fiscal deficits have another appeal for right parties when capital is internationally mobile: deficits financed by capital inflows tend to raise asset prices, and the gains of asset price appreciation go disproportionately to right-party constituents, namely homeowners and older asset holders. In trying to convert lower-income minority voters into home-owning Republicans, the Bush administration merely pushed this strategy to its logical end. By undermining the appeal of balanced budgets and providing a way to generate short-run wealth effects for asset-owning constituents, international capital mobility may have caused a fundamental shift in the right's electoral strategy. Unfortunately, this shift exposed other OECD countries, like Germany, to a higher risk of financial crisis.

The German case is a mirror image of the U.S. case. Before the crisis, the left was in power pursuing restrictive fiscal policies and accumulating large external surpluses. These policies reduced domestic demand and the odds of a home-grown financial crisis. But Germany was vulnerable to an imported financial crisis because the left did a poor job regulating how the nation's surplus savings was invested overseas. In the 2009 elections, the SPD was punished by the electorate, and the biggest winner was the free-market party that had railed against state bailouts for the Landesbanks. As in the United States, voters in Germany appear to have held the party responsible for the crisis to account.

4

THE POLITICS OF HARD TIMES

Fiscal Policy and the Endogeneity of Economic Recessions

Pablo M. Pinto

The causes and consequences of economic crises have become a recurrent theme in political and academic debates. Recent empirical work focusing on financial crises has documented how severe recessions cause business failures and bankruptcies and lead to unemployment and raising poverty levels in economies experiencing those recessions.[1] The short-run economic changes and the alleged long-term consequences have a direct impact on the well-being of individuals, which in turn is likely to trigger political responses of various kinds.

Economic theory in several different strands provides a clear prescription regarding optimal responses to economic crises. During expansions, the government should reduce spending in order to "cool off" the economy and contain inflationary pressures. During recessions, as public demand for protection and compensation increases, spending should be increased in order to stimulate aggregate demand and protect vulnerable groups. In sum, fiscal policy should be countercyclical in order to perform its stabilization function. Recent literature in the political economy tradition has tried to explain deviations from these optimal prescriptions; scholars explore explanations based on credit constraints, terms of trade and output volatility, or even different sources of preference heterogeneity.

I would like to thank two anonymous reviewers, Suzanne Berger, Lawrence Broz, Peter Cowhey, Peter Gourevitch, Stephan Haggard, Peter Hall, Gordon Hanson, Miles Kahler, Peter Katzenstein, David Lake, Isabela Mares, M. Victoria Murillo, Megumi Naoi, Ron Rogowski, Sebastian Saiegh, Steve Nelson, and David Soskice for comments on earlier versions of this chapter. Matt Getz provided excellent research assistance.

1. On the consequences of banking and financial crises, see Cerra and Saxena 2008; Reinhart and Rogoff (2009); Griffith-Jones, Ocampo, and Stiglitz (2010).

Most empirical studies on the consequences of recessions, on the other hand, focus on the variation in the fiscal responses to sharp downturns in economic activity. These studies report that during recessionary times some governments are willing and able to expand spending in order to sustain aggregate demand, while others are more prone to retrench the public sector to encourage the expansion of the private sector. A common premise in these analyses is that the orientation of the ruling coalition should help explain the observed variance in the policy responses aimed at dealing with crises and distributing the burden of adjustment to the sharp changes in prices and economic activity. Fiscal responses to recessions, for instance, would be more expansionary under left-leaning governments; austerity and contractionary policies would result when a right-leaning party is in power (see Broz, chapter 3, this volume).

To conduct the analyses of political responses to economic crises, scholars implicitly or explicitly assume that economic shocks are exogenous to the political processes that they affect. Yet we have good reason to believe that this is not the case, as persuasively argued by Schumpeter (1939, 1961), Minsky (1975, 1982), and Hibbs (1977). In this chapter, I will show that the occurrence, timing, and severity of economic crises are directly related to political decisions made along the backdrop of the business cycle. Most instances of crisis, including the Great Recession of 2008, are far from the ideal exogenous shock: they result from policy choices made along the business cycle that have direct bearing on how economic activity plays itself out. Although the downside of the economic cycle is likely to place constraints on government activity, political conditions in the run-up to a recession have potential not only to precipitate the likelihood that the downturn would occur, but also to restrict the options available to policymakers when dealing with the negative consequences of the drops in output. The assumption that crises are exogenous shocks makes researchers mistakenly attribute to a crisis what is actually a direct consequence of political choices made before the crisis occurred. This is the core of the problem of identification that has become central to social science research.

If economic shocks are endogenous, a different theoretical apparatus is needed to explain economic policymaking along the business cycle. Rather than explaining the size and timing of the adoption of stimulus packages across countries *after* a recession, what we need is an explanation of what governments do *along the business cycle*. In this chapter, I present an interest-based theory aimed at explaining the commonplace observation that governments often engage in suboptimal pro-cyclical behavior. Focusing on cyclicality, rather than on higher or lower spending in response to economic shocks, is a better way of addressing the endogenous relationship between economic and political outcomes. One of the main corollaries from this argument is that both the likelihood and severity of economic crises are functions of political conflict around trade, taxation, and regulation of economic activity in the country. Political conflict rooted in redistributive motivations can create a perverse incentive structure. The inability of winners to credibly commit to compensating the losers encourages coalitions representing the latter to adopt more inefficient forms of redistribution, which in turn increases political contestation by the opposition. Political contestation escalates as the redistributive effort—and its expected distortions—intensify. The risk of being unseated by the opposing coalition makes political actors run scared. This problem is exacerbated when the coalition is built around heterogeneous groups who could potentially defect. The end result is a shortening of time horizons, which forces governments off the more desirable, and less disruptive, optimal policy path. The nature of political competition and coalition dynamics makes some governments more likely to adopt unsustainable policies, while others are more willing to strike political compromises that allow them to better absorb the ups and downs in economic activity.

I illustrate this problem by looking at the evolution of fiscal policy in Argentina, a crisis-prone country notorious for its poor record in macroeconomic management. The argument could also explain the interconnection between political and economic outcomes in developed countries as well, as suggested by the U.S. experience discussed by Gourevitch (afterword, this volume). The unfolding of the subprime crisis in the United States provides additional support to the coalitional argument: financial deregulation, an accommodating monetary policy, lax oversight, and dual deficits were undeniably the permissive conditions for the occurrence of the Great Recession of 2008 and framed the policy options available to the Obama administration. Moreover, the ripple effects on the rest of the world that resulted in the collapse of global finance and the slump in economic activity in the North Atlantic economies were far from homogeneous. The difference lies in policy choices made by countries prior to the crisis: it was felt less severely in places with lower dependence on trade with the North and on global capital.

The politics of booms and busts in Argentina has been documented in the work of Díaz Alejandro (1970), Dornbusch and Edwards (1991), and Rodrik (1995). Yet in this chapter I present an argument that makes apparent that the pattern of pro-cyclical spending in the country is far from exceptional. I also provide evidence that suggests that the degree of political conflict that resulted from distributional motivations had a direct bearing on the adoption of unsustainable fiscal policies, which were both a cause and a consequence of the country's poor economic performance. Moreover, the very same political motivations help explain why the country managed to tread the early stages of the Great Recession of 2008 relatively unscathed: just like in the run-up to the Great Depression, the country had abandoned old orthodoxies that sheltered the transmission effect of the drop in activity in the transatlantic economies. Yet the incentive structure faced by the ruling Peronist coalition ultimately resurfaced: as the country's economy started contracting the government's fiscal position followed the traditional cyclical path.

In the ensuing sections, I will first review the literature on cyclical spending. Next, I introduce a political economy argument aimed at identifying the fundamental relationship between political and economic outcomes. I illustrate the argument with a historical analysis of the evolution of fiscal spending in Argentina and the unfolding of the Great Recession in the United States, which suggests that fiscal policy is as much a cause of economic crises as it is a response to them. Taken together, the Argentine and U.S. cases help illuminate the close link between economics and politics along the business cycle, rendering problematic the assumption of strict exogeneity of economic crises. In the conclusion, I discuss how the evolution of public finance and its degree of cyclicality can be better understood under a political economy lens.

Determinants of Fiscal Policy in Good and Bad Times

How do governments choose their fiscal policy in response to aggregate economic shocks? Governments can rely on different policy instruments to deal with the risks associated with movements along the business cycle.[2] In particular, tariffs, subsidies, fiscal and monetary policies, and the exchange rate are the main tools that governments can deploy to smooth externalities generated by "bad" states of the economy.[3] The analysis of changes in public spending as a result of external shocks has been a central concern in the comparative literature explaining economic policy reform in the 1990s and has become a source of heated policy debates these days.[4]

According to several important strands of economic theory, fiscal policy should be countercyclical in order to perform its stabilization function. As demand for protection and compensation increases during recessions, spending should be increased in order to stimulate aggregate demand and to protect vulnerable

2. On the political determinants of fiscal policy outcomes, see Alesina and Perotti (1995) and Eslava (2006).

3. For example, in the classic work of Musgrave (1959), stabilization is one of the three objectives or functions of fiscal policy in modern economic systems. The other two being efficiency and redistribution.

4. On crises and policy reform, see Fernandez and Rodrik (1991); Cardoso and Helwege (1993); Drazen and Grilli (1993); Rodrik (1995); Tornell (1995); Martinelli and Tommasi (1997).

groups such as the working class and the poor.[5] During expansions, the government should reduce spending in order to "cool off" the economy and contain inflationary pressures. Although this "benevolent planner" prescription is followed to a great extent among member countries of the Organisation for Economic Co-operation and Development (OECD), fiscal policy in many developing countries is actually pro-cyclical (Kaminsky, Reinhart, and Vegh 2004; Alesina, Campante, and Tabellini 2008). In other words, total government spending as a share of GDP goes up during booms and down during recessions, a policy pattern that adds to macroeconomic instability and hurts the poor the most because they lack the assets or the access to financial markets that would allow them to smooth out adverse income shocks. Previous studies have shown that pro-cyclicality is a particularly acute problem in Latin America (Gavin and Perotti 1997).

Economists usually answer these questions using credit constraint arguments. For example, Gavin and Perotti's (1997) seminal contribution argued that developing countries find it hard to follow countercyclical policy because they lack access to international credit during recessions, suggesting that any explanation of pro-cyclical behavior needs to take into account credit constraints or creditworthiness.[6] The problem with this economic explanation is its inability to provide answers to the following: why are countries not able to self-insure by accumulating reserves in good times? Why would lenders not provide funds to countries if they were convinced that borrowing would help smooth out the cycle in the first place?

Policy legacies play a major role in determining credit constraints: as incumbents deplete the fiscal coffers to fend off attempts at replacing them, governments are left empty-handed when a recession hits and foreign finance dries up. This lesson, which became obvious to Latin American governments in the last quarter of the twentieth century, is being hammered into Greek, Portuguese, Spanish, and Irish leaders in the wake of the Great Recession of 2008. Yet we still need to explain why some incumbents establish automatic stabilizers and entitlement programs in anticipation of bad times, while others are more prone to enact unsustainable policies that ultimately place their constituents in harm's way.

A similar problem pervades arguments that link pro-cyclical policy with the nature of the tax base (Talvi and Vegh 2005) or integration with the world economy (Wibbels 2006). Output and consumption in developing countries are highly volatile. When revenue is raised mainly from taxes on trade and consumption,

---

5. Both Keynesian macroeconomic policy and tax smoothing arguments (Barro 1979), for example, prescribe countercyclical fiscal policy.

6. Access to credit is central to understanding the variance in responses to the Great Recession of 2008: due to the prominent role of the dollar in international finance, the United States has been able to stimulate its economy by adding to the ever-growing fiscal deficit.

and access to finance is limited, it is no surprise that governments are unable to follow countercyclical fiscal policies (Talvi and Vegh 2005). Increasing trade exposure and specialization around the country's comparative advantage has the potential to exacerbate volatility (Wibbels 2006). In theory, output volatility and trade openness are neither necessary nor sufficient conditions for pro-cyclical spending. On the contrary, one could imagine that the more volatile and exposed to international trade an economy is, the higher the incentives for politicians to behave in a countercyclical way would be, leading to the creation of stabilization funds or automatic stabilizers in the budget. After all, that is the lesson from the experience of small and open economies in the developed world (Cameron 1978; Katzenstein 1985; Rodrik 1998).

Ultimately, it is uncontested that policy responses adopted under political influence as motivated by distributive concerns usually differ from the optimal policy adopted by an agent who maximizes aggregate welfare.[7] Under most circumstances, policy choices are made under political constraints and may reflect demands for redistribution, which create the incentives to depart from the welfare-maximizing policy regime. The bottom line is that under fairly broad conditions economic downturns and political choices are jointly determined, forcing researchers to identify testable implications under the assumption that both processes are endogenous.

Politics in Hard Times

Although policy responses adopted during crises are allegedly aimed at redressing the duress created by the sharp downturns in output, they ultimately reflect actors' incentives to shape the political and economic environments to their benefit. As Peter Gourevitch eloquently puts it in his seminal book *Politics in Hard Times*:

> History has its points of critical choice, moments of flux when several things might happen but only one actually does. For years afterward, that winning alternative will preempt other possibilities, and things will seem more closed. Economic crises create one such set of points of choice. (1986, 9–10)

The specific content of those responses depends on the expected distributional consequences of the changes in relative prices—which generate the demand for policy responses—and on contemporaneous political conditions that

7. Findlay and Wellisz (1982) present an excellent example of this problem in the political support function literature on tariff formation.

determine who is more likely to mobilize politically and whose preferences will be reflected in the policies implemented.

Although crises are usually associated with misery and deprivation for individuals, for social scientists these hard times offer unparalleled opportunities: "Moments of flux are fruitful for evaluating theoretical debates and for analyzing historical patterns" (Gourevitch 1986, 10). The depth and breadth of the policies adopted in the shadow of sharp recessions are also likely to reflect the underlying distributive cleavages in the polity. And the content of the policies adopted in times of major economic crises depends on the nature and orientation of the ruling coalitions. The Great Recession of 2008 should be no exception.

Yet, while I agree with Gourevitch's assessment that coalitional dynamics trump ideology, institutions, and international factors in explanations of policy choices, in this chapter I caution against using downturns in economic activity as the identifying strategy to assess deviations in policy responses. I will argue that policy choices made along the business cycle have the potential to exacerbate or to smooth out the naturally occurring peaks and troughs of the business cycle.

Pre-existing political conditions reflected in lax regulation of financial markets, large current account deficits, and unhindered capital mobility were the permissive conditions for the sharp contraction of economic activity experienced in the United States and western Europe, and hence hardly exogenous for that set of countries. The diffusion of the contractionary pressure resulting from the collapse at the global centers of economic activity onto peripheral economies is hardly exogenous, as Haggard demonstrates in his analysis of the responses to the crises by developing countries in Europe, Latin America, and Asia (chapter 2, this volume). However, the performance of the Argentine government suggests continuity with prior policy choices: the conflict over export taxes and the seizure of pension funds in 2008 are vivid reminders of the redistributive motivations and shortening of time horizons looming over the political calculus of the ruling coalition.

In more technical terms, the key insight is associated with issues of identification in social science research. If exogenous to the outcome of interest, economic crises could arguably provide researchers a sound empirical strategy to analyze divergence in policy responses to common price and output shocks. Exposure to these common, contemporaneous, and arguably exogenous shocks would allegedly isolate the effect of specific political processes. This strategy is adopted by Gourevitch (1978) in his seminal *International Organization* article on the second image reversed and more thoroughly in his book *Politics in Hard Times* (1986); it is also present in other influential works in international political economy.

The problem of identification—which aims at addressing issues of endogeneity and selection bias—is pervasive to all but a few empirical exercises in social sciences.[8] Ideally, the researcher would identify a natural experiment or quasi-experiment that creates a shock that is completely exogenous to the system under analysis. However, the take-home point of this chapter is that most instances of crises in the empirical literature, and economic downturns in particular, are a far cry away from fulfilling the exogeneity requirement: economic crises and policy choices are jointly determined.

Economic Policymaking along the Business Cycle

To develop a political economy analysis of fiscal policies, we need an analytical model that fully accounts for demand and supply conditions in policymaking. Political actors' interests and their abilities to overcome collective action problems figure prominently on the demand side of politics; on the supply side of politics, politicians' preferences and political institutions are the key analytical concepts. Political actors, individual or collective, are usually construed as holding clearly defined objective functions; they are embedded in an economic environment and operate under an institutional setting that creates benefits and opportunities as well as costs and constraints on their ability to attain preferred outcomes. It is therefore incumbent on those actors to engage politically to effect the policy changes that would benefit them.

This element is present in several political economy accounts of policymaking in times of crises and parallels a development in the endogenous tariff-formation literature in economics (Caves 1976; Baldwin 1985; Gawande and Krishna 2003). In the political economy of trade literature, politics is both the process of intermediation of interests—mobilized politically as groups with different degrees of influence and coalition potential—and the institutional environment that makes some coalitions more likely to arise (Gourevitch 1986, 9, 33, 227–40; see also the introduction and the afterword in this volume).

The supply side of politics could be augmented for analytical purposes. We could, for instance, identify the policy choices available to policymakers. Researchers usually make simplifying assumptions about the existence of policy bundles associated with certain schools of thought, which allow them to sidestep the issue of identifying the optimal policy responses when the policy space is multidimensional. Protectionism, lax monetary policy, and tax-and-spend policies, for instance, are usually assumed to go hand in hand. Although the historical

8. See also Green and Gerber (2007) and Humphreys and Weinstein (2009) for a review of this literature. The problem of identification is now a central theme in economics including behavioral game theory, applied micro, the empirically oriented, and at the New School of Economic Development (Banerjee et al. 2007; Banerjee and Duflo 2008; De Mel, McKenzie, and Woodruff 2008) in the cutting-edge empirical literature in political economy (Habyarimana et al. 2007; Blattman and Annan 2010), and is percolating into international political economy (Wantchekon 2003; Hyde 2007).

record suggests that a combination of these policies usually fall on the same left-right dimension in the policy space, governments could choose a combination of these policies depending on the circumstances.

The restrictiveness of this assumption becomes apparent when analyzing the regulatory conditions leading to the financial crisis of 2007 and the policy responses to the Great Recession of 2008. The divergent choices made by western Europe and the United States on one hand, and emerging markets on the other hand (especially in the latter group where countries such as Argentina, Brazil, or South Africa were historically affected by changing financial conditions), demonstrate that actors are not restricted in their policy choices.

The simplicity of this setup is elegant and powerful. However, two analytical issues immediately arise. First, it is far from apparent that the timing, geographic coverage, and magnitude of downturns in economic activity are independent of political conditions in the run-up to the downturn. There are certain shocks to economic activity that could be considered to be truly exogenous to politics.[9] These usually result from sudden changes in prices and output as a function of the weather, natural disasters, or even sharp demographic and technological changes. Yet other drops in economic activity are usually the natural course of the business cycle, which actors could and should be able to anticipate. (This does not necessarily mean that they would be willing to act in anticipation of those expected shocks, as the subprime crisis in the United States suggests.) Recessions, on the other hand, are drastic drops in output caused by actors' behavior in the political marketplace. The disposition to absorb those shocks or to transfer their costs to other actors depends on political actors' position in the economy, access to finance, and risk aversion. These are the very same conditions that lead to the adoption of policies that raise the probability that a recession will occur.

A second issue is the role of economic, policy, and institutional legacies, which further underscores the link between politics and economics along the business cycle. Although comparing cross-sectionally within each episode could be defended as a sound empirical strategy, drawing conclusions across time periods violates the assumption of independence, invalidating any exercise in causal inference. Choices made in the past affect the probability of a crisis and condition actors' ability to cope with the consequences of the downturn. Legacies are central in many contributions to international and comparative political economy. A prominent example is the literature on varieties of capitalism (Berger

9. Although the three instances identified in *Politics in Hard Times* (*PHT*) clearly stand out as qualitatively different from other downturns in the business cycle, only the first of those instances (the Crisis of 1873–96) is triggered by sudden changes in relative prices; the shock resulting from the oil embargo of 1967 is only a proximate cause of the last instance of crisis included in *PHT*. To show that this problem is far from innocuous, I will later discuss an extension of Gourevitch's framework that views economic crises as endogenous to the political process.

and Dore 1996; Hall and Soskice 2001). In other accounts, legacies emerge in the form of policy bundles available to political leaders and the constraining or enhancing effects of domestic and international institutions that determine the relative influence of political actors and the policy alternatives available to them. Legacies are also present in the form of technological development (see, for instance, the skill-biased technological change of the late twentieth century), in the organization of production, and the international division of labor.

To analyze policymaking in good and hard times, analysts must account for political, institutional, and economic legacies. Past choices affect current conditions and even have the potential to restrict the policy choices available when reacting to those conditions. Given the alignment of preferences and specific processes of political intermediation, some governments will be more prone to adopting unsustainable policies (even if they represent constituents who would benefit from countercyclical spending), while others would be able to strike political compromises that allow them to better absorb the ups and downs of the economic cycle.

Unsustainable Policies, Legacies, and the Endogeneity of Economic Crises

To identify the effect of economic crises on economic policymaking, an analyst must persuasively show that the asserted economic shocks are indeed exogenous to political processes. Yet we have good reason to believe that this is not the case: political conditions preceding a downturn not only precipitate the likelihood that the crisis would occur but also to restrict the options available to policymakers. The assumption that crises are exogenous to politics would attribute to the economic crisis what are actually direct consequences of political choices made prior to the crisis.

The analytical problems associated with endogeneity of economic outcomes, including sharp recessions that result from financial and exchange rate crises, should not preclude the analyst from tackling substantive issues in political economy. If economic shocks are endogenous, we need to shift our focus: rather than exploring the size and timing of the adoption of stimulus packages *in times of recession*, we need a theoretical apparatus that helps explain what governments do *along the business cycle*. Focusing on cyclicality rather than on the response to economic shocks is a better way to address the endogenous relationship between economic and political outcomes.

I present a stylized model aimed at explaining fiscal choices in the shadow of distributive conflict. The argument combines elements usually associated with a country's position in the international division of labor, domestic actors' position in the economy, and fiscal policy.[10] Specifying the underlying model of the economy and the boundaries of political exchanges helps derive the scope conditions under which unsustainable policies may arise in equilibrium. Incentives to deviate from the optimal path depend on the time horizons of political leaders, which in turn are endogenous to their redistributive motivations.

Although securing tenure in office is usually a balancing act for any ruling coalition, the problem is compounded for those coalitions representing fragmented or heterogeneous interests. The likelihood of being voted out of office is greater when the heterogeneous coalition enacts policies that redistribute wealth in favor of their followers against the will of those who bear most the cost of the redistribution. The losing side will usually mount political opposition against this effort. Political conflict around redistributive motivations creates a perverse incentive structure that leads governments to engage in pro-cyclical spending. Redistributive conflict simultaneously raises the incumbent's incentive to cater to followers to prevent defections while reducing the leader's incentive to internalize the future consequences of the policy choices.

This framework helps explain why governments enact unsustainable policies. It also offers a key insight to the endogeneity of economic crises. The risk of being unseated by the opposing coalition makes political actors run scared. The problem is exacerbated when the coalition is built around heterogeneous groups who could potentially defect. The end result is a shortening of time horizons, which forces governments off the optimal policy path.

The politically motivated adoption of unsustainable policies makes recessions more likely to occur and forces governments to respond in suboptimal ways. Moreover, those incentives grounded in political economy motivations reduce the room to compromise and make coalitions representing economic actors who would benefit the most from the adoption of countercyclical policies, such as the Peronist coalition in Argentina, engage in pro-cyclical behavior.

In terms of fiscal policy, an incumbent facing shorter time horizons has lower incentives to defer expenditure and is therefore more likely to deviate from the optimal. Political instability reduces the incumbent's "discount factor," so the level of public expenditure will go up when the government can tax more (such as in the up side of the business cycle), borrow from abroad, or both. Yet credit market imperfections may prevent the government from borrowing.[11] With complete markets, the optimal fiscal policy consists in completely smoothing out government consumption. However, governments in developing and emerging markets with shallow domestic financial systems typically face rationed foreign

10. The framework is presented in more detail in Ardanaz, Pinto, and Pinto (2011).

11. Specifically, consider a capital market imperfection that generates a positive association between public debt and the risk premium (Aizenman, Gavin, and Hausmann 2000).

finance due to lack of confidence. These credit constraints are especially binding during bad macroeconomic times, hence reinforcing the pro-cyclicality generated by political distortions. Limited access to financial markets makes it virtually impossible to run a countercyclical fiscal policy, particularly when the government was unwilling or unable to self-insure by stashing funds away during good times (Gavin and Perotti 1997).

The type of fiscal policies implemented by a government affects the risk premium charged on its sovereign debt. The risk premium tends to increase in bad times, making borrowing more costly. As a result, the incumbent is forced to raise taxes and/or reduce government consumption, further fueling the pro-cyclicality of fiscal policy. In good times, the opposite would take place: a lower risk premium would encourage more borrowing, more government spending, and lower taxes.

As a review, I expect fiscal policy to be countercyclical or acyclical when the policymaker is insulated from political demands and internalizes the future. Yet political conflict resulting from distributional motivations has the potential to prevent incumbents from adopting the optimal policy; those constraints are particularly prevalent for those incumbents representing economic agents who need protection to survive in the marketplace. The end result is the adoption of suboptimal policies along the business cycle, which increase the likelihood of economic recessions and magnify their consequences.

Endogenous Time Horizons and Fiscal Policy: Lessons from Argentina's History

The evolution of fiscal policy in the Argentine case discussed in this section can be best understood under the lens of a distributive conflict between rural and urban interests that has dominated the country's history since its political consolidation. The centrality of this conflict affects the time horizons of political leaders, creating incentives to spend in the up cycle and constraining the ability to spend in the down cycle. This pro-cyclical behavior has also resulted in a higher likelihood of experiencing recessions, suggesting that at least in the Argentine case economic and political cycles are jointly determined.

Given its vast extensions of arable land and its temperate climate, Argentina's comparative advantage has historically lain in its agricultural sector. Historically, agricultural producers have not demanded government support to stay competitive, especially in the up side of the business cycle, and have fought to fend off attempts at taxing their gains, as reflected in the country's political instability and fluctuation between democratic and autocratic governance. Producers of import-competing manufactured products who had been sheltered from foreign competition in the interwar era, on the other hand, were only able to survive in the shadow of protectionism and with the help of government transfers that resulted in the country's embrace of import substitution industrialization (ISI). Yet the adoption of the ISI strategy was not fortuitous (Galiani et al. 2008). Technological changes in the production of food in the early twentieth century, the arrival of migrants from the Old World (Zimmermann 1995), and the collapse of the trading system in the interwar era provided incentives for emergence of import-substituting manufacturing firms, particularly in Buenos Aires. These firms would gradually employ all surplus workers who had been expelled from the countryside as well as those arriving to the port.

During the twentieth century, incumbents of different orientations were subject to demands for government spending from starkly different political groups. Traditionally, agriculture producers have been represented by the conservative and military governments; the coalition formed by labor and producers in the urban sector, on the other hand, is represented by Juan Domingo Perón and his followers. Last, the Radical Party has historically represented the middle class and professionals in the urban sector and usually clashed with organized labor, industrialists, and agricultural producers; yet their tenure was unstable and usually punctuated by electoral upsets or authoritarian coups.

Despite their ability to win elections, all Peronist leaders (who ruled Argentina in the periods 1946–55, 1973–76, 1989–99, and 2002 to date) have systematically behaved as if in fear of being toppled either by military coups or even from within their own coalition. The subjective expected probability of staying in power affects an incumbents' discount factor; that probability, in turn, is endogenous to the political process, as it results from the government's motivations to redistribute.[12]

The Peronist party is a heterogeneous coalition of workers and industrialists in urban centers; it is characterized by a higher level of political fragmentation or heterogeneity than the coalition built around agricultural interests. For several reasons, the Peronist coalition may face more difficulties in keeping government expenditure under control. First, as a catchall coalition, the Peronists have a more heterogeneous support base, are subject to greater fiscal pressure, and have a limited ability to force coalition members to compromise. Second, it is built around organized labor, a formidable political resource that can deliver votes and block political change through strikes and political mobilization. At the same time, or-

12. Additional tests of the link between politics and fiscal policy are presented in Ardanaz, Pinto, and Pinto (2011). The emphasis on distributive politics is an important addition to traditional explanations of cyclical spending based on the role of preferences, institutions, and veto players (Kontopoulos and Perroti 1999; Velasco 1999; Tsebelis and Chang 2004).

ganized labor has little power to implement its own program without the support of other groups in the polity. Organized labor could coalesce with capital owners in manufacturing whose preferences toward the country's insertion in the international division of labor are congruent to those of its own, yet are potentially in a collision course with workers on their claims over their respective share of output and government spending. Finally, the distributional conflict with agricultural producers has the potential to escalate, thus making incumbents feel insecure and less willing to internalize the value of long-term commitments. To the extent that a pro-manufacturing government requires increasingly larger transfers from other sectors to satisfy the demands of its constituencies, political tensions eventually arise, decreasing the probability of staying in power and further reducing the government's time horizon. Hence the expectation of being toppled reduces the incentives to cooperate.[13]

Statistical analyses discussed in the ensuing section suggest that fiscal responses to the business cycle in the Argentine case depend on the nature and orientation of the ruling coalition as predicted by the political economy framework. Yet the evidence suggests that both the magnitude of cyclical swings in economic activity and the timing of sharp recessions are also affected by those politically motivated changes in spending. The evidence suggests that the prevailing assumption that crises are exogenous is highly problematic.

Political Coalitions, Cyclical Spending, and the Likelihood of Recessions

The evolution of Argentina's public accounts from 1900 to date allows an exploration of the predictions from the framework. The pro-cyclical nature of government spending in Argentina is evident early in the series, when government revenue depended on taxes on consumption and foreign trade, a trend that has been persuasively explained by Talvi and Vegh (2005). The correlation between output and spending becomes stronger toward the second half of the twentieth century, an era characterized by stop-go cycles usually attributed to the problems that arise from the adoption of import substitution as a developmental strategy (see table 4-1 and figs. 4-1 and 4-2). Figure 4-2 in particular suggests that access to credit is key when government needs to finance shortfalls in revenue.

Using time-series data on the evolution of government spending in Argentina, I can explore more directly the claim that politics is directly linked to the

13. On the role of time horizons in fostering (or hindering) political cooperation, see Alesina (1988) and Dixit, Grossman, and Gul (2000). Spiller and Tommasi (2007) provide an application of this framework in the Argentine institutional context.

TABLE 4-1. Argentina: Pro-cyclical spending by decade

DECADE	CORR. COEFF.
1900–1910	0.38
1911–20	0.52
1921–30	0.23
1931–40	0.26
1941–50	0.50
1951–60	0.03
1961–70	0.72**
1971–80	0.53
1981–90	0.76***
1991–2004	0.79***

Notes: Significance levels: * 1%, ** 5%, *** 1%.
Correlation between cyclical components of Ln GDP/cap. and Ln Govt. Spend./cap. using the Hodrick-Prescott filter.

Source: Ardanaz, Pinto, and Pinto (2011).

cyclicality of spending and that changes in public spending are strong predictors of the onset of the fourteen recessions that the country has experienced throughout the twentieth century.[14] The results suggest that pro-cyclical spending makes economic recessions both more likely and more frequent. (See table 4-2.)

While countercyclical spending would have benefitted their constituency base—workers and other economic agents who have limited access to financial markets to smooth their consumption—when in power the Peronists have engaged in pro-cyclical behavior. Consistent with our argument, the Peronists, who represent a coalition of industrialists and workers in the comparative disad-

14. The results presented in table 4-2 are from fitting an error correction model (ECM) using data on the evolution of government spending for the period 1900–2004. The series are integrated of *I(1)*, i.e., stationary after first-differencing, hence the ECM specification. The coefficients are from the second-stage regression of change in spending on change in output interacted with variables aimed at capturing the partisan orientation of the incumbent government. The second-stage regression has the following functional form: $\Delta\ G_t = \mu_0 + \mu_\lambda\ \lambda + \lambda\ \beta_\lambda\ \Delta Y_t + \beta_1\ \Delta Y_t + \gamma\ (G_{t-1} - \delta\ Y_t -_1) + \varepsilon_t$ where λ isan indicator variable that takes the value of 1 when the Peronist coalition is in power (or *Peronist-like* coalition such as the GOU (Grupo de Oficiales Unidos, or United Officers' Group) that ruled the country between 1943–46, paving the way for Peron's election in 1946). The expectation is that spending will be more pro-cyclical when the ruling coalition represents workers and capitalists in the urban sectors. The models include the lagged residuals from a first-stage regression of spending in levels on output; thus captures the adjustment rate in each period when the series move away from their equilibrium relationship. For a discussion on the sample and methods used for these tests, see Ardanaz, Pinto, and Pinto (2011).

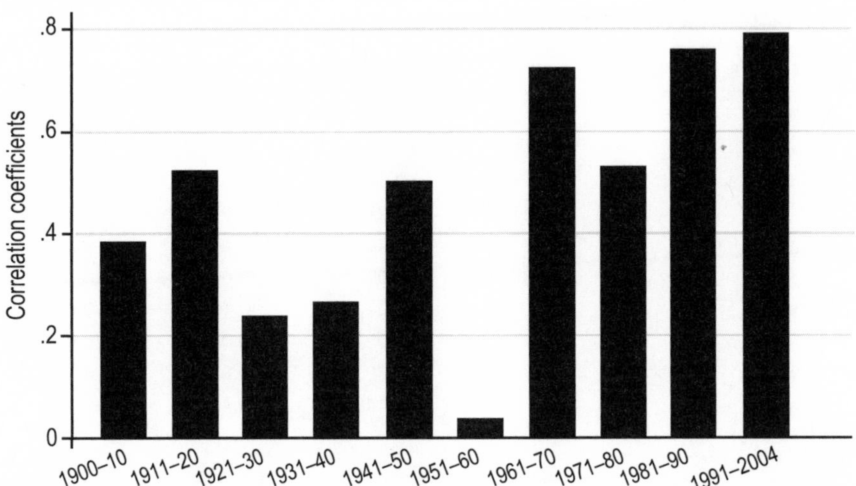

FIGURE 4-1. Argentina GDP and government spending: Correlation by decade.

Source: Ardanaz, Pinto, and Pinto (2011).

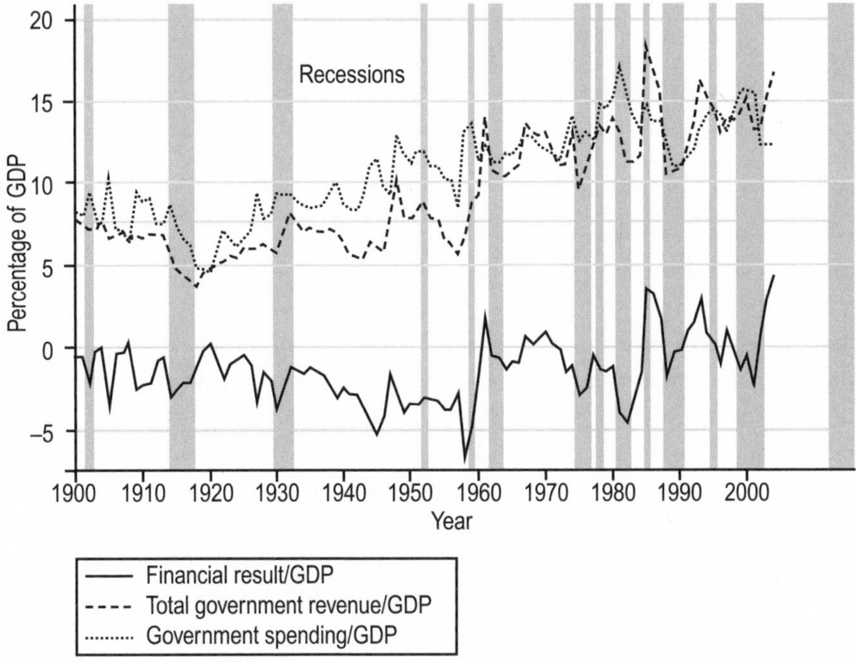

FIGURE 4-2. Argentina government spending and revenue

TABLE 4-2. Error correction models: Baseline

MODELS	(1)	(2)	(3)	(4)
Constant	0.006	0.008	–0.024	–0.024
	(0.011)	(0.012)	(0.028)	(0.028)
Δ Ln GDP/capita	0.817***	0.583**	0.597**	0.576
	(0.241)	(0.284)	(0.275)	(0.481)
γ (θ_{t-1})	–0.430***	–0.414***	–0.463***	–0.461***
	(0.090)	(0.091)	(0.097)	(0.098)
Peronist		–0.013	–0.024	–0.023
		(0.022)	(0.022)	(0.023)
Peronist × ΔLn GDP/cap.		0.895**	0.87**	0.992**
		(0.446)	(0.421)	(0.484)
ISI (1930–75)			0.061*	0.058*
			(0.035)	(0.034)
ISI × ΔLn GDP/cap.				0.145
				(0.567)
Reform (1976–2004)			0.028	0.027
			(0.032)	(0.032)
Reform × ΔLn GDP/cap.				–0.183
				(0.600)
N	104	104	104	104
R^2	0.338	0.363	0.395	0.397
$F_{(8,95)}$	14.62	12.89	10.23	7.65
Durbin-Watson d-stat$_{(9,104)}$	1.947	1.939	1.934	1.912

Notes: DV: Ln Govt. Spend./capita; omitted categories: non-Peronist incumbents.
Huber-White robust std. errors in parentheses; significance levels: * 1%, ** 5%, *** 1%.
γ: coeff. on lagged Residual (θ_{t-1}) from first stage regression, where $\theta_{t-1} = G_{t-1} - \mu_0 - \hat{\delta} Y_{t-1}$.
ISI: Import Substitution Industrialization; Reform: economic and trade liberalization.

Source: Ardanaz, Pinto, and Pinto (2011).

vantage sector of the economy, have systematically used spending as a political tool when the economy expanded and were forced to retrench spending at times of economic crises. The case suggests that the adoption of suboptimal policies is not grounded on structure or ideology, but on the salient role of coalition bargaining across policy dimensions (see table 4-3).

Table 4-4 explores the link between changes in government spending with the probability of the onset of a recession.[15] The results suggest that recessions in Argentina are positively and statistically associated with lagged changes in gov-

15. I fit a probit model where recession is a dummy variable, which is set to 1 during the year of the onset of a recession, and 0 otherwise. Note that I am trying to estimate the probability that lagged values of the right-hand side variables and their lagged changes are associated with the probability that the country will fall into a recession in year *t*.

TABLE 4-3. ECM models: Alternative hypotheses

VARIABLE	COEFFICIENT	(STD. ERR.)
Constant	−0.118**	(0.053)
ΔLn GDP/cap.	−0.130	(0.758)
γ (θ_{t-1})	−0.622***	(0.119)
Peronist	−0.006	(0.029)
Peronist × ΔLn GDP/cap.	1.511**	(0.631)
GOU	0.054	(0.047)
GOU × ΔLn GDP/cap.	1.713**	(0.654)
Radical	0.053	(0.035)
Radical × ΔLn GDP/cap.	0.827	(0.554)
Conservative	0.142**	(0.069)
Conservative × ΔLn GDP/cap.	1.386	(0.945)
Nat. Coal.	−0.067*	(0.038)
Nat. Coal. × ΔLn GDP/cap.	2.082	(1.710)
Nat. Dem.	0.038	(0.036)
Nat. Dem. × ΔLn GDP/cap.	0.714	(0.614)
Δ Ln ToT	0.132	(0.097)
Δ Ln US int. rate	−0.042*	(0.024)
Δ Ln Imports	−0.091	(0.079)
ISI (1930–75)	0.126**	(0.053)
ISI × ΔLn GDP/cap.	0.280	(0.645)
Reform (1976–2004)	0.113**	(0.047)
Reform × ΔLn GDP/cap.	0.419	(0.633)
N	104	
R^2	0.498	
$F_{(21,82)}$	11.087	
DW d-statistic$_{(22,104)}$	1.805	

Notes: DV: Ln Govt. Spend./capita; omitted category: Military government
Significance levels: * 1%, ** 5%, *** 1%; Huber-White robust std. err. in parentheses.
γ: coeff. on lagged Residual (θ_{t-1}) from first stage regression, where $\theta_{t-1} = G_{t-1} - \mu_0 - \delta Y_{t-1}$.
ISI: Import Substitution Industrialization; Reform: economic and trade liberalization; ToT: terms of trade; U.S. interest rate: short-term U.S. interest rate.

Source: Ardanaz, Pinto, and Pinto (2011).

ernment spending, with the level of short-term interest rates in the United States, and with changes in import penetration, and negatively correlated with changes in the country's trade balance.

In combination with the results presented in tables 4-2 and 4-3, we can conclude that recessions are endogenous to politics; analyses of politics in hard times should embrace this endogeneity and model political and economic outcomes

TABLE 4-4. Probit regression: Probability of onset of a recession

VARIABLE	(1)	(2)
Δ Ln Spend/cap$_{t-1}$	2.730**	3.397***
	(1.150)	(1.285)
Δ Ln US int. rate$_{t-1}$	0.278	−0.0243
	(0.258)	(0.522)
Δ Ln ToT $_{t-1}$	−0.995	−0.783
	(1.441)	(1.826)
Δ Ln Trade Balance $_{t-1}$	−0.659	0.0747
	(0.636)	(0.817)
Ln Spend/cap$_{t-1}$		−1.002
		(0.850)
Ln US int. rate$_{t-1}$		0.839**
		(0.371)
Ln ToT $_{t-1}$		1.488
		(1.209)
Ln Trade Balance $_{t-1}$		−1.596**
		(0.715)
ISI (1930–75)	0.110	1.469
	(0.447)	(1.000)
Reform (1976–2004)	0.692	2.058
	(0.513)	(1.326)
Constant	−1.579***	−4.032
	(0.438)	(5.606)
Observations	104	104
Pseudo R^2	0.1135	0.2358
Wald χ^2	12.10	16.21
Prob > χ^2	0.0599	0.0938

Notes: Significance levels: * 1%, ** 5%, *** 1%; Huber-White robust std. errors in parentheses.
ISI: Import Substitution Industrialization; Reform: economic and trade liberalization; Ln ToT: natural log of terms of trade; Ln US int. rate: natural log of short term US interest rate; Ln Govt. Spend./cap: natural log of government spending per capita. Δ: first difference.

as jointly determined. Moreover, the limited effect of the global recession of 2008 on the Argentine economy can be also understood under the lens of the distributional conflict and cyclicality of spending discussed in the previous section. The same distributional motivations that explain cyclicality and the link between spending and recessions in the Argentine case have reduced the transmission pulleys through which the crisis initiated in the United States and western Europe.

Extending the Framework: The Subprime Crisis and the Great Recession of 2008

Although Ardanaz, Pinto, and Pinto (2011) test the predictions from the model with data from one country by fitting a model that directly incorporates the joint determination of economic and political outcomes, figure 4-3 suggests that Argentina is far from an exceptional case. The basic setup on which the model presented earlier is built could be extended to capture this dynamic in a more complex policy space, such as the regulation of finance, exchange rate politics, and government finance.

Moreover, the modeling strategy could be applied to any setup where demands from redistribution create a political rift among different groups in the polity, including cleavages between those in the comparative advantage and disadvantage sectors in the economy; producers versus consumers; producers of traded goods and producers of nontradables; or Wall Street versus Main Street. These rifts could be ameliorated through compromise, yet this compromise is usually inhibited by the inability of winners to credibly commit to compensating losers, a problem that is at the center of most accounts of distributive politics in the positive political economy literature.

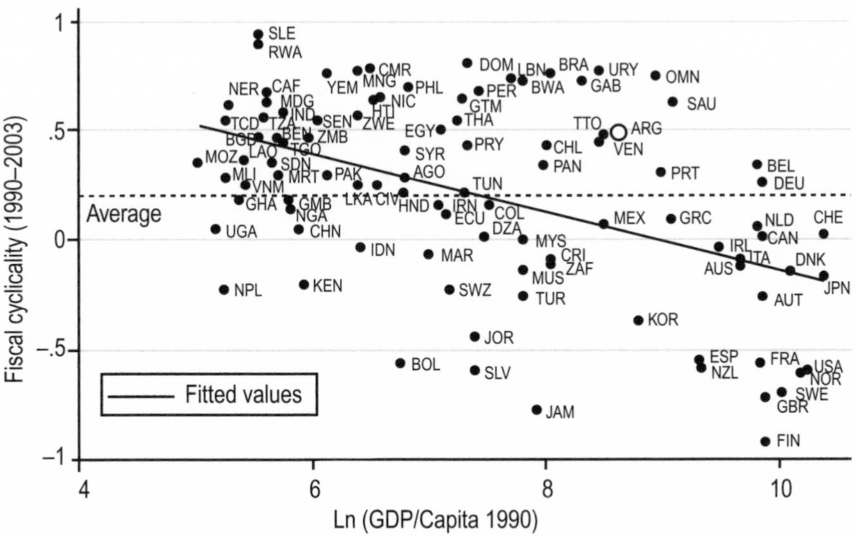

FIGURE 4-3. Constant GDP per capita (natural log) and pro-cyclical government spending.

Source: Ardanaz, Pinto, and Pinto (2011).

Other contributions to this volume (Broz; Hall; Haggard; Gourevitch) explore the political economy of economic policymaking in good times that led to the Great Recession of 2008; the run-up to the burst of the real estate bubble and the subsequent subprime crisis that froze economic activity in the United States is widely documented by academics and pundits (Reinhart and Rogoff 2009; Lewis 2010). While several accounts point to the peculiar conditions in this specific instance of financial collapse, the similarities to other episodes of boom-and-bust cycles suggest that, paraphrasing Reinhart and Rogoff, "this time is far from different": the proximate causes of the Great Recession become clearly apparent in the times of the Great Delusion.[16] Just like the well-documented Latin American debt crisis of the 1980s, the Tequila crisis in the early 1990s, or the Asian financial crisis of the late 1990s, the U.S. subprime crisis is tightly linked to the problems caused by international capital mobility in countries where economic actors (public and private) engage in excessive financial leverage to finance consumption and investment at unsustainable levels, pitting economic actors in a war of attrition that delays adjustment.[17]

After the fact, it becomes apparent that while the peaks and troughs in economic activity can be partially smoothed out, the business cycle cannot be tamed (Reinhart and Rogoff 2009, 270). The depth and length of the waves of the cycle are exacerbated by policy legacies such as implicit guarantees that encourage risk-taking; unsustainable policies, including overvalued exchange rates that exacerbate the wealth effect; fiscal profligacy, which could be attributed to political logrolling, flypaper effects (expansion of public spending in previous crises that ratchets up); or desperate attempts by political leaders to consolidate political power and remain in office. The proximate answer to the problem is thus political: changes in the structure of the American economy have exacerbated the privileged position of financial and service sectors.

The main lesson from Argentine case discussed in the previous section, the Latin American experience in the 1980s, and the Asian financial crisis of 1997 is the following: when financial regulation is lax, excessive dependence on short-term foreign capital to finance current account and fiscal deficits increases the likelihood of sharp recessions and magnifies the consequences of those recessions when foreign sources of finance dry up.[18] The main difference in the U.S. case is the role of the greenback as a store of value, which could be attributed to the productivity of dollar-denominated assets and a history of repayment that

16. I use the term "Great Delusion" to describe the pre-subprime crisis period in the United States. The term comes from Charles Mackay's 1840 writings on asset bubbles. See Lewis (2008).

17. Fernandez and Rodrik (1991); see Rodrik (1995) for a discussion on the literature on economic reform.

18. See Chinn and Frieden (2009, 2011).

boosts the government's credibility. Yet reputations can be shattered, as suggested by the market reaction to the deal struck by Obama and the Republican congressional leadership that extended the Bush-era tax cuts and passed a sizable stimulus package during the 2010 lame-duck session of Congress, thereby adding to the government deficit.[19]

One could attribute those choices to historical accident, ideological blinders, or market folly. Yet it becomes apparent that political choices were central: in the U.S. case, a coalition of financial capital owners, producers of nontradables, and homeowners coalesced around cheap credit and a relatively strong currency, as has been extensively documented by Reinhart and Rogoff (2009), Chinn and Frieden (2011), Gourevitch (2013), as well as Kahler and Lake (this volume) and Gourevitch (this volume). The financial sector's demand for lax regulation (which led to excessive risk-taking) and the Fed's willingness to accommodate its monetary policy (a stark departure from the Taylor rule, as documented by Taylor 2009) resulted in the availability of cheap money that led to overleveraged investment and fed the stock and real estate bubbles. Paraphrasing Taylor, had there been no boom, we would not have suffered the bust (Taylor 2009, 3).

The problem was compounded by an ever-increasing government deficit resulting from the war effort, the expansion of public services and tax cuts, and the implicit guarantees that encouraged risk-taking by banks and reduced incentives to innovate for automakers and other large employers in manufacturing.

Far from smoothing economic activity, policy decisions made along the business cycle exacerbated the negative consequences of the economic contraction and constrained the policy choices available for dealing with those consequences. Those in privileged political positions were not willing to forsake short-term gain for long-term welfare, and political agents were in no position to turn against them.

That the Great Recession originated in the United States should come as no surprise given the policy choices made at the time of the Great Delusion (Reinhart and Rogoff 2009; Chinn and Frieden 2011). And responses to the crisis are clearly constrained by those policy legacies. For instance, with reference interest rates close to zero, the Fed learned from the Japanese experience in the 1990s that stimulating the economy would require innovative mechanisms such as asset purchases and quantitative easing. Although the sharp fall in economic activity of the largest world market had ripple effects throughout the planet by causing a drop in demand of imports, the speed and extent of those effects were far from uniform (Baldwin and Evenett 2009). The effect of the crisis was magnified

19. Christine Hauser, "Bonds Fall on Fear That Tax Cut Deal Will Add to Deficit, but Stocks Are Steady," *New York Times*, December 8, 2010, B12.

in countries whose manufacturing sectors are tightly integrated to United States producers' supply chains (such as Mexico; see Yi 2009); countries that could not switch to domestic demand to mitigate the drop in trade (compare the United Kingdom, Ireland, Greece, Portugal, and Spain to surplus countries like Germany or China); countries running large current account and fiscal deficits, particularly those with lax financial regulation and oversight, and/or weak institutions of financial intermediation; countries with pegged and/or overvalued exchange rates; and countries with accommodating monetary policy.[20]

Argentina and the Great Recession of 2008: How Loud Must the Dog Bark?

To many pundits and scholars, the fact that Argentina (along with other emerging economies in the Southern Cone) has emerged relatively unscathed from the global recession of 2008 is surprising: its history of unstable political coalitions, pro-cyclical spending, and recurring economic recessions should have driven the country to the edge of the cliff and forced yet another free fall in economic activity as the global economy contracted and financial markets dried up. Yet just as in 1929, policies adopted previously in the shadow of the distributive conflict and a strong tailwind from the steady rise in prices of Argentine exports both delayed and reduced the effects of the global contraction and mitigated the pressure to adjust spending.

Argentina's sovereign default in 2001 and subsequent renegotiation virtually severed the country's link to international finance; the reduction in interest rate payments also provided a strong relief to the fiscal authorities. When international financial markets dried up after the subprime crisis, the Argentine economy hardly suffered. The country had also benefitted from the sharp rise in the price of agricultural products, particularly resulting from the demand for food from the quickly growing economies of East and South Asia. The government responded to this demand by increasing the taxes on agricultural exports, particularly on the export of foodstuff, and by banning the export of meat to protect the urban population that consumes but does not produce food. These policies resulted in extra government revenue, reducing the strain created by higher spending, particularly under the under the presidencies of Néstor Kirchner and Cristina Fernandez de Kirchner. Moreover, the consolidation of Mercosur and the increasing demand from Asia decoupled the Argentine economy from the

20. These conditions are present in most historical accounts of financial crises (Kaminsky and Reinhart 1999; Reinhart and Rogoff 2009). Note, however, that several countries such as South Korea, Taiwan, Indonesia, and India, which are also highly integrated in manufacturing supply chains, were able to avert the crisis. See Kahler and Lake, this volume.

North Atlantic markets, making it less vulnerable to the drop in aggregate demand from the Great Recession.[21] The Argentine economy did contract in 2009, yet this contraction was much less severe than those experienced by Mexico and countries in Central America and the Caribbean, which were more exposed to the U.S. market.

Consistent with previous episodes, the recession put pressure on government spending; yet this pressure was mitigated by the government's seizure of the funds managed by the private pension funds, which allowed sustaining the public works, subsidies, and other social programs at least until the 2011 reelection of Cristina Kirchner.[22] The seizure of pension funds is not unique to Argentina: Hungary, Latvia, Poland, and Romania have tapped into private pension funds to finance public spending, either totally (as in Hungary) or partially undoing their pension reforms of the 1990s (Aslund 2011).

That the policy course in the wake of the 2001 crisis was unsustainable is already apparent in the imposition of import restrictions, elimination of subsidies, and fiscal retrenchment strategy that Kirchner government enacted in early 2012, as soon as the electoral dust cleared.

Conclusion

In this chapter, I have argued that treating economic crises as exogenous to the political process that they affect is problematic. Post-crisis decisions are not made in a vacuum: decisions made in the run-up to a crisis have the potential not only to precipitate the likelihood that the crisis would occur but also to restrict the policy options around which political actors can coalesce. The assumption that crises are exogenous would drive researchers to mistakenly attribute to the drop in economic activity what are actually direct consequences of political choices made before the crisis occurred. This assumption is the core of the problem of identification that has become central in social science. Yet I have argued that the analytical problems associated with endogeneity of economic outcomes, including sharp recessions that result from financial and exchange rate crises,

21. The Mercosur (Mercado Común del Sur, or Southern Common Market in English) is a customs union formed in 1991. Its original members were Argentina, Brazil, Uruguay, and Paraguay. Venezuela formally joined the group in 2012. Bolivia, Chile, Colombia, Ecuador, and Perú are associate members of the group.

22. Miguel Jorquera, "Hacia el principio del fin para las AFJP" [Toward the beginning of the end of the AFJP], November 7, 2008, 12. Both sources are from the online archives of the newspapers: www.pagina12.com.ar and www.lanacion.com; Silvia Stang, "Admiten que los fondos jubilatorios son usados para enfrentar la crisis" [(Government officials) admit that the retirement funds are being used to face the crisis], *La Nacion*, May 21, 2009.

should not preclude researchers from tackling substantive issues in the political economy of foreign economic policymaking.

To illustrate this point, I discuss the evolution of fiscal policymaking in Argentina where the probability of a severe crisis is a function of decisions made along the business cycle as a result of political conflict and coalition bargaining. This discussion suggests that the theoretical framework presented in the chapter could be extended to capture this dynamic in a more complex policy space, such as the regulation of finance, exchange rate politics, and government finance, where distributive concerns are paramount. The Great Recession of 2008 also seems to support the conjecture that crises are as much the consequences as the causes of political choices along the business cycle, and therefore these crises cannot be treated as exogenous shocks to identify political effects.

Part II

INTERESTS, COALITIONS, AND CONSEQUENCES

5

THE POLITICAL ORIGINS OF OUR ECONOMIC DISCONTENTS

Contemporary Adjustment Problems in Historical Perspective

Peter A. Hall

The financial crises and recession of 2008–9 are the worst experienced by the developed democracies since World War II. Will this crisis inspire radical changes in policies or in the economic models that underlie them? How do we explain the adjustment paths countries take in the wake of such a crisis? These are economic questions about the sources of demand and supply in a chastened world, and political questions about how the will to adjust is generated. Such issues can be approached in various ways, but in the political economy as in the forest, if we want to know where we are going, it is useful to know from where we have come. Therefore, this chapter considers how the developed democracies addressed parallel challenges over the past seven decades with a view to understanding better how they are responding to the current ones.

To this problem, I bring a synoptic perspective that emphasizes the architecture of the political economy, seen as a set of interdependent institutional structures, encompassing organizational relations among economic actors, the policy regimes supporting those relationships, and the international regimes in which they are embedded (Eichengreen 1996b). Drawing on a well-established literature, I outline the institutional architecture of the developed political economies

Although he may disagree with the arguments in this chapter, Peter Gourevitch will recognize the inspiration I have drawn from his writing and our many conversations. I am grateful to Catherine Yang for efficient research assistance, to the Hanse-Wissenschaftskolleg for its hospitality while this chapter was revised, and to Chris Allen, Albena Azmenova, Arie Krampf, Waltraud Schelkle, Herman Schwartz, David Soskice, Peter Swenson, Mark Thatcher, and Kathleen Thelen for helpful comments on an earlier version.

during the Keynesian era of the 1950s and 1960s. I then try to construct a parallel account of that architecture for the neoliberal era of the 1980s and 1990s. This analysis yields a set of claims about the economic formulas underpinning economic growth in these eras, but it generates a puzzle: On what political conditions did these economic formulas depend? The institutions of the political economy do not spring full-blown from the head of Zeus. Moving beyond accounts that treat national economic models as matters of effective institutional engineering, I inquire into the politics that makes them possible. From this analysis, I then draw some conclusions to explain variation in the initial response of governments to the crisis of 2008–9 and some propositions about the paths ongoing economic adjustment is likely to follow.

The Institutional Formulas of the Keynesian Era

The operation of the developed political economies during an era stretching from the 1950s into the 1970s illustrates the importance of the institutional architecture of the political economy. These were decades of high growth, when the size of the German economy quintupled, the French quadrupled, and the British tripled. Of course, postwar growth had many sources, including a transition from agricultural to industrial production (Crafts and Toniolo 1996). But there are strong grounds for thinking that the economic success of these years also depended on a set of institutional frameworks and supportive policy formulas, nicely described by the regulation school of economics and analysts of the social structures of accumulation (Noel 1987; Boyer 1990, 2002; Kotz, McDonough, and Reich 1994).

Based on this literature, we might say that the success with which a political economy secures economic growth and social peace depends on arrangements in four institutional fields. The first is that of the production regime, reflected in the organization of firms, of work relations, and of the production process more generally. The second is the industrial relations regime, marked by the ways in which bargaining over wages and working conditions is organized. The third is the socioeconomic policy regime, which distributes the fruits of production, determining who secures work on what terms and what social benefits go to those who do not get paid work. The fourth is composed of the international regimes relevant to the operation of domestic political economies, including those regulating trade, exchange rates, and international finance.

During the 1950s and 1960s, mass production in industry was at the heart of the production regime. Using Fordist techniques, the production of complex goods was divided into simpler tasks, often accomplished by semi-skilled workers on automated production lines. One result was rapid productivity gains, as laborers who had been only marginally productive on the farm could be mobilized to create products of higher value (Boyer 1990). The expansion of industrial production was crucial to the resolution of the unemployment problem following World War II. However, mass production requires high levels of long-term capital investment likely to be forthcoming only if investors receive assurances that aggregate demand will rise steadily over the long term and that profits will be high enough to sustain such investments. Reforms regularizing collective bargaining in this period served these purposes. By granting trade unions an established role in wage determination, they made possible steady wage increases that fueled aggregate demand but encouraged unions to leave room for profits by giving them the long-run power to punish firms that did not translate profits into subsequent wage gains (Przeworski and Wallerstein 1982; Boyer 1990; Howell 1992, 2005).

The policy regimes of this era were built around the development of a Keynesian welfare state also crucial to sustaining aggregate demand. Although countercyclical fiscal policy was practiced in only a few countries, and with more fanfare than effectiveness, the Keynesian principle that governments would "manage the economy" underpinned most policy regimes, including indicative planning in France, the social market economy of Germany, and the Rehn-Meidner model of Sweden, enhancing the confidence of investors and consumers about the trajectory of employment and demand (Hansen 1968; Martin 1979; Hall 1989; Sally 2007). The increasing social benefits of the Keynesian welfare state gave workers enough assurances about their income during retirement or unemployment to persuade them to invest in skills and to spend, rather than save, their income (Estevez-Abe, Iversen, and Soskice 2001). As Eichengreen (1996) has noted, the international regimes established after World War II were equally important. The General Agreement on Tariffs and Trade and the European Economic Community increased demand steadily through trade, while the European Payments Union and Bretton Woods monetary regime provided stable monetary frameworks for that trade, limiting the capacity of governments to protect industry through exchange-rate manipulation.

Of course, my account of this era is a stylized portrait that emphasizes similarities across countries in order to highlight the changes that subsequently took place (cf. Piore and Sabel 1982; Streeck 1991; Hall and Soskice 2001; Amable 2003). However, the developed political economies had a distinctive institutional architecture during the 1950s and 1960s, marked by Fordist production regimes, organized collective bargaining, a Keynesian welfare state, and outward-looking international regimes.

Where did this institutional architecture come from? Its origins are complex and inflected by national histories (Shonfield 1969; Manow 2001; Streeck and Yamamura 2001; Thelen 2004; Iversen and Soskice 2009). However, to see this institutional architecture as economically determined would be to miss important parts of the picture. The collective bargaining arrangements, socioeconomic policies, and international regimes of the Keynesian era had important political roots. Three sets of political factors made the development of these regimes possible during the 1950s and 1960s.

The first was a historical memory, still fresh in the public mind during the 1940s and 1950s, of the intense class conflict that had polarized electoral competition in the 1930s, under the shadow of mass unemployment and Bolshevik Revolution, with disastrous consequences manifest in the Weimar Republic (Abraham 1988). The political elites of western Europe and America left World War II determined to avoid the social unrest of the interwar years, of whose relevance they were reminded by a new Cold War (Maier 1981). Thus, concerns about class conflict provided much of the initial *motivation* for the construction of the Keynesian welfare state.

The *means* were provided by Keynesian ideas applied in diffuse forms across a wide range of countries. As they were taken up by postwar economists, those ideas gained economic credibility, and they had political appeal because they provided the rationale for a class compromise that had eluded interwar governments (Hall 1989; Fourcade 2009). At the heart of the Keynesian compromise was the notion that governments could ensure full employment, the key demand of the working class, by pursuing active fiscal or industrial policies, without depriving businessmen of control over the means of production, which was the key demand of capital. At conferences from Brighton to Bad Godesberg, this formula encouraged mainstream parties of the left to make peace with capitalism, and it allowed parties of the political right to accept responsibility for employment without alienating their business allies (Offe 1983, 1985).

However, the *motor* driving the construction of the Keynesian welfare state was the logic of partisan electoral competition in the 1950s and 1960s. At a time when social class still structured much of the vote, lining up parties of the political left that claimed to represent the working class against middle-class parties that sought cross-class appeal, class-based distributive issues held center stage, and both sides of the spectrum began to offer social benefits and active economic management in return for electoral support. The result was a new kind of political convergence around the managed economy and the welfare state from which only those at the margins of the political spectrum in Europe and America dissented (Lipset 1964; Beer 1969; Shonfield 1969).

The institutions of collective bargaining were built for similar reasons and in much the same way. Governments of the left and right supported the extension of collective bargaining in order to move class conflict out of the political arena into the industrial relations arena where it could be contained (Pizzorno 1978; Goldthorpe 1984). By enabling trade unions to secure better wages and working conditions, they hoped to weaken the abilities of the radical left to exploit issues of class in electoral politics. Even the shape of international institutions was influenced by such concerns. Their architects designed the postwar international regimes to accommodate the policies of the Keynesian welfare state, partly to limit the influence of western communist parties in the midst of a new Cold War (Ruggie 1982).

In short, the institutional architecture of the postwar political economies rested on a particular set of political conditions defined by the prominence of social class in the politics of the day. If concern to avoid class conflict provided the initial impetus and Keynesian ideas the means, class-oriented electoral competition drove the development of those institutions forward.

From this perspective, the 1970s were years of transition, when the institutional architecture of the Keynesian era broke down, partly under the weight of its own liabilities and partly in response to international developments led by large rises in commodity prices and the collapse of the Bretton Woods monetary regime.[1] The result was stagflation, marked by simultaneous increases in unemployment and inflation. In response, governments turned to more interventionist measures. Many increased social and industrial subsidies (Berger 1981). In economies where wage bargaining could be coordinated by powerful trade unions and employer associations, governments used neocorporatist bargaining to contain inflation, often with favorable results (Schmitter and Lehmbruch 1979; Goldthorpe 1984). In liberal market economies, where decentralized systems of wage bargaining threatened wage-price spirals, governments often resorted to incomes policies that imposed direct controls on wages and prices, thereby shifting distributional conflict back from the industrial to the political arena.

However, these policies failed to restore previous rates of growth, thereby discrediting Keynesian policy formulas and setting governments in search of new ways to cope with what some called "Eurosclerosis" (Hall 1993). The result was a profound backlash against state intervention. In liberal market economies, where unwieldy attempts at incomes policies generated political conflict over wage differentials, the authority of the state suffered deeply from crises of governability,

1. For more detailed studies of this period, offering different perspectives, see Crouch and Pizzorno (1978); Ferguson et al. (2010); Sandbrook (2010).

often linked to apprehensions of national decline (Crozier, Huntington, and Watanuki 1974; Goldthorpe 1978; Krieger 1986). This was the tide that Margaret Thatcher and Ronald Reagan rode to power. Even in continental Europe, the political backlash against stagflation and slower rates of growth was significant. For the 1980s and 1990s, the climacteric of the 1970s became what the interwar years had been for the 1940s and 1950s, a totemic set of events that would condition the course of policy for another generation (cf. Kingdon 1995; Sewell 1996).

The Institutional Formulas of the Neoliberal Era

In response to these and other developments, the structure of the developed political economies shifted during the 1980s and 1990s, as did policy, in terms that marked the end of the Keynesian era and the inception of what might be called a neoliberal era. Although I have relied on a familiar literature to describe the former, we do not yet have parallel accounts of the latter. Therefore, the initial question must be: Can we identify an analogous institutional architecture for this neoliberal era, whose component parts reinforced each another to produce distinctive aggregate and distributive economic outcomes?[2] Key developments in each of the relevant institutional spheres gave rise to such an architecture.

The production regime of the neoliberal era was deeply affected by two central developments. One was a shift in employment away from manufacturing to services, including well-paid employment in high-end sectors such as health care and finance, and low-paid positions in sectors such as retailing, restaurants, and tourism. This shift was the result of long-term secular trends whose effects became pronounced in the neoliberal era (Iversen and Cusack 2000). The second defining feature of that era was a shift away from Fordist modes of production toward methods that made more intensive use of knowledge, high technology, and skilled labor, often embedded in global supply chains (Womack, Jones, and Roos 1991).[3] Enterprises once interested in vertical integration turned to outsourcing: the traditional Fordist enterprise became a thing of the past in the developed democracies, demand for semi-skilled industrial labor fell, and job creation took place mainly in services (Berger 2005).

These changes were encouraged by developments in international regimes during the 1980s and 1990s that increased the flows of goods and capital across national borders (Berger and Dore 1996; Keohane and Milner 1996). One of

2. For insightful reviews bearing on this topic, see Glyn (2006) and Eichengreen (2007).
3. I am indebted to David Soskice for drawing my attention to this feature of the neoliberal era.

Margaret Thatcher's first acts was to eliminate currency controls. The Single European Act of 1986 and trade agreements such as the Uruguay Round promoted the movement of low-cost manufacturing offshore, thereby accelerating the shift to services and knowledge-intensive manufacturing in Europe and America (Wood 1994; Leamer 1996; Antràs, Garicano, and Rossi-Hansberg 2006).

Collective bargaining arrangements moved in tandem with these developments. More intense global competition opened up cleavages in bargaining systems, between more and less competitive firms and the traded and sheltered sectors (Pontusson and Swenson 1996; Thelen and Kume 1999). As a result, the locus of bargaining shifted downwards and firm-level bargaining became more important in most countries, as firms reorganized production in the face of global competition (Iversen 1999; Lallement 2007; Baccaro and Howell 2011). The power of trade unions declined, as average union density in the OECD dropped from 33 percent in 1980 to 18 percent in 2008, leaving many workers outside the scope of collective agreements.

Socioeconomic policy regimes also changed dramatically during the 1980s and 1990s. If Keynesians had treated unemployment as a demand-side problem, requiring active macroeconomic management, the new policy formulas treated unemployment as a supply-side problem that could be alleviated only by structural reforms to labor, capital, and product markets. Industrial policies targeted on promising industries gave way to manpower policies designed to push people into employment. Symbolic of the shifting approach were the steps taken in the 1990s to make central banks more independent of political control.

These developments fit the circumstances of more open economies, where the effects of a fiscal stimulus leak abroad, as it always has in the small northern European states. Economic doctrine gradually converged on a "new Keynesianism," and most governments pinned their hopes for growth on the expansion of trade. There was some variation in national strategies. The Nordic countries used public employment to create jobs in services without lowering wage floors, while liberal market economies promoted low-wage employment in services by making part-time work and layoffs more feasible (Esping-Andersen 1990, 1999; Iversen and Wren 1998; Scharpf and Schmidt 2000). After experimenting with costly early retirement programs to shrink the workforce, the continental coordinated economies used manpower policies featuring large subsidies to employers to expand employment. In the liberal market economies, measures that weakened trade unions were used to lift profits, while coordinated market economies relied on coordinated wage bargaining to restore profits and competitiveness.

In short, the neoliberal era had mutually reinforcing production, industrial relations, policy, and international regimes analogous to those of the Keynesian era. But the economic results were quite different. Wage inequality rose faster during the 1980s and 1990s, especially in liberal market economies, and rates of growth were slower, partly because productivity gains were harder to secure in services than in manufacturing.

The Political Formula of the Neoliberal Era

How is this shift in institutional architecture to be explained? Most accounts cite the inexorable pressures of globalization, and they played a role, but the international regimes that opened up emerging markets were created by governments. Global competition put enormous pressure on firms to change their business practices, and business lobbied governments for supportive policies (Berger and Dore 1996; Keohane and Milner 1996). Governments saw many of these policies as the most feasible way to create jobs in services. However, to view the institutions and policies of this era as a "natural" response to economic circumstances is to neglect the extent to which they had to have a political underlay. The policy formulas of this era were not simply reflexive responses to economic conditions but artifacts of a certain kind of politics. What then were the political conditions that made this new architecture possible?

The answer is not obvious. The Keynesian welfare state can be seen as a class compromise, but it is difficult to view the policies of the neoliberal era in such terms, because they have not delivered benefits in anything like equal measure to both sides of the class divide. In many countries, the affluent have enjoyed significantly greater increases in income and well-being over the past thirty years than those at median or below-median incomes (Kenworthy and Pontusson 2005; Barnes and Hall 2013). However, the case of the Keynesian welfare state is instructive. I have argued that three factors underpinned its construction: it was motivated by a historical memory, given shape by Keynesian ideas, and put into place by electoral competition around a class cleavage. The same types of elements made the transition to neoliberal policies possible, but in new forms dictated by the historical circumstances of the 1980s.

The crisis of the 1970s provided the initial motivation for the shift to neoliberal policies. If the specter of class conflict inspired the Keynesian welfare state, the neoliberal policies of the 1980s were initially a reaction to the traumatic events of the 1970s, when stagflation and the failure of assertive government intervention discredited activist states more generally. Disillusioned by the failure of activist policies, political elites emerged from the 1970s looking for alternatives and open to the view that renewing market competition might be a better way of reviving economic growth. Of course, the subsequent reforms entailed assertive state action, but the common objective of the new policies was to increase the role of markets relative to states in the allocation of resources and to intensify market competition (cf. Gamble 1994; Vogel 1998).

The means for this shift were supplied by a "new classical economics" built on monetarist foundations. Although available in some form since the 1960s, monetarist perspectives remained a minority view until the 1980s, when they were assimilated into mainstream economic doctrine and succeeded by a wave of work built on rational expectations frameworks. By the middle of the 1980s, the result was an economic orthodoxy skeptical about the value of active macroeconomic management and convinced that countries face a "natural rate of unemployment" reducible only by structural reforms (Crystal 1979; Cuthbertson 1979; McNamara 1998). These doctrines gained credibility as they secured traction within the economics profession, and they appealed to politicians interested in shifting the blame for high unemployment from governments to markets. Party platforms on both the political left and right moved in neoliberal directions during the 1980s and 1990s (Cusack and Englehardt 2002; Iversen 2006).

However, in democracies, changes in the views of elites are rarely enough to explain major changes in the direction of policy (Hall 1993). We also have to ask: what happened in the realm of electoral competition to make the market-oriented policies of the neoliberal era feasible? The effects of those policies were adverse for large numbers of workers. They made jobs more insecure, reduced social benefits, and increased income inequality. Why did parties running on platforms opposed to those policies in the name of working-class defense not emerge and win elections?

In large measure, those policies seem to have been made possible by a fragmentation of the electorate. In the years after 1970, the electoral space of most western democracies became disorganized, in both ideological and institutional terms. Long-standing divisions, rooted in class or religion, lost their hold over the attitudes of the electorate. The most obvious indicator was a decline in the class alignment of the vote, but most important were corresponding changes in how people thought about politics (Dalton, Flanagan, and Beck 1984; Clark and Lipset 2001).[4] The result was a permissive electoral dynamics, in which durable electoral coalitions to promote neoliberal policies were rarely formed, and the opposition that might have been mounted to such policies was effectively undercut, allowing governments to pursue neoliberal agendas.

Three factors lie behind the declining electoral salience of class. The first is a familiar set of socioeconomic changes identified by Lipset (1964) long ago.

4. Whether the extent to which social class structures voting has declined is an issue hotly debated. Much depends on how class is measured and decline defined. My reading is that there has been decline in the dimensions relevant to this argument, but for a range of alternative views, see Manza, Hout, and Brooks (1995); Evans (2000); Elf (2007); Oesch (2008).

Thirty years of prosperity improved the living standards of ordinary workers enough to reduce their sense of grievance vis-à-vis the upper classes. Shifts in occupational structure eroded class boundaries, as deindustrialization decimated working-class communities and employment in services blurred the lines once separating blue-collar and white-collar workers. Second, political developments were equally important. In some ways, the Keynesian welfare state was a political accomplishment that sowed the seeds of its own demise. Contemporary analyses emphasize the sense of entitlement that social programs create but neglect their ancillary effects on social democracy (cf. Pierson 1996). As social benefits became more generous, they eroded the material insecurity central to working-class mobilization. The welfare state was the historic achievement of postwar social democratic parties, even if they were not its sole sponsors; but once its programs were in place, social democracy was left without a distinctive political mission around which to mobilize.[5] On other fronts, reaction against the experiences of the 1970s discredited its interventionist stance. In many respects, the decline of the class cleavage was the reflection, as well as the cause, of the exhaustion of social democracy.

The third important factor was the appearance of a new cleavage, crosscutting the traditional left-right spectrum. This is the right-authoritarian/left-libertarian divide identified by Inglehart (1990) and Kitschelt (1997). On one side of it are those who embrace the post-materialist values promoted by decades of postwar prosperity and reinforced by the new social movements of the 1980s. On the other side are those attached to more traditional values, not only because of lingering material concerns but also in reaction to the cultural revolution of the 1960s. Of course, this cleavage is about more than values (Martinez-Alier 2003). In Europe, its salience was raised during the 1980s and 1990s by a reaction against immigration and the market initiatives of the European Union (EU), seen by many as threats to their material well-being (Kriesi et al. 2008). In the United States, it mobilizes many who associate post-materialist values with unpatriotic opposition to the military, disregard for religion, or sympathy for waves of immigration that are changing the racial complexion of the country (Carmines and Layman 1997; Frank 2004; cf. Bartels 2008).

This new cleavage is significant because it crosscuts the class cleavage in two ways. Because right-authoritarian voters are more likely to be working-class, it drove a wedge through the constituency that social democracy might otherwise have mobilized in opposition to platforms of neoliberal reform. Significant proportions of the European working class now vote for parties of the radical right.

5. For an alternative view that ascribes more importance to religious cleavages, see Manow (2001) and Van Kersbergen and Manow (2009).

Many Americans have been drawn away from the segments of the Democratic and Republican parties sympathetic to activist government. Moreover, by drawing a middle-class constituency of post-materialists to the Democrats and social democratic parties, this cleavage also undercuts the inclination of those parties to operate as parties of working-class defense, since middle-class voters are more likely to benefit from neoliberal reforms.

In sum, if the policies of the postwar era reflected a class compromise, born of electoral competition around the agendas of working-class parties, the policies of the neoliberal era have rested on a different politics, marked by class dealignment, rising electoral volatility, and a shift away from class-based political competition.

Cross-National Variation

In order to make comparisons over time, I have emphasized commonalities across the developed political economies during the Keynesian and neoliberal eras. Social and economic policy became more market-oriented during the 1980s and 1990s. However, we can also distinguish four different growth models in the recent period, based on how countries mobilized economic demand for their products and political consent for their policies. These differences bear emphasis because they significantly affect the dilemmas facing those countries today.

The first is a liberal growth model adopted with some variation in virtually all the liberal market economies described by Hall and Soskice (2001) but exemplified by the United States and United Kingdom. In these political economies already dominated by market competition, neoliberal reform went farthest (Hall and Gingerich 2009). Margaret Thatcher and Ronald Reagan took pioneering steps to intensify competition, privatize national enterprises, and contract out public services (Gamble 1994; Thatcher 2004). In high-profile battles with miners and air controllers, they broke the power of trade unions, and their successors tightened controls on social benefits with a view to turning "welfare" into "workfare."

For most of the period, such measures kept average real wages in these countries low, thereby promoting employment growth in services such as retailing, restaurants, tourism, and child care. Loose regulatory environments promoted job growth in finance and health care in the Unites States, where the financial sector was responsible for almost a third of all profits by 2008. The result was a "jobs miracle' " envied in continental Europe, but the distributive consequences were stark. At one point in the 1990s, almost a fifth of the U.S. labor force worked for wages and benefits lower than those available at the minimum wage in

France, and real median income stagnated while below-median incomes declined (Hacker and Pierson 2010). More than half of total growth in U.S. GDP over this period went to the top 10 percent of income earners.

The danger, of course, was that this approach would depress aggregate demand and make the mobilization of political consent for neoliberal policies difficult. However, the Anglo-American model spoke to these problems with deregulatory measures that promoted housing booms, an influx of cheap consumer goods from emerging economies, and unprecedented expansion in consumer credit (Crouch 2009). Thanks to a number of programs symbolized by federal support for Freddie Mac and Fannie Mae, the proportion of people owning their own home rose to 69 percent in the United States in 2008; and house prices in the United States and United Kingdom doubled between 1990 and 2008, giving many people the sense that their wealth was increasing even if their incomes were stagnant (Schwartz and Seabrook 2009; Rajan 2010).

An influx of cheap goods from Asia helped sustain purchasing power, and the opportunity to borrow freely became a crucial complement to the "privatization of risk" that was a feature of Anglo-American policy in this period (Hacker 2004). Credit cards and home equity loans were the safeguards that carried many people exposed to highly flexible labor markets through fluctuations in the economy and adverse life events. In these respects, loose financial regulation was a substitute for social policy (Schelkle 2010). Since the establishment of the Household Finance Corporation in the 1930s, Britain and the United States had pioneered the use of consumer credit, but between 1980 and 2008 American household debt expanded from about 70 percent to 122 percent of disposable household income (Trumbull 2012). This formula allowed these countries to run growth models led by consumer demand, even though median incomes were rising only slowly; and its wealth effects, however illusory, mobilized political consent for neoliberal initiatives whose acceptance is otherwise hard to explain.

In the coordinated market economies of continental Europe, such formulas were not available. Trade unions were more powerful and wage coordination so central to the strategies of firms that it made no sense to try to break the power of the unions, aside from marginal steps epitomized by the French Auroux laws (Howell 1992). Moreover, stronger traditions of social solidarity made it difficult for governments to mobilize political consent for neoliberal reforms. The solution, on which the governments of the European Community (EC) agreed, was to inflect their institutional architecture for a global age. The decisive innovation was the Single European Act of 1986 that transformed the EC from an association to promote free trade and agricultural protection into an agent for market liberalization. Although its member governments were always in the driver's seat, the move to qualified majority voting ensured that they could take shelter from the political flak generated by neoliberal initiatives behind the protective shield of EC action (Hall 2006).

Facing trade unions willing to defend wage floors, the European governments also had to find another approach to the creation of employment in services. As Esping-Andersen (1990, 1999) has observed, the Nordic countries developed a second growth model based on expanding public employment in health care, education, and child care, funded by high tax rates that depressed disposable income and thus limited the growth of private services (Iversen and Wren 1998). In keeping with the policy legacy of the Rehn-Meidner approach, they also operated "flexicurity" systems in which low levels of employment protection were combined with generous wage-related unemployment benefits to allow firms to rationalize in the face of global competition while still encouraging workers to invest in skills (Martin 1979; Estevez-Abe, Iversen, and Soskice 2001; Campbell, Hall, and Pedersen 2006). These strategies were highly successful.

The approach to the employment problem initially pursued in a third growth model adopted by the continental coordinated market economies such as France and Germany, which was to encourage exit from the labor force through early retirement, soon proved so costly that it was abandoned in favor of active manpower market policies, which subsidized the costs to employers of training or taking on new workers. By the 1990s, France was spending almost 4 percent of GDP on such policies, and active labor market policy had become a pillar of the EU's Lisbon strategy (Levy 2005). However, employment expanded significantly only when these countries developed secondary labor markets, by relaxing restrictions on part-time work and temporary contracts. Much as Japan had done earlier, these economies developed dual labor markets, marked by stable employment in the manufacturing or public sector and precarious employment often in private-sector services (Visser and Hemerijck 1997; Palier and Thelen 2010).

To mobilize political consent for such initiatives, these continental countries increased spending on social benefits, however counterintuitive that might seem to apostles of neoliberalism. By the end of the 1990s, French social spending had reached Nordic levels, and even after the Hartz reforms, the German welfare state remained generous. One of the characteristic features of European growth models is the extent to which taxes and transfers are used to offset the effects of earnings inequality on the distribution of disposable income (Kenworthy and Pontusson 2005).

The other constitutive feature of European growth models was the Economic and Monetary Union (EMU) established in 1999. The EMU was designed to bind Germany to Europe and counteract protectionist pressure building up in the European monetary system (Dyson and Featherstone 1997; Eichengreen

1997). Its "convergence criteria" forced firms in many parts of Europe to rationalize in the face of a new single market joined to relatively high exchange rates. Once established, however, the EMU induced a further bifurcation in growth models, between northern and southern Europe. At issue was the familiar question of how to ensure levels of demand sufficient to sustain investment and economic growth. Designed along neoliberal lines that gave short shrift to fiscal policy, the EMU provided no institutional mechanisms for the long-term coordination of fiscal policy across Europe, aside from a Stability and Growth Pact limiting national deficits to 3 percent of GDP. This arrangement privileged the member states capable of restraining labor costs in order to stimulate growth led by exports. Given their capacities for coordinated wage bargaining, the small states of northern Europe were well placed to implement such strategies of export-led growth; and over the ensuing decade, Germany, Belgium, and the Netherlands did so with considerable success (Katzenstein 1985).

By contrast, with labor movements divided into competing groups that could not readily coordinate wages, the countries of southern Europe were poorly equipped to pursue such strategies and can be said to have pursued a fourth growth model. Many, such as Portugal and Greece, lacked strong export sectors. In the short term, they were rescued from this dilemma by entry into a strong currency union awash in funds generated by Germany's trade surpluses. Led by the public or private sector, they used that bonanza of cheap credit to fuel domestic growth, centered on a construction boom in Spain, commercial lending in Portugal, and public spending in Greece. These were rational short-term responses to the prevailing incentive structure. In the longer term, however, this formula left southern Europe vulnerable to the kind of credit squeeze induced by the recession of 2008, which forced deflation on them when concern in the bond markets rose about their elevated levels of debt.

The Implications for Adjustment

What does this historical analysis imply for the contemporary politics of economic adjustment? The global recession of 2008–9 marked an inflection point in the neoliberal era. As large financial institutions collapsed and unemployment rose, many governments rediscovered the value of what has sometimes been called "emergency Keynesianism," stepping in with massive support for the financial sector and stimulus packages, but rates of unemployment in the Eurozone and the United States were still close to 10 percent of GDP in 2012. Governments faced continuing adjustment problems of substantial dimensions. How might national variations in their responses be explained? This problem can be approached as one of understanding the initial response to the crisis, the medium-term response, and the long-term prospects for more radical change in economic policies.

My analysis highlights the extent to which each nation's initial response to the crisis was conditioned by its institutional architecture. If recession floods the basement and financial crises set fire to the roof, the first reaction of governments will not be to tear the edifice down but to address their problems with the building materials on hand. Thus, the initial response of the governments of liberal market economies, where growth had long been led by domestic demand, was to expand consumer demand through cuts in taxation and increases in public spending, letting flexible labor and capital markets reallocate resources.[6] By contrast, in many coordinated market economies, the stimulus was designed to preserve existing jobs. This type of approach makes sense in countries whose manufacturing regimes depend on employees with high levels of industry-specific skills. In such regimes, firms need to retain skilled labor and, once lost, such jobs are difficult to recreate. Thus, key components of the German stimulus included a pioneering subsidy for automobile purchases (soon copied by other countries) that sustained employment in metalworking, and a large program of subsidies for short-time working so that employees in core manufacturing could be retained. Although widely criticized by the Anglo-American media, the German response was highly successful at preserving jobs.

One of the lessons of the 1970s is that governments are likely to revert, even in the medium term, to strategies on which they have relied in the past. In the face of stagflation with which Keynesian policies could not cope, the governments of the 1970s struggled to make those policies work for more than half a decade before moving to different strategies (Hall 1986, 1993). The medium-term strategies pursued by both the American and German governments conform to this template. From 2009 through 2011, the American government desperately tried to revive the housing market, arguably the source of the financial crisis, pouring billions of dollars into Freddie Mac and Fannie Mae in addition to subsidies for first-time homebuyers. Despite calls for fiscal discipline, the Bush-era tax cuts were extended, and the Federal Reserve Bank mounted two programs of "quantitative easing" worth more than $1 trillion to encourage lending, indicating a tolerance for inflation that has historically been one way to erode national debt.

The political structure of the United States encourages such an approach. Although nominally independent, the Federal Reserve Bank is sensitive to political pressure and hence inclined to target unemployment as well as inflation. A system

6. Initially, cuts in taxation figured more prominently in the response of liberal market economies, while the stimulus packages of coordinated market economies relied more heavily on public spending (OECD 2009b).

that combines undisciplined political parties, frequent elections, and unbridled campaign finance confers unparalleled political influence on business interests (Hacker and Pierson 2010). It is not surprising to find that tax cuts for the wealthy and subsidies to the financial sector figure prominently in the American response, accompanied by calls to cut social programs in order to finance them. Although tighter financial regulations have been mandated in the wake of the crisis, business retains enough influence to ensure those regulations do not significantly reduce the role of credit in the American growth model (Hacker and Pierson 2010).

In international terms, the American economy is also well placed to pursue growth led by consumer demand. A floating exchange rate allows the government to cushion adjustment by using depreciation to erode real wages rather than depending on domestic deflation to make such adjustments. The principal threat to such a strategy stems from the large reserves of American securities held by other countries. If they were to develop a sudden reluctance to hold American assets, a precipitous decline in the dollar could make adjustment painful. However, China has no incentive to pursue such a policy and few substitutes for American securities. The more likely scenario is one in which depreciation gradually erodes the purchasing power of American consumers without plunging the economy into another recession: by 2011, the real value of the dollar in trade-weighted terms had already fallen to its lowest level since the dollar was floated in 1973.

Across the Atlantic, the German government also reverted to a familiar strategy, built on export-led growth in manufacturing that takes advantage of Germany's formidable capacities for wage coordination and the strong demand for capital goods from emerging economies. The government modified this strategy slightly in 2010 by encouraging a large wage settlement in metalworking in order to fuel domestic demand during a year of multiple state elections and, since the Hartz reforms of the early 2000s, employment has been increasingly reliant on part-time jobs. But the striking feature of continuity in German policy was the government's refusal to treat Germany's trade surplus as a problem for Europe and its insistence that fiscal discipline, rather than coordinated reflation, was the only way to resolve the crisis in the Eurozone.

Although this stance was of dubious value from a European perspective, it was conditioned by the institutional structure of the German political economy. Demand-led growth is difficult to inspire in an economy dominated by a manufacturing sector dependent on unionized workers with high levels of industry-specific skills. On the one hand, expansionary fiscal policies encourage wage settlements that threaten the competitiveness of the export sector at the core of the German economy. On the other, even in the context of expansion, the German savings rate tends to remain high, because workers with industry-specific skills worry that equivalent jobs would be hard to find if they were to become unemployed (Carlin and Soskice 2009). Germany's view of what is best for Europe has been driven by its view of what is best for Germany; and just as the American government was influenced by a powerful financial sector, the German government has remained in thrall to export-oriented manufacturing.

What does this analysis imply about the longer-term prospects for more radical changes in policy? I have argued that the transitions to both the Keynesian and neoliberal eras required motivation, means, and a motor. Do we see those elements in the current conjuncture?

The search for new policies that marked the advent of the Keynesian and neoliberal eras was motivated by widespread perceptions that existing policies had failed. The sense of failure present today varies across countries, largely in line with how they have fared in the wake of the recession. High levels of unemployment trouble Americans, but similar levels in Europe during the 1980s and 1990s induced only incremental changes to policy. If the United States settles into a decade of sluggish growth, pressures for more radical shifts in policy are likely to mount. Recall that it took almost a decade for the Keynesian consensus to unravel in the 1970s.

In some other countries, such as Greece, Spain, Portugal, and Ireland, where up to a fifth of the workforce has been unemployed, the effects of the recession have been devastating enough to motivate a search for new policies. But their governments are currently constrained by pressure from the bond markets and the deflationary conditions attached to rescue packages from the EU. Reflecting standard neoliberal doctrines, the latter were imposed by governments in northern Europe, which have seen few reasons to change direction because their economies recovered relatively rapidly from the recession. EMU itself clearly failed and is being reconstructed. However, there is no consensus about what precipitated the failure or what reforms will rectify it. Many northern Europeans cling to the view that the crisis of the euro was caused by the fiscal profligacy of southern European firms and governments, while others point to the structural asymmetries in the political economies of the member states. Efforts to reform the EMU have been correspondingly slow and disjointed (Baldwin, Gros, and Laeven 2010). Although the capacities of the EU to enforce fiscal rules and to subsidize the debt of its member states are being reinforced, it remains to be seen whether the EU will acquire the capacities for coordinated reflation over the medium-term that are arguably more important to its future. Here, too, much will depend on the continent's growth trajectory. Unless deflation in southern Europe significantly depresses the economies of northern Europe, consensus on a new growth strategy is unlikely to emerge.

Equally important to dramatic shifts in policy is the matter of means. The transitions to the Keynesian and neoliberal eras were made possible by the availability of new policy paradigms with appeal for politicians and credibility among economists. It is illuminating to compare the British governments led by Edward Heath and Margaret Thatcher. Both entered office determined to make radical changes to the course of policy, but Heath soon retreated, in no small part because he lacked the alternative policy paradigm that Thatcher had in the form of monetarist economics, which had substantial support among economists by the time she became prime minister (Hall 1982). Although the current recession has discredited some of the tenets of neoliberalism, such as the efficient markets hypothesis, there are still no alternative paradigms available with sufficient credibility among economists to constitute clear alternatives to the "new Keynesianism" that has been guiding policy for some years (Fox 2009).

Thus, debate has been concentrated between those who favor a sustained fiscal stimulus directed at unemployment and others who are concerned to reduce the sizable debt burden left in the wake of an initial stimulus; and the latter have had the upper hand. In the emerging economies, there is renewed interest in the doctrines associated with a developmental state. But in both Europe and North America, widespread support for large programs of public investment substantial enough to have a major effect on unemployment has been notably absent.

Movement in that direction cannot be ruled out, since the oft-repeated injunction that "structural reform" is the only way to promote higher growth is largely empty. Making competition in product markets more intense and employment less secure may improve the competitiveness of some economies, but it is unlikely to build a strong export base where one is lacking. In this respect, the managers of the euro look increasingly like defenders of the gold standard during the 1920s. The dominant motif of policymaking in the OECD has been confusion, among officials torn between the desirability of sustaining demand and the dictates of international bond markets urging fiscal prudence. Nothing illustrates that better than the divergence between American and British policy in 2009–11. The default option has been fiscal tightening amidst monetary easing, which sustains the financial sector but does little to address the immediate hardships suffered by the unemployed and others on low incomes.

I have argued that radical shifts in policy also depend on the character of partisan electoral competition. What are the coalitional possibilities today? Many hope that economic recession will swing the political pendulum to the left, ushering in more interventionist policies, as the depression of the 1930s did in the United States and Sweden (Gourevitch 1986). But, in politics, there is no Say's law: economic crisis does not necessarily inspire political mobilization, let alone effective mobilization on the political left. The secular socioeconomic changes that undermined class boundaries have not disappeared, and the neoliberal era has seen new conflicts of interest arise inside the working class, between "insiders" and "outsiders" and older and younger generations (Chauvel 1998; Rueda 2005).

Thus, the main effect of the crisis has been to inspire a *sauve qui peut* politics that eschews redistribution, as everyone lobbies to retain what they have at the expense of others (Alt 1979). Where economic recovery is improving the security of those who have jobs, while leaving others unemployed, it is gradually translating economic dualism into political dualism. The Tea Party, for instance, ranges older Americans defending their Medicare and Social Security benefits against those seeking more social support for the young and unemployed (Palier and Thelen 2010; Skocpol and Williamson 2011). In similar ways, successive attempts to resolve the euro crisis have been stymied by the efforts of the relevant actors to ensure that others pay the costs of adjustment.

In this context, the dominant motif of politics has been dissatisfaction with the government in power whatever its partisan complexion. Deep recessions typically inspire a reaction against the governments of the day. Virtually every government in office during the recessions of the 1970s was turned out at the next election. Contemporary governments face a similar backlash from electors outraged that many of the financial institutions seemingly at the root of the crisis have been rescued, while their neighbors paid the costs of recession in the form of lost jobs or higher impending tax burdens. Seventy-seven percent of Americans have indicated they are "frustrated" or "angry" with the federal government (Pew Research Center Survey, March 11–21, 2010, Q. 20). The result is a diffuse discontent, visible in Ireland, in Länder elections in Germany, in the American Tea Party movement, and in Britain where a government committed to social justice was turned out for one committed to fiscal austerity. The corollary has been growing hostility to immigration, born of the nativist reactions that recessions typically fuel.

How this discontent will play out is dependent, to some extent, on electoral rules. Social progressives have applauded systems of proportional representation because they are more likely to elect redistributive coalitions (Iversen and Soskice 2006). However, those are the politics of good times. Amid hard times, proportional representation is no longer so clearly an advantage, as Weimar demonstrated (Abraham 1988). This crisis is moving voters to the radical right and left of the political spectrum. Under systems of proportional representation, that increases the vote for smaller parties on the political extremes, making it more difficult for mainstream parties to retain control of governments and forcing some into fragile coalitions with some strange bedfellows. This makes for an unpredictable and indecisive politics. Even majoritarian systems are betraying such strains, visible in unprecedented ideological polarization in the United States, coalition government in Britain, minority government in Canada, and significant support for the Front National in France.

In sum, although discontent with governing parties is palpable, new electoral coalitions offering alternative policies are not yet in sight. Meanwhile, producer group politics goes on as usual, conditioned by each country's distinctive economic model. Although the financial sector faces heavier regulation on both sides of the Atlantic, its strictness is still in doubt as the details are negotiated. The United States and Britain continue to argue for latitude on behalf of their financial *entrepôts*, while the governments of continental Europe generally favor more restrictive regulation. The striking feature of these negotiations is the determination of each government to preserve the advantages of its own firms (Clift and Woll 2012). Although lending is likely to be less expansive in the next decade, the era of finance capitalism is far from over.

Moreover, the crisis does not as yet seem to have thrown national varieties of capitalism off course. Although the crisis initially brought more assertive state intervention, the liberal market economies continue to pursue growth models based on highly flexible labor and capital markets. Thanks to continuing growth in the emerging economies, the coordinated market economies of northern Europe recovered well based on classic export-led growth strategies. However, the euro crisis has left the southern European economies in disarray and a question mark hanging over Europe: Can the Eurozone prosper without a balanced growth strategy that entails more expansion of domestic demand in northern Europe and some kind of coordinated reflation in the south? To date, the German, Dutch, and Finnish governments have refused to move in that direction, but the result is hardly a stable equilibrium. The draconian deflations imposed on southern Europe are inspiring deep political discontent and a backlash against the European Union that could plague the continent for some years.

However, these are still early days from which to identify the political fallout from this economic crisis. As Peter Gourevitch (1986, 239–40) reminds us, there is an intrinsic openness to politics at such conjunctures. As governments look for new ways to cope with new problems, this crisis will inspire experimentation with new policies, as earlier crises did in the 1940s and 1970s. In the Eurozone, that process is manifestly under way. In many countries, the politics is complicated by the simultaneous emergence of demands to create jobs and to reduce debt, which have set in motion intense conflicts about who is to pay the costs of adjustment. That politics calls for complex bargains, not only across sectors, but across countries and generations, in which the already tenuous capacities for redistribution of many political economies are at stake.

In sum, the political tail of this crisis has not yet stopped wagging. This account yields an explanation for the initial response of governments to the recession and a cautionary tale about whether it will usher in radical changes to policy. The ultimate lesson, however, is that in order to find durable new paths for policy, governments have to address not only the economic dilemmas of our time but also the problem of assembling political support in electoral arenas beset by tides of discontent. History suggests that any new economic formula will have to be rooted in a corresponding political formula and that has yet to emerge in any of the developed democracies.

6

PUZZLES FROM THE FIRST GLOBALIZATION

Suzanne Berger

In the first globalization, 1870–1914, as in our own times, debates raged over the impact on domestic life of free movement across borders of goods, people, and capital.[1] Then as today in the hard times that have followed in the wake of financial crisis, many saw that open borders brought uncontrollable risks and vulnerabilities. Even a hundred years ago, without benefit of sophisticated statistical analysis, it was generally understood that cross-border capital flows greatly increased the potential for crisis as the troubles of other financial markets poured in unimpeded by national controls, and financial market distress turned into credit blockages to the real economy (Stevens 1894).[2] As the *Economist* wrote about the 1907 New York banking crisis:

> The fact seems to be that when a sudden collapse of speculation is accompanied by a banking panic, all the machinery of a great modern industrial society goes out of gear. Even in the vast territory of the United States, with all its diversities of soil, climate, industry, agriculture, and even law, the network of railways is so complete, and interchange of commodities and credit so intimate and complex, that every part seems to be dependent on some other part, while all are related

1. This chapter draws on arguments I developed in Berger (2003) and incorporates some text from that work. Translations from French texts are mine.

2. On the intellectual history of attribution of blame for crises to "international contagion," see Kindleberger and Aliber ([1978] 2005).

> more or less closely in a common dependence upon their great financial metropolis—New York. (*Economist*, November 16, 1907, 1965).

Thus far, policy proposals have been limited and without major consequence. On balance, as Miles Kahler and others in their contributions to this volume convincingly argue, the dominant fact is how little effect the current crisis has had in stirring up opposition to the open institutional architecture of the global financial market. The puzzle that motivates this chapter is why—even in the wake of financial crises that wreaked great damage on the economy—states did not raise barriers to capital flows. The current situation seems in this respect similar to that of the first globalization, where even as major battles were waged over tariffs, the free flow of capital across borders was contested, but remained largely unimpeded. In the social sciences, exploring events that did not happen is usually considered a futile pursuit. But this case of the "curious incident of the dog that did not bark in the night," to borrow from Sherlock Holmes, is fascinating because it turns on a contentious issue in political economy: how to conceptualize interests and their mobilization.

In a number of the contributions to this volume the explanation for the current quiescence of groups that might have risen up in reaction against goods, services, and capital moving across borders is that today these groups themselves have far more complex, interwoven, and contradictory interests than in the past. As Peter Gourevitch (afterword, this volume) summarizes, an orthodox "open economy politics" (OEP) perspective conceives interests as springing out of the production profile of groups variously located in the international economy; these interests and their location in the economy directly determine policy preferences. As Helen Milner has expressed it: "Interests are the stable foundation on which actors' preferences over policy shift as their situation and the policy area vary . . . Preferences are a variable; interests are not" (Milner 1997, 15). Even in the early nineteenth-century crises he considers, Gourevitch finds that interests did not directly determine policy outcomes; rather a variety of intermediating agents and institutions shaped or "packaged" these interests in different ways with different policy outcomes. About the later periods he analyzes, Gourevitch discovers (afterword, this volume) that the "stripped-down interest group model of the first crisis seemed increasingly insufficient," because ideology and institutions entered ever more directly into interest formulation.

This analytic move to identify a process of interest "complexification" over time with changes in the economy and in politics plays a major role in explanations of the current situation in which groups apparently adversely affected by capital and trade flows do not react as a simple OEP readout of interests might predict. With the expansion of foreign direct investment into emerging economies and the fragmentation of national production systems and their reorganization into networked global supply chains, interests have become far more complicated. They have been redefined in ways that undermine the common ground under old protectionist coalitions (Milner 1988; Kahler, chapter 1, this volume). Also, as Peter Hall (chapter 5, this volume) emphasizes, divisions within the old class boundaries (e.g., within the working class between "insiders" and "outsiders") have made it ever more difficult to rally around common interests.

In all of these accounts of stability in the present, there is at least implicit comparison with a past in which interests with respect to international capital and trade flows were in some sense "pre-political" and more clearly and antagonistically defined than today. But is it really the case that interests in some past incarnation of an open world economy were simple and compelling, and that policy preferences could be read off the production profiles of different economic groups? When we return to the late nineteenth- and early twentieth-century battles over capital flows and examine the positions of major political and economic actors in the wake of banking crises and in periods of high tension over sovereign borrowing (e.g., during the 1905 Russian revolution), we do not find a past in which interests were prior to the politics that created them. It is not only that interests entered politics through the intermediation of leaders and political organization and through the transforming filters of different institutional constellations (although they did, *pace* Gourevitch). It is that interests as such emerged as the product of politics. Groups "discovered" their interests through a process of contention and coalition with others. For interest formation in the first globalization, it was politics all the way down.

The Dangers of Open Borders

If the gold standard had become virtually inevitable for advanced economies by the last quarter of the nineteenth century, the openness of borders to portfolio and foreign direct investment had not. The gold standard involves a commitment to freely move gold across borders in response to demand. But how much and what other kinds of capital could be shifted across national borders and what kinds of regulations should apply to such flows remained open for debate. In Germany and France during the first globalization, there was political demand for regulating capital flows well after the adoption of the gold standard, and there were policy levers already in place that might have been used and enhanced. Given the vulnerabilities that borders open to capital flows created for domestic economies, why were there not stronger movements to close up or to regulate these flows? How was openness sustained against challenges? Who favored no regulation or less regulation? Who advocated regulations and/or closure? How was capital mobility sustained during periods of contestation?

As the Bretton Woods accord showed, it is possible to design an international regime with a single monetary standard and a commitment to lowering barriers to trade and to couple these policies with national regulation and limitations on flows of capital across borders. In the nineteenth century, an international consensus on capital controls was highly unlikely. But even short of such an international agreement, there were possible domestic, unilateral moves, and at times the demands to make such moves were loud. Who supported such restrictions and why they ultimately failed to have significant impact will be discussed in this chapter. But to start, a few examples taken from German and French debates over capital control may serve as reminders that throughout the first globalization, regulating capital flows was seen as a plausible option and keeping the borders open was a recurrent political challenge.

In Germany, after the 1907 banking crisis, a national commission was charged with examining the causes and consequences of the outflows of gold from Germany during the crisis and, more generally, of German investment abroad and of foreign investment in Germany. The objective was to consider policies to reduce German vulnerability to future financial crises (German Bank Inquiry 1910). The participants debated at length whether lending abroad helped industry by winning foreign markets or penalized industry (and agriculture) by making money more expensive domestically. Did foreign investment in Germany add to Germany's strengths, or was it a source of vulnerability because foreigners could withdraw their capital in bad times? Should the Reichsbank intervene to limit the amount of German capital invested abroad? Should government regulate the flotation of foreign securities on German markets? A number of speakers berated the government for not intervening more forcefully to exercise its existing powers over capital flows. The Stock Exchange Law of 1896 had instituted a system of regulation over capital by prohibiting a foreign security from listing on a German exchange if it had been denied access in any German state. This law gave Prussia and the German chancellor a de facto veto over the listing of foreign securities (Laves 1927).

The Banking Inquiry considered more far-reaching controls. One proposal was for setting up a second "Juliusturm." The Juliusturm was gold, locked up in the Spandau fortress, which was to be used in the event of outbreak of war. The funds had been siphoned off from the huge indemnity paid by the French after the Franco-Prussian War. Some of the members of the Banking Commission demanded a "Juliusturm No. 2" to protect the economy against disruptions from capital flows. As one of the Krupp directors on the commission expressed it, "Just as the Juliusturm forms a war reserve in the event of mobilization, this

Juliusturm No. 2 would form a cash reserve. . . . If we had such a reserve, it would open in a time of gold scarcity and stabilize the situation" (German Bank Inquiry 1910, 2:649–50).

In France as well, the state had some leverage over capital flows through control over the listing of foreign securities on the Paris Bourse (Ribière 1913).[3] A para-public body, the Chambre syndicale d'agents de change formally regulated listings on the Paris exchange, and for foreign offerings, authorization was required from the Ministry of Finance and the Ministry of Foreign Affairs. The government refused all listings of German securities; otherwise instances of rejection were rare. The tax system also provided a lever for public control of capital flows. In theory, taxes on all issues, domestic or foreign, were levied at the same rate, but the collection system was different, resulting in a lower rate on foreign investments. Over the years, there were a number of legislative proposals to reform the collection system, including a Socialist proposal to encourage relatives to denounce family members who inherited foreign assets and failed to declare them at the time of an inheritance, with the incentive that the denouncing relative would be granted the foreign property as a bounty. This idea, like other less draconian ones proposed by successive ministers of finance, failed. But in moments of crisis, proposals for tightening up the controls always resurfaced.

Objections to the free movement of capital across national borders fell into four categories. First, some argued that letting domestic capital (or letting "too much" domestic capital) be invested abroad would starve the economy of resources needed to fund infrastructure, innovation, industries, and job creation. What might be profitable for the individual investor might mean less housing, less investment in domestic industries, and less investment in innovation and development at home. As J. A. Hobson famously put it, "Although the new Imperialism has been bad business for the nation, it has been good business for certain classes and certain trades within the nation" (Hobson [1902, 1905] 1965). In France, the great debate over the impact on the domestic economy of the outflow of French capital played out around exchanges in the press between "Lysis" and "Testis," the pseudonyms of a left-wing journalist and of an economist close to banking circles.[4] Lysis claimed that bank-led export of capital was the principal cause of economic stagnation in France. Whether investment abroad weakened investment at home is still contested by economic historians.[5]

3. The classic study of government controls over foreign capital flows between 1870 and 1914 is Feis ([1930] 1965).

4. "Lysis" was Eugene Letailleur, who published a number of articles in *La Revue* and *L'Humanité* and in Lysis (1912). His ideas were attacked by "Testis" (pseudonym of Raphael-Georges Lévy) in Testis (1907).

5. In the British debate, among those who see such an effect, is Cairncross (1953). For research suggesting the contrary, see Edelstein (1982). For France, see Lévy-Leboyer and Bourguignon (1985).

But at the time, many believed it, and the fact that academic controversy has continued so long suggests that contemporary policymakers might reasonably have regarded it as at least an open question.

Second, left parties and unions argued that allowing capital to freely exit might block social reform because capitalists could evade new burdens by shifting investment to less-exigent countries. In the nineteenth century as today, every new proposal for taxes or capital controls generated predictions about capital flight. Third, another class of objections to free capital mobility was nationalist. The French nationalist right saw Germans as the illegitimate beneficiaries of French portfolio investment abroad (and it was true that significant French outward investment ended up in Germany). For the left, the enemy was tsarism, and during the 1905 revolution French left parliamentarians demanded that the government deny access to French capital markets for new loans to Russia. In American political debates over the monetary standard and, more generally, over the role of the state on the economic borders of the nation, there was also a strong nationalist charge. William Jennings Bryan's speech on acceptance of the Democratic nomination and *Coin's Financial School*—the 1894 best seller on the monetary standard—show how powerful the idea of struggle against a hated English enemy was in these debates (Harvey [1894] 1963).[6] Distant resentments may have been revivified by the bitter disputes between the United States and England over the Venezuelan border in 1895. But above all, the British enemy was conceived to be the British banker—seen as a predator ready to grab American resources and as a master eager to maintain subordination.

Finally, and perhaps closest to current anxieties about the dangers of open capital mobility, people grasped that a world of open borders was one in which misbehavior and failures in the financial market of some other country could rapidly be propagated through the multiple connections of the international economy into troubles and disaster at home. Responses to the 1907 financial crisis illustrate this vividly.[7] At the height of the crisis, the *Economist* traced out the mechanisms of financial contagion. It reminded its readers that the crisis had roots deep in the international system, not just in the corrupt malfeasance of New York trust companies.[8] It identified the origins of the crisis in the vast devastation of capital in the Boer War and the Russo-Japanese War, and the issuance of large amounts of debt. Then abundant harvests led to an expansion of trade and inflation of credit. Together with increased production of gold, this combination of circumstances

6. The book sold around a million copies. On the anti-British sentiment in Coin, see Richard Hofstadter's introduction to Harvey ([1894] 1983).

7. On the crisis of 1907, see Bruner and Carr (2007) and Tallman and Moen (1990). Both emphasize the domestic sources of the crisis.

8. A similar account by a contemporary American observer who attacked domestic explanations of the crisis may be found in Noyes (1909).

led to price inflation. Then some "bubble companies" in Japan collapsed, followed by a fall in Japanese stock prices. There were troubles in Genoa and Egypt. Prices became unsteady on the American exchange, and rumors spread about weakness in the German and the U.S. economies. Then came "the sensational break in copper, and the failures in Amsterdam, Hamburg, Boston, and New York [which] provoked the final crisis that found theatrical expression in the run on the Knickerbocker Trust" (*Economist*, November 2, 1907, 1854).

For some English, it might be a source both of profit and of pride to be so centrally located in the midst of these tangled webs of connections among economies around the world. As the *Economist* declared with satisfaction: "London, the capital of Free-trade and the great emporium of gold plays the lucrative but onerous part as the distributor and collector of credit, the clearinghouse of the world. We have no reason to be ashamed. The collapse of the American system has bought our supremacy into relief" (*Economist,* December 28, 1907, 2286). But the more common effect of the 1907 crisis was to demonstrate how the interconnected capital markets of stocks, bonds, and direct investment made German shopkeepers, French peasants, and millions of other savers and small-scale borrowers vulnerable to the failure of the American regulatory system to constrain crooked American bankers. As observers noted, this crisis, in contrast to earlier ones, highlighted the dangers of capital mobility. Small wonder, then, that cries went up everywhere demanding buffers to protect and insulate national resources against the dangers of open capital markets. The question is, Why did these demands have so little effect?

Of the major advanced industrial countries, the case of France is, in many respects, the most puzzling. The willingness to let capital flow in and flow abroad virtually unimpeded was, understandably, strong in Britain and the United States. Most British overseas investment went into New World (United States, Canada, Australia) infrastructure projects and rather successful enterprises, and rates of return were higher for British foreign investors than for others. Even so, afterwards, there would be questioning of whether such high levels of foreign investment had been a good idea. John Maynard Keynes, writing in 1924, concluded: "The nineteenth century, as in so many other respects, came to look on an arrangement as normal which was really most abnormal. To lend vast sums abroad for long periods of time without any possibility of legal redress, if things go wrong, is a crazy construction; especially in return for a trifling extra interest" (Keynes 1924, 585). But before the war, the challenges to heavy foreign investment were minimal in Britain. This was also the case in the United States—understandable since it was a net capital importer until immediately before World War I. In Germany, the issue of capital mobility was hotly debated, as the previously given brief account of the Banking Inquiry suggests, but the levels of capital invested abroad never came close to those of the British or the French.

The French stand out as exceptional both in the magnitude of the capital they sent abroad (second only to Britain) and (in contrast to Britain) for the disastrous outcome of this investment. Two-thirds of France's outstanding foreign investments in 1914 were lost by the end of the war. At the war's outbreak, about 40 percent of all private French wealth had been invested in securities of one or another kind (Michalet 1968, 138–39). About a half to a third of those securities were foreign (Cameron 1961, 487).[9] This meant that between one-quarter and one-third of total French wealth other than land and consumer capital was in foreign investments, by Cameron's calculations.[10] The French invested abroad sums equal to about 10 billion dollars at pre–World War I gold parity (50 billion gold francs). Only the British invested more, with foreign investments in 1907 amounting to about 40 percent of British savings (Cairncross 1953, 104).

Analyses of inheritances show a diffusion of these securities across urban and rural France. Surprisingly, small French savers seem to have bought foreign securities in heavier proportions than the richest savers (Michalet 1968; Daumard 1977). French investors abroad initially bought government and railroad bonds, but in the decade before the war, increasingly funds flowed into foreign direct investment in enterprises. The ratio of foreign direct investment to portfolio capital on the eve of the war may have been considerably greater than generally recognized (Svedberg 1978). In contrast to Britain, which sent about 30 percent of its foreign investment to the Empire and 70 percent to politically independent countries such as the United States, France sent very little to its colonies before World War I. In 1900, only 1.5 billion out of 28 billion francs of French-held foreign securities were in the colonies; by 1914, only 4 out of 45 billion in foreign holdings (Feis [1930] 1965, 51). The lion's share of French foreign investment went to Russia, the Near East, and Latin America. Russia was the largest single destination and absorbed about a quarter of all French foreign investment.

So France before World War I is a promising case in which to examine more closely the political challenges to capital mobility, since the sums at stake were enormous and there were millions of lenders. Why did the French accept the investment of so large a proportion of domestic savings overseas? As I have previously suggested, it was neither for lack of critics nor for lack of the means of control (however imperfect they might have proved). Nor do "interests" explain it, if we conceive interests as deriving from some more or less fixed and objective

9. On the calculation of French foreign investment and returns, see also White (1933); Lévy-Leboyer (1977a, b).

10. Cameron (1961, 64) and Michalet (1968) conclude for a lower figure: 14% of total private fortunes were in foreign securities.

economic location of actors in the domestic and international economies. For many of the important social actors, "interests" regarding open borders for capital flows were indeterminate in two fundamental respects. First, no individual investor could calculate with any degree of certainty what his own "naked" interest might be, let alone which forms of collective action would advance it. Rates of return on domestic and foreign securities varied too much from year to year—and the differences were usually too small—to make for clear conclusions. Second, "interests" in free capital flows were inextricably connected by politics to other highly salient and significant stakes, so that no actor could regard action on this issue as separable from outcomes on other high-valence priorities. For this reason, political actors could not reasonably hope to shift position on one part of a coalition's policy package and to leave other parts of the constellation intact.

Calculating Interests in Foreign Investment

The consensus among mainstream economists then and now—setting aside the realm of speculation and irrational expectations—is that there is no mystery about why people invest abroad instead of at home: they do it for higher returns.[11] France was in recession and stagnation from 1873–97, and over these decades grew at a rate slower than other European economies. Between 1865 and 1895 Britain's GDP doubled, Germany's more than tripled, while France's GNP grew only by a third (Broder 1997). French shares of world markets were shrinking. And the French population was growing at a slower rate than that of any other European country. In the view of liberal economists of the times, slow growth, demography, excess savings, and too few good opportunities for domestic investment explained why French investors chose to invest abroad. Maurice Brion in 1912 summed up these conclusions, writing:

> In France, as in other long-established societies, the resources of nature have already been exploited: there's nothing much left to create. There are no more railroads to build, no more cities to electrify or supply with tramways, no more natural resources to discover and extract. Germany, in contrast, whose economic birth is relatively recent, has still not fully developed its resources. (Brion 1912, 82–83)

Paul Leroy-Beaulieu, a well-known political economist, advised first-time investors against investing in domestic industry as far too risky for anyone ex-

11. For recent contributions on how professional investors evaluated sovereign borrowers, see Flandreau (2003) and Tomz (2007).

cept experts and the very rich (Leroy-Beaulieu 1905, 50). The prudent investor should buy foreign securities, even though the rate of return on them might be only a little higher than on domestic securities: "It would be turning one's nose up at wealth to turn down an interest differential of ½ percent" [i.e., between foreign and domestic securities] (107–8).

Calculating the rates of return on domestic and foreign investment in France before the war remains controversial, and the results vary greatly depending on time period and the methodology. Harry Dexter White, who calculated the 1899 yields of foreign and domestic securities at the price of issue found that the yield on domestic securities was higher relative to the issue price (4.28%) than on foreign securities (3.85%) though the rate at the price of February 1900 was lower (3.23%) than on foreign (3.84%) (White 1933, 271–72). Others have reached opposite conclusions. Debate about the relative profitability of investment at home and abroad continues among economic historians analyzing British domestic and imperial investment in the prewar period. Lance Davis and Robert Huttenback (1982) and Sidney Pollard (1985) have shown there were many years in which domestic securities had higher returns than those abroad. For Germany, where a far larger share of savings were invested in domestic infrastructure and industry, Richard Tilly concluded that on the average over the forty years before World War I, the annual rate of return on Prussian government issues (consols) was 4.3 percent; on domestic industrial shares, 9.35 percent; and on foreign securities traded on the Berlin Stock Exchange, 6.7 percent (Tilly 1991, 95). But the basic fact, as the advice of Leroy-Beaulieu to the neophyte investor implied, was that the gap between the rates was usually not so great—in either direction—that an individual could read his interest off a table of bond yields or stock market returns. It was impossible to calculate from year to year whether the best investments would be at home or abroad. Interests, even narrowly economically defined, were not obvious. How, then, did savers actually decide where their interests lay?

The Structures of French Capitalism

For politicians in left and right opposition parties and for the journalists who led the attack on the export of capital, the point was that it was a mistake to think of the world as one in which individuals face an array of rates and choose. Lysis—the pseudonymous left journalist who launched the great debate over the outflow of French capital—argued it was the institutions of French capitalism that shaped the choices and responses of investors. "How can competent writers attribute the fall in French securities to spontaneous decisions of capitalists and make no reference at all to the formidable organization of French financial markets or to its uncontestable power?" (Lysis 1912). Lysis claimed that it was the banks that channeled individual savings into foreign investment, and not a process in which individuals responded to different interest rates or were swept away by irrational "animal spirits." Individual investors can only choose among the institutional options they find already in place. So the real factors shaping interest formation were the structure of French capitalism and the patterns of French commercial banking.

The banks that were attacked by Lysis and by the deputies who rose to speak against foreign loans in the parliamentary debates over the export of capital were recently founded commercial banks that channeled the savings of millions of depositors. As critics pointed out, these banks earned large commissions on the sale of foreign securities and on manipulating the margins between the rates at which they negotiated the loans and the rates at which they sold them to their French customers. Between 1897 and 1903, the largest of these commercial banks, the Credit Lyonnais, made 30 percent of its profits in Russian affairs. The defenders of the banks responded that French banking laws and practices were not any different than those of other countries. It's not the fault of the banks if economic growth in France is sluggish: the maturity of the economy, a stagnant demography, the lack of natural resources, a contentious workforce are simple facts, they reasoned (Testis 1907, 60–61).

State-Led Capital Exports

Political economists disputed whether capital exports represented rational individual responses to market signals or the institutional effects of the French variety of capitalism, but others claimed that money flowed out of France because the government used capital exports as an instrument of state power. Foreign investment was a lever with which France could expand its influence in the international arena. Capital exports could be seen as a kind of substitute for French deficiencies: for a stagnant economy, for an inadequate military buildup, or as a vehicle of French influence in the world. As Brion wrote: "Exporting our capital is in a way the ultimate form of our glory in the world" (1912, 219).

The strongest evidence for the case of state direction comes from the loans to Russia. French diplomacy since the 1870 war had been obsessed with breaking out of isolation. French diplomats considered the loans to Russia from 1888 on as instruments for prying the Russians out of their alliance with the Germans.[12] At first the loans were almost exclusively for government bonds to support gov-

12. See Girault (1973) and Kennan (1984).

ernment deficits and for infrastructure projects like railroads, bridges, and harbors (Girault 1973; Anan'ich and Bovykin 1991). But increasingly, French funds flowed into foreign direct investment in Russian firms and into firms the French themselves established in Russia (Crisp 1960). The big sectors of French investment were metalworking, steel, iron, mines, infrastructure projects, and textiles and apparel. By 1910, five major French textile firms employed 10,000 workers in their own firms in Russian Poland. By the 1917 revolution, 44 percent of Russian banks were owned by foreigners (half of which was held by French investors.)

As loan followed loan, and as French governments began to have a better understanding of the state of Russian public finances, the French realized that, as a senior official in the Ministry of Finance suggested in 1905, the ruin of the debtor would be a disaster for the creditor (Girault 1973, 22). It became impossible to reverse course. The real test for this policy was the period 1904–6, when the Russo-Japanese war and the outbreak of revolutionary violence in Russia panicked foreign investors with evidence of the ramshackle state of Russian finances and the weakness of the tsarist regime. Under considerable pressure from the government of Maurice Rouvier, the French banks kept lending to the Russians (Guilleminault and Guilleminault 1991). The loan of April 1906 was the biggest of them all.

Even if we recognize the French government's interest in pursuing a Russian alliance, though, the puzzle of large-scale private investment remains, for the state had no way of compelling or even incentivizing private investors to place their money in Russia.

One factor was the interpenetration of governmental and financial elites with many of the most influential deputies and ministers sitting on the boards of banks, railroads, shipping companies, and industrial firms (Garrigues 1997). In ordinary times, the arrows of influence in these tight networks undoubtedly went from the world of business to the world of politicians. But in situations of high tension in international affairs as in 1906, the politicians could push businessmen and bankers, however reluctantly, to support state policy.

The second mechanism by which the government intervened to induce private savers to invest in ways that supported France's foreign policy objectives was colluding in the corruption of journalists who were paid by the Russians to report favorably on economic conditions in Russia. The archives of the Russian ministries of Foreign Affairs and of Finance, opened after the Bolshevik Revolution, document the links between glowing articles in the French press about the prospects of investment in Russia and the money that the Russians passed to newspapers and to particular journalists identified by the French government as the most influential (Raffalovitch 1931). One can roughly match up the recipients of the money and the newspapers with good news about Russia. For example, in 1909 the *Semaine financière*, which received money, wrote: "Political crises are no longer to be feared. The time for big loans is over. If Russia needs to borrow again, it will only be for extending the railroads" (28 August 1909). This was written at a time when Russia was borrowing simply to repay previous loans. Another newspaper on the payoff list wrote:

> In every domain, Russia appears to us as disposing of an almost inexhaustible mass of resources and forces and with a very large margin for expansion . . . The Russian state today—just considering its Treasury—is the richest in Europe. Since finances are the sinews of war, our readers can judge how fortunate France is to have its Russian alliance. (*France économique et financière*, March 12, 1913)

These rosy visions were contested by other journalists who detailed the disastrous state of Russian finances and indebtedness and speculated about why the French were so willingly ignorant. After all, Saint Petersburg was only two days away from Paris, and anyone could see the true state of affairs. The information was there—but private investors mostly turned a blind eye.

The Politics of Openness

Neither the evidence of clear self-interest nor that of state directives supports any simple theories about why investors sent savings out of France into countries with dubious public finances and very risky infrastructural and industrial enterprises or why the politicians let them do so. The puzzle becomes even more challenging when one focuses on the support that left parties and unions provided at all those political junctures—particularly after financial crises—when major steps to regulate capital mobility were proposed. Why should the left and the working-class movement, which might have expected to suffer from, and hence, to be opposed to, the mobility of capital, labor, and goods across boundaries, have accepted the legitimacy of the internationalization of capital? Like many of the critics, the French left understood that if the capital that was invested abroad had been invested in France, the rate of economic growth might have been higher, jobs might have been more abundant, and wages would have risen.

But the abundant evidence we have from Socialist and trade union congresses and publications and from the parliamentary debates over capital flows in the years before World War I shows the French left as a consistent opponent of efforts to stop the investment of French capital abroad. In fact, across the full range of political battles over border-level controls to stop the flow of goods, immigration, and capital, the French left parties and unions, like the German Social Democrats and unions and the English, were staunch opponents of protectionism. The Belgian Socialist leader Emile Vandervelde expressed the general point in arguing that nationalist autarchy was antithetical to the socialist internationalist ideal of abolishing boundaries and assuring a decent life for workers all over the world. In debates over tariffs, the positions of these parties and unions varied from a kind of neutrality justified on grounds that the issue was a distraction from class struggle to a passionate defense of free trade for providing cheap food and basic commodities and thus raising the standard of living of workers. On internationalist grounds, the Socialists even refused to support legislation for limiting immigration, despite strong pressures from their base (Prato 1912).

On each of these issues—trade, immigration, capital mobility—the left struggled with those in its own ranks who wanted some kind of protection, but perhaps on none of these questions was the "interest" of the left in openness less evident—hence requiring of more interpretation and defense—than on capital mobility. Yet in each of the great parliamentary debates over foreign loans before the war, the Socialists consistently supported the basic principle that capital should freely circulate among nations. French investors should be able to place their funds in developing countries, even if the result might be less investment in France, hence fewer new jobs at home. The left's support for open borders for capital faced even tougher challenges than hypothetical future growth rates and job loss in France. The debates in the Chamber of Deputies over the export of capital coincided in time with two other burning problems: French policy toward Russia during the 1905 revolution and its aftermath and Minister of Finance Joseph Caillaux's efforts to pass income tax legislation. When considered in conjunction with each of these two issues on which the left had intense preferences, capital mobility seemed extremely dangerous, for it threatened to help out Russian reactionaries and, at home, it threatened to undermine the chances for progressive tax reforms.

On the first point, the Socialists strongly opposed authorizing new loans to Russia while tsarist police were still shooting protesters and instigating pogroms. As Léon Remy wrote in *L'Humanité* (January 7, 1908): "We're providing abominable Tsarism with a knife to stab the revolution in the back, and we're providing the Tsar's supporters with easy rents. It's just a little sordid! Socialists should protest!" Socialists insisted that any further loans to the Russian government be approved by the newly elected Duma.

Centrist deputies also urged making the loans conditional on the tsar's agreement to political concessions. Georges Clemenceau wrote:

> We French are the ones who gave the Tsar the means to go to Manchuria and show the incompetence of his bureaucracy. After giving him all the financial resources he needed to be defeated by a foreign army, now we are supposed to give him the financial resources he needs to assure his victory over his very own subjects. . . . If he can put together a government capable of real reforms, then he can receive support from the French Republic. But if it's to keep Barbarism going, let him get his loans from Kaiser Wilhelm. (*L'Aurore*, January 30, 1906)

In 1907, the Socialist leader Jean Jaurès developed the same themes and argued that tyranny was the real cause of social and economic unrest in Russia: "In allowing new loans to go forward, you are giving arms to despotism against the people, and preparing the ruin of Russia's credit (Chamber of Deputies, *Journal Officiel*, session of February 8, 1907, 339). But even in the case of Russia, Jaurès continued, he would not favor restricting French capital exports:

> **J. Jaurès:** I am not opposed in principle to investment of French capital abroad. Yesterday, the Minister of Finance accused one of our Socialist colleagues of economic nationalism. No, Mr. Minister. It's a question of degree and of prudence. It is impossible, and—at a time when the whole world is in a phase of economic growth—it would undoubtedly not be a good idea to prevent French capital from participating.
>
> **J. Caillaux, Minister of Finance:** But that runs contrary to all your doctrines.
>
> **J. Jaurès:** It would be contrary, in a sense, though one should not confuse the internationalism which brings nations together with a false cosmopolitanism . . . But what I'm saying is that it's a matter of prudence and . . . moreover it's inevitable and in a sense positive that French savings participate abroad in human economic development. It's important that this expansion of French savings, of our national capital take place in a prudent fashion, while leaving a fair share to domestic industry and overseeing the securities that are allowed to be publicly listed. (Chamber of Deputies 1907, 338)

The Socialists' concerns about the export of capital focused not only on the political impact of these investments on foreign governments but on the impact of these monetary flows on French politics. For virtually all the reforms of the period—from the limitations of hours of work to income taxes—Socialists had to battle against the Right's threat that social reform and the passage of an income tax would drive capital out of France. Jaurès used Lysis's arguments to drive home points about the extraordinary monopoly of control over French savings in the hands of a few banks and to warn that if this power were used to subvert reform that the Socialists would mobilize to regulate the stock market as well as the commercial banks (Chamber of Deputies, *Journal Officiel*, session of February 8, 1907).

The concern that the banks' control over savings and their bias toward foreign investments would undermine reform at home and the attack on French loans to repressive governments were themes throughout the debates of the first decade of the century. Sometimes the Socialists joined the majority in pressing governments to condition approval for foreign loans on the provision of contracts for French industries.[13] But still, the left of the first globalization always came around to support for open borders for capital, goods, and labor.

Why and how did the French left come to conceive its interests as aligning with support for open borders—despite what might have been considered much evidence to the contrary? One possible approach to this question has been provided by Frank Trentmann's (1998, 2008) work analyzing the passionate support for free trade across broad and diverse sectors of English society over the period of the first globalization. Trentmann argues that the resilience of support for free trade, even as British interests in the international economy changed, derived from potent popular beliefs that associated freedom in trade with basic civil rights. He suggests we need to examine how interests are constructed out of the moral and political conceptions people bring to bear in interpreting the world. On this reading, it was the broadly shared ethical assumptions of British political culture that allowed conservatives, liberals, and labor—each with very different views about the international economy—to find common cause in support of free trade. Its proponents were imbued with a sense of moral rightness, not only with an unshakable conviction that prices of food would be lower under this trade regime than any other.

In France, there was nothing similar. No political symbols expressed as the "cheap loaf" did for the English the association between economic openness and the freedom and well-being of the public; there were no mass mobilizations over these issues. There was deep attachment on the left to internationalism and a certain cognitive belief that different dimensions of internationalism were connected. But the commitment of the French left to internationalism did not translate into passionate conviction in the virtues of free trade or, even less, in those of capital mobility.

Rather, as the passages quoted above from the French parliamentary debates over foreign loans suggest, the leaders of the left were always weighing in the

13. Linking loans to guarantees of foreign contracts was a major demand of trade associations and a major source of contention between industrialists and the banks (Rust 1973).

balance one set of possible gains and dangers against another. In the debates over Fashoda, the Moroccan crisis, the Turkish loan, Jaurès denounced the role of powerful interest groups in driving colonial policy and warned that the conflicts with the British and the Germans could spin out of control into war. He condemned "an internationalism of bombs and profits." But still the Socialists saw the internationalization of the economy as creating a world in which democratic politics might gain. As Jaurès expressed it in 1905: "The world today is ambiguous and mixed. There's no inevitability, no certainty. The working class is not strong enough to create the certainty of peace, but it is not so weak that war is inevitable. In this uncertainty of things and the unstable equilibrium of forces, human action can truly make a difference" (*L'Humanité*, July 9, 1905). On the eve of the war, Jaurès saw the foreign investments of capitalists and the web of interdependencies in the international economy as among the last possible bulwarks against the outbreak of conflict.

These political reflections suggest political leaders moving on to new and uncharted territory without a map. Working-class internationalism as an ideological grid did not provide good guidelines for dealing with capital flows. Rather the left's support for open borders suggests a different mode through which groups may identify their interests. They search for familiar features of the political terrain even when in new territory, and one feature in particular helps to establish such landmarks. Where groups see their old enemies gathering, there be dragons, as on medieval maps that marked off blank spaces of unidentified lands and oceans. What helped the left define and consolidate its positions on trade, immigration, and capital flows was that they could identify on the other side a familiar enemy in nationalism.

The pressures of economic changes in the first globalization, as today, come to bear on an already constituted set of political actors and alliances. The groups in contention did not emerge and mobilize in response to the forces of globalization. Rather these were actors already present, who had coalesced in the great political battles of democratic development: battles over the republic, church-state relations, and socialism. In closest proximity to the great parliamentary debates over the export of capital was the near civil-war strife over the Dreyfus case and the separation of church and state. The groups were ones whose politics had been forged in struggles over issues quite distant from the international economy. Their ideologies, constituencies, alliances, and connections to power were tied to old political cleavages. The actors tended to perceive and interpret the disruptions and opportunities of the new international economy by reference to a set of benchmark political struggles in which they were already engaged. For example, during the 1906–7 parliamentary debates over authorizing new loans to Russia, different groups on the left seized on the republican stakes in the issue—despotism, arbitrary rule, the crippling of the Duma—rather than on the impact on employment or investment in France. There were indeed voices in the labor movement who found hope in the Russian events that "strike fever" in French-owned factories in Russia might spill over into France (*Voix du Peuple* [*CGT*], January 29–February 5, 1905, and February 19–26, 1905). But the dominant chord was the reaffirmation of the republican values at stake in supporting a repressive Russian regime with French savings. On these issues, Jaurès and the centrist Clemenceau could find common cause.

The internationalism of French working-class organizations and the left thus had two strong anchors that moored these groups, even when particular groups within the Left camp came under pressure from international competition. First, internationalism was anchored by the Marxist convictions of the Socialists, who understood socialism to mean that solidarity extended across national boundaries, encompassing even Italian immigrant workers, who might drive down wages, or Russian workers, whose jobs in a French-owned factory in Russia replaced jobs the French firm might have created at home. Second, and perhaps most important, internationalism was anchored by the legacies of republicanism and by a past in which republican allies had been located in a free-trade camp aligned in opposition to reactionary foes in the protectionist camp. The battles of the turn of the century between right-wing nationalists and the republican camp worked to reinforce this identification of republicanism and internationalism.

The anchors that attached French political coalitions to internationalism and republicanism and served to define interests on free capital movements have long ago slipped their moorings. With the Bolshevik Revolution, internationalism became identified with subservience to Comintern directives. With the erosion of religious practice and a massive shift to the left of many Catholic regions, the old left-right divisions and alliances were undermined. The result has been to unfreeze old definitions of interest and to open a new phase of interest identification and mobilization. Some groups within the left have joined antiglobalization movements; others support open borders. As Marcos Ancelovici has shown in research on the shifts in French unions and parties on economic protection and openness, there is little direct connection between the socioeconomic location of groups and their positions on globalization (Ancelovici 2002, 2009, forthcoming). Rather the dynamic of political competition among factions of the left drives these positions.

To the question of how capital mobility survives politically in a world it makes more dangerous, the case of the French in the first globalization offers some interesting possible approaches. It suggests we need to widen our focus from the politics of those with clear and unconflicted material interests (as a first approximation, the bankers in our example) to a much broader field of actors who do not know and perhaps cannot know with any certainty where their interests lie with respect to the flow of capital across national borders. How these actors puzzle out their interests has much to do with the legacies of ideas, cultural norms, and cognitive maps they bring to the task. But to regard the determination of interests in such cases—which are ubiquitous in politics—as a process of cultural construction of interests suggests a tighter congruence between the most deeply held values of the actors and their positions on this issue than ever existed. Rather in this case, politics shaped interests from their very inception as the actors sought to figure out how this issue connected them to their allies and distinguished them from their enemies. Interests with respect to capital mobility emerged not as the first and most desired set of outcomes; then at some later stage of the political process, compromises were made and such interests became joined with others as strategic behavior. Politics entered from the first moments in the process of interest formation as a process of reasoning over how to conceive one's ends, not as a set of strategic calculations over how to achieve one's ends. As the French Socialists asked themselves what it meant to be on the left on an issue such as capital mobility, they looked at their friends and allies and they looked across the way at their long-standing opponents. In such a process, interests emerge not mainly as points that can be read off an ideological grid but as extensions of political choices, compromises, and alliances made on quite unrelated prior issues. This process accounts for the incompleteness of the "interests" that come to be affirmed over time and for the continuous reworking and renegotiation characteristic of this phase of politics. Despite the evidence all around us of the same processes at work today in shaping choices over the regulation of financial flows within and across borders, this phase of interest formation remains a domain that we political scientists have barely begun to explore.

7

PORTFOLIO POLITICS IN THE NEW HARD TIMES

Crises, Coalitions, and Shareholders in the United States and Germany

James Shinn

Prosperity blurs a truth that hard times make clearer.

—Peter Gourevitch (1986)

The Great Recession of 2007–8 induced a sideways slip in a decades-long trend of improved minority shareholder protections, blunting the effects of global investors on corporate governance while amplifying the effects of pension losses on support for shareholder protections. In two illustrative and contrasting country cases, painful stock market losses energized broad political support for governance reforms in the United States, given the wide exposure of American citizens' pension savings to financial markets, but had little effect in Germany, where there are much lower levels of private-pension assets and equity. But in both countries, a broad public perception that Wall Street and international financiers were a proximate cause of the Great Recession undercut coalitions supporting minority shareholder protections on both sides of the Atlantic.

Two parallel trends favoring enhanced minority shareholder protections in all countries of the Organisation for Economic Cooperation and Development (OECD) are described in *Political Power and Corporate Control* (Gourevitch and Shinn 2005), one working through pension preferences in individual countries and the other by means of global investors' price incentives working across countries. The first, which we termed the "pension preferences mechanism," is an example of public ordering of governance institutions, in which voters support laws and regulations that impose minority shareholder protections on listed firms because of the benefits of good governance—and the costs of poor governance—to their individual retirement portfolios. The second trend, which we termed the "global investor mechanism," is an example of private ordering of governance institutions, whereby the owners of firms voluntarily adopt minority shareholder protections because of the superior returns that they in turn receive from portfolio investors.

The effects of the Great Recession on these two trends occurred in two phases. The first phase was relatively short, a matter of months beginning in the middle of 2007, and concentrated in the financial sector. The second phase took several years as the financial crisis worked its way into the real economy, beginning in 2008 and still unfolding as of the time of this writing. Phase 1 was a liquidity squeeze, followed by a steep fall in asset prices, in all OECD countries. Phase 2 was characterized by a steep contraction in private consumption and business investment throughout the OECD, as governments scrambled to adopt expansionary monetary and fiscal policies to offset the demand contraction. What started as a draught of liquidity in the two financial centers of New York and London ultimately turned into a river of red ink in all OECD capitals.

Despite the sideways slip in corporate governance reform caused by the Great Recession, persistent fiscal deficits in the OECD countries will ultimately reengage the pension preferences trend, as the liabilities for defined benefit plans from public entities become sharply visible and increasingly fragile to beneficiaries, taxpayers, and cold-eyed sovereign debt markets alike, a striking example of how crises induce the redefinition of interests. The funding (or default) of public-pension liabilities, as well as the compensatory growth of private-pension assets as a hedge against government claims, will ultimately reengage the global investor trend as well. The combined effect in the long run is likely to be slow but steady gains in minority shareholder protections in all the OECD countries—at least until the next hard times.

Cross-Class Coalitions and Minority Shareholder Protections: Contrasting Germany and the United States

In *Political Power and Corporate Control*, Peter Gourevitch and I argue that improvements in minority shareholder protections rest on cross-class coalitions that cut across traditional capital-labor and right-left distinctions in complex and sometimes unexpected ways (Gourevitch and Shinn 2005, 5).

For example, in the case of the United States, we argue that a broad basis of support for minority shareholder protections was rooted in a mosaic of interests:

- Both blue- and white-collar workers held dual identities as workers and as shareholders. Many blue-collar workers came to think of themselves as shareholders as well as employees because of the large equity holdings of their pension plans and 401(k) savings—the unexpected transformation described by Peter Drucker in *The Unseen Revolution* more than three decades ago (Drucker 1976). Many white-collar workers also thought of themselves as shareholders because of stock-option plans as well as their pension and savings equity holdings.

- Public- and private-sector labor unions had different preferences, with private-sector union employees exposed to the vagaries of stock markets through their defined contribution plans, as defined benefit pensions were largely eliminated by their sponsoring corporations. In contrast, public-sector employees were buffered from direct exposure to financial markets by their defined benefit pension plans, in which the financial risk was born by the sponsor—governments—rather than the beneficiaries.
- The financial industry was also divided, with some institutional investors and other market participants, such as activist hedge funds, often pressing for greater minority shareholder protections. Other intermediaries, such as investment banks and mutual funds, usually sided with incumbent managers and had little taste for governance activism.
- Some wings of the Democratic Party were linked closely to Wall Street, while others were more populist. The nervous ambivalence with which Democratic politicians reacted to the so-called Occupy Wall Street movement in 2011 reflected this cleavage. Conservative forces were also fractured, with some elements also linked closely to Wall Street and resistant to changes in governance rules, even as other elements of the Republican Party were aligned with so-called Main Street groups that supported corporate governance reforms. The Tea Party movement within the Republican Party in 2011 and its hostility to the Republican "establishment" reflected this cleavage.

In contrast, the cross-class coalition in Germany that supported and sustained steady improvements in corporate governance in that country was built on a narrower, ultimately more fragile base, with different lines of cleavage.

- Far fewer German workers viewed themselves as shareholders, given the much lower equity exposure of their private portfolios and their greater dependence on industrial pension plans (often co-administered by firms and unions) or on state-backed defined benefit plans. Moreover, equity-sharing arrangements were relatively rare in Germany compared to the United States, so fewer German white-collar workers were beneficiaries of stock option plans.
- German unions were united in their fundamental opposition to minority shareholder protections and to other corporate governance rules that, in

their view, served to privilege shareholder value creation over stable employment. These unions were particularly neuralgic about the prospects for hostile takeovers that could reduce employment or even remove union representatives from German firms' supervisory boards.

- The financial industry in Germany was also split on the question of shareholder protections, with firms such as Deutsche Bank (DB) and Dresdner Bank opting to compete in global capital markets and fully embracing the principle of maximizing shareholder value, whereas institutions such as insurance firms and Landesbanks remained linked to traditional "Rhenish capitalist" firms by means of cross-shareholdings and overlapping boards. As Deutsche Bank and the other "globalist" German financial firms almost collapsed and were bailed out, ironically, by the U.S. Federal Reserve Bank (which paid $12 billion dollars to DB in order to redeem its derivatives claims on AIG [American International Group] at 100% of par value), the Great Recession cast these contrasting choices in a particularly harsh light.
- By the same token, the German right was fractured, with some wings supporting globalized finance and competition even as others supported traditional linkages and practices such as Mitbestimmung. The German left, in turn, favored minority shareholder protections as a way to split the right, exploiting corporate governance as a wedge issue. As Martin Höpner observes, "With respect to the enforcement of share markets and the conflicts between shareholders and managers, the SPD [Social Democratic Party] is the market-enforcing party, whereas the CDU [Christian Democratic Union] is the market-restricting party" (2003, 35).

As we noted earlier, according to the pension preferences mechanism, worker-voters are more likely to make common cause with shareholder-voters if they are shareholders themselves via their personal savings and/or pension claims.[1] Pension assets as a percentage of gross domestic product (GDP) have grown rapidly in those countries in which pension claims are funded by financial markets, known as pillar 2 and pillar 3 assets in the pension lexicon, but have lagged in those countries in which pension claims are relatively more dependent on the state. Appendix 7-1 at the end of this chapter shows this bimodal distribution for

1. It matters how these pension claims are structured, whether in the form of defined benefit or defined contribution plans, and whether (or how much) the claims are actually funded. The beneficiary of a defined benefit plan is hostage to the performance of a particular firm or government entity and thus has a strong interest in the solvency and governance of that firm or entity, though not necessarily in governance practices in financial markets more broadly. The beneficiary of a defined contribution plan is hostage to the performance of the financial markets in which his or her contributions are invested and thus has a strong interest in the solvency and governance practices of those markets broadly, though not in the governance or solvency of any single firm or government entity.

TABLE 7-1 Percent of GDP and equity exposure of pension assets in Germany and the United States, 2005 and 2008

	PA/GDP	EQUITY%	EXPOSURE
United States			
2005	74.15	0.68	50.42
2008	58.41	0.55	32.12
Germany			
2005	4.04	0.35	1.41
2008	4.73	0.36	1.70

the years 2005 through 2008 for twenty-two countries, while table 7-1 highlights the sharp contrast between the United States and Germany in this regard. In 2005, the ratio of private-pension assets to GDP for the United States was just over 74 percent, versus just over 4 percent for Germany. The percentage of these assets held in listed equities—as opposed to other assets such as fixed income or real estate—was 68 percent in the United States compared to 35 percent in Germany, so the net exposure to equities as a percentage of GDP was 50.42 percent in the United States and only 1.41 percent in Germany.

Although the pension preferences mechanism works primarily within countries in the context of domestic politics, the global investor mechanism works through cross-border transactions between global investors and majority shareholders (albeit sometimes with side-payments to workers and managers). Unlike the pension preferences mechanism, the global investor mechanism is not based on any explicit political agreements about corporate governance principles, but it does embrace the principles of capital mobility and relatively free flows of equity portfolio investment—both basic principles of the OECD, by the way.

Over the past four decades, both the pension preferences and global investor mechanisms have been driven by the remarkable accumulation of pension assets and expansion of foreign portfolio investment, combining to produce a slow but steady improvement in minority shareholder protections, at least until the Great Recession. For the sample of countries in *Political Power and Corporate Control*, the mean value of the percentage of the total market capitalization held by foreign investors doubled, from 12.6 percent in 1900 to 25.1 percent in 2000 (Gourevitch and Shinn 2005, table 5.1). The estimate of foreign portfolio investment (FPI) in Germany's stock market expanded to 21 percent in 2007 from 18 percent in 2005 but was still the second lowest in the European Union (EU), after Italy, and well below the EU mean FPI estimate of 39 percent.

TABLE 7-2. RiskMetrics Group (RMG) and GovernanceMetrics International (GMI) country-level indices for the United States and Germany and 23-country sample means, 2005 and 2009

	RMG			GMI		
	2005	2009	CHANGE	2005	2009	CHANGE
United States	53.8	62.6	0.16	7.06	7.18	0.02
Germany	38.4	48.3	0.26	5.12	5.7	0.12
Sample Mean	39.7	48.7	0.26	5.27	5.58	0.06

Minority shareholder protections in all the OECD countries have improved in line with the growth of both pension assets and FPI over the last two decades.[2] As table 7-2 highlights, the level of minority shareholder protections in Germany were about three-quarters as high as those in the United States for the period in question.

The Impact of the Great Recession

The Great Recession started on Wall Street, as losses on securities in financial firms' inventories—particularly securitized real estate—undermined the solvency of counterparties, and quickly spread through the global banking system. Interbank lending and the short-term securities repurchase market ("repo") rapidly dried up on both sides of the Atlantic. All risk assets fell sharply, as investors "fled to quality" to U.S. Treasury obligations. The cross-correlation between traded financial assets snapped almost to one, including equities, bonds, real estate funds, and even commodities, with only Treasuries moving in the opposite direction. Institutional and personal investors sustained dramatic losses.

Phase 1: Portfolio Losses Sink In

The dramatic losses incurred by institutional investors in their foreign and domestic portfolios between 2007 and 2008, including the huge amounts lost in financial firms' equity value, had a galvanizing influence on citizens' views of

2. A recent careful revision of one of the most popular academic indices of shareholder protections, the so-called LLSV index, showed a steady annual increase, from a mean country value of 13.2 in 1990 to 17.6 in 2005 (see La Porta et al. 2002 and Martynova and Renneboog 2010).

corporate governance in the United States. In turn, the losses in private-pension funds attributable to asset repricing were huge in the United States and in other high private-pension countries (see app. 7-1). Moreover, because of the relatively high exposure of U.S. private-pension assets to equities—two-thirds of the total U.S. portfolio as opposed, for example, to one-third in Germany—the beneficiaries of U.S. private-pension assets lost huge sums during the Great Recession, amounting to 18 percentage points of GDP. By contrast, with their low holdings of private-pension assets and relatively low-equity exposure, the holders of German private-pension assets rode through the Great Recession unscathed (see app. 7-1 and table 7-1).

The pension preferences model depends on a chain of cause-and-effect that translates losses in citizen-voters' private pension assets into political support for public ordering changes in corporate governance. Two of the evidentiary steps in this chain require us to establish that (1) citizen-voters' losses in the equities that they hold are material, and of sufficient magnitude as a percentage of personal net worth to command the holders' attention; and (2) citizen-voters make a logical connection between these losses and corporate governance.

The Federal Reserve's periodic survey of household finances shows evidence for the first of these steps. According to 2007 data, the most recent available, 51.1 percent of U.S. households reported holding publicly traded stocks, which accounted for 54 percent of their total financial assets. The median value of these household stock holdings at the end of 2007 was $35,000, slightly more than one-quarter of the median household total net worth of $120,000. The Federal Reserve estimated that the median value of these equity holdings fell by 35.7 percent, from $35,000 to $22,500, between the end of December 2007 and October of 2008 (Federal Reserve Board 2009, A27). This translates to a 10 percent loss of net worth in ten months, a loss that is clearly both material and large enough to command citizen-voters' attention. Combined with the decline in real estate prices, this dramatic fall in equity values accounts for the total 21.7 percent fall in household wealth between 2007 and 2009 in the United States that is cited in the introductory chapter of this volume.

Evidence for the second causal step can be gleaned from opinion polling in the United States. In June 2009, the Opinion Research Corporation (ORC) conducted a telephone survey in which 2,006 randomly selected adults were asked questions regarding corporate governance.[3] The results showed a high degree of

3. According to ORC, 19% of respondents had lost up to 10% in the value of their investment portfolio in the prior year, 24% had lost up to 25%, and 38% had lost up to 50%. The query "What best describes the way you feel about the financial markets today as it relates to your investments, retirement fund, or savings?" garnered the following responses: 34% affirmed, "I am ANGRY about what has happened and want to see strong action taken to correct the problems that exist," while another 44% of respondents were "NOT ANGRY" but said that they "still want to see action

anger and political support for reforms, including otherwise arcane issues such as "say on pay," executive compensation "clawback" in cases of fraud, and proxy access—not usually bread-and-butter issues for the average voter. U.S. citizens appeared to be particularly inflamed by news reports of big Wall Street executive payouts in 2009 and 2010.

In contrast, a German household with the equivalent net worth of approximately 85,000 euros would have lost virtually nothing through equity losses in pension assets over the same period. This is not to say that the average German citizen-voter was untroubled by the Great Recession, or that there was not widespread anxiety about the financial consequences of the Recession, but that this anger was not connected to minority shareholder protections by means of the pension preferences mechanism. The financial trigger of the Great Recession had other consequences in Germany as well as the United States, however, to which we now turn.

The Financial Trigger

Because of the financial trigger, a series of administrative measures and legislative acts were passed in the United States to tighten corporate governance rules in order to improve minority shareholder protections. These actions were driven in large part by public indignation at the terms of the Wall Street bailouts, as the details trickled out through news reporting, congressional hearings, and a series of books including a surprisingly frank memoir by former U.S. Treasury Secretary Henry Paulson (2010). The sustained appearance of these otherwise arcane books on best-seller lists reflects the "what caused this?" debate that often follows major crises. There was widespread belief on Main Street that the Great Recession was an endogenous event caused in part by poor governance of financial firms rather than an exogenous financial tsunami that submerged Wall Street, as ex-Lehman chief executive officer (CEO) Richard Fuld claimed in his testimony before the Financial Crisis Inquiry Commission: "Lehman's demise was caused by uncontrollable market forces and the incorrect perception and accompanying rumors that Lehman did not have sufficient capital to support its

taken to correct the problems." In follow-up questions, 81% supported "new laws and regulations to crack down on stock market abuse," 77% supported "strengthening the legal rights for investors," 65% supported "more investor involvement in CEO pay," 58% supported "more power for stock market regulators," 51% wanted investors to have a "say on pay" for CEOs, and 49% thought it "very important" for shareholders to have the ability to "vote on issues through the proxy ballot." The poll was commissioned by Shareowners.org, a grassroots activist organization with labor union and pension fund affiliations (http://www.shareowners.org).

investments. All of this resulted in a loss of confidence, which then undermined the firm's strength and soundness."[4]

But official Washington was initially cautious in imposing any corporate governance reforms on the firms that it had bailed out. In the "fog of crisis," the risk of financial collapse apparently pushed concerns about corporate governance far down the list of priorities for the Treasury Department, judging by the Paulson memoir, among others. For example, the October 2008 recapitalization of the banks was done by purchasing restricted preferred stock from the banks in exchange for the cash injections, but the term sheet specified no voting rights for the government unless the banks missed dividend payments for six successive quarters (Johnson and Kwak 2010, 154). When the U.S. Treasury appointed a "pay czar" in mid-2009 and proposed compensation guidelines for banks, the biggest financial institutions competed with each other to pay back the government equity funds as quickly as possible. As one (politically conservative) pundit acidly observed, "The U.S. Congress was angry enough to vote once against the $700 billion troubled asset relief program in 2008, but not angry enough to demand a seat on the executive compensation committees of those banks they had committed the U.S. taxpayers to bail out."[5]

More intrusive reforms reflecting a deeper distrust of the corporate governance of financial firms were embedded in the omnibus Dodd–Frank Wall Street Reform and Consumer Protection Act (Public Law 111-203), which became law in July 2010. Dodd–Frank altered the rules of corporate governance in the United States by means of a series of provisions within Title IX of the legislation, including the following:

- Subtitle C, which created an Office of Credit Ratings (OCR) to provide oversight of "nationally recognized statistical rating agencies."
- Subtitle E, which imposed tighter disclosure rules on executive compensation (including severance packages such as the so-called golden parachutes), required shareholder approval of some aspects of executive compensation, provided for conditional "clawback" of executive compensation in defined cases of malfeasance, and tightened the conditions of independence of board compensation committees.
- Subtitle G, which gave the Securities and Exchange Commission (SEC) authority to enforce shareholder access to proxy solicitation materials

4. Richard Fuld, "Written Statement of Richard S. Fuld, Jr. before the Financial Crisis Inquiry Commission," September 10, 2010, http://fcic-static.law.stanford.edu/cdn_media/fcic-testimony/2010-0901-Fuld.pdf.

5. Christopher Caldwell, "Politicians Take Note," *Financial Times*, January 28, 2012, 7.

(subject to certain threshold conditions) and to require explanations of boards' policies on separating the CEO and chairman functions.

For better or for worse, Dodd–Frank was an example of how crises can render interests "more malleable or plastic" as the introductory chapter of this volume suggests. Until Dodd–Frank, defenders of the corporate governance status quo opposed attempts to extend minority shareholder protections on the federal level by the SEC on the grounds that company law in the United States was a matter of primarily state-level jurisdiction. The financial crisis of the Great Recession was a national-level problem, requiring national-level policy responses, and so Dodd–Frank was passed in the "political moment" when a national-level coalition coalesced.

State-level political entrepreneurs competed to ride the wave of public anger against financiers, such as the cases that New York's then-attorney general Eliot Spitzer pursued against securities and insurance firms, most notably AIG. An unexpected consequence of these state-level inquiries into Wall Street malfeasance were several investigations and prosecutions involving public employee pension funds over allegations of so-called pay to play, in which investment managers offered campaign contributions and outright kickbacks to pension fund managers and trustees. Andrew Cuomo, Spitzer's successor as New York State's attorney general, for example, piled on to an SEC investigation to prosecute Steven Rattner and his Quadrangle Group for transactions involving the New York State Public Employees Pension Fund. California's then-attorney general Jerry Brown brought a similar indictment against several former executives and board members of the California Public Employees' Retirement System (CalPERS).[6] Ironically, state pension funds, especially the New York State Common Retirement Fund and CalPERS, had been among the most outspoken advocates of good corporate governance in their portfolio firms, first in the United States and subsequently abroad.

The financial-sector trigger of the Great Recession also gave Wall Street and the City of London a political bad name in the other OECD countries, particularly in Germany. German media made much of the fact that the financial crisis had begun in New York and London—the centers of Anglo-Saxon-style "good governance." Despite considerable resistance across the political landscape to

---

6. "In May, the California attorney general's office sued Alfred Villalobos, a CalPERS board member from 1993 to 1995 who became a so-called placement agent, accusing him of trying to improperly influence CalPERS personnel to favor Apollo Global Management LLC and other private-equity clients. On August 26, Leon Shahinian, head of CalPERS private equity team, resigned after the lawsuit alleged he accepted a private jet flight, a $200 bottle of champagne, and other gifts from Villalobos in May 2007. The next month, Shahinian called for a $700 million investment in Apollo, says the suit" (Bloomberg News, September 9, 2010).

activist foreign investors, the global investor mechanism steadily improved minority shareholder protections in Germany throughout the 1990s, with a series of legislative milestones. These included the Control and Transparency Act (Gesetz zur Kontrolle und Transparenz im Unternehmensbereich—KonTraG, for short), which validated the one-share-one-vote principle, tax rules that permitted the unwinding of cross-shareholdings by banks, the adoption of International Accounting Standards for reporting, the creation of a powerful securities regulator (Bundesanstalt für Finanzdienstleistungsaufsicht—BaFin for short), and even an initial embrace of a European takeover directive (the Federal Financial Supervisory Authority). These milestones were justified as the cost for allowing German firms to participate in, and benefit from, global capital markets. As John Cioffi recounts in his analysis of the impetus behind minority shareholder protections in Germany, during the 1990s Deutsche Bank and Dresdner Bank made common cause with international investment banks such as Goldman Sachs to press for corporate governance reform inside Germany through the Bundesverband für Deutsches Banken (BDB).[7] The BDB lobbied for shareholder protections against resistance from the Bundesverband für Deutsches Industrie (BDI), which represented the traditions of so-called Rhenish capitalism, including union representation on boards (Mitbestimmung) and resistance to hostile takeovers. Until the Great Recession, the BDB largely prevailed.

During the Great Recession, the BDI and Germany's powerful labor unions pushed back, hard. The financial-trigger aspect of Phase 1 discredited a key element of the political coalition underlying the global investor mechanism in Germany. Indeed, both Goldman Sachs and, arguably, Deutsche Bank were bailed out by governments during the financial crisis. For example, Goldman received $12.9 billion and, as noted earlier, Deutsche Bank received $11.8 billion in the AIG bailout alone to satisfy its derivative claims against AIG, at 100 percent of face value, in cash.

In the meantime, both the managers of traditional firms and labor unions in Germany had already chosen sides against the corporate governance reform block, a movement that began in 2001, when the European Union submitted a draft takeover directive to the European Parliament. As Cioffi observes, "Organized labor saw the takeover directive as a means of decisively shifting power and income from employees to shareholders. German managers and labor thus formed a potent coalition across class and ideological lines to opposed the directive and

7. "The entry of American investment banks into the German market during the 1990s . . . altered policy preferences in the financial sector. . . . The enhanced political influence of the banks and the BDB contrasted with the diminished influence of the peak industry association, the BDI, a redistribution of influence that continues to this day. . . . Thus, by the mid-1990s, the most powerful financial and industrial firms had realigned their preferences in favor of a reform agenda that served their interests by favoring those of shareholders" (Cioffi 2010, 147–8).

its supporters in the financial sector and government" (2010, 162). The financial-trigger aspect of the Great Recession only served to harden this alignment against public ordering of minority shareholder protections in Germany, a sharp contrast to the parallel events in the United States.

Phase 2: Liquidity Drought and Cash Hoarding

The sustained drought in many financial markets during the Great Recession served to shut down several of the alternative pathways by which the global investor mechanism works. In both the United States and Germany, nonfinancial firms engaged in a sustained paydown of bank borrowings, substituted relatively low-interest long-term debt for short-term borrowings, and accumulated a striking amount of cash, even as they reduced capital expenditure. Rather than return this cash to their investors through dividends or share buybacks, firms held onto the cash to a remarkable degree. In the United States, by midway through 2010, U.S. nonfinancial firms held $1.93 trillion in cash on their balance sheets, equal to 7.4 percent of total assets, the highest percentage of total assets in cash for 50 years (*Wall Street Journal*, December 10, 2010, A1). The hoarding of cash by large listed firms during the Great Recession was equally salient in Germany, with firms running a net cash surplus ranging between 0.1 and 0.5 percent of GDP in the period from 2007 to 2009 (*Economist*, July 10, 2010).

These cash hoards reduced the dependence of firms in both the United States and Germany on financial markets, both equity and debt markets, thus making the managers of these firms relatively impervious to the governance preferences of outside investors, particularly those of minority shareholders. This trend reduced the appeal of the good governance premium, at least from the standpoint of the firms (blockholders and incumbent managers alike), and thus served to attenuate the global investor mechanism's private reordering of governance bargains.

For those firms that were susceptible to good governance incentives because they still needed external sources of capital, the Great Recession's liquidity drought further blunted three interrelated alternative pathways of the global investor mechanism: private-equity good-governance deals, blockholder depository receipt (DR) issues, and the partial privatization via stock offerings of state-owned enterprises (SOEs).

PRIVATE EQUITY

In good times, private equity firms provide a channel through which outside investors can purchase a controlling interest in firms from their previous blockholders (usually founders or families); restructure the firm in a variety of ways including adopting more attractive corporate governance practices of accounting, disclosure, executive compensation, and board oversight; and then float the firm with a public offering. In this process, outside investors can reap the global investor mechanism's "good governance premium" from institutional investors that the firms' previous blockholders had not exploited.

In the period from 2008 to 2009, however, any number of private equity deals were stopped dead in their tracks at various points in the pipeline, from acquisition right on through to stock floatation, thereby blunting the private equity work-around associated with the global investor mechanism.[8]

DEPOSITORY RECEIPTS

In good times, blockholders in emerging markets have the option of issuing equity through DRs in developed financial markets such as those of the United States, the United Kingdom, and Hong Kong and complying with the corporate governance standards of these markets, thereby reaping their own good governance premium despite lagging minority shareholder protections in their home markets.[9] However, the global market for new DR issues dried up in the bad times of the Great Recession as equity markets plunged, emerging markets in particular were sold off, risk premia expanded everywhere (back to historic levels), and the dollar appreciated in response to the "flight to quality." Funds raised in global DRs totaled $42.6 billion in 2006, $57.3 billion in 2007, and $14.7 billion in 2008—almost a 75 percent plunge as the effects of the Great Recession were felt. The 2009 figure recovered to $20.3 billion, but this was still far below levels in good times; German firms, moreover, accounted for less than 1 percent of the 2009 offering total.[10]

STATE-OWNED ENTERPRISES

Share offerings in SOEs provide yet another channel by which the global investor mechanism serves to enhance minority shareholder protections, as government

8. Many of the large international private equity firms were flush with cash collected from their institutional investors at the front end, even as many cash-strapped investors were pleading with the private equity firms to return some of these committed funds; but the liquidity crunch and collapsed equity prices made it difficult to finance the deals since many of these transactions depended on large amounts of relatively low-rated debt. Moreover, the "flight to quality" associated with the financial-sector trigger quickly devalued the currencies of many overseas private equity acquisition targets, making their future earnings streams less attractive from a dollar-denominated investor's point of view.

9. In the case of the United States, foreign firms may issue DRs on U.S. stock markets (thus termed American Depository Receipts, or ADRs) if they comply with a set of standards regarding accounting, disclosure, and oversight through Level II (listing) or Level III (issuing) rules.

10. Reflecting this abrupt contraction, the JP Morgan DR Composite Index fell by 46% in value terms year on year during calendar 2008. See J.P. Morgan and Company, "Global Depository Receipts: Year in Review 2008," 2–3; and "Global Depository Receipts: Year in Review 2009," 8–9, both available at http://www.adr.com.

blockholders adopt higher standards of accounting, disclosure, and oversight in order to reap the good governance premium and thereby maximize their privatization proceeds. These share offerings can take place in several ways, including share issues on national stock markets and depository receipt offerings abroad.

As tracked by the Privatization Barometer Database, global share offerings of SOEs were $18.2 billion (26 transactions) in 2006, $24.9 billion (16 transactions) in 2007, $31,784 billion (8 transactions) in 2008, and $2,282 billion (4 transactions) in 2009 (http://www.privatizationbarometer.net/database.php). However, the 2008 figures include a "mega" share offering by Electricite de France (EDF) of $21.2 billion that was a follow-on transaction from 2007; if the EDF offering is removed, the total figure for 2008 actually fell by about 60 percent, to $10,514 billion (7 transactions). By another measure, SOE share proceeds in 2007 of 19 billion euros plunged to a total of 1 billion euros in the first half of 2008 (Megginson 2010, 26). The last German privatization issue, that of Hamburger Hafen und Logistik AG, took place in November 2007. By any measure, bad times rudely interrupted the SOE privatization flow, thereby shutting down that part of the global investor mechanism.

Fiscal Policy Response

In response, central banks stepped in with vast amounts of liquidity and direct intervention to buffer the financial meltdown. Nonetheless, distress in the financial sector and asset repricing quickly spread to the real economy. Consumption dropped sharply as households began a process of financial de-leveraging (by saving more or defaulting on their debts), even as banks also began to de-leverage, thereby further tightening credit to firms and households.

Governments in the OECD countries responded with fiscal stimuli in ways shaped largely by pre-recession practices and institutional choices: tax rebates and transfers to "pump prime" consumption in countries such as the United States and direct transfers to buffer unemployment in countries such as Germany. As Peter Gourevitch observes:

> When faced with economic crises, all governments' first reaction is to take out the same playbook they used the last time. For example, after the 2007–08 crisis, the Americans tried to expand consumption, the Europeans tried to expand exports, the Asians hunkered down, and so on. This is because the politics of shifting course in economic policy requires governments to upend the interests of the many groups in society who have a stake in the status quo, and governments usually lack

the political support or the urgency to switch gears like that. (As quoted in Shinn 2011a, 87)

As tax revenues fell off, fiscal stimulus by OECD governments aggravated the already deep structural deficits.[11] The additional claims on government revenues that emerged just as the recession deepened posed a significant risk to the beneficiaries of government-sponsored pension plans, both partially funded and conventional pay-as-you-go (PAYGO) plans. Other things being equal, this risk is higher for the pension claims of citizens in Set B countries than for the pension claims of citizens in Set A countries (see app. 7-1).

All of the OECD countries, Set A and Set B alike (and therefore with the United States and Germany both in the same leaky boat), are heading into a slow-motion fiscal train wreck of their national social security systems. This problem is driven primarily by demographics, although the ultimate crunch will be far worse for the Set B nations with relatively smaller pillar 2 and pillar 3 pension assets. In this sense, the effects of the Great Recession on corporate governance through the pension preferences mechanism are part of a slow-moving but powerful crisis, an extended grinding of fiscal tectonic plates rather than a sudden financial earthquake, as the introductory chapter to this volume suggests.

As we argued in *Political Power and Corporate Control* (Gourevitch and Shinn 2005), implicit pension debt (IPD) is inversely correlated both with the ratio of private pension assets to GDP and with indices of corporate governance. This inverse correlation suggests that efforts to reform corporate governance that are based on a political appeals to citizen-voters whose retirement assets have been reduced or put at risk by corporate governance failures could collide with efforts to protect PAYGO pensions, efforts that are based on a political appeal to citizen-voters whose retirement claims have been put at risk by shrinking government revenues and fiscal deficits. The beneficiaries of state pension claims are usually aware that they face some combination of reduced benefits, delayed vesting, and/or much higher taxes unless their pension claims are given priority in government budget-making. This collision of preferences, moreover, is sharper for citizens in Set B countries than in Set A countries.

Indeed, prospective pensioners in the European Union have their eyes nervously set on the example of Greece, a Set B Country, whose pension obligations are largely unfunded and thus compete with other general obligations of the Greek state for current tax revenues, and were therefore cut back as part of the

11. "Amidst continued uncertainty about the pace of recovery as well as the timing and sequencing of the steps of the exit strategy, gross borrowing needs of OECD governments are expected to reach almost USD 16 trillion in 2009, up from an earlier estimate of around USD 12 trillion. The tentative outlook for 2010 shows a stabilizing borrowing picture at around the level of USD 16 trillion" (Blommestein and Gok 2010, 2).

austerity program imposed by the European Union and the International Monetary Fund (IMF). As reported by Rachel Donadio in the *New York Times* (September 24, 2011): "Since 2010, the government has raised taxes and slashed pensions and state salaries across the board, in an effort to rein in the bloated public sector that today employs one in five Greeks. Last week, the government announced it would put 30,000 workers on reduced pay as a precursor to possible termination and would cut pensions again for nearly half a million public-sector retirees."

This contrast in the basic funding of pensions suggests a divergence in the tone of the political debate over public ordering of corporate governance between Set A and Set B countries—which is to say, in this regard, with the United States and Germany in separate boats. Citizens in Set A countries, such as the United States, will have a debate over the sustainability of pensions within the context of financial markets and fiscal budgets, a debate in which most citizens perceive a clear link between the viability of their pensions, financial market health, and corporate governance broadly writ. In contrast, citizens in Set B countries, such as Germany, will experience a debate over the sustainability of pensions that is largely disconnected from financial markets or corporate governance but that features an intense contest between pension claims and other fiscal claims on government revenues.

Long-Term Implications

In the longer run, the pension preferences and global investor mechanisms will probably become conjoined. Sovereign debt markets will continue to impose ever-higher standards of accountability and transparency on OECD governments, particularly with regard to retirement and health care promises made to their citizens.[12] Differential risk-based pricing of sovereign debt, of national authorities, as well as of subnational provinces and states, will force states to account properly for their pension obligations. States will be forced to reduce these obligations by trimming benefits, capping eligibility, or pushing out benefit dates. Or they will have to fund these obligations by imposing higher taxes or by diverting other funds into the retirement schemes. At stake is not just corporate governance, but governance broadly writ: the credibility of financial commit-

12. "Fiscal restraint tends to deliver stable debt: rarely does it produce substantial reductions. And, most critically, swings from deficits to surpluses have tended to come with either falling nominal interest rates, rising real growth, or both. Today, interest rates are exceptionally low and the growth outlook for advanced economies is modest at best. This leads us to conclude that the question is when markets will start putting pressures on governments, not if" (Cecchetti, Mohanty, and Zamponi 2010, 1).

ments by political authorities, and the persistent unwillingness of politicians to acknowledge (in hard financial terms) the net present value of future commitments.

As an early example of a trend that is likely to become more widespread in other countries, a draft law entitled the Public Employee Pension Transparency Act was introduced in the U.S. Congress in late 2010. The bill pressures states to adopt the stricter financial disclosure, accounting, and transparency rules with regard to their pension liabilities that are observed by private firms according to the terms of the Employee Retirement Income Security Act (ERISA). For any U.S. states refusing to adopt these higher ERISA standards of accounting disclosure, the statute would remove their ability to make debt issues tax deductible for federal income purposes.[13] The original target of this draft federal law, submitted by a Republican congressman from the state of California, was the large unfunded liabilities of California's public employee pension funds.

We are already seeing pressure for similar changes in the accounting and disclosure rules for pension obligations of governments in Europe, particularly for EU peripheral states such as Greece, Ireland, and Portugal, in the evolving mechanisms of the European Financial Stability Facility (EFSF), European Union fiscal surveillance, and European Central Bank lending. Restatement of its budget by Athens to properly account for undisclosed liabilities such as pension obligations was an element in the near-meltdown of Greek sovereign debt in financial markets in late 2010. Ironically, much of this new accounting rigor for the EU peripheral states is being imposed at the insistence of Berlin, which was opposed to having German workers subsidize generous (and unfunded) retirement benefits for Greek workers.

In the long run, too, the global investor mechanism will shape and reshape political coalitions in all OECD countries, including the United States and Germany, through the mechanism of global market pricing of sovereign debt. The terms of retirement will become even more intensely politicized, as the "Greek Disease" reappears in the credit default swap premia for Ireland, Portugal, and

13. According to the language of the draft statute, "The extent to which State or local government employee pension benefit plans are underfunded is obscured by governmental accounting rules and practices, particularly as they relate to the valuation of plan assets and liabilities. This results in a misstatement of the value of plan assets and an understatement of plan liabilities, a situation that poses a significant threat to the soundness of State and local budgets. . . . This lack of meaningful disclosure poses a direct and serious threat to the financial stability of such plans and their sponsoring governments, impairs the ability of State and local government taxpayers and officials to understand the financial obligations of their government, and reduces the likelihood that State and local government processes will be effective in assuring the prudent management of their plans. The status quo also constitutes a serious threat to the future economic health of the Nation and places an undue burden upon State and local government taxpayers, who will be called upon to fully fund existing, and future, pension promises" (H.R. 6484, 11th Congress, 2nd Session, December 2, 2010, http://nunes.house.gov/_files/BILLS111hr6484ih.pdf).

Spain, as well as for U.S. states, particularly California, New York, and Illinois. Trimming benefits and increasing taxes will cause political heartburn on a vast scale, with irate pensioners in the streets of Athens and Paris merely the first minor acts in a long and disruptive play, one that has future bookings in Dublin; Lisbon; Madrid; Madison, Wisconsin; Springfield, Illinois; Albany, New York; Trenton, New Jersey; and Sacramento, California. In short, pension portfolio politics will be the epicenter of partisan and ideological struggles for decades to come.

It is possible that citizens throughout the OECD will be sufficiently discomfited by the Great Recession to master the intricacies of market returns, the fine print of pension benefits, or at least the basic mathematics of net present value. This could well lead to a new kind of confrontation at the notional barricades of political debate, with one group clutching their 401(k) reports and copies of the *Financial Times* and the other group grasping their social security checks and copies of the federal budget. More likely, however, this collision will take place through dueling narratives of wealth creation, dependency, and social justice, and the "logic of appropriateness" about what constitutes legitimate corporate governance. As the introductory chapter to this volume suggests, as interests are redefined and crystallized by crises such as the Great Recession, political contests may draw on pension mathematics but will be expressed in metaphors of resentment and cross-class conflict. In other words, the governance tropes of corporate governance may well figure as prominently in this debate as the financial corporate aspects of minority shareholder protections.

Meanwhile, the relentless pricing of sovereign risk and government funding requirements will grind away in the background. States (sovereign, provincial, and municipal) will be submitted to unpleasant scrutiny and differential pricing, and politicians will forge coalitions to oppose or exploit these market pressures. Some politicians will rail against faceless capital markets and attack the reputational intermediaries involved in sovereign financial transactions: speculators, "bond vigilantes," and even "wolf packs" will be and indeed already have been invoked in the debate. Other politicians will use the pressures of the "new austerity" to renegotiate institutional choices, including the terms of public employee bargaining, wage compensation, and retirement conditions. We have, in fact, already seen evidence of these realignments appear in Greek and Irish politics, as well as in several U.S. states. For example, Stephan Haggard (chapter 2, this volume) describes how Konstantinos Karamanlis and George Papandreou took opposite sides of the pensions versus austerity debate in the hotly contested Greek election of 2009.

As this political debate rages, citizens in all OECD countries whose future pension payouts depend on governments making good on unfunded promises—

which includes many public sector employees in the United States as well as most German citizens—are likely to take steps to hedge their risk by means of private savings and pension asset accumulation. For example, in a 2010 Gallup Poll, 56 percent of nonretired adults believed there would eventually be cuts in their social security retirement benefits (*USA Today*, July 8–11, 2010).

The more shrill the debate, and the more hotly debated the facts and figures of the public-pension funding gap, the more these rational actors will incline toward pillar 2 and pillar 3 pension plans. At some point, these asset holdings will draw citizens into the pension preferences mechanism for enhancing minority shareholder protections. The gears of these mechanisms grind slowly, but over time they grind with considerable force.

In the very long term, too, the funding of their pension obligations by governments in all countries will expand the pool of investible cash searching for risk-adjusted returns in financial assets as good times return. These pools of cash will join, sooner or later, the global pools of return-seeking assets that power both the pension preferences and the global investor mechanism. On the supply side, mobile capital may find the terrain less open than in previous decades, particularly in emerging markets, where capital controls (or penalties) may be back in vogue, and also in some developed markets, as fiscal authorities are tempted to engage in fiscal repression by means of exchange and capital controls.

Nevertheless, the volumes of capital crossing borders, currencies, and asset classes in the pursuit of risk-adjusted returns will almost certainly continue to expand. On the demand side, as the business cycle improves, firms will ramp up capital expenditure and run down their hoarded cash reserves, and states will still need to tap sovereign debt markets for the indefinite future.

It is not clear whether the coalitions for minority shareholder protections induced by the pension preferences and global investor mechanisms will offset the distributional tensions and other antagonisms induced by the Great Recession described elsewhere in this volume, but it is clear that these mechanisms are deeply embedded in the larger trend of economic globalization and capital mobility. OECD governments and their citizens are probably irreversibly engaged in financial globalization, and the Great Recession's sideways slip of corporate governance reform will almost certainly get back on the track of steady incremental improvement in minority shareholder protections, at least until the next hard times.

APPENDIX 7-1. Pension assets and equity exposure, A and B countries, 2005–8

	2005			2006			2007			2008		
ABV	PENSION	EQUITY	EXPOSURE	PENSION	EQUITY	EXPOSURE	PENSION	EQUITY	EXPOSURE	PENSION	EQUITY	EXPOSURE
Set A												
AUS	80.38	0.80	64.30	90.40	0.84	75.94	110.36	0.80	88.29	91.78	0.79	72.50
CAN	50.26	0.64	32.17	53.88	0.66	35.56	62.33	0.64	39.89	50.58	0.58	29.34
DNK	33.71	0.38	12.81	32.43	0.42	13.62	32.36	0.41	13.27	47.55	0.18	8.56
FIN	68.61	0.38	26.07	71.33	0.44	31.38	71.05	0.47	33.39	58.70	0.33	19.37
IRL	48.26	0.65	31.37	50.22	0.63	31.64	46.62	0.66	30.77	34.14	0.28	9.56
NLD	121.73	0.46	55.99	125.74	0.47	59.10	1*38.05	0.40	55.22	113.66	0.37	42.05
CHE	117.03	0.45	52.66	119.97	0.48	57.59	119.18	0.48	57.21	101.07	0.43	43.46
GBR	78.63	0.60	47.18	83.43	0.57	47.56	78.90	0.53	41.82	59.20	0.55	32.56
USA	74.15	0.68	50.42	78.92	0.58	45.77	79.40	0.66	52.40	58.41	0.55	32.12
Mean	74.75	0.56	41.44	78.48	0.57	44.24	82.03	0.56	45.81	68.34	0.45	32.17
Std Dev	29.72	0.15	16.65	31.02	0.13	18.55	34.58	0.14	21.08	27.08	0.19	19.66
Min	33.71	0.38	12.81	32.43	0.42	13.62	32.36	0.40	13.27	34.14	0.18	8.56
Max	33.71	0.38	12.81	32.43	0.42	13.62	32.36	0.40	13.27	34.14	0.18	8.56

Set B												
AUT	4.78	0.37	1.77	4.94	0.36	1.78	4.82	0.35	1.69	4.44	0.21	0.93
BEL	4.41	0.84	3.70	4.22	0.88	3.71	4.47	0.84	3.76	3.31	0.79	2.62
FRA	1.16	0.00	0.00	1.11	0.00	0.00	1.06	0.00	0.00	0.00	0.00	0.00
DEU	4.04	0.35	1.41	4.21	0.34	1.43	4.65	0.39	1.81	4.73	0.36	1.70
GRC	0.00	0.00	0.00	0.00	0.00	0.00	0.01	0.05	0.00	0.01	0.11	0.00
ITA	2.79	0.20	0.56	3.01	0.22	0.66	3.27	0.19	0.62	3.42	0.17	0.58
JPN	6.63	0.00	0.00	0.00	0.00	0.00	0.00	0.00	0.00	0.00	0.00	0.00
KOR	1.85	0.01	0.02	2.99	0.06	0.18	3.07	0.06	0.18	2.99	0.25	0.75
MEX	9.95	0.11	1.09	11.50	0.14	1.61	11.54	0.13	1.50	10.42	0.11	1.15
NOR	6.71	0.29	1.95	6.79	0.33	2.24	7.05	0.36	2.54	6.03	0.30	1.81
PRT	12.73	0.41	5.22	13.64	0.51	6.96	13.74	0.50	6.87	12.20	0.34	4.15
ESP	7.22	0.30	2.17	7.52	0.30	2.26	7.54	0.30	2.26	7.13	0.15	1.07
SWE	9.07	0.35	3.18	9.26	0.39	3.61	8.68	0.40	3.47	7.38	0.30	2.21
Mean	5.49	0.25	1.62	5.32	0.27	1.88	5.38	0.27	1.90	4.77	0.24	1.31
Std Dev	3.70	0.24	1.63	4.26	0.25	1.99	4.22	0.24	1.97	3.83	0.20	1.20
Min	0.00	0.00	0.00	0.00	0.00	0.00	0.00	0.00	0.00	0.00	0.00	0.00
Max	12.73	0.84	5.22	13.64	0.88	6.96	13.74	0.84	6.87	12.20	0.79	4.15

8

COALITION OF LOSERS

Why Agricultural Protectionism Has Survived during the Great Recession

Megumi Naoi and Ikuo Kume

The politics of the Great Recession illuminate the surprising disparity between the rise of public protectionist sentiments and the lack of protectionist policy responses (Kahler and Lake; Haggard, this volume). This chapter seeks to solve this puzzle by showing that the rise of mass protectionist sentiments did not translate into protectionist policies because these sentiments were not rooted in existing institutions, such as political parties and labor unions. Rather, protectionist sentiments were formed through social psychology of individuals, in particular, their sympathy for globalization losers and the projection of their own job insecurity onto struggling industries.

We substantiate this claim using evidence from a survey experiment we conducted in Japan during the Great Recession (December 2008). We focus on the public's support for protecting a symbolic declining industry in Japan, agriculture, and document the emergence of a "coalition of losers" between workers with high job insecurity and farmers to sustain agricultural protectionism. This emergence of a "coalition of losers" is paradoxical as workers with high job insecurity should be the prime beneficiaries of cheaper food imports as consumers.

We further test two mechanisms for determining why workers with high job insecurity would support agricultural protectionism: (1) institutional mechanisms, such as through the coalition of political parties and cooperation among occupational associations; (2) social-psychological mechanisms, such as through sympathy for farmers and projection of their own job insecurity onto farmers.

The results lend strong support to social-psychological mechanisms and very weak support to the institutional mechanisms. In particular, projection hypothesis finds strong support: those who fear future job insecurity and loss of income are the ones who become more supportive of agricultural protectionism with the activation of a producer perspective. Our results help us solve the paradox of persisting mass support for agricultural protectionism in the midst of the worldwide recession and surprising lack of protectionist policy responses by elites. They also force scholars to reconsider the institutional approaches used to study how coalitions formed during the financial crisis. The dynamics of coalitional politics in economic crisis might have changed from the ones that are organized around political parties and sectoral interest groups to the ones that are less institutionalized, more diffuse, and transient.

The Puzzle

The Great Recession has posed threats to the job security of low-income and low-skilled citizens in advanced industrialized nations. During such hard times, access to cheap goods, especially cheap food, is more critical for low-income citizens as they experience layoffs and wage cuts (Broda, Leibtag, and Weinstein 2009).

However, a series of public opinion surveys, which directly measures individual preferences for regulating food imports, suggest that around half of citizens seem to be *willing* to bear the cost of supporting farmers even during the Great Recession. Forty-seven percent of U.S. citizens in March 2009 thought that "it is the wrong thing that the Obama administration will reduce agricultural subsidies for many farms," while 40 percent of them thought "it is the right thing."[1] Fifty percent of European respondents in the Eurobarometer (fall 2007) support the status quo level of tariffs and quota protection for agricultural commodities, while 37 percent oppose it. In a nationally representative survey we conducted in February 2009, 55.6 percent of Japanese citizens thought that "we should not accept import liberalization of agricultural products in order to protect Japanese agriculture" while 37.8 percent thought "we should accept import liberalization of agricultural products in order to maintain Japanese manufacturing exports."[2] The high level of mass support for protecting agriculture is even more surprising given the estimates of the Organisation for Economic Co-operation and Development (OECD) that consumers in advanced industrialized countries spend 10 percent of their annual consumption on agricultural products to support

1. These figures are taken from a survey report released by Pew Research Center on March 16, 2009, http://people-press.org/report/?pageid=1485. The final survey data published later indicates that 43% of respondents think "it [reducing agricultural subsidies] is the wrong thing" and 44% think "it is the right thing."

2. Waseda University (2009). Farmers constitute 3.9% of the total respondents; among farmers, 90% support protectionism.

farmers. In countries such as Switzerland, Norway, Japan, and South Korea, more than 40 percent of consumers' expenditures on domestically produced commodities went to support farmers during the Great Recession in 2009.[3]

Two common explanations for agricultural protectionism are not helpful in making sense of this puzzle. The first focuses on the collective action capacity of interest groups: producers (i.e., farmers) are concentrated and better politically organized than are diffused and unorganized consumers (Olson 1965). The second focuses on political mobilization by elites: legislators exchange trade protection and subsidies for rural and agricultural votes (Gawande and Hoekman 2006; Grossman and Helpman 1994; Kabashima 1984; Magee, Brock, and Young 1989; Park and Jensen 2007; Rogowski and Kayser 2002). Because of its focus on producer power, however, the literature simply makes assumptions about consumers' preferences for free trade. The two conventional accounts do not help us understand why the public seems to be willing to accept high-priced agricultural products to support farmers during the Great Recession. These limitations force us to think how actors assess their own interests and the interests of others in relational and institutional contexts.

A Situational Account: Institutional Mechanisms to Forge Interests

Peter Gourevitch's *Politics in Hard Times* provides a more situational and relational account for why labor demanded cheaper food imports in some recession cases, while they aligned with industry for higher tariffs in other cases: "Identically situated actors may adopt different policies . . . workers in cheap-food countries and those in high-cost-food countries may think differently about tariffs" (Gourevitch 1986, 58).

Specifically, Gourevitch identified two situational factors that determined labor's coalitional choices. One was the cost of food in a given country, which shaped how labor weighed the importance of their consumer interests (preference for cheaper food) and occupational interests (preference for employment and wages). When food was cheap as was the case in the United States, labor aligned with industry for higher tariffs as they weighted occupational interests (employment and wages, which were tied to industry's survival) more than further lowering the cost of food; when food was expensive, as was the case in

3. The estimate is a percentage of Consumer Support Estimate (CSE) per total expenditures on domestically produced commodities. CSE is "an indicator of the annual monetary value of gross transfers from consumers of agricultural commodities, measured at the farm gate (first consumer) level, arising from policy measures which support agriculture" (OECD 2009a).

Europe, labor aligned with farmers of high-quality foodstuffs in favor of free trade as they weighed their consumer interests more. Although not couched in the following terms, Gourevitch (1986) shows how workers chose a coalitional partner by strategically weighing the dual interests they had as income earners versus consumers.

The second situational factor was the institutional context in which private actors were embedded, such as the party politics and industry associations. "Nearly everywhere agriculture and labor found it difficult to cooperate" (Gourevitch 1986, 24), yet through institutional mechanisms for forging interests, such as the alliance of agrarian parties and labor parties and corporatist arrangements, labor-farmer alliances did emerge during the crisis of 1873–96 in the United Kingdom (for free trade), during the 1929–49 Depression in Sweden as the cow trade between the Swedish Workers party and the agrarian party (both of which supported the welfare state expansion), and during the New Deal in the United States as the corporatism of the National Recovery Administration (NRA) (which supported protectionism).

Do these two factors account for the high level of public support for agricultural protectionism during the current Great Recession? It does not appear to be so. In countries both where the costs of food are high (Japan and many of the EU member countries) and low (the United States), the public shows a high level of support for assisting domestic farmers. Party politics and corporatist arrangements seem to play limited role as well. Even in countries without strong labor party or corporatist arrangements with centralized labor unions (for example, Japan and the United States), around half of consumers are willing to accept the high price of agricultural products. Furthermore, those who support agricultural protectionism in these surveys are cross-partisan. The same survey report of Pew Research Center (March 16, 2009) cited earlier in this chapter indicated that 57 percent of Republican supporters think reducing agricultural subsidies is the wrong thing, whereas 43 percent of Democrats do so. In Japan, 54 percent of Democratic Party of Japan (DPJ) supporters think increasing food imports is bad or very bad, and 52 percent of Liberal Democratic Party (LDP) supporters do so. In sum, a cursory look at cross-national and individual patterns of support for agricultural protectionism does not lend strong support to the arguments about the cost of food or the institutional mechanisms for forging interests of consumers and farmers.

If not institutions, then, what gives rise to a consumer-farmer alliance to sustain agricultural protectionism during the recession? To answer this question, we conducted an online survey experiment in Japan during the midst of Great Recession (December 2008). The experiment randomly assigns visual stimuli to activate respondents' identification with either producer or consumer interests, then proceeds to ask attitudinal questions regarding food imports. The next section describes the design and procedure of this experiment in detail.

Research Design and Method

Why Experiment? Priming without Framing

The duality of interests workers (or citizens) have as income earners and as consumers complicates our inquiry into how citizens' occupational and consumer interests shape their attitudes toward food import as discussed previously. Gourevitch's discussion of labor's coalitional choices during past recessions demonstrates that even well-organized labor unions weighed their occupational and consumer interests in forming their attitudes toward trade. Declining labor union membership and increasing number of nonorganized workers in developed economies today means that workers are even more torn between their occupational and consumption interests when they puzzle out their attitudes. A key question then is not *whether* consumers' interests matter more than producers' interests; rather, we need to ask whether citizens' support for agricultural protectionism differs when they assess their positions in the global economy as producers versus as consumers. This question calls for an experimental research design that randomly primes citizens to think about globalization as a producer or as a consumer.

What complicates our endeavor further is that, in reality, consumer interests do not equate with their preferences for free trade. The emerging research suggests various parameters beyond price sensitivity that make some consumers more protectionist than others: the type of consumption basket (Baker 2005, 2009), safety and quality concerns (Kono 2006; Vogel 1999), ethical concerns (Ehrlich 2010; Hiscox and Smyth 2009; Maclachlan 2001), the love of variety (Broda and Weinstein 2004; Krugman 1980), and community and family concerns (Goldstein, Margalit, and Rivers 2008). In light of studies that suggest consumers' preferences are indeterminate and complex, we should not frame respondents to think about the positive or negative consequences of food import when we ask about their attitudes toward it. Instead, we need to design an experiment that primes respondents to think about food import from a consumer versus a producer perspective without framing its distributional consequences.

The Experiment

We conducted an online survey experiment in Japan with a sample of 1,200 respondents between the ages of twenty and sixty-five during the first week of December 2008, when media coverage of the world financial crisis and the rise of unemployment among the temporary workers was extensive (Kono 2006; Vogel 1999). Japan is an appropriate case for our research as the public strongly supports agricultural protection despite the fact that more than 40 percent of food expenditures go to support farmers through agricultural subsidies and the prevalent form of this protection is price support, which directly burdens consumers (Davis and Oh 2007). To understand the sources of support for agricultural protectionism, we randomly assigned visual stimuli to three experimental groups. The experiment consists of two groups that receive the treatment ("stimulus") and another control group without any stimulus (400 respondents each).

The producer-priming group is shown three photographs: a typical white-collar office, a car factory, and a rice field (see fig. 8-1). The images were chosen

■次の写真をよく見て以下の質問に答えてください。

Q2 ここはどのような業種の人が働く職場だと思いますか。

(回答は1つ)

○ 金融
○ 製造業
○ 出版
○ 役所
○ その他

FIGURE 8-1. Producer-priming (photos 1, 2, and 3). Note: These three photos were used for the producer-priming. Before showing the photos, we asked: "Please carefully look at the photos below and answer the following questions" (translated by the authors).

Source: For the first (white-collar office) and the third (harvesting) photos, Copyright © Kenji Hall-Creative Commons Attribution Licensed. For the second photo (car factory), Copyright © Chang-Ran Kim.

■次の写真をよく見て以下の質問に答えてください。

Q5	この食料品店は以下のどのタイプのお店だと思いますか。

(回答は1つ)

◯ 個人商店
◯ コンビニエンスストア
◯ 有機/自然食品店
◯ 大型スーパー
◯ その他

FIGURE 8-2. Consumer-priming (photos 4, 5, and 6). Note: These three photos were used for the consumer-priming. Before showing the photos, we asked: "Please carefully look at the photos below and answer the following questions" (translated by the authors). Photos courtesy of the authors.

to represent three major sectors of the economy (service, manufacturing, and agriculture) to activate respondents' consciousness as producers (or, their occupational interests).

The consumer-priming group is shown three photographs: a supermarket with food, a consumer electronics retail store, and a large-scale casual clothing store (see fig. 8-2). These images encompass three areas of basic consumer goods that citizens purchase regularly regardless of their income, gender, family status, and age. These visual stimuli are intended to activate respondents' consciousness as consumers. The control group receives no stimulus.[4]

4. The treated and control groups are balanced in their key demographic characteristics such as age, gender, income, and respondents' self-assessed difficulty finding a comparable job. See Naoi and Kume (2011, table 1).

Using images to prime respondents has two advantages over framing experiments that supply respondents with opinions about how trade affects consumers and producers (Hiscox 2006). First, priming differs from framing in that the former makes some issues more salient than others and thus influences the standards by which the subject is evaluated, while framing characterizes issues negatively or positively (Iyengar and Kinder 1987, 63; Scheufele 2000). This characteristic of priming allows us to manipulate respondents' "standards" by which food import is judged (producer versus consumer) without imposing on them the judgment itself (that is, food import is good or bad for producers/consumers). This is critical for the purpose of our study as we do not yet know whether activation of a consumer perspective uniformly leads to lower or higher support for agricultural protectionism. Instead, the visual stimuli simply prime respondents to think of themselves as consumers rather than producers. Second, our visual stimuli do not explicitly convey information about either trade or globalization. This omission is appropriate for the purpose of our study, as not all production and consumption activities are linked, in reality or in citizens' minds, to trade or globalization. After the treatment, we proceeded to ask attitudinal questions about food import and general trade issues.[5] The survey instruments are described in the results section that follows.

The Results: Aggregate Effects of Priming

Figure 8-3 summarizes the distribution of responses for questions on food imports and general trade. The former question is, "Food imports from foreign countries have been increasing. What is your opinion on this?" The latter question is, "Imports from foreign countries have been increasing. What is your opinion on this?" Respondents choose answers from a five-point scale (very good, good, can't say one or the other, bad, and very bad).[6] For each experimental group, a black bar describes the proportion of protectionist responses ("bad" and "very bad"), a gray bar describes the proportion of neutral responses, and a white bar describes the proportion of respondents that supports increasing food imports ("good" and "very good").

---

5. We embedded two checks in the survey to ensure that the priming worked in a way we expected. The results of these manipulation checks are discussed in detail in Naoi and Kume (2011).

6. Note that this question asks respondents' opinion about "increasing food imports," not about protecting agriculture or farmers. We chose this form of question instead of "trade policy" questions (e.g., asking respondents' opinions about subsidies, tariffs, or new limits on import) for three reasons: (1) it does not directly remind respondents about "jobs" (theirs or farmers) or "consumption"; (2) the wording is less technical than asking about tariffs or subsidies, and thus is better suited to solicit a gut reaction from the public; and (3) it parallels the survey instrument we used for the general trade issue, which is similar to the one that was used for Pew Global Attitudes Survey and Hiscox (2006).

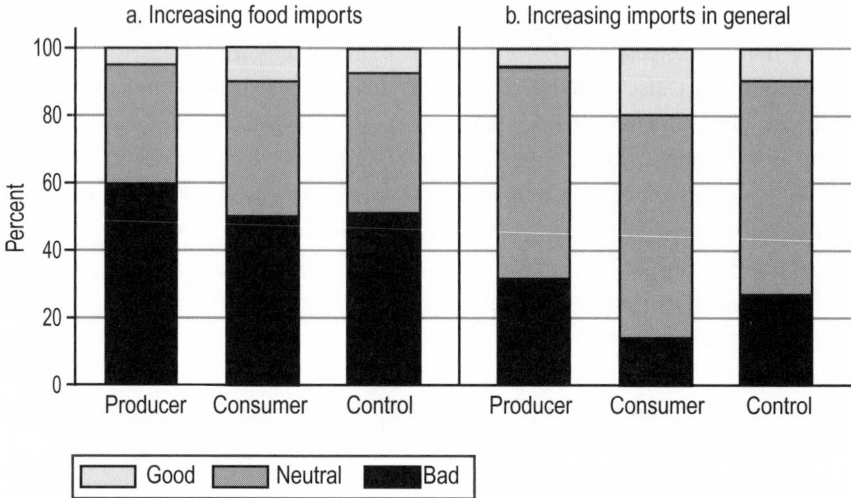

FIGURE 8-3. The effect of priming in aggregate: (a) increasing food imports, (b) increasing imports in general. Note: The *x*-axis is three experimental groups, and the *y*-axis is the proportion of total respondents (%) choosing each answer. The difference-in-means tests for protectionist responses (%) show that the difference between producer treatment and the control groups for the food import issue is 0.09 ($0< x <1$, standard error 0.035) and statistical significance at $PR(|T|>|t|)=0.011$. Difference between consumer treatment and the control groups are 0.01 (standard error 0.035) and is not statistically significant.

The figure shows that, in all groups, the proportion of protectionist responses roughly doubles for the issue of food imports compared to the issue of general trade. This result is counterintuitive in light of the two conventional approaches, one emphasizing individual occupational profiles of respondents and the other looking at their ideological predisposition as determinants of trade attitudes (Hainmueller and Hiscox 2006; O'Rourke and Sinnott 2001). The former would predict a higher proportion of protectionist responses on the issue of general trade than the issue of food imports as the latter only affects the jobs and wages of farmers, which constitute 0.7 percent of our sample. The latter would predict that respondents exhibit similar ideological predispositions for the import of goods in general and the import of food. Yet, respondents clearly view the import of goods in general differently from food imports: more than half of respondents across the three groups think increasing food imports is "bad" or "very bad." Why?

Possible explanations for stronger opposition to food imports are protectionist sentiments that consumers might have, such as food nationalism, safety and quality concerns, and food security concerns (e.g., food self-sufficiency ratio), which have been all observed in Japanese elite discourse (Goudo 2006; Maclachlan 2001; Vogel 1999). Yet these accounts would predict that consumer-priming increases opposition to food imports. Contrary to this prediction, figure 8-3a suggests that consumer-priming does not provoke higher or lower levels of opposition to food import than in the control group. On the other hand, producer-priming increases opposition to food imports by 9 percentage points compared to the control group, and the difference is statistically significant at the 5 percent level.

This leads to two questions. First, why does the activation of a producer perspective lead to higher support for agricultural protectionism? Second, why do citizens think of agricultural trade differently from general trade? These questions force us to think beyond how individuals perceive their own interests and to pay due attention to how they perceive interests of "others."

Disentangling the Puzzle "Consumers Think Like Producers"

We disentangle this puzzle along two possible explanations: (1) the existence of institutional mechanisms to forge common interests between consumers and farmers, such as through the coalition of parties or cooperation between occupational associations; or (2) noninstitutional, social-psychological mechanisms, such as sympathy for farmers and projection of respondents' own job insecurity onto farmers. Both mechanisms force us to move beyond occupational theories of trade policy preferences, based on Stolper-Samuelson and Ricardo-Viner models, which derive individual policy preferences from their occupations' relative positions in the international economy. Instead, these mechanisms consider how individuals perceive other occupations or sectors (such as agriculture) when forming their own attitudes toward trade. To do so, we analyze which subgroups of respondents are sensitive to producer- and consumer-priming and identify the direction of their attitudinal differences among the three experimental groups.

Institutional Mechanisms: Partisan Identity and Associational Membership

For the institutional mechanisms for a coalition of losers, we conduct two separate tests. The first is to analyze respondents in the control group only ($n = 400$) to investigate whether a labor-farmer coalition exists to support agricultural protectionism even without producer or consumer treatment. The second is to use data from all the three experimental groups and test whether subgroups of respondents with particular partisan identity or membership in associations are more likely to become protectionist with the viewing of producer treatment.

For the partisan identity, we examine whether the supporters of the LDP and the DPJ responded differently to the producer and consumer treatments. The LDP, which was in power when the survey was conducted (December 2008), is known to voters as a pro-rural, pro-farmer's party. The major opposition party, the DPJ, mainly represents urban constituents and labor union members who support the expansion of the welfare state. The DPJ has also been flirting with farmers by pledging to grant income compensation for future agricultural liberalization in order to compete against the LDP in rural districts.[7] Thus, if a "coalition of losers" emerges through the partisan identity and the coalition of parties, we expect to see that the nonfarming LDP supporters become more protectionist with the viewing of the producer treatment, forming an alliance with the LDP's longtime core constituents, farmers. On the other hand, we expect the DPJ supporters to split between those who become less protectionist with the viewing of the consumer treatment (urban consumers) and those who become more protectionist with the viewing of the producer treatment (public sector, labor union members).[8]

We also examine subgroups of respondents who are members of one of the following occupational and consumer associations that directly benefit or incur loss from agricultural protectionism: labor unions, agricultural cooperatives, and consumer cooperatives (*seikatsu kyodou kumiai*). Respondents who are members of each association constitute 12.6 percent (labor unions), 7.5 percent (agricultural cooperatives) and 25.1 percent (consumer cooperatives) of our sample. Labor unions in Japan are within-enterprise, decentralized unions without a strong national center (Kume 1998). Public sector unions, especially unions of local governments, tend to support agricultural protectionism, and the metal unions have been a strong advocate for free trade.[9] Such conflict within labor unions suggests little possibility for a red-green coalition at the national level.[10]

On the other hand, consumer cooperatives in Japan were established in 1951 to promote consumer-driven society and domestically-produced, safe, high-

---

7. The two-party competition between the LDP and the DPJ is a relatively new phenomenon as the LDP has formed a coalition government with the Clean Government Party (CGP) since 1994. The two-party competition has generated convergence of policy positions especially in agricultural policy. In an effort to compete with the LDP's popularity in rural districts, the DPJ pledged to provide all the farmers income compensation for further agricultural liberalization since the 2007 Upper-House election.

8. CGP supporters constitute 2.5% of our sample, and thus we are not able to test the effect of treatments on this group due to the small sample size.

9. Rengo, "Rengo no Jutenseisaku, 2010," http://www.jtuc-rengo.or.jp/kurashi/seisaku/index.html.

10. Japan Council of Metal Workers' Unions, "2010–2011 Seisaku/Seidokadai," http://www.imf-jc.or.jp/.

quality food. One of their main activities is farm-to-table delivery of agricultural produce and processed food. As of 2009, the local-level consumer cooperatives, which handle the food delivery service, boast 18 million members (Okumura 2010). The farm-to-table delivery service has fostered a collaborative relationship between the agricultural cooperatives and consumer cooperatives. Among our respondents, 12.6 percent of members of the agricultural cooperatives also belong to consumer cooperatives. Members of the consumer cooperatives are expected to become more protectionist with the viewing of the consumer treatment.

Table 8-1 summarizes the results for analysis using the data from the control group. It suggests that the only institutional mechanism that works to mobilize agricultural protectionism is respondents' membership in consumer cooperatives. This finding suggests that the coalition of losers between consumers and farmers forms at the level of organized interest groups as well. Respondents' party identity or membership in labor unions and agricultural cooperatives do not turn out to be significant. The results suggest that even with the retirement of older farmers and shrinking membership of agricultural cooperatives, agricultural protectionism might survive with emerging protectionist consumers, such as co-op members, who are sympathetic to domestic farmers.

Figure 8-4 summarizes the experimental results for institutional mechanisms for forging interests of consumers and farmers. The overall results lend very weak support to the functioning of institutional mechanisms. The *x*-axis is three experimental groups, and the *y*-axis is the percentage of respondents choosing protectionist responses regarding food import (increasing food import is "bad" or "very bad"). The producer treatment increases the opposition to food import among DPJ supporters by 16.3 percentage points, and this increase from the control group is statistically significant at 5 percent. The effect of producer treatment in increasing protectionism, however, is only statistically significant among the DPJ supporters. The LDP supporters do not increase their opposition to food import with the viewing of producer or consumer treatment. These results are against the conventional wisdom that the LDP supporters are more sympathetic to protecting farmers.

Consistent with our expectation, furthermore, the DPJ supporters decrease their opposition to food import by 10.4 percentage points with the viewing of the consumer treatment, although this difference is statistically significant only at 11 percent. Other respondents do not become more protectionist or free trading with the viewing of consumer treatment, including co-op members.[11]

11. The difference-in-means tests between consumer-treatment and control groups show the difference is statistically insignificant.

TABLE 8-1. Institutional mechanisms for a coalition of losers.

	(CONTROL GROUP ONLY)			
	(1:PROBIT)	(2:OPROBIT)	(3:PROBIT)	(4:OPROBIT)
Institutions				
LDP	–0.009	0.034		
	(0.05)	(0.18)		
DPJ			0.176	0.092
			(0.93)	(0.56)
Non-Partisan	0.190	0.113	0.265	0.140
	(1.26)	(0.89)	(1.68)*	(0.98)
Labor Union	0.115	–0.042	0.114	–0.043
	(0.55)	(0.24)	(0.55)	(0.25)
Agr Coop	0.097	0.139	0.089	0.138
	(0.35)	(0.52)	(0.32)	(0.51)
Consumer Coop	**0.308**	**0.296**	**0.322**	**0.303**
	(1.79)*	**(1.87)***	**(1.86)***	**(1.93)***
politics_index	0.043	0.013	0.043	0.014
	(0.92)	(0.35)	(0.93)	(0.36)
Controls				
Low Income	0.103	0.052	0.094	0.043
	(0.62)	(0.40)	(0.57)	(0.33)
High Income	0.277	0.087	0.277	0.087
	(1.60)	(0.60)	(1.61)	(0.60)
Female	0.075	–0.010	0.070	–0.015
	(0.52)	(0.08)	(0.49)	(0.11)
College	0.052	0.036	0.045	0.032
	(0.37)	(0.31)	(0.32)	(0.27)
Age over 50	0.140	0.006	0.147	0.013
	(0.94)	(0.05)	(0.99)	(0.10)
Married	0.217	0.309	0.212	0.304
	(1.26)	(2.19)**	(1.23)	(2.15)**
Have Kids	–0.167	–0.331	–0.169	–0.332
	(1.05)	(2.53)**	(1.06)	(2.52)**
Constant		–0.475		–0.542
		(2.29)**		(2.62)***
Observations	384	384	384	384

Notes: Robust z-statistics in parentheses.

* significant at 10%; ** significant at 5%; *** significant at 1%.

The dependent variable is a protectionist response (dummy variable one for increasing food import is "bad" or "very bad," and zero otherwise) for the food import question for models (1) and (3). Models (2) and (4) use a five-point ordered responses that increasing food import is "very good" (zero) to "very bad" (five). Cut points for models (2) and (4) not shown.

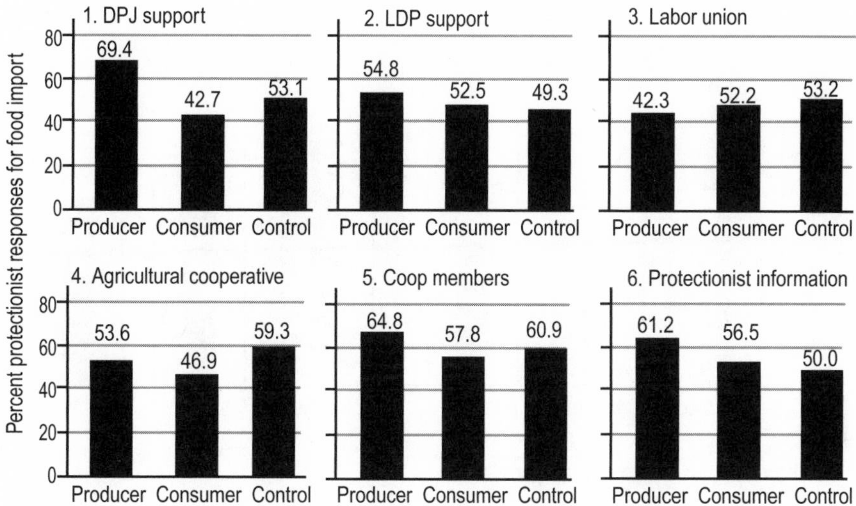

FIGURE 8-4. Institutional mechanisms: Only DPJ supporters become more protectionist with the viewing of producer treatment. Note: Respondents do not become more protectionist or free trading with the viewing of consumer treatment for any of the above subgroups (the difference-in-means tests between consumer treatment and control groups show the difference is statistically insignificant). The producer treatment increases opposition to food import only among DPJ supporters, and the 16.3 percentage point difference between producer treatment and the control groups is significant at 5%.

We further disaggregate the DPJ and the LDP supporters into three income groups (low, middle, and high) to identify which subgroups of respondents are likely to become more protectionist with the viewing of producer treatment. Figure 8-5 shows that only middle-income DPJ supporters become more protectionist with the producer treatment and this increase is statistically significant at 5 percent. The increase is quite dramatic, almost doubling the baseline proportion of protectionists from 37.8 percent to 73.5 percent. On the other hand, low- and high-income DPJ supporters become less protectionist with the consumer treatment, by 31.7 and 21.7 percentage points respectively. Among the three income groups of LDP supporters, however, neither producer or consumer treatments produce statistically significant differences from the control group. The results suggest that a coalition of losers emerges through the interaction between partisan identity and respondents' level of income, probably because some citizens support agricultural protectionism as a redistributive policy. A more systematic test of this claim, however, is a task for another paper.

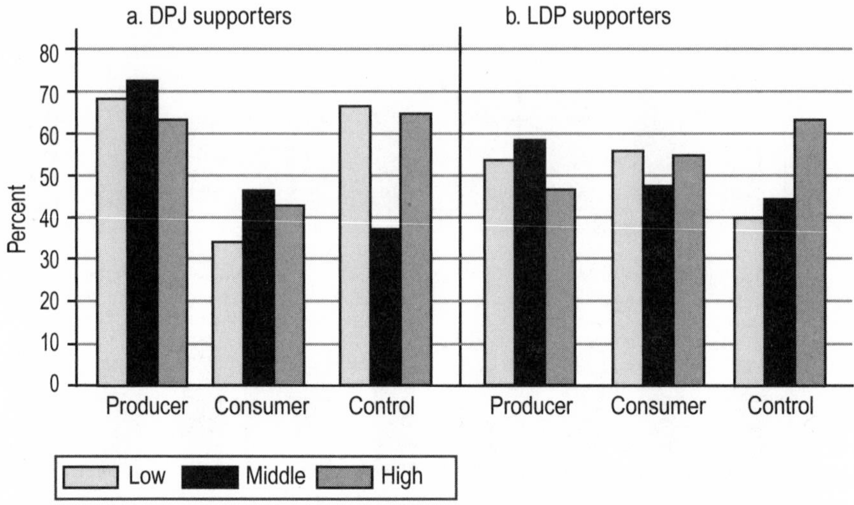

FIGURE 8-5. The effect of treatments on partisan respondents by income group. Note: The *x*-axis is three experimental groups, and the *y*-axis is % protectionist responses for food import question. A light-gray bar indicates the bottom 33% of income group, a black bar indicates the middle 33%, and a dark-gray bar indicates the top 33% income group. Difference-in-means tests suggest that the difference is statistically significant only for (1) producer treatment and the control groups for the middle-income DPJ supporters and (2) consumer treatment and the control groups for low- and high-income DPJ supporters.

Noninstitutional Mechanisms: Social Psychology

For noninstitutional mechanisms, we test two possibilities suggested by experimental studies on mass support for income redistribution: sympathy in the public for "poor" and "hardworking" people (in our case, farmers), and the public's projection of their own job insecurity onto a symbolic declining industry (agriculture).[12]

SYMPATHY

One possible explanation for the puzzle is that producer-priming provokes agricultural protectionism because of sympathy that consumers have for farmers: the dominant occupational image of farmers is that they work hard for low pay

12. We tested the effect of respondents' levels of exposure to protectionist discourse on food nationalism, safety and quality concerns, and food security and found no effects. See figure 8-2.

in a declining industry. Indeed, despite the fact that the household income of farmers has exceeded that of the average employee since 1975, sociologists have found that farmers' "occupational prestige scores," in which citizens have ranked the socio-economic prestige of more than 80 occupations since 1955, have been extremely stable and low throughout 1990s (Hara 1999; Moriguchi 2008; Naoi 1979).[13] Citizens might perceive agricultural protectionism as a redistributive policy (Calder 1988; Kabashima 1984).

Experimental studies also lend support to this intuition by showing that the level of respondents' income is only a partial predictor of attitudes. Survey experiments suggest that public support for redistribution increases when they sympathize with the recipients and feel that they "deserve" it due to bad luck and despite hard work (Harris-Lacewell, Imai, and Yamamoto 2009). Lu, Scheve, and Slaughter (2012) also demonstrate that altruism explains why low-skill and labor-intensive industries, such as agriculture, receive high levels of protection across countries with different factor endowments such as the United States and China.

To identify whether sympathy is a source of support for protectionism, we asked the respondents to choose three words that characterize their images and feelings toward producers and consumers before they received the visual stimuli.[14] Among twenty word choices, the top four producer images chosen were "responsibility" (48.3%), "sweat" (48.1%), "rural" (43%), and "factories" (36.7%). On the other hand, the top four consumer images are "money" (57.9%), "citizens" (46.0%), "information" (28.6%), and "urban" (27.7%). We test whether respondents who choose "sweat" as one of the three producer images (*Sweat*) are more likely to become supportive of protectionism with the viewing of producer treatment.[15]

The second operationalization of "sympathy" is the respondents' attitudes toward redistribution (*Redistribution*). We recode respondents' five-scale responses to a question, "What is your opinion about a policy to redistribute wealth

13. The occupational prestige score for farmers (*jisakunou*) is 51, 43, 45, 46 for years 1955, 1965, 1975, and 1995, respectively. These scores are comparable to taxi drivers, workers at train stations (*ekiin*), and hair stylists (*riyoushi*) but much lower than white-collar employees.

14. The question was worded as follows: "We call those who produce manufactured and agricultural products as well as those who provide service to customers "producers" (*seisansha*), and call those who purchase these goods and consume "consumers" (*shohisha*). Among the 20 words below, please each choose three images or feelings you have about producers and consumers: trust (*sekinin*), suspicion (*utagai*), urban (*tokai*), rural (*inaka*), money (*okane*), leisure (*goraku*), responsibility (*sekinin*), information (*jouhou*), weekdays (*heijitsu*), off days (*kyujitsu*), sweat (*ase*), factories (*koujou*), government (*seifu*), citizens (*shimin*), progressive (*kakushin*), conservative (*hoshu*), men (*dansei*), women (*josei*)."

15. Alternatively, we also include an interaction term between "sweat" and "rural." The results do not change.

from the rich to the poor using taxation and the social insurance system?" so that the higher the number, the higher the support for redistribution. We expect those who support a redistributive policy are more likely to become supportive of protectionism with the viewing of producer treatment.[16]

Likewise, we test whether respondents who have used a "farm-to-table" service to buy food directly from farmers in the past year are more likely to become supportive of protectionism with the viewing of producer treatment (*Farm-to-Table*).[17] Finally, we test a popular social network argument that consumers support agricultural protectionism because their family members are engaged in farming (*Social Network*). *Social Network* takes a value of one when a respondent has a family member or relatives who engage in farming, including part-time farming, and zero otherwise.

PROJECTION

The second hypothesis we test is that citizens might support agricultural protectionism because they project their own job insecurities onto a symbolic declining industry, agriculture. Projection is a concept developed in social psychology to understand how people make inferences about "others" using their own mental states as a benchmark (Ames 2004a, b). Daniel Ames develops "projection" and "stereotypes" as two inferential strategies people use to understand what others want. With lab experiments, he demonstrates that when the perceived similarity between self (a perceiver) and others (a target) is high, respondents are more likely to use projection as a tool to infer others' preferences. On the other hand, when the perceived similarity between self and others is low, respondents are more likely to use stereotypes as a mechanism of inference.

In the context of our research, we can infer from Ames's findings that when the level of respondents' perceived similarity with farmers is high, respondents are more likely to project their own mental states onto what farmers want regarding food imports (that is, protectionism). We derive three potential similarities that respondents might perceive with agricultural workers: declining industry, high job insecurity (difficulty finding a comparable job), and older age. In projection research, these perceived similarities are usually recorded before asking respondents to infer the targets' positions. We did not want to ask about respondents' perceived similarities with farmers before our question about food imports, however, based on our concern that the similarity questions could risk priming respondents to think about farmers. Thus, these potential similarities are derived from conven-

16. Alternatively, we also include an interaction term between "sweat" and "rural." The results do not change.

17. Alternatively, we also include an interaction term between "sweat" and "rural." The results do not change.

tional occupational images of farmers found in existing public opinion and social surveys (Hara 1999). We aim to test whether the subgroup of respondents who are likely to perceive potential similarity with agricultural workers shows higher opposition to food import interacting with the producer and consumer stimuli.

Thus, if the projection hypothesis holds, we expect to see respondents with high job insecurity or perceived risk of income loss in the future show higher support for agricultural protectionism with the viewing of the producer treatment. The subgroup of respondents *Difficulty Finding a Job* comprises those who answered "very difficult" or "difficult" to the following question: "If you were to quit your current job, do you believe it would be difficult to find a similar job that pays a comparable salary?"

Likewise, older respondents face a higher risk of income loss because of approaching retirement or increasing difficulty in finding their next job. Also, the average age of agricultural workers in Japan is 57.6 for all farmers and 64.6 for farmers whose main source of income is farming (Japanese Statistics Office 2008). *Age over 50* is a subgroup of respondents whose biological age is over 50 years old. We also test whether temporary workers and factory and construction workers are more likely to become supportive of protectionism with the viewing of the producer treatment.

Figure 8-6 summarizes the results for the five subgroups. No subgroup of respondents increases or decreases its opposition to food imports by viewing the consumer treatment. The producer treatment, on the other hand, increases opposition to food imports among respondents with high job insecurity, such as those who responded that once they quit a job, finding a comparable job will be "difficult" or "very difficult" (1); temporary workers (3); and those who are over 50 years old (4). The protectionist effect of the producer-treatment is substantial, ranging from 12.1 percentage point increase for respondents over age 50 to 17.6 percentage point increase for temporary workers. The difference-in-means tests show that these differences are statistically significant at 5 percent. The sympathy hypothesis also finds partial support. Those who have a family member or relatives who engage in farming, including part-time farming, become more protectionist by 15.5 percentage points with viewing the producer treatment.

These results suggest that a labor-farmer coalition emerges more through individual-level, social-psychological mechanisms than institutional mechanisms through political parties and organized interests. Thus we can infer that the new politics of hard times are less institutionalized and more diffused and transient than the previous ones that involved party realignment and organized lobbying.

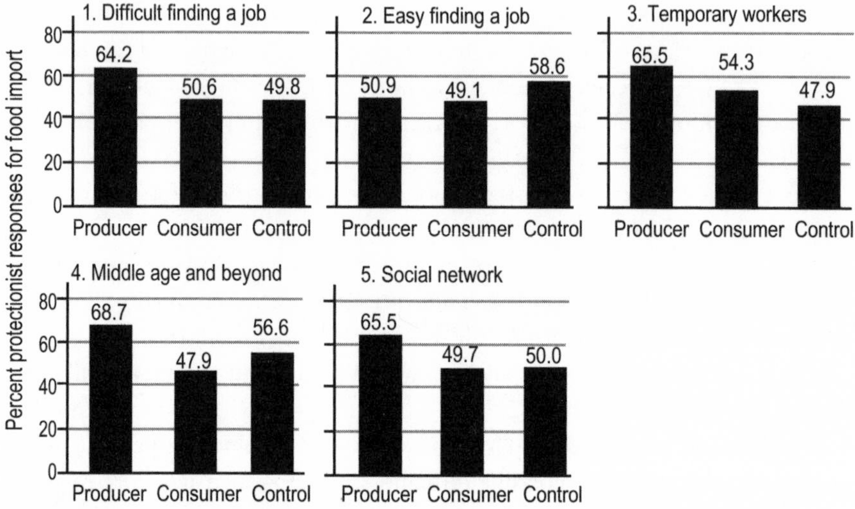

FIGURE 8-6. Social-psychological mechanisms: Projection hypothesis finds strong support. Note: The *x*-axis is three experimental groups. The bars and numbers indicate the proportion (%) of protectionist responses (increasing food import is "bad" or "very bad") for each group. The difference-in-means tests suggest that differences between producer treatment and the control groups are statistically significant at 5% for all five subgroups.

Discussion: From Cyber Space to the Real World

Although our findings in cyberspace suggest that photo images that have no obvious connection to political agents (such as political parties or bureaucracy) can change citizens' support for agricultural protectionism, in reality, political actors actively prime and frame citizens' minds. Two forms of framing have been particularly prevalent: the declining food self-sufficiency ratio and produce local–consume local movements. In 2008, the Ministry of Agriculture, Forestry, and Fishery set up its Food Action Nippon Program, which aims to educate consumers about the declining food self-sufficiency ratio in Japan and to encourage consumption of domestically produced foods.[18]

The ministry has extensively used popular media outlets to achieve this goal, such as buying full-page ads in daily newspapers; airing an "Eat Breakfast" cam-

18. Despite extensive media reports on consumer safety issues related to imported foods, especially from China, the Ministry of Agriculture, Forestry, and Fishery and legislators have been careful not to use this framing to mobilize consumer support for protectionism as it will upset Japanese food-processing and trading companies who invest and harvest in China.

a.

b.

FIGURE 8-7. (a) Cover of *Brutus* magazine's special issue "Let's All Farm." (b) Image used to explain Japan's food self-sufficiency ratio problem.

Source: Food Action Nippon program, http://syokuryo.jp/fan/japanese-problem.html.

paign ad on television in which they promote eating rice and bread made from rice powder; and funding and designing a special "Let's All Farm" issue of *Brutus* magazine, an art and fashion magazine targeted at young urban males. At the website of the Food Action Nippon program, the image of hardworking farmers, such as a farmer manually harvesting rice, has been extensively used to mobilize consumer support for protectionism, while in reality, machine harvesting is dominant (see fig. 8-7).

In 2005, the coalition government of the Liberal Democratic and Clean Government parties passed the Basic Food Education Law, which aims to educate school-age children about healthy eating habits, locally grown food, and cultural traditions of farming and eating in Japan.[19] The law explicitly promotes the consumption of locally grown food through school lunch programs at public schools. In addition to these framings by political actors, the private media also promotes consumption of domestically produced food through sensational reporting on food safety crises and the health benefits of domestically produced food.

In our survey, we have measured the levels of respondents' exposure to these protectionist discourses, such as whether a respondent has heard about or discussed issues such as the food self-sufficiency ratio, food safety crises such as the Chinese poisoned dumpling incident, or the produce local–consume local movements. The cumulative index we created as a measure of citizens' exposure to these discourses, however, turns out to have no systematic effect on their attitudes toward food imports. Furthermore, we identified no partisan effects on the levels of respondents' exposure to the protectionist discourse, again confirming that the role of institutions in aggregating individual preferences into the coalition of losers is weak and limited at best. The next step of our research should investigate how citizens' support for agricultural protectionism changes with the viewing of these real-world framings from political sources, such as the Ministry of Agriculture, Forestry and Fishery and the LDP.

Conclusion

High public support for agricultural protectionism in developed economies during the recession, combined with the lack of protectionist policy responses by elites, poses a puzzle. This chapter demonstrated that what gave rise to high consumer support for agricultural protectionism in Japan were not institutions, such as political parties and cooperation among organized interest groups, but rather the social psychology of individuals. In particular, making citizens think about their jobs mobilizes a "coalition of losers" between workers with high job insecurity and farmers. These sentiments did not translate into protectionist backlash precisely because they lacked institutional foundations to translate sentiments into politics.

To what extent are our findings generalizable beyond the Japanese case and the Great Recession? The survey data from a monthly Gallup poll on American citizens' preference for buying American cars corroborates with our finding. As Detroit struggled with a 41 percent decline in sales and the media extensively covered Obama's bailout program, the percentage of respondents who would

19. The legal text of the Basic Food Education Law is available at http://law.e-gov.go.jp/htmldata/H17/H17HO063.html.

"only consider buying foreign cars" decreased sharply from 15 percent at the onset of the recession (December 2008) to 6 percent in March of 2010. By contrast, percentage of respondents who would "only consider buying American cars" has increased from 30 percent to 37 percent.[20] Low-income respondents and youth (18–34 age group) were the two subgroups who showed a 10 percent point increase in their preference for American cars.

The finding is consistent with our projection findings in Japan and suggests that producer-priming might mobilize the coalition of losers supporting protectionism only during the hard times, while the consumer-priming might mobilize free trade coalitions during the good times. The decreasing role of sectoral and class-based organizations, the increasing importance of diffused and unorganized publics, and the expanding role of the media in shaping the minds of the public are ubiquitous among advanced industrialized nations.

We should not hasten, however, to conclude that our findings are broadly generalizable beyond the Japanese case. Relatively new two-party competition and policy debates, decentralized labor unions and weak left-leaning parties in Japan certainly did not favor the institutional hypothesis. French labor during the first globalization (1870–1914) used ideological conflicts between internationalism/Marxism and right-wing nationalism as an anchor to guide their preference formation toward capital liberalization. Such a strong ideological heuristic is not available to guide Japanese citizens today.

A promising line of future research is to examine how an economically unorganized public's attitudes toward trade and globalization are shaped through communication with elites, such as media and legislators.

Another promising line of research is to explore the external validity of our projection finding by bringing this experiment to racially and ethnically diverse societies such as the United States or India. Along the line of observational studies on racial diversity and income redistribution in U.S. cities (such as Alesina, Baqir, and Easterly 1999), we expect that the projection mechanism is more prevalent in homogenous societies (Japan) than in heterogeneous societies (the United States and India). Another possible line of research is to test the income threshold of our projection hypothesis by bringing this research to developing economies with a comparative advantage in agriculture.

---

20. Gallup Poll 2010, http://www.gallup.com/poll/126548/fewer-americans-set-buying-foreign-cars.aspx[0].

9

CRAFTING TRADE STRATEGY IN THE GREAT RECESSION

The Obama Administration and the Changing Political Economy of the United States

Peter Cowhey

As President Obama took office, many global leaders cautioned that the Great Recession could ignite a new era of protectionism. Pessimists warned that the new president's campaign had hedged on free trade and the Democratic Congress was skittish about trade. They said that the administration was not moving quickly to confirm the three pending free trade agreements (FTAs) with Panama, Colombia, and Korea or to conclude the World Trade Organization (WTO) Doha Round of negotiations. Moreover, the new Congress had attached "Buy America" provisions to the stimulus bill (Suominen 2009). Amid these fears, the Group of Twenty (G-20) met urgently to coordinate macroeconomic stimulus policies, fashion short-term relief packages, pledge to reject protectionism, and renew their vows to reinforce free trade by completing the Doha Round.

One year later (February 2010), the worst of the recession was over, although recovery in the wealthy economies remained slow. Trade wars had not broken out, the usual array of scattered protectionist acts notwithstanding. Despite sharp American disputes over currency exchange rates with China, reminiscent of clashes with Germany and Japan in the 1970s and 1980s, congressional legislation calling for retaliation was designed with an eye to WTO compliance and never moved on a fast track. Still, trade policy analysts worried that the delay by the United States, still the heart of the world trade system, on further liberalization—think of it as "preventive liberalization"—increased the odds that delayed protectionism could erupt.

I thank Michael Plouffe for his statistical analysis and research assistance.

The economic crisis had crystallized a "turning point" in the words of Kahler and Lake (introduction, this volume) in American political economy. Despite a massive economic shock, sustaining past trade liberalization was far less difficult than trade Cassandras feared. But efforts to liberalize further had become very challenging. As other papers in this volume (e.g., Kahler and Lake, Haggard) observe, the pace of globalization slowed after the recession, but it did not decline. The incentives for trade policy point to more selective integration to address emerging features of the world economy.

This chapter focuses on the height of the crisis, the first year of the Obama administration, to offer a two-fold explanation.[1] First, I argue that the political institutional structure and party politics of the United States combined to make protectionism very unlikely but required revisions of the pending FTAs. This political story ran parallel to changes in the structure of the American political economy, the "materialist" base for trade interests that Gourevitch's work on sectoral politics (1986) in the Great Depression and application of Stopler-Samuelson models of economic factors (Rogowski 1987; Ladewig 2006) have embedded in contemporary political economy models of trade. Second, I explain how these shifts both blunted protectionist incentives and altered the demand for further liberalization in ways not easily addressed by traditional trade agreements.

Why Didn't We Backslide to Protectionism?

This section argues that the institutional structure and party politics of the U.S. government made backsliding on trade commitments much harder than pessimists feared. But the academic literature often omits opportunity costs for legislation and "branding" by political parties that were critical considerations in Obama's trade strategy. These strongly influenced the approach to the FTAs inherited from the departing Bush administration.

Political Institutions and Open Markets

Although presidents try to pursue their vision of the public interest, they live in a world driven by elections and political institutional dynamics that shape how the pursuit of votes and the response to economic interests play out. So, any account of trade politics has to consider voter sentiment, and the life experiences that shape them. The following is a simple version of the story.

1. During this time the author served as a member of the leadership team for trade policy in the administration. References to internal discussions in the administration on policy come from the author's notes at the time. The opinions are those of the author.

Voter sentiment about trade had grown steadily gloomier. A trade deficit growing to $698 billion in 2008, a swelling trade deficit with China along with charges of exchange rate manipulation, and stories of worker dislocation dominated coverage of trade.[2] Unsurprisingly, a 2010 Pew survey showed that only about 35 percent of Americans supported free trade agreements.[3] Unfortunately, trade policy cannot easily reverse some of these "bad" political facts. The arithmetic of national income accounting shows that the trade deficit will remain large until we rebalance national savings, investment, and demand (including the federal deficit). The impasse on budget and tax policies makes this unlikely, thereby keeping the trade deficit large.

The second part of this chapter parses the changing economic incentives for trade policy in detail. But, as a first cut, in 2009 Republicans still interpreted their voters and business supporters as being more favorable to free markets and free trade than Democrats.[4] Rising manufacturing and employment in Red (predominantly Republican) states in the prior 20 years bolstered this conviction. Democrats more closely identified with unions and many of their House members were particularly ardent on issues concerning manufacturing. Although U.S. manufacturing output rose steadily from 1990 through 2008, and the United States topped the world with the largest manufacturing output in 2008 (Manufacturing Institute 2009), employment plunged and the trade deficit in manufacturing grew steadily, peaking at 4.3 percent of gross domestic product (GDP) in 2005 before receding.[5] This record posed a problem for the trade policy of any Democratic president. Moreover, the Democratic electoral coalition also features voters with reservations about free markets, such as environmentalists (Weller 2009).

Still, the Democratic coalition is not tilted one-sidedly against trade. The Democrats have constituents in unionized firms that win from trade (e.g., chemicals, aerospace) and major support in knowledge-intensive industries (such as technology and finance) that favor trade. Thus, Democrats favor liberalization

---

2. The deficit in trade in goods was $834 billion and the surplus in services was $135 billion (Bureau of Economic Analysis [BEA] 2010, numbers rounded).

3. The October 2010 Pew People and the Press Survey reports that 44% of Americans believe that FTAs and WTO dispute settlement are harmful for the United States; this contrasts with relatively high percentages of respondents preferring increased trade with key partners. Traditional Republicans are more sympathetic to trade than Tea Party sympathizers. Pew Research Center, Global Attitudes Project, 2010, http://pewglobal.org/files/pdf/Pew-Global-Attitudes-Spring-2010-Report.pdf.

4. Weller (2009) and Fordham (2008) parse the relative weights of ideology and party versus economic interests in congressional voting.

5. In 2008, the United States had about 21% of world manufacturing output. Manufacturing output in 2008 was about 65% larger than in 1990 (according to OECD estimates). But Helper, Krueger, and Wial (2012) show that manufacturing employment had plummeted in the George W. Bush presidency at a rate far beyond explanations based on rising productivity or high wages. There was an employment shock in these industries, particularly in the unionized North.

targeted especially toward their constituent winners from trade while trying to aid losers from trade liberalization through labor policy, such as the Trade Adjustment Assistance Act of early 2009. Similarly, Democrats seek "green-friendly" features for trade agreements.

Institutional analysis of American politics shows how voter sentiment and economic interests intersect with decision making and political party dynamics. The United States has a divided government with power split between the executive and legislative branches. It also has a large number of veto points when making policy (Milner and Rosendorf 1997b; Cox and McCubbins 2005). One effect of divided government on the Obama administration's trade policy was straightforward. Multiple veto points, including the division between the president and Congress, made the rollback of existing free trade agreements very hard. The bigger question was how to move new trade agreements forward, as the discussion of the three pending FTAs in 2009 will show.

A head count of probable votes showed why protectionist legislation was unlikely. The sponsorship of the Michael Michaud (D-ME) trade bill was a good proxy for the maximum size of the anti–free trade bloc in the House in the 111th Congress; its co-sponsorship had a slender majority of the Democratic caucus (with very few Republican backers). Of course, sponsorship was only a symbolic act for some who wavered on trade because the members knew the bill would fail. But the bloc of strong trade skeptics ran at around 90 to 100 Democratic members.[6] (The leaders and members of the key committee on trade, Ways and Means, were notably not co-sponsors.) In contrast, the proportion of senators against trade was much smaller, in part because larger constituencies cancel out some particularistic dynamics of individual districts. But the extreme division within the Democratic caucus was striking. Democratic senators who firmly or likely leaned toward free trade totaled 26 to 29. The number firmly or likely against was 21. And the number where the track record was too limited (or the prior behavior was very mixed) numbered 10 to 13 votes. Only 3 Republican senators clearly opposed or were skeptical of trade deals. Thus, there was a potential super-majority for trade, if a sizeable majority of the Democrats "leaning" favorably toward trade and some of the "unknowns" came around; there was certainly a simple majority. Clearly, there was a coalition that could block passage or sustain a certain presidential veto of a bill that would roll back existing trade agreements. Indeed, a potential majority existed to approve new trade agreements, but the political opportunity cost for a Democratic president was steep.

A test of this logic came in the first weeks of the Obama administration when House skeptics on trade attached a "Buy America" requirement for all

6. I have used estimates of veteran vote counters in the private sector, not Executive Branch analysts.

procurement done under the massive stimulus bill. However, the administration successfully amended the bill in the Senate to say that the Buy America requirement could not override U.S. obligations on procurement under the WTO. In short, it reaffirmed trade policy commitments. Regrettably, this trade victory got lost when Canada argued loudly that the bill was still unfair because stimulus spending funneled through the states was not covered under Canada's rights to market access. Countries eager to pressure the United States into agreeing to the Doha WTO package used this complaint as proof of U.S. susceptibility to protectionism. However, Canada only lacked these rights because it had previously refused U.S. firms reciprocal access to its provincial markets. (In 2010, Canada and the United States agreed to reciprocal market opening.)

A massive move to protectionism by other countries might have changed American political dynamics, but the administration did not expect this. True, trade volumes fell dramatically, about a 27 percent decline in U.S. exports in 2009, but this was a macroeconomic problem. Everywhere, firms and consumers postponed purchases of consumer durables and investment goods (Baldwin 2009). Further, after prices dropped in 2008, trade in food, fuel, and raw materials collapsed, leading to a large drop in both volumes and value traded. This decline in trade was not caused by the type of protectionism associated with the Great Depression, which resulted from a second-best macroeconomic policy that adhered to the gold standard to bolster the domestic economy (Eichengreen and Irwin 2009). The stimulus measures endorsed by the G-20 fended off recourse to protectionism. Monitoring of the G-20, the key nations in the world economy, by the WTO and the Office of the U.S. Trade Representative (USTR) uncovered no rising wave of protectionism.[7] Furthermore, the Council of Economic Advisers expected that, as the stimulus and financial stabilization defused the crisis, exports would lead U.S. growth and job creation. So, at worst, the White House just had to hold the line on trade policy until exports rebounded.

The Politics of the Free Trade Agreements

New administrations wrestle with legacy legislative agendas. The Bush administration left three FTAs pending before Congress. As the world fretted over the trade intentions of the United States, leaders in the G-20 and international organizations (such as the WTO) argued that the crisis made it urgent for the Obama adminis-

7. According to the G-20 endorsed monitoring exercise, one hundred seventy-nine trade restricting measures were implemented by G-20 members. However, these measures were not necessarily protectionist by design; many were side products of bailouts, especially of the financial sector. The number of protectionist measures following the Great Recession was slightly higher than in normal years (Evenett 2009).

tration to conclude these trade deals promptly as an inoculation against a possible aftershock of protectionism during a slow world recovery. Republicans argued that the president could easily move the pacts forward; Democrats controlled both Houses and Republicans backed the FTAs. This common attitude, caught precisely in the editorial pages of the *New York Times* (July 6, 2010, A18), had minimal patience for President Obama's decision that the FTAs should only go to Congress after amending them to address his concerns raised during the campaign.

There were, to be sure, debates within the White House about the merits of when to move on the FTAs. But Obama's approach reflected the political logic of divided government. Divided government can cut both ways when a president chooses to move off the status quo to embrace more trade liberalization. The divided-government literature rightly notes that a pro-trade president can use a pro-trade congressional opposition party to enact trade legislation over his own reluctant congressional party (Karol 2000). However, this ploy has significant political opportunity costs. This analysis will capture the legislative costs by analyzing choices about "issue bundling" and "clock management." It analyzes national political costs by examining "brand management" by "reframing" and "adjusting" policy.

The large number of FTAs under President Bush had left Washington exhausted by the ratification fights, but firms strongly pressed for the pending FTAs for three reasons. First, in what were still asymmetric negotiations (given the scale of the U.S. market), the United States had leverage to push on some pinpointed tariff, nontariff barrier (NTB), intellectual property (IP), and service issues that were of consequence to key producer groups (Government Accounting Office [GAO] 2009). Even if the total size of the national market was small, specific business units were enthusiastic for the smaller pacts. Second, the "laboratory of states" logic, experiments on a decentralized basis as models for grand bargains, still has appeal. Trade agreements are about both bargaining and creating policy options to resolve mutual problems. The Korean FTA, for example, has innovative market commitments on services that can be built upon in WTO or other regional FTAs. Third, business focuses on defensive interests. American firms fear losing advantages to the proliferation of FTAs by other countries and prefer to operate under an American FTA where their influence on implementation is greatest.

When examining the FTAs of the Bush administration, three political structural constraints—the treatment of agriculture, labor and environment provisions, and opportunities for key American firms who are critical to advocating trade pacts—mattered greatly. The catch phrase for these constraints is that FTAs must be "comprehensive high-standard" agreements. (In contrast, many countries brush over tough issues lightly to complete a deal.)

First, despite its shrinking role in the U.S. economic output, agriculture is ubiquitous. More importantly, for a wealthy country, U.S. agriculture is unusually dependent on exports—almost one-quarter of its revenues flows from exports. Agriculture has to be satisfied because no winning coalition for trade is possible without the votes of farm and ranch state senators from both parties (Gawande and Hoekman 2006). Therefore, FTAs required major agriculture features. The three FTAs did well on this score except for Korean barriers to some American beef products, a key concern of Senator Baucus (D-MT), the chair of the Senate Finance Committee that had jurisdiction over trade.

Second, to sway the Democratic caucus, Obama had to reduce opposition from labor and environmental groups.[8] The pressure was to "upgrade" the labor and environment provisions of the "May 10th" bipartisan, bicameral agreement that propelled the passage of the U.S.-Peru FTA in 2007, a set of delicate compromises to win enough Democratic support to pass the Peru FTA. Any revision had to be done carefully, or the Republicans would revolt. In general, progress on issues of value to environmental organizations was easier to demonstrate. The "achievable" regarding labor provisions did little to ameliorate the distress of U.S. organized labor directly, although it might help pro-union groups in the other country (Hafner-Burton 2005). The biggest problem for the FTAs involved the security of labor organizers in Colombia.

For a Democratic president, especially one who had helped to organize unemployed auto workers, the courting of business support for trade pacts is mixed with special attention to opportunities for market gains for unionized firms. Firms like Caterpillar fit the bill and were eager to support the FTAs. But, as will be explained, Ford, Chrysler, and their unions adamantly opposed the Korea FTA as inherited from President Bush.

All this said, the Obama White House might have lightly tweaked the pending FTAs in 2009 to provide a Democratic spin and then used Republican support to pass the pending FTAs and build further momentum for free trade. Why didn't this occur?

Divided-government strategy posed difficult political opportunity costs for the Obama administration. Republicans were willing to support trade deals, but in the context of the larger legislative gridlock, this support was a tricky gift. Once the president committed to pushing for a specific free trade vote, thus raising the political stakes for the White House,[9] would the Republicans sud-

8. The pressure on FTAs to deal with labor was even greater because Doha could not address the issue. President Clinton's unexpected, last-second decision to push a labor agenda at the WTO Seattle ministerial, partly to protect Vice President Gore's electoral flanks on trade, precipitated a diplomatic backlash that killed labor as a Doha issue (Blustein 2009).

9. Incumbent administrations fear that they are much weakened if they start a major vote on foreign economic policy and then lose. A major push on a trade agreement is a risky undertaking.

denly put conditions on their support tied to other bills (e.g., health care)? Further, given the need to pass most domestic legislation only with Democratic votes, what would be the impact of a divisive trade debate on the president's domestic agenda? Thus the legislative opportunity costs involved calculations about "managing the legislative clock" and how much "bundling" of bills was possible.

To understand the intertwining logics of clock management and bundling, consider the following questions: Was it better to take up a relatively innocuous FTA (say the approval of the Panama FTA) early on to establish the principle that trade bills could be passed (thus showing the White House could succeed and would fight), thereby invigorating pro-trade advocates among Democrats?[10] Or was it better to wait on all trade bills until health care passed? And given that each trade bill would heighten legislative rancor, multiple bills could crowd out the domestic legislative calendar and also impede the administration's own trade initiatives later on. So, was it possible to bundle the FTAs for approval, and then just shoot for one legislative window to consider them as a group? Did such a window really exist? (In 2009, some argued that December 2010 after mid-terms was the window.) But, of course, bundling would intensify the debate. The administration continually revisited the questions of timing and bundling.

Trade negotiators recognize that diplomacy matters in domestic ratification games (Putnam 1988; Milner and Rosendorff 1997a; Pahre 2006). President Obama's concerns about the FTAs meant negotiations before the FTA could go forward. Panama proved trickier than expected, but still was quickly manageable. The issue tied to Colombia (murders of labor leaders that could negate the commitments on labor rights made in the FTA) required creative solutions to address the problem. (Colombia also hesitated on difficult reforms until it knew the FTA would go up for approval.) The Korea issue was primarily access to the auto vehicle (and parts) market (with secondary issues on beef products); the issue was how to craft side agreements that would address the remaining wariness of Detroit about market access on autos.[11] A side agreement with Korea might convince the companies and the United Automobile Workers (UAW) that the worst risks of the pact for Korean expansion in the United States had been mitigated, and significant export opportunities had opened up. It took nearly a

10. Some saw this option as calling the bluff of Democrats who wanted it both ways (not to oppose trade in a final vote but wanting to engage in rhetoric and symbolic complaints against trade). If members of Congress finally have to reveal their bottom line, it reduces posturing.

11. Detroit is a surrogate for a combined management-union attack on the FTA. GM was silent because of its joint venture with Daewoo and the bailout. Chrysler and Ford bitterly opposed the FTA because the provisions would accelerate lower tariffs for Korean vehicles with higher profit margins while perhaps not reducing the costs of complying with Korean vehicle regulations sufficiently to make an entry into Korea's market economically feasible.

year to convince Korea that a fresh solution was necessary, and yet another year to negotiate a compromise.

Domestic political considerations constantly shifted because the bitter politics of health care consumed all of 2009, thus slowing all initiatives. Perhaps health care might be dismissed as a quirky anomaly for models of divided government. But, if not health care, it could have been climate and energy or financial reform. The degree of cleavages and the ambition of the broader legislative agenda change the risks and rewards of "grand bargains" on trade for the White House. Just as importantly, if national politics are about building coalitions and "brand identities," then political strategy and governing are about how to meld good policy, economic interests, and political considerations.

The Obama administration sought to lower the heat from Democratic congressional opponents so that the aftermath of trade votes was less painful. The White House had to be particularly sensitive to union concerns. Labor has increased its favoritism in campaign contributions toward Democratic members of the House since 1990, and business has not offset this giving (with the notable exception of the influential Ways and Means Committee). This proves nothing about the specific reasons behind members' trade votes, but it underscores Washington's "folk wisdom" that the influence of organized labor over the House Democratic Caucus is potent. Perhaps most interesting, the greater the fraction of a district's employment in exporting industries, the greater that organized labor contributions to that district's representative will be.[12] This pattern may offset some leaning toward more trade liberalization by those members.

Still, the Democratic Party needs to appeal to workers outside the unions in the long run to succeed electorally (Mansfield and Mutz 2009). Under Clinton, the technology boom helped to create full employment and high growth with rising wages. In 2009, there was no similar uplift during the jobs downturn. By 2010, the president opted to craft a story around export-led growth's impact on jobs as part of an economic strategy to "brand" trade policy through the tools of reframing and adjusting.

Presidents routinely "brand" trade pacts by "reframing" them as part of national security goals. But in 2009, reframing meant redefining trade strategy as part of a new economic strategy tied to jobs. Emphasizing a goal of doubling exports, and the two million jobs supported by more exports, would frame trade

12. These observations are based on statistical analysis of campaign contributions and a dataset constructed by Christopher Magee. It contains five major trade bills, incorporating the North American Free Trade Agreement (NAFTA) and the Central America Free Trade Agreement (CAFTA) (1993 and 2005), and three fast-track bills (1991, 1998, and 2001). It also includes a measure for a district's percentage of workers in exporting firms. Contributions to members of the House of Representatives in the preceding elections are linked to their votes on trade bills at the district level.

agreements as part of an export strategy.[13] The growing concentration of trade in multinational corporate channels, which I discuss later, has reinforced the tendency in Democratic circles to treat trade as a game of multinational giants, not "grassroots" American firms. As a result, the White House also focused on export promotion for small- or medium-sized enterprises (SMEs). If SMEs could participate directly in expanded exports, it would create a new "grassroots" story on trade, an effort to change the information "framing" U.S. trade policy.[14]

"Adjusting" meant that the president would inject some special Democratic features into trade initiatives. More attention to environmental considerations in trade pacts was one candidate. Continual work on labor rights in FTAs and labor training policies at home was another (Tyson 2009). A practical expansion of labor rights by revising the Colombia FTA to include new commitments on protecting labor organizers (for example, by expanding judicial enforcement resources) took until 2011. And adjusting also had to address popular concerns in both parties that other countries did not play by the trade rules. Congress always suspects that the executive branch would sacrifice trade enforcement for other foreign policy priorities. Mistrust on enforcement had become epic in the Democratic caucus. The administration had to show that it would take on hard challenges, especially on China, in greater numbers. This topic became a major focus starting in 2009 and grew into a feature of the 2012 State of the Union Address.

It took until July 2010 for the administration to be close to completing a side deal on new features for the U.S.-Korea agreement. It was also clear by then that legislative opportunity costs would be low—the next Congress would feature few major legislative initiatives from the White House, so trade was a possible bipartisan spotlight feature. (There was the added boost of growing congressional concern over North Korea and China.) The president set the goal of resolving final issues on the pact by the Seoul G-20 meeting in November 2010. The eventual agreement, focused primarily on a side agreement involving the implementation of the auto provisions of the FTA, won support from both the companies and the UAW (to the displeasure of other unions) (Greenhouse 2010).[15] The approval of this agreement demonstrated that a key FTA could be "branded" as pro-manufacturing and pro-jobs. Once Korea fell into place, it was easy to bundle the other two pacts and send the three up for a successful Senate vote (83 in favor) backed by many Democratic senators.

13. The president's 2010 State of the Union address crystallized this strategy.

14. The key was changing the story about jobs and workers at the local level. Hiscox (2006) discusses framing and voter attitudes toward trade.

15. The complex side deal on autos (and smaller adjustments on beef and pork that won support of the United Food and Commercial Workers) demonstrated the administration's negotiating and political skills but also illustrated the hurdles of winning union support. Rep. Sander Levin (D-MI), the chair of Ways and Means, was a key player in the process.

What's Next?

Turning points spur choices about both continuities and new directions. If the established base of trade liberalization is largely secure, what new ground can be broken? Many trade policy analysts consider the old and the new to be inseparable because they believe that "preventive liberalization," a steady diet of trade initiatives to keep political economic momentum for trade, is essential. This section argues that a closer parsing of the changing structure of U.S. economic interests in trade gives important clues about which initiatives are feasible. It will apply these insights to the Doha WTO talks and the Trans-Pacific Partnership (TPP) negotiations.

Economic Incentives for Trade Policy

While the press dwelled on import competition as the cause of major disruptions of long-established U.S. industries, the U.S. economy had changed in ways that Stolper-Samuelson models of trade politics do not fully illuminate.[16] Beginning in the WTO Uruguay Round (concluded in 1994), the range of issues on the trade agenda grew dramatically, including services, investment, and intellectual property. This pressure to chart new territory in trade policy intensified as the fundamentals of global production changed. And the shift in the center of economic growth to big emerging markets further drove changes in the policies and politics of American trade (Prasad and Kose 2010). This discussion reviews the detailed implications for the Obama White House.[17] Particularly important were the following:

1. Changes in who trades
2. Blurring of sector winners and losers
3. Knowledge economy demands on trade liberalization
4. Role of organized labor in the economy

The first significant shift in trade and manufacturing is its growing reliance on multinational corporations. Today, about 60 percent of U.S. imports and exports flow through the internal channels of multinational corporations (either U.S. or foreign based). Moreover, as foreign direct investment (FDI) into the United States has risen, it has reshaped U.S. manufacturing exports. In 2007,

---

16. To be sure, the models predict some of these changes. The United States exports much more, for example, in skills (capital) intensive products, as the factors model predicts (Bernard et al. 2007; Bernard, Jenson, and Schott 2009).

17. I omit the work on strategic trade theory that first captured the effects of imperfect competition because it played a large role in trade policy in the 1980s.

more than one in three U.S. manufacturing export dollars was earned by a foreign controlled plant in the United States ($370 billion of $900 billion) (Manufacturing Institute 2009). FDI was particularly important for some industries. These multinational investors (like American multinationals), along with their regional communities and supply chains, are usually a force for trade liberalization even in sectors undergoing dramatic changes in winners and losers.

A sharp concentration of who trades, even at the SME level, also occurred. Only about 18 percent of manufacturing firms export. Of these, 22,000 firms account for over 90 percent of U.S. manufactured goods' trade. Firm-specific attributes matter greatly for participation and success in trade. The transaction costs (and risks) of entering and servicing foreign markets remain significant even though tariff levels have dropped. Only a small fraction of firms surmount them, and an even smaller fraction dominates trade flows.

Even among SMEs, the firms engaged in trade are bigger (in revenue and employment) and more productive than their rivals in the same industry who do not trade; their revenues grow faster, they add more jobs, and they are more profitable than firms that do not trade. Given their low engagement in trade, but their high returns when they trade, SMEs constitute a relatively untapped constituency for trade policy (U.S. International Trade Commission [USITC] 2010). Moreover, standard trade models do not capture a major impact from trade; capital and labor shift to the more efficient trading firms at the expense of less efficient firms in the same industry. In effect, trade bolsters overall American productivity (Bernard et al. 2007; Bernard, Jenson, and Schott 2009).

The second impact on trade politics from the reorganization of the U.S. economy is the blurring of winners and losers by sector. To be sure, some sectors still clearly win and lose, but navigating splits within industries are now much more central to trade policy dynamics, and there is now a concentrated set of winners (both large and small firms) among exporting companies who can be organized as easily as firms facing import competition. This blurring weakens the classic axiom that it is easier to organize concentrated pools of losers than diffuse pools of winners from trade liberalization.

The changing composition of trade flows and the firms engaging in trade further blunt traditional dynamics of "winners and losers."[18] Rising intra-industry trade is particularly vital. Horizontal industry differentiation looms large in the trade picture because of the impacts of economies of scale, lower logistics costs, and product differentiation. Grossman and Rossi-Hansberg (2006) have dubbed

18. Market winners with growing resources for political action do not necessarily dominate politically. Workers are voters. Most manufacturing employees do not work for firms that depend directly on exports (USITC 2010). Moreover, even in factor-abundant industries, firms with lower productivity may lose and become protectionist.

this "trade in tasks" (the supply chain phenomenon). The political economy consequence is that firms can prosper (faster productivity growth and higher returns) by sharper specialization. Therefore, even while the prospects for individual sectors may shift, "winner takes all" shifts matter less because specialist firms can prosper in losing sectors, and sectors themselves may restructure, splinter, and change course with surprising volatility.

Consider the situation in manufacturing where, as a first approximation, there is both growth and dislocation. U.S. manufacturing output kept growing and remained diversified—it is more than aerospace and military—but the composition of manufacturing changed significantly. The biggest losers were in the print and paper industry and in the textile and apparel industry. The leaders, constituting 44 percent of manufacturing GDP in 2007, were computers and electronics, plastics and chemicals, food products, and fabricated metal products (Manufacturing Institute 2009). But total manufacturing jobs declined sharply from 1990 to 2008, while nonmanufacturing civilian employment grew substantially (Bureau of Labor Statistics [BLS] 2010; Helper, Krueger and Wial 2012).

Manufacturing also shifted away from the Midwest and the Northeast to the West Coast and the Southeast. This shift occurred partly because of the rise of FDI from countries outside of Europe. The newer FDI has sought out non-union areas for installing plants and design centers.[19] Another reason was that knowledge-intensive industries were especially associated with the West Coast and parts of the Southeast (Texas and North Carolina).

Even as winners and losers blurred and exporters consolidated, a third major shift in the U.S. economy, the growth of the knowledge economy, further changed the political economy of trade. The role of knowledge, understood as a good with nonrivalry in supply but potential excludability, has grown dramatically in the modern economy. Drawing on Paul Romer's work (Romer 1990), Warsh (2006) pithily summarized the shift as "people-ideas-things" replacing "land-labor-capital" as our factors of production. However summarized, the U.S. economy is increasingly driven by knowledge inputs.

Predictions about which industries would favor protectionism were blurred by the splits between more or less product or knowledge sophistication among firms even in traditional industries. Thus, when the 2009 debate over the surging imports of low-cost Chinese tires in the United States occurred, the major American tire manufacturers were silent. Their unions opposed the imports, but these

19. While the Big Three's Midwest auto production shrank, FDI-fueled production of foreign rivals swelled, especially in the non-union Southeast. (Kia and Hyundai are the latest to join the ranks of major foreign producers with plants in Alabama and Georgia.) This import-substituting FDI has not ameliorated trade tensions as much as some (Goodman, Spar, and Yoffie 1996) predicted because of the politics of locational decisions for FDI and because displaced American workers are less mobile than once supposed (Autor, Dorn, and Hanson 2011).

firms were already irreversibly exiting the market's low end to more capital- and technology-intensive tires.[20] The shift in industrial composition and the move to higher-value-added products underscore the reasons why manufacturers, while sensitive to tariffs, focus even more on intellectual property, nontariff barriers, and rights concerning FDI.

Knowledge also had implications for the increasing sophistication and globalization of the services industry. In 2008, about 25 percent of U.S. trade was in services, and the United States ran a trade surplus in services. Although the service sector remains predominantly local, it is significant when the market leaders in 75 percent of the U.S. GDP (and the majority of private-sector jobs in the United States) become tied to the global economy. The big service firms became major supporters of open U.S. trade policies. Moreover, their expansion is partly intertwined with the expansion of the "trade in tasks," such as FedEx and IBM's logistics and information services.

The sale of high-end hardware is linked with the provision of services, leading to new forms of trade disputes. For example, China is pursuing a renewed industrial policy to upgrade its global position in advanced technology markets, using a full spectrum of tools. They range from purchasing policies of state-owned enterprises through manipulating technology standards, failing to protect intellectual property, and setting "milieu" policies that work against foreign-owned service firms, such as Internet service providers, allied to foreign hardware products.[21]

Even as changes in what, who, and how America produces for world markets influences trade strategy, no Democratic White House can ignore transformations in the American labor market and the role of unions in the economy. Although politicians respond to short-term electoral concerns, presidents deal with the bigger shifts that go beyond the immediate claims of interest groups. The issues involving labor epitomize these complexities. The role of labor in the American economy was the fourth big issue confronting the political economy of trade.

One clue to the complexity is the impact of productivity gains that occur as resources shift to more efficient firms in the same industry. Rises in productivity can even raise the real income of labor (the scarce factor of production in Stolper-Samuelson models) by driving down the price of goods (Bernard et al. 2007, 115). Thus, the distributional politics between abundant and scarce factors could be, ceteris paribus, less extreme than in the past. But these changes became entangled in the changing composition of the workforce.

---

20. Some major U.S. tire producers are also foreign owned.
21. A milieu policy may have other purposes, such as censorship, but also harms foreign firms.

This shift in the unionization of the workforce and the composition of manufacturing (by industry, by region, and by skill mix) has altered the politics of labor and trade. Overall, most private-sector employees are not unionized. Union manufacturing jobs are only about 12 percent of total manufacturing jobs (BLS 2010). Indeed, unionization has shifted decisively to the private services sector and government (BLS 2010). Government unions place a lower priority on trade policy, and the services industry unions may be a "jump ball" on trade policy in the long run. Teamsters vehemently oppose opening U.S. trucking to other NAFTA nations. But such unionized firms as Las Vegas hotels, telecommunications carriers, UPS, and United Airlines may benefit from services liberalization. Interestingly, while incomes in traded professional services (e.g., law) tend to be higher, some polling indicates that these professionals are skeptical about free trade.[22]

In an era of continuous restructuring of traditional manufacturing industries, including a growing share of production in non-unionized plants, the politics of trade among industrial unions might change as some industries go through deep restructuring with new union contracts aligned with the global strategies of American multinational exporters, as painfully happened in 2009 in the auto industry. Furthermore, regional variations matter for politics. In the Midwest, the decline in traditional manufacturing led to the painful accounts of swapping GM jobs for Walmart jobs, the concern of many Midwest Democratic politicians. In the Southeast, the rise of non-union auto plants created good jobs, but without the pay premium once enjoyed in GM plants. One popular story, told by the region's Republicans, was the following: Toyota creates decent jobs and Walmart's low prices (enabled by imported goods) make the standard of living associated with the jobs even better.

These shifts have shown up in national political strategies. The Republican Party base moved strongly to the Southeast, parts of the Great Plains, and the Mountain states featuring non-unionized manufacturing (often through FDI) and agriculture. In the core Blue (predominantly Democratic) states, the Democratic Party was split between its union wing and the technology and high-end services faction of the party.[23] Both parties want to be known as the champions of growth and innovation. It is not in the political cards to abandon rapidly expanding industries and their regional communities because of traditional constituencies. A winning trade strategy has to address issues about nontariff

22. They may worry that globalization threatens their professions. For example, higher manufacturing productivity is partly the result of outsourcing lower-end service jobs tied to manufacturing (Feenstra and Hanson 2003; Slaughter and Scheve 2004; Chase 2008).

23. The two largest exporters are Texas and California—one state is predominantly Republican and predominantly pro-trade while the other is predominantly Democratic and has a split senatorial and House Democratic delegation on trade.

barriers, intellectual property protection, and trade implications of domestic regulatory policies on services, not just tariffs. It also has to deliver on the highest growth markets for these products and services, Asia and the big emerging markets. Democratic trade deals also need to show gains for the unionized manufacturers who were succeeding (such as chemicals).

The realities of the American political economy of 2009 posed difficult issues for trade policy. The next two sections explain why they weighed heavily against traditional WTO trade rounds and in favor of new FTAs in the Asia-Pacific region.

Doha and the Changing Structure of the American Economy

As the Obama administration looked past the FTAs, the question was what could be done next to strengthen the global trade system? Any discussion had to consider the prospects for action at the WTO, the clearest embodiment of the multilateral trading system and to some economists (Bhagwati 2009) the far superior alternative for trade liberalization. No one in the Obama team doubted that the WTO was valuable. Its past comprehensive "rounds" produced big economic benefits and, in theory, could yield further big gains. But could the WTO Doha Round deliver what is valuable to organized interests who favor free trade?[24]

The staunchest supporters of the WTO process argued that it would only take the president standing firm to overcome divisions on trade and carry the day for a Doha agreement. Republican support, reinforced by a massive campaign by business, would be the trump card. (The head of the WTO, Pascal Lamy, also privately and vigorously argued this.) However, Obama's trade team soon discovered minimal business support. The lengthy Doha process had eroded faith in its prospects, but all recent WTO rounds were lengthy. The key issue was skepticism about Doha's benefits, symbolized by the opposition of the National Association of Manufacturers, the American Farm Bureau, and the Coalition of Service Industries.

The problems of Doha emerged from its terms for negotiation, the changes in global power during the round, and the fit with the big opportunities for American growth through trade liberalization.

In order to salvage the launch of the Doha Round, and to bolster global solidarity after 9/11, the United States agreed to cast Doha as a "development round" to show developing countries that trade could benefit them significantly. As a

24. The Peterson Institute calculated the gains from WTO rounds as having enriched the U.S. GDP by about 9%. And it estimated that an elimination of all remaining trade barriers would add about another 4 to 5% to GDP, a big win if achievable (Bradford, Grieco, and Hufbauer 2006).

result, reciprocal market opening was downgraded because the round was supposed to be asymmetrical (Collier 2006; Erixon 2008; Blustein 2009). This approach ignored a key political strength of the WTO process: its emphasis on reciprocal opening catalyzed coalitions of exporters in each member country to support expansive trade deals in order to achieve new market access. Asymmetrical access immediately dampened this political benefit in the United States.[25]

Agriculture reform was set as a top priority, while many new issues pertinent to the changing U.S. economy were excluded or downgraded.[26] Furthermore, developing countries were to enjoy various "flexibilities" (of ill-defined dimensions) in implementing their commitments. This substantive slant had a procedural counterpart. The negotiation process emphasized "modalities" (formulas to cut tariffs) that shielded the emerging market powers (which were treated as developing countries) from intensive bilateral bargaining over their specific market commitments and "flexibilities."

Crucially, the Doha Development Round coincided with the emergence of new market powers (most notably, China, Brazil, and India along with South Africa and Indonesia) (Prasad and Kose 2010). Given the already low level of U.S. tariffs, many businesses believed Doha would sacrifice the remaining U.S. "negotiating chips" without significant progress on lifting barriers to the most promising U.S. exports in the major emerging markets.

When compared to the American political economy at the time, the problems of Doha in 2009 became evident:

1. Agriculture: Whatever the United States yielded on curbing subsidies to its farmers and ranchers, it needed some offsetting gains on market access. This change in policy could yield modest gains for the key players (Tokarick 2008). But the flexibilities in schedules of emerging markets made this hard to achieve. And the European Union (EU) rejected moving off its WTO offer generated by its internal farm market reform—thus thwarting a creative endgame.
2. Manufacturing tariffs: Tariffs remain substantial (both at the bound and applied levels) for the faster-growing U.S. manufacturing exports in the largest emerging markets. Tariff cuts in these markets would matter to U.S. industries such as chemicals. The emerging market nations again declined to participate in sector-specific, tariff-cut negotiations (separate from the modality formulas). They also declined to waive their flexibilities, thereby leaving uncertain what was gained for American exports.

25. See Koremenos, Lipson, and Snidal (2001); Bagwell and Staiger (2009).
26. Gawande and Hoekman (2006) argue that framing a round around agriculture was not prudent.

3. Nontariff barriers and intellectual property protection: A knowledge-based export mix is particularly sensitive to nontariff barriers (such as technical standards). The Doha negotiations had made modest progress and promised little on IP protection.
4. Foreign direct investment/Services: The services negotiations were moved to the backburner until meeting the ambitions of developing countries on modalities for goods. It was hard to start belatedly on a comprehensive package of the conceptually and legally complicated innovations necessary for services. Moreover, looming behind these challenges was the India–U.S. split over cross-border liberalization of movement of service workers.

Ramming the existing Doha deal through Congress with tepid business support might fail and would certainly poison all subsequent trade politics. Therefore, the Obama administration used 2009 (and much of 2010) to convince countries that, although the president wanted multilateral economic cooperation, the United States would not yield to repeated diplomatic pressure from the EU and key emerging markets to accept the Doha package.

The political stalemate in 2009 led to G-20 calls for rapid conclusion of a "balanced and ambitious" Doha deal, an acknowledgment that the United States wanted more while other countries thought that the current package was sufficiently balanced (Group of Twenty [G-20] 2009). The Obama administration believed that progress required getting the larger market powers to turn to small group (sector) and bilateral negotiations. Most countries could leave their offers unchanged; the improved returns particularly hinged on Brazil, China, and India. The administration hoped these countries had enough to gain from a Doha deal that a revamped negotiation could succeed. However, those countries resisted shifting negotiating formats because it weakened their protections under modalities and flexibilities. Most critically, these countries were skeptical about opening their key growth sectors to each other, yet a market concession to the United States was a concession to all under WTO rules.

Although some shifts in the negotiating format emerged in late 2010, the success of the Doha Round remained in doubt. By late 2011, the administration began to float ideas about a possible role for the WTO in an era without major trade rounds. This might feature smaller partial agreements on, for example, trade facilitation, environment and trade, and services liberalization (particularly on information technology) among "plurilateral" groups of WTO members. The questions for the WTO were, first, would the emerging trading powers be willing to liberalize with each other and, second, would the WTO membership be willing to shift from a failed comprehensive round to "plurilateral" agreements on particular bundles of issues subject to the WTO's framework of rules. For example, a services pact might only have commitments from 65 WTO members, but would constitute such a large share of the prospective world market that the participating parties would be willing to unilaterally offer its benefits to nonparticipating WTO members (as demanded by the most favored nation rule).

Asia-Pacific: Regionalism and the Changing Political Economy of Trade

In its opening months, the Obama administration searched for a new initiative, geared to significant export and job expansion in emerging markets while meeting the "comprehensive high-standard" deals that captured the Democrats' aspirations for trade. The Trans-Pacific Partnership negotiation (the United States joining Australia, Brunei, Chile, New Zealand, Peru, Singapore, and Vietnam), as redefined by the Obama administration, became its preferred option.

The Obama administration inherited the TPP from President Bush. After a careful review, it upgraded its ambition in order to fit the political strategy for trade. The TPP aims to build from a significant economic base; the largest export returns from trade policy can come from further integration of the United States with the rapidly growing Asia-Pacific (including major Latin American) markets. Its core group of members already had FTAs with the United States; the TPP will knit the FTAs together while adding one "high-value" emerging market (Vietnam) that is eager to strengthen its ties to the United States and to balance China's influence. (The China goal was shared by other TPP members.) This core group can then provide a platform for adding later partners to an already approved agreement (thus simplifying ratification debates later).[27] By 2011, Canada, Mexico, and Japan had requested TPP membership (although agriculture issues foiled the Japanese bid). Malaysia had joined as well.

The TPP negotiating partners are pre-committed to accepting a comprehensive agreement (including goals for stronger labor and environment provisions) that also reflects special concerns of high-value-added exporters, such as technology and service industries, who require strong IP protection, favorable policies on nontariff barriers and service markets, and rights of foreign investment to compete effectively. It also puts a strong emphasis on small- and medium-sized enterprises as a goal for the negotiation's beneficiaries, thus fulfilling another political economic goal. And it set ambitious goals for liberalizing trade in agriculture. In short, the TPP represented the effort of the Obama administration to find a new formula, attuned to Democratic political constraints, to move

27. TPP's critics question its feasibility because knitting together diverse FTAs into a consistent whole as a platform for other nations is a formidable task.

trade forward on a basis pinpointed by region and particular economic considerations.[28] As it does so, it will face numerous political issues in the United States about the intersection of trade commitments with domestic policymaking on hot topics such as intellectual property and the regulation of service markets. These political fights have a logic and dynamic very different from the sector clashes of prior decades, and their successful resolution by a creative presidential administration could earn significant political capital while advancing the cause of open global markets and growth.

Just as significant as what TPP does is what it does not do initially. Considerable discussion in the administration went into figuring out how to bring India into an Asia-Pacific strategy. Using the Asia-Pacific Economic Cooperation (APEC) organization as a vehicle for ad hoc engagement with India was one early initiative, but a combination of Chinese resistance (as an APEC member) and Indian reluctance scratched this option. Bilateral probes with India on the feasibility of information and communications agreements, a seeming natural for common work, met with bureaucratic reluctance, masking internal turf fights, despite enthusiasm from Indian business. And Indian interest in a FTA that did not meet the test of being "high-quality comprehensive" was a political nonstarter in Washington.

Meanwhile, TPP raised issues immediately for China and ultimately for Brazil about their trade strategies. If TPP emerged as a strong agreement with expansive membership, it raised concerns of "trade diversion" as potential exports of China and Brazil, particularly in higher value products, might suffer from lack of preferred access to TPP markets. This concern is a persistent snag to the rise of regional accords at the expense of comprehensive WTO rounds (Bhagwati 2009).[29] Similar concerns applied to the European Union as it built trade agreements with Korea and perhaps with India. Where FTAs are politically difficult, but the economic and political stakes are considerable for countries such as India and Brazil, FTAs may be supplemented by more efforts to do "quasi"-

28. Sometimes official statements are good guides to political economic strategies. The TPP statement from U.S. Trade Representative Ron Kirk on the USTR website reads: "We will . . . confront big challenges, from rationalizing rules of origin amongst our current FTA partners to addressing agricultural, developmental, and labor challenges elsewhere to . . . ensure that we maintain a comprehensive, high standard agreement. . . . we expect the TPP agreement to serve as a model for the future of American trade. We recognize that today's workers, businesses, and farmers have different concerns than they did a generation ago, and we intend to update our approach to trade in keeping with a changing world. . . . we will talk about new technologies, emerging business sectors, and the needs of small businesses alongside labor, environmental, and more traditional trade concerns." http://www.ustr.gov/about-us/press-office/press-releases/2009/december/ustr-ron-kirk-remarks-trans-pacific-partnership-n>.

29. Bhagwati (2009) also argues that many of the issues in expanded trade agendas are little more than pandering to domestic lobbies, not legitimate trade issues, and may weaken support for free trade in developing markets. Whatever the merits of this view, and they are decidedly mixed, even the Bush administration rejected them as politically unrealistic.

trade agreements—bilateral or regional agreements on regulatory cooperation that would ease market-access problems impeding high-growth sectors that employ trade concepts (such as the ones for technical standards) but are not formal trade agreements.

In the end, it may be concerns over trade diversion that cause major trading economies to agree to global plurilateral agreements for the most dynamic industries at the WTO.[30] Such pinpoint pacts allow the deep policy coordination necessary to tackle knowledge economy issues while leaving less-promising industries to FTAs that may be more amenable to compromise among smaller groups of bilateral or regional partners.

Conclusion

The Great Recession sharply revealed the challenge for proponents of trade policy—how to build from a secure base of existing liberalization to a new set of trade options that meet changing demands of the American political economy and the constraints of party political dynamics in a system of divided government.

If the TPP is successful, it symbolizes the further movement of U.S. trade policy in alignment with economic forces that first played out in the WTO's Uruguay Round concluded in 1994. In that round, services and the introduction of intellectual property issues, tied to a new mechanism for enforcing trade rights, propelled the negotiation to success. Since then, the forces that surfaced in the Uruguay Round have grown even more important. With the political energy for the WTO exhausted by the Doha Round, experiments in trade liberalization to meet new demands moved to the Asia-Pacific region, the new center of global growth.

From the viewpoint of American political economy, can global trade negotiations ever again succeed? There are few signs of backsliding on the binding trade dispute mechanism of the WTO. But the comprehensive round may be a "bridge too far" for the new world economy. In short, the new structure of economic interests and trade politics suggest selective liberalization through a variety of policy instruments, not the end of integration of global markets.

30. Mansfield and Reinhardt (2003) analyze the interplay of WTO and regional pacts.

10

WORLDS IN COLLISION

Uncertainty and Risk in Hard Times

Peter J. Katzenstein and Stephen C. Nelson

In a decade marred by manias, panics, and crashes (Kindleberger 1978), our analytical worlds are in collision. Economists for the most part hold firmly to the view that the world of finance is a world of calculable risk. Other social scientists disagree and insist that we live not only in a world of risk but also in a world of uncertainty. A world of risk assumes that agents act on material incentives and respond to regulatory institutions, conventions, and norms. A world of uncertainty assumes that actors can, in addition, be motivated by social or constitutive institutions, conventions, and norms. Most scholars of international political economy (IPE) and financial economics base their analyses on the dubious assumption that we live only in a world of risk. In this chapter, we develop a contrarian argument that underlines the centrality of uncertainty. Without concepts that capture the element of uncertainty, our analysis of economic life will remain partial, even stunted.

We support our view of the importance of uncertainty with illustrative evidence drawn from financial markets and central banking. Specifically, the

---

For their critical comments and suggestions on earlier drafts of this paper, we would like to thank Rawi Abdelal, Jens Beckert, Mark Blyth, Jeffry Frieden, Joanne Gowa, Douglas Holmes, Robert Keohane, Jonathan Kirshner, Eric Maskin, Helen Milner, Julio Rotemberg, David Spiro, Richard Swedberg, Hubert Zimmerman, the editors of this volume—David Lake and Miles Kahler—and the participants at two workshops on Politics in the New Hard Times, held in honor of Peter Gourevitch at the University of California, San Diego, April 23–24, 2010, and January 7–8, 2011. Katzenstein would like to acknowledge the generous financial support of the Louise and John Steffens Founders' Circle Membership at the Institute for Advanced Study at Princeton, where he spent the academic year 2009–10 working on early drafts of this chapter.

financial crisis of 2008 shifts the burden of proof to rationalists who believe that we are living only in a world of risk. The definition of "actor interest" contains variable social elements that our analytical lenses must identify rather than blend out systematically. "Nobody knows anything but everyone knows someone" is a bon mot that captures nicely the social element in economic life.[1] As was true of the International Geophysical Year half a century earlier, in a social science replay of the Velikovsky affair, the financial crisis of 2008 is providing us with enough evidence to make it worthwhile to integrate uncertainty systematically into our analysis of international and comparative political economy.[2]

Our argument is rooted in a distinction drawn ninety years ago by Frank Knight (1921) and John Maynard Keynes (1921). Knight and Keynes delineated choice settings marked by risk, in which decision makers can access reliable probability distributions based on past observations, from choices made in the presence of uncertainty, in which probabilities are unknown.[3] It is very compelling to view actors adhering to consistent and rational decision rules in a world of risk. But that assumption is implausible when actors are unable to form well-grounded probabilistic assessments of future developments (Keynes 1937; Lawson 1985, 915–16).

This distinction between two worlds is especially helpful as the biblical fat seven years end and we enter, once again, into hard times (Gourevitch 1986, afterword, this volume). Although we lack historical distance and intellectual consensus, the baseline model of the 2008 crisis is consistent with the world of risk. It weaves together a handful of causal factors including foreign and domestic investors who made available massive pools of savings at ultra-low interest rates that stoked demand for high-yielding assets; bankers and financial engineers who supplied investment vehicles carved out of pools of mortgages (many of which were low quality); credit raters who, locked in intense competition over market share, overlooked evident flaws in the securitization process to give their

1. We are indebted to Peter Cowhey for this pithy formulation.

2. In 1950, Immanuel Velikovsky published *Worlds in Collision*, in which he argued that many global natural disasters were related to near-collisions between Earth and other celestial bodies. Influential American astronomers were so outraged by the book that they tried to prevent its publication (see Goldsmith 1977).

3. Theoretically, there is a third world between pure risk and pure uncertainty, in which we form subjective probabilities (we believe, based on past observations, that an outcome is more or less likely than the alternatives), but the choice setting is sufficiently uncertain that the probabilities cannot be quantified, even with a wide confidence interval. We stick to the two-worlds imagery in this chapter, but note that the possibility of a third world was briefly explored by Keynes in his 1921 *Treatise on Probability* (but did not play a role in Keynes's theorizing in the *General Theory* and its extensions). See also Dequech 2000. In private communication, David Spiro (June 22, 2011) has pointed out to us that the distinction between uncertainty and risk leaves out the possibility that "we are living the null hypothesis of arbitrary and capricious randomness" in markets and institutions. If true, "the 2008 crisis can be explained by hindsight, but it does not deserve a characterization of rationality, whether in terms of risk or uncertainty."

seal of approval to the marketing by banks of a dizzying variety of financial instruments; the banks that ratcheted up their leverage ratios in order to maximize short-term profits, with the implicit guarantee that if market conditions soured they would be bailed out by the government; and government regulators who stood by idly or looked the other way as the crisis was building because they were convinced of the power of risk management models.

Conventional explanations share in the two core assumptions of a rationalist-materialist style of analysis. First, the interests of agents are derived primarily from income effects generated by the interaction of policy choices and the position that agents hold in the international division of labor. Second, once agents know what they want, they make, on average, consistent choices that are in line with the axioms of subjective expected utility theory. Peter Gourevitch's historically informed single- (1986) and co-authored (2005) work reflects these two assumptions and thus has provided a signal contribution to the scholarship informed by the open economy politics (OEP) approach to the study of IPE. At the same time, Gourevitch's work has differed sharply from OEP approaches by highlighting the importance of domestic politics.[4]

The subprime meltdown and the global credit crunch provide evidence that contradicts the approaches that eliminated uncertainty and reduced the world of finance to one of risk. Political and economic agents, we argue, make many of their most important decisions under conditions of uncertainty, or in ambiguous situations that mix risk and uncertainty. When actors lack reliable estimates of probabilities, they rely on social conventions such as risk management models while making their investment decisions. We discuss the world of risk in the first part of this chapter. In the second part, we inquire into the world of uncertainty, analyzing, among others, the decision making in the U.S. Federal Reserve. Our analysis is suggestive, not conclusive. The evidence we adduce is, however, substantial enough to throw into doubt the basic assumptions on which scholars working in the tradition of OEP have interpreted the financial crisis and approached most issues in IPE. In a world of risk *and* uncertainty, we argue, social conventions, constitutive institutions, norms, and practices must be part of our analytical toolkit.

4. To state that Gourevitch highlighted the importance of domestic politics is not to argue that there has been no evolution in Gourevitch's thinking on this central issue. His analysis was quite ecumenical in his first book as ideas, institutions, and other factors also were considered, although normally playing second fiddle to the material interests induced by position in the international economy. Although his views became largely, though not totally, rationalist in his co-authored book with Shinn, Gourevitch has been given a highly selective reading by adherents of the rationalist OEP approach who are either neglecting uncertainty altogether or argue it out of existence, insisting that we live only in a world of risk.

The First World: Risk in Hard Times

Peter Gourevitch's (1986) landmark study and its partial modification through a better specification of institutions in his co-authored work with James Shinn (2005) focus attention on the domestic determinants of political economy. In contrast to OEP, for Gourevitch international constraints and opportunities are always underdetermining in accounting for policy choices that could have gone another way. Shaped by material interests, domestic politics supplies the mechanisms that determine policy choice.

Materialism and Ideas in Gourevitch's Analysis

Gourevitch (1986) analyzes three economic crises in five countries. Across the three crises, the causal weight of factors changes. "Raw and naked" social actors in the first crisis of 1873–96 give way to polymorphous political coalitions in the second crisis of 1929–49, and a complex politics in the third crisis of the 1970s and 1980s (Gourevitch 1986, 23–28, 32, 228; Blyth 2009). Across all three crisis periods, position in the international economy remains the driving structural factor that largely shapes coalitional politics. This insight is central to OEP scholarship.

Gourevitch's work has been validated by what he dubs as a widespread, almost universal move in the social sciences to the micro level. His most recent book on corporate governance (Gourevitch and Shinn 2005) also pushes toward the micro level. As before, the causal priority that Gourevitch accords to various factors is grounded in the assumption that actors make probabilistic guesses in the pursuit of their interests. Since Gourevitch is not a strict materialist, in his view it matters greatly who promotes and who opposes specific ideas and policies. Over the last five decades, Gourevitch (afterword, this volume) argues, this concern has become deeply problematic as scholars have become more aware that actors can understand their situation in numerous ways.

There exists, then, a gap in Gourevitch's reasoning, between the ready acknowledgment of the profound problems involved in the process of preference formation and the alacrity to move on to the analysis of strategic action among players with well-defined interests. That gap is bridged by invoking the standard assumption, shared by all scholars working in the OEP tradition, that individual or collective actors have a rational, risk-calculating way of establishing and advancing their interests. This assumption helps explain the one-sided reading of OEP scholars who invoke the roots of their work in Gourevitch's coalitional analysis. Institutions do not anchor actors in some fundamental way as they are seeking firm footing in an uncertain world. Instead institutions and interests are malleable and can be used for very different political purposes. "The impact of rules and institutions depends on who tries to use them" (Gourevitch 1986, 229). In this mode of analysis, constitutive institutions, norms, and processes are neglected and the identity of actors and their ability to calculate risks is unproblematic.[5] In the OEP approach, institutions shape risk-calculating actors' strategies and regulate which societal groups have access to the levers of power.

Gourevitch and Shinn (2005) start their book with the analytical premise that *Politics in Hard Times* observes empirically only in its third and final case. Institutions and regulatory norms rather than the position actors hold in the international division of labor are vitally important in shaping risky decisions. This point of departure leads to an important shift away from a materialist argument that sees interests determined largely by the position actors hold in the international division of labor and by the dynamic of their political conflicts. This move grounds their analysis firmly on a simplifying assumption that is fully consistent with a rationalist OEP approach; that is, a view in which governance and government are solely responsive to economic incentives that are unproblematic in a world of calculable risks, illuminated by incomplete contracting, transaction costs, and principal-agent relations. The structure of incentives can be explained adequately only by studying how preferences are aggregated politically and mediated by institutions (Gourevitch and Shinn 2005, 27).

Gourevitch and Shinn (2005, 41) insist that we are living in a world of coalitional politics and norms in which subjective probability estimates are taken for granted and choices are shaped by regulatory norms, processes, and institutions. The world of uncertainty in which actors look to constitutive norms, processes, and institutions to inform their definition of "self"-interest and their strategies is not in their purview. The self-imposed one-sidedness of their analysis is the subject of a few trenchant pages (2005, 87–91) that discuss and dismiss the social embeddedness of the economy. Unlike economic sociologists, Gourevitch and Shinn argue that economic incentives motivate strategic decisions. Social conventions, roles, and scripts that typically shape the practices of actors moving in an uncertain world are irrelevant. Put differently, Gourevitch and Shinn regard as unproblematic and leave unanalyzed the common knowledge within which

5. In rationalist-materialist accounts (Frieden and Rogowski 1996), interests are determined by the structure of the economy; in the case of Gourevitch (1986), this means a country's position in the international economy. In rationalist-ideational accounts (as in the chapter by Peter Hall in this volume; at times Gourevitch 1986; and occasionally even Gourevitch and Shinn 2005), politics and institutions create interests that are frequently in flux. In these accounts, institutions typically are defined in terms of their regulatory norms and processes, without regard to their constitutive aspects. Thus the analysis tends to underrate or neglect the importance of social factors that can help stabilize interests and make the pursuit of rational strategies possible, especially in times of uncertainty.

strategizing, signaling, bargaining, and choosing occur. On this central point, their analysis is a close cousin of OEP.

Rationalist, Risk-Based Analysis and Open Economy Politics

Invoking Gourevitch's work and drawing on deductive economic models, OEP supplies a clear answer about the origins of agents' interests. As Gourevitch (1986, 58) writes "the behavior of economic actors is affected by preferences and these in turn are affected by situation [in the domestic and international economy]." David Lake calls the assumption that interests can be read off the agents' situation in the international division of labor the "hard core" of this research tradition (2009a, 231).

To the extent that there is an "American school" of IPE (Cohen 2007, 2008a, b; Phillips and Weaver 2010), it has at its center OEP as outlined by David Lake (2006, 2009a, b).[6] In Lake's presentation, OEP formalizes the approach that motivates Gourevitch's work. Actors are price takers with clearly ordered preferences. Interests are deduced from the actor's position in the international economy, or what Gourevitch (1986) calls the "production profile." Interests are aggregated by institutions that in turn structure the bargaining that occurs. Policies and outcomes are ranked according to how they affect the actor's expected future income stream. The main advantage of OEP, as Lake correctly emphasizes, is its deductive argument about preferences. OEP scholars start with sets of actors who "can be reasonably assumed to share (nearly) identical interests . . . Deducing interests from economic theory was the essential innovation of OEP" (Lake 2009a, 226–27, 230–31; 2009b, 50). OEP derives parsimonious theories of politics from sparse economic theory. The flow is from micro to macro in an orderly and linear progression. To simplify analysis, work in the OEP tradition adopts a partial equilibrium analysis by focusing at most on one or two steps in this causal chain and treating the others in reduced form, an analytic simplification that holds constant many elements that otherwise would make analysis intractable. In principle, however, all partial analyses can be assembled into one integrated whole.

In this theoretical formulation, agents' material (not social) interests are stipulated to exist (not inquired into). Informed by rational expectations, OEP

---

6. Lake (2006) summarizes the OEP approach, engages the TRIPS survey (Lake 2009a), and responds to Cohen (Lake 2006, 2009a, 2009b) by defending the OEP approach; he also offers (Lake 2009b) an extended summary of his previous writings and develops three "inside the Church" criticisms of the approach. Lake regards the 2009b version of his writings as the "most authoritative" and also the "most critical" one of the OEP approach. Hence we rely on it in our more far-reaching critique. David Lake, personal communication, March 29, 2010. For critical discussions that differ from our concerns see Hainmueller and Hiscox (2006); Mansfield and Mutz (2009); Oatley (2011); Blyth (2012).

moves exclusively in the world of risk.[7] Institutions provide the rules and procedures that normally reflect the strength of different social groups. As is true of Gourevitch and Shinn (2005), OEP holds a truncated view of what institutions and conventions are and do, focusing largely on their regulative characteristics and denying for the most part their social and constitutive features. OEP thus overlooks the possibility that institutions can shape both actor identities and interests and their capacities for acting on them. It is thus difficult to accept the ambitious claim that such a narrow perspective will help us understand fully how institutions "serve to define what political power means in a particular society . . . and how different political assets are valued" (Lake 2009a, 227).

Questions of meaning and value in institutions and of individual and collective action under conditions of uncertainty become more accessible with an analysis that includes also the social and constitutive aspects of politics. OEP's always rationalist and often materialist conception of actor interest and its persistent neglect of social and constitutive politics are treated, at least to date, as hard-core assumptions. Modifying them would mean vitiating the entire paradigm (Lake 2009a, 231–32). OEP thus insists, erroneously, that we live only in a world of calculable risks.

The Second World: Uncertainty and Risk and the Crisis of 2008

To support our view, we offer in this section illustrative evidence drawn from financial markets, policymaking by the U.S. Federal Reserve, and discursive politics.

Uncertainty in Finance

Most economists assume that finance lies squarely in the world of risk. Financial markets, however, are realms of uncertainty. In very short time periods, asset prices can wildly veer away from their historical benchmarks. During the October 1987 stock market crash, in just over an hour of trading the Dow Jones index

---

7. Rational expectations, in its strongest form, means that agents have full knowledge of the true structure of the economy and are not prone to any *systematic* biases in information processing and terminal decision making. The assumption imposes "equality between agents' subjective probabilities and the probabilities emerging from the economic model containing those agents" (Hansen and Sargent 2010, 4). In a paper addressing the effects of uncertainty, Lake and Frieden (1989, 6–7) concede that uncertainty increases in crises and then proceed to argue that risk and uncertainty "are similar enough to be conflated for our purposes." They follow a long line of economists who treat the difference between risk and uncertainty as semantic rather than substantive (Nelson and Katzenstein 2011).

fell by 300 points, "three times as much . . . as it had in any other full trading day in history" (Bookstaber 2007, 87). Data indicate that volatility in the U.S. stock market is on the rise: eleven of the twenty largest daily drops since 1980 have occurred in the past three years (Story and Bowley 2011).

Extreme price swings in equity and foreign exchange markets defy the laws of normality. In August 2007, David Viniar, Goldman Sachs' chief financial officer, declared that his risk management team was "seeing things that were 25-standard deviation moves, several days in a row" (quoted in Chinn and Frieden 2011, 91). On September 6, 2011, the Swiss Franc fell by 8 percent against the Euro—a move that exceeded previous moves by more than twenty standard deviations (sigmas).[8] If returns were Gaussian, we would observe an event that is five sigmas away from the mean about once every 14,000 years; by contrast, "the waiting period associated with a 20-sigma event is a number, in years, that considerably exceeds recent estimates of the number of particles in the known universe" (Dowd and Hutchinson 2010, 89).

How do traders and fund managers view financial markets? In 2007, the psychologist David Tuckett conducted a series of interviews with top financiers. His subjects described "trying to decide what they thought were the various uncertain futures that might unfold for the future price of various financial assets . . . the information they had was always *both* too much to be examined exhaustively and never enough to give any certainty about choices" (Tuckett 2011, xvi, 51). Over decades of investing, thinking and writing about financial markets, one of the world's most successful financiers, George Soros (1987, 1998, 2008, 2009), has grappled with the behavioral consequences of the uncertainty he experienced firsthand. For Soros, market participants seek to impose some order on a complex reality and an unknowable future. The mental constructs that inform their expectations do not simply mirror underlying economic fundamentals; rather, the partial and distorted views that market participants impose on the world shape markets. And these views evolve in a social environment in which "rumors, norms, and other features of social life are part of their understanding of finance" (Sinclair 2009, 451). In "reflexive feedback loops," these views drive markets which then subsequently shape beliefs and thus can generate far-from-equilibrium situations.

As a stand-in for many others, Nobel laureate Robert Solow (1999, 31) takes Soros to task for a multiplicity of sins and calls his work "embarrassingly banal." Reading Soros's work and Solow's review is like watching the two proverbial ships of theoretical and practical knowledge of financial economics passing at night. Solow's incisive review glosses over a central point in Soros's argument.

8. http://blogs.reuters.com/felix-salmon/2011/09/06/charts-of-the-day-swiss-franc-edition/.

Unlike the rationalist economic models that Solow references, Soros assumes knowledge in and about financial markets to run up against fundamental uncertainty, "unknowable unknowns" (Dequech 2000). Reality exists independently from individual understandings and expectations of the kind that economists try to model. Why? Because of the power of collective beliefs. As Justin Fox (2009) has shown in great detail, the creation of the common knowledge assumption about the world of risk is a complex historical and deeply social process involving scholars and policymakers; that process eventually took on a life of its own, governing policy for a while, before being assaulted recently by the harsh facts the world of uncertainty revealed in the financial crisis and its aftermath.

Economic models of manias, panics, herd behavior, bandwagons, fads, bank runs, and other phenomena are analytical specifications of that collective process. They are based on the assumption of the aggregation of individual perceptions, volitions, and behavior. Put differently, they all move in the world of subjectivity rather than intersubjectivity, of the additivity rather than the superadditivity of parts. That assumption undervalues the power of collective beliefs. In the words of George Akerlof and Rachel Kranton (2010, 6), in economics tastes vary with social context. "Identity and norms bring something new to the representation of tastes . . . The incorporation of identity and norms then yields a theory of decision making where social context matters." Bias cannot be reduced to individually held beliefs and is inconsistent with the assumption of an asocial, individual rationality (Cassidy 2009). Market prices are never independent of the views of market participants, and sometimes they express prevailing bias rather than correct valuation. This social character of financial markets gives them the power to shape underlying economic fundamentals (Soros 2009, 59, 71). And it is these social qualities that can drive financial markets far off their equilibrium path (Calandro 2004, 45–49).

This view is dramatically at odds with the twin ideas of rational expectations and efficient markets. In that view, today's prices incorporate all available information, and any errors made by agents forecasting future market conditions are random and uncorrelated. For Emanuel Derman (2011, 140, 156), this is simply wrong-headed since "financial modeling is *not* the physics of markets . . . the Efficient Market Model stubbornly assumes that all uncertainties about the future are quantifiable. That's why it is a model of a possible world rather than a theory about the one we live in." Inhabiting the real world, and informed by his practical knowledge, Soros argues that reflexivity introduces an inescapable element of uncertainty into financial markets. And that uncertainty affects both the views of market participants and the real world. Instead of basing their actions on an unknowable "true" model of the economy, market participants substitute a variety of social conventions such as guesswork, instinct, emotion, experience, and rituals. Rather than assuming, as does rational expectation theory, that all market participants ultimately come to share in accurate, common knowledge of how the world works, Soros (2009, 8, 11) argues that this is simply impossible. James Shinn's (2011a) analysis of the reference models of the traders in the global macro hedge fund world supports this view. All of them focus on the same, small number of major events and trends, and all of them are ready to throw their models overboard should markets behave differently. In sum, in a world of uncertainty and ambiguity, social conventions play a large role.

The catastrophic failure of forecasting models employed by banks and credit rating agencies makes more sense when, following Soros, we view finance through the lens of uncertainty. On average, the projections of banks underestimated the actual default rates for collateralized debt obligations of mortgage-backed securities by 20,155 percent.[9] Why did banks, hedge funds, credit rating agencies, and regulators all come to rely on quantitative risk models that were deeply flawed? In the presence of uncertainty, financial market actors make use of rules of thumb, embedded in social relations, to guide their decisions. In their practical application, risk management models proved to be social conventions offering the illusion that uncertainty could be made into manageable risks (Latsis, de Larquier, and Bessis 2010).[10] Therefore, they do not provide strong evidence of an emerging science of financial economics that can be imported readily into the field of international political economy. Risk models are a conventional source of confidence that enables investors, financiers, bankers, and government officials to take decisions and act, as they must.[11] As Keynes (1937, 214) wrote long ago, "knowing that our own individual judgment is worthless, we endeavor to fall back on the judgment of the rest of the world which is perhaps better informed . . . [this] leads to what we may strictly term a conventional judgment."

Uncertainty at Work: Policymaking in the Federal Open Market Committee

In its regular functioning, members of the Federal Reserve hold to a world view that combines risk with uncertainty. Situating central banks exclusively in the world of risk misses a key fact: decision making in the Federal Reserve often

9. We averaged the percent difference between estimated and realized default rates across ten ratings classes (BBB–AAA) for collateralized debt obligations (CDOs) issued in 2005–7; the data were supplied by Donald MacKenzie and reported in the *Economist* ("The Gods Strike Back: A Special Report on Risk," *Economist*, February 13, 2010, 6).

10. Bernhard and Leblang (2008, 7, 60), for example, build from the assumptions that "market actors engage in economic activity in efficient markets" and "that economic actors have rational expectations." Armed with those assumptions, the authors build models of investor behavior rooted in portfolio theory.

11. For further elaboration of this point, see Nelson and Katzenstein (2011).

takes place in the presence of uncertainty. We find evidence of the role of uncertainty in deliberation at the Federal Reserve in three places. The "Summary of Economic Projections" that is appended at irregular intervals to the "Minutes of the Federal Open Market Committee [FOMC]" contains a section on "Uncertainty and Risk" that has appeared twelve times between 2008 and 2010 in contrast to only one time between 2005 and 2007.

One of the tasks of FOMC members involves forecasting near-term macroeconomic conditions. Policymakers, working with data and reports supplied by the staff of Federal Reserve, submit forecasts of output growth, inflation, and unemployment prior to the semi-annual publication of the Fed's Monetary Policy Reports to Congress. We treat the degree of forecast error as an indirect measure of uncertainty facing the FOMC. We draw on David Romer's (2010) dataset, which records every forecast provided by members between 1992 and 1999, to track individual members' forecasting errors (calculated by subtracting the forecast from realized values for the four indicators) as well as the average forecasting error in each year.[12]

Figure 10-1 reveals two important patterns. First, monetary policymakers' forecasts about important macroeconomic variables vary widely. Second, accurate forecasts are extremely rare. According to Alan Greenspan, policymakers and forecasters are doing "exceptionally well" if they can get projections right 70 percent of the time (2010, 209). FOMC members fall well below this benchmark: out of 360 separate forecasts for each of the four variables, we observe 25 perfect forecasts of inflation, 21 for unemployment, 8 for real GDP, and not a single correct forecast of the growth of nominal GDP. Less than 4 percent of all forecasts issued between 1992 and 1999 were correct.[13]

The best source of evidence on decision making in the Fed comes from transcripts of the FOMC meetings. Because the FOMC releases transcripts with a five-year lag, we rely mainly on meetings from the period just prior to the invasion of Iraq in 2003 when the war and its uncertain effects on markets was all-pervasive. It is likely that we would see more evidence of the impact of uncertainty on FOMC deliberations if we had access to transcripts from meetings

12. The FOMC released the information on member forecasts with a ten-year lag. See also Bailey and Schonhardt-Bailey 2005.

13. A skeptic might argue that FOMC forecasts deviate from reality for good reason: voting members are being strategic. Forecasts are intended to influence the Fed's policy stance. If that is true, then we would expect to see evidence that members from depressed regions (who would likely prefer a more accommodative policy) would forecast very low inflation and GDP growth and overstate unemployment. Specifically, one might expect those regional bank presidents with unemployment rates higher than the national rate may become increasingly dovish and those with rates below the national rate may become increasingly hawkish. But there exists no evidence that regional conditions influence the degree of forecasting error (McCracken 2010). It seems more plausible to assume that the poor track record of the FOMC forecasts is due to uncertainty.

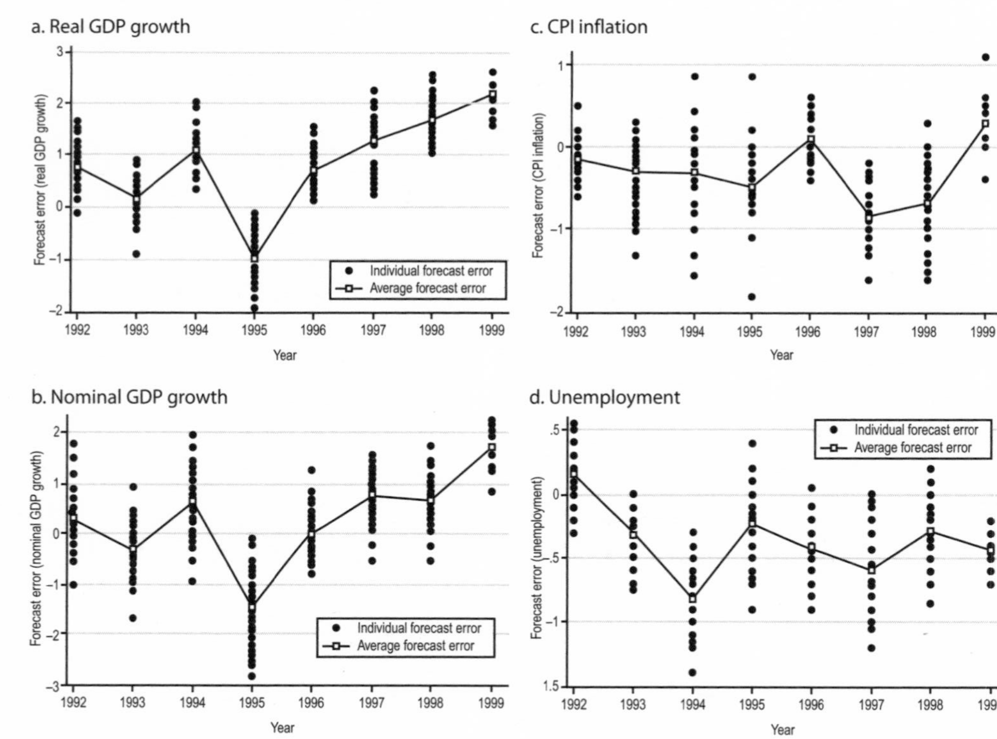

FIGURE 10-1. The accuracy of economic forecasts of the members of the Federal Open Market Committee (1992–99). Note: CPI is Consumer Price Inflation.

Source: Romer (2010).

during the height of the crisis in September 2008. Nonetheless, the discussion from the years before the crisis reveals that policymakers framed their choices in Knightian terms. A number of policymakers noted that the institution was operating in the fog of uncertainty.

We are presenting brief excerpts of the minutes verbatim with the single aim to convey more accurately than a synopsis could the reasoning process of central bankers who must deal with the issue of uncertainty and risk.

On January 28, 2003, for example, Alan Greenspan reflected on the relation between uncertainty and economic models:

> **Chairman Greenspan:** In other words, we start with a degree of uncertainty that is very high; it is much higher than it is for those who take the data and put them into a model and do projections. Most modelers are dealing with a controlled environment in which the number of variables is well short of a thousand. In the real world there are a million, and we don't know which ones are important. So it really matters. Lots of technical things that we do would seem to be wrong in a sort of optimum sense. Yet we do those things because we don't trust the models to be capturing what is going on in the real world. (Federal Open Market Committee [FOMC] 2003, 37–38)

Greenspan's comments prompted a debate about the prudence of the Fed's accommodative stance (specifically, deviating from the so-called Taylor Rule). The debate prompted Anthony M. Santomero, head of the Federal Reserve of Philadelphia, to reflect on why the Fed cannot rely on fixed decision rules:

> **Mr. Santomero:** I think in fact our policy behavior was more symptomatic of an environment of uncertainty than we give ourselves credit for. In my view, our actual behavior looks more like a rational response to the uncertain world in the dimensions I just laid out. So rather than try to chase the optimal rule, I suppose my reaction is that we're probably doing a better job than the optimal rule suggests. (FOMC 2003, 48)

Later the discussion turned to monetary policymaking in the face of saber-rattling by the Bush administration. Cathy Minehan of the Federal Reserve of Boston, William McDonough of New York, and Chairman Greenspan ruminated on how geopolitical conditions made policy choices little more than guesswork.

> **Ms. Minehan:** It seems to me that if all the uncertainties center on a discrete geopolitical event—a go/no-go decision such as we go to war or we don't go to war—that has one implication for how to look

at the second half of the year. As in the Greenbook, one could look at various scenarios that make some big assumptions about the shortness of a war or whatever. If the uncertainties hedge around underlying fundamentals—growing out of the view that this is a very different kind of recession than that around which our models and people's memories are built because this "recovery" compared with previous ones is so slow—then that says something different about the role of uncertainty. (FOMC 2003, 65)

Vice Chairman McDonough: May I slide a comment in here? In talking with people in the New York, London, and Paris financial centers, it's very, very hard to determine to what extent they are saying that the uncertainty is geopolitical when it's really a cover story for uncertainty about economic issues. (66)

Ms. Minehan: Clearly, uncertainty is a major factor in the economic outlook. What will cause that uncertainty to subside, however, is difficult to determine. Will the go/no-go decision about war make businesses more confident about the future? Or will the economy's current soft patch have to show real signs of firming to achieve that end? Or, as Dave Stockton suggested yesterday, are these two sources of uncertainty so intertwined that it's hard to tell one from the other? (118–19)

Vice Chairman McDonough: We do have an enormous amount of uncertainty. So the question is, What does the prudent central banker do in an atmosphere of enormous uncertainty? It seems to me that one should think very hard, do nothing, and stay extremely alert. (127)

Chairman Greenspan: All this raises the interesting issue as to what will happen if and presumably when the geopolitical risks are removed. Will we be looking at a bounceback as this particular risk is removed, or will we be shocked to find that the sluggishness is still there? I don't know any way to judge analytically the relative probability of those two potential outcomes. We can guess. We may say that history suggests such and such, but we really can't assess with confidence the probability of the two events. The bottom line to all of this is that the military uncertainty is so overwhelming with respect to the question of potential monetary policy actions that the less we do, even in how we phrase our post-meeting statement, the better off we are. The problem, as the Vice Chair of the Board said, is that we do not know what will happen, and like him I think that it's important for us to hedge our judgment at this stage. (146)

Even though there are other threads of the FOMC discussion that we could have cited (Nelson and Katzenstein 2011), illustrative quotes from transcripts do not permit us to make strong claims about how central bankers react in times of financial crisis. And it is true that Alan Greenspan's (2010) reflections on his time in office say virtually nothing about the importance of uncertainty while he was in office. This omission we take to be an indication of the ways in which the conventional wisdom of economics can shape the memory of key decision makers. Together with other evidence and arguments presented in this chapter, the tenor of the discussion among the Federal Reserve's Board members in 2003 is, however, strong enough, we believe, to shift the burden of proof to scholars who argue that we live only in a world of risk.

Discursive Politics

Attention to language offers additional evidence to support the view that we need to pay attention to both risk and uncertainty. Central banks talk to politics and markets. How they talk to politics depends on the degree of their independence, which can raise vexing questions of democracy (Johnson 1998, 195–217). "Talking to markets" is about conveying meaning as much as conveying information, as "the Oracle of the Fed," Chairman Greenspan, understood only too well. Douglas Holmes (2010, 1–4, and 2009; see also Hellwig 2009, 161–62) has developed a compelling argument that shows how stabilization of expectations in a world shot through with both risk and uncertainty is a matter of discourse. Central bankers have embraced transparency so that markets now do a substantial amount of the Federal Reserve's work (Krippner 2007, 505).

Communicative action has revolutionized central banking practices during the last two decades. Rather than presiding over secret and esoteric institutions dealing with arcane subjects such as inflation targeting (the focus of Holmes's extensive field research), central banks have become very transparent and open. In their effort to control the evolution of prices, they seek to influence both collective sensibilities about and in the future. Relying on the interpretive and scholarly writings of Ben Bernanke and, especially, of Alan Blinder, public statements and interviews, Holmes (2010) shows that central banks manage individual expectations and social biases through official statements, interviews, press conferences, and other ways of "talking to markets." This "talk" is a self-conscious and concerted effort to make all market participants assimilate central bank policy intentions. "Econometric allegories," as Alan Blinder and Ricardo Reis (2005, 5) call them, draw on the intellectual resources, policy judgments, political experiences, and economic preferences of central bankers. Prices become anchored in the expectations and assumptions of market participants who take these allegories seriously and adjust their practices, and thereby become active participants in the banks' preferred policies. The economic narratives of central banks thus have become an important determinant for market developments. Central banks reduce uncertainty through discursive practices that rely on strategic rhetorical action with essentially pedagogical aims. Central bank statements, Holmes (2010, 4, 7–9, 13) argues, "are not merely expressing an interpretative account or commentary: they are making the economy itself as a communicative field and as an empirical fact" (4). Central bank narratives activate the reflexive capacities of actors, all in the interest of creating a predictable future in a world fraught with risk and uncertainty.

Economic models thus do not only analyze financial markets. They alter them. In the words of Donald MacKenzie (2006, 25), they are not only cameras, passively recording developments in markets, but engines which actively transform the very same markets. Representation and action are part of the same story. The issue is not only about being right or wrong in our knowledge about the world but also about being able or unable to transform that world (MacKenzie, Muniesa and Siu 2007, 2).

The effect of economic theory on markets can be more or less visible (MacKenzie 2006, 16–19). The "Chicago Boys" were economists at the Universidad Católica de Chile who had been trained at the University of Chicago between the mid-1950s and the mid-1960s. After General Pinochet's military coup of 1973, this group of economists not only analyzed the Chilean economy but sought to reform it along free-market and monetarist lines. Other interventions by economists though less visible, can also be very consequential. Economic theory, as Miyazaki (2007) argues, not only stands outside of markets as an external object but often is intrinsic to market processes. In the form of self-validating feedback loops, the practical use of economic theory thus can make market processes more like their depiction in theory. For example, index funds have altered fundamentally the operation of financial markets. Anomalies discovered in the course of testing the efficient-market hypothesis have encouraged investment practices that often led to the reduction or elimination of these anomalies. And options were priced more accurately as predicted by the Black-Scholes-Merton model before than after the crash of 1987. In brief, finance theory has been incorporated into markets—technically, linguistically, and as a legitimating device (MacKenzie 2006, 29–30, 32–33, 255–59; MacKenzie, Muniesa, and Siu 2007, 4–5). In the words of Alan Blinder (2000, 16, 18; quoted in MacKenzie 2006, 25), "Economists . . . have bent reality (at least somewhat) to fit their models." And financial market actors bent models to fit reality. A trader involved in developing Salomon's option pricing model described how the Gaussian assumption was built into the model: "Sometimes we'd assume normal just to make it even more simple" (MacKenzie 2006, 215).

Blinder's qualification—"at least somewhat"—agrees with Michel Callon and Fabian Muniesa's (2005, 1229–31) view of markets as "calculative collective devices." The characteristics of financial goods and services are often extremely uncertain and the number of actors involved in financial markets is often very large and highly dispersed. Callon (1998, 6) thus asks, "How can agents calculate when no stable information or shared prediction on the future exist?" Markets are such effective institutions because they make possible complicated calculations that yield practical solutions that could not be reached by theoretical reflection only (Callon 1998, 23–32).

Callon and Muniesa's (2005) analysis sidesteps the one-sided views of neoclassical economics and anthropology. Economists take an abstract and formal view of markets, which, they assume, are governed by impersonal laws and populated by agents who are inherently calculative. Anthropologists prefer to dissolve the calculative competence of actors in rich ethnographies that view quantitative practices as rationalizations for choices that are based on other logics. Neither view is very satisfying. The first overlooks the diversity of economic practices and forms of calculations that can be observed in markets; the second denies that economic forms of behavior have any specificity whatever. The first thinks in terms of pure calculation; the second marginalizes all calculative practices. Both seem inappropriate for an analysis of the ambiguity that marks financial markets with their characteristic mixture of risk and uncertainty. Calculative behavior includes but goes beyond mathematical or numerical calculations. It is a hybrid of calculation, judgment, and imagination. Avoiding positivist and constructivist preconceptions, economists can view the laws of the market as neither discoveries that reveal hidden truths, nor as constructions that illuminate an opaque reality. Economic laws account instead for "regularities progressively enforced by the joint movement of the economy and economics." Such regularities connect the obduracy of the real world with the contingency of the artifact of reason (Callon 1998, 46).

A financial crisis is therefore not only an event "out there in reality" but also a set of interpretive and rhetorical acts "in here," which can have different effects over time. The degree of congruence between "out there" and "in here" is a central stabilizing or destabilizing element of the financial order. Economists are part of a social performance by which their ideas are assimilated by experts and policymakers who, against their better knowledge, pretend that they are true. Economic ideas are thus put into the service of making rather than merely representing reality.[14] Furthermore, these ideas are built into the operation of both the financial system and the system of government regulation (Hjertaker 2011; Riles

14. Douglas Holmes, personal communication, December 13, 2010.

2011). Jens Beckert (2010, 2, 7, 9, 25, 30) offers an explanation that is congruent with this work. Going beyond the collective identities, calculative tools, judgment devices, and cultural frames invoked by economic sociologists, he focuses on the central role of fictions for decisions made under conditions of uncertainty. A fictional or imagined future is not disclosed as such and regarded as separate from the real world. Instead it is perceived by relevant communities as a natural though contestable representation of the future that emerges in the process of social interaction. When calculation-based expectations under conditions of uncertainty are beyond reach, fictional rather than rational expectations are the foundation for noncapricious action. This view is shared by one of the leading "quants" in the world of finance, Emanuel Derman (2004, 266–69), who views his models as "imaginary" inquiries. "In physics you're playing against God . . . When you've checkmated Him, He'll concede. In finance, you're playing against God's creatures, agents who value assets based on their ephemeral opinions. They don't know when they've lost, so they keep trying . . . The right way to engage with a model is, like a fiction reader or a really great pretender, to temporarily suspend disbelief, and then to push it as far as possible." It is not only the world of models that has fictitious elements. In the real social world we all inhabit, "the imagined future can affect the present, and thereby the actual future too" (Derman 2011, 142).

Discursive politics shows that stability and instability in finance are not the outcome of autonomous market dynamics as much as they are deeply intertwined with those dynamics. For this reason, economic sociologists emphasize the relevance of social institutions and conventions in their analyses of markets (Dobbin 2004). We observe the centrality of social conventions in legal fictions sustaining neoliberal ideas as recently as the last few decades (Riles 2011), and as long ago as in the common commercial law for merchants that developed in Europe over several centuries prior to the emergence of domestic commercial regulations in nascent states (Swedberg 2004). Rationalist explanations of risk are not only challenged but also complemented by the call heard from many different quarters: it is time to put the social back into the science with which we analyze financial markets.

Conclusion

Living in the worlds of both uncertainty and risk, traders and central banks point the way for scholarship. They rely on often large, methodologically sophisticated research departments that have access to a rich trough of quantitative and qualitative data. Yet central banks in particular also engage in communicative action that helps create the economy as an empirical phenomenon. As their reasoning process illustrates, inquiring into conditions of uncertainty does not require a new theory of interest but attention to the meanings of words. Aware of living in two worlds, central banks are able, imperfectly, to describe, to explain, and to predict stability and change. There are good reasons for students of political economy to adopt a similarly ecumenical approach to the analysis of financial markets and economic life. Yet judging by current standards of political economy scholarship, there is scant evidence that good reason is prevailing.[15]

Both rationalist and social approaches are useful for an analysis of a world that mixes uncertainty with risk. That mixture is readily acknowledged by the insurance industry when it deals with financial markets (Munich Re Group 2009, 2010, 2011) and underground transportation systems and occupational diseases (Munich Re Group 2004a, b). It is a prominent feature in the analysis of climate change (Geneva Association 2009; Lohmann 2010), science and technology policy (Wong 2011), and environmental law (Farber 2011). And it is readily apparent in financial markets where, according to James Shinn (2011a), four subtle trends are nudging an uncertain world just a little over toward a world of risk: the growth in hedge fund resources, an expansion and acceleration of news cycles, the diffusion of policy elites, and the consolidation of legal and intellectual regimes in the international economy. Rather than favoring an academic division of labor that typically rests on little more than shaky or spurious claims of the stipulated superiority of one or the other version of social science, we are, it seems, much better off when we subscribe to a dialogical model of scientific inquiry (Sil and Katzenstein 2010). It is unwise, even foolish, to force on paradigmatic grounds a choice between risk and uncertainty without any knowledge of the specific situation at hand. Although distinguished economist and policymaker Charles Schultze's trenchant observation—"when you dig deep down, economists are scared to death of being sociologists" (quoted in Beckert 2002, 42)—may create some resistance to importing sociological approaches built on uncertainty to the field of international political economy, we contend that pragmatic reasoning should trump paradigmatic purity in our analysis of a world that often is ambiguous in mixing risk with uncertainty.

The end of the Cold War and the collapse of the Soviet Union did to the analysis of security studies what the sinking of the *Titanic* did to the field of naval engineering. As a result, existing approaches were not replaced but refurbished and complemented by new ones that pointed to different questions and lines of

15. Benjamin Cohen, one of the doyens in the field, observes that mainstream IPE scholars by and large failed to even anticipate the crisis—a "myopia" that he blames on the "distinct loss of ambition, reflecting the gradual 'hardening' of methodologies" (2009, 442). The counterpoint to Cohen is the more optimistic view of Helleiner (2010a).

arguments, thus helping reinvigorate a field of scholarship mired in arcane debates as the world changed dramatically. In underlining the importance of uncertainty and reintroducing social styles of analysis into the field of international political economy, the financial crisis of 2008 might have a similarly salutary effect.

Afterword

YET MORE HARD TIMES?

Reflections on the Great Recession in the Frame of Earlier Hard Times

Peter A. Gourevitch

What politics produced the Great Recession of 2008–10, and what politics shape the responses to it? Situating this crisis as another in the sequence examined in *Politics in Hard Times* (*PHT*) casts a shadow backward, compelling an appraisal of what was obscured about the earlier crisis, as well as a shadow forward, using the past to provide insights into what we are experiencing today. While we hate the effects of crises on our lives, they fascinate us in the same way that moths are famously attracted to flame. In examining all of these crises, I continue the search for political explanations of economic policy choices.

This crisis of 2008 is striking for the centrality of finance. Financial instruments generated in the United States and sold around the world globalized the pain as the expanding bubble of previous years finally burst. European policy contributed as well (Shinn, chapter 7, this volume). The burst produced the sharpest economic downturn since the Great Depression of 1929, bad enough to make the ranks of Reinhart and Rogoff's (2009) classification, although only as far as number 4.

Financial lobbies caused not only the bubble that led up to the current crisis but have greatly shaped the policy responses to it. U.S. policy relaxed controls on credit, fiscal policy, housing, taxation, and corporate governance in ways that made for great public and private debt, substantial leveraging, and financial innovations that proved destabilizing. The United Kingdom, Spain, Ireland, and Iceland pursued similar policies. Germany, China, Japan, and other countries did not. Regulation in Europe seems also to have been lax and may have contributed to the bubble (Shinn 2011a).

To prevent economic collapse, U.S. financial interests received substantial bailouts, protecting most of the institutions and the wealth of the people who ran them, and the loans of investors around the world who had bought into these risky assets. In contrast with earlier bailouts in Sweden, the "haircut" on investors and managers was low (Johnson 2009; Johnson and Kwak 2010). There has been no great reversal of policy profile. The United States remains dependent on cheap credit, high consumption, low saving, and deficit financing, while China, Germany, and Japan continue to export heavily, keep consumption down and savings up (Rajan 2010). Top managers are still able to pay themselves huge bonuses. The U.S. model has created growing income inequality, and now high unemployment. In Europe, as in the United States, the central bank has been lending large sums to financial institutions to prevent banking collapse.

Three problems have interwoven into a larger crisis: (1) the credit crunch and liquidity crisis of collapsing banks; (2) the structural imbalances among creditor and debtor nations; and (3) the recession, and specifically, the argument austerity versus demand stimulus to fix economic contraction.

Understanding the comparative responses to the global crisis requires that we situate the influence of finance in the context of the political economy of the industrial countries, most notably the United States: the various interest groups that have participated with finance in a policy coalition, and the political institutions and ideas that keep that coalition in power. Why in the run-up to the Great Recession did no one "take away the punch bowl just as the party gets going" (William McChesney Martin's pithy summary of the job of the Fed Reserve governor, quoted in Mankiw 2007) when previous U.S. governments had pursued more balanced policies? Why were no dogs barking in the night to sound the alarm about the accumulation of risk? The answers lie, I argue, in understanding the vast growth in the relative power of financial interests, what McCarty and others (2010) call the "regulatory financial complex." In the American context, the influence of the "money" economy over the "real" economy shaped the weak regulation, the tolerance of deficits that led to the bubble, and the fear of collapse after it burst that meant no strong punishment or strong shift of policy regime. Reform so far (the Dodd–Frank bill of 2010) has been modest, and its implementation seems limited.

And yet the power of finance itself requires further reflection: it has influence because of its wealth and role in the economy, but also because "countervailing forces," advocates for alternatives, have been weakened by globalization, deregulation, and technology. The shift of manufacturing abroad, the spread of global value chains, the decline of manufacturing, the growth of financial concerns in manufacturing, the decline of trade unions, all helped alter interest and power relations, enabling a financial view of policy options to grow. While the importance of finance as an explanation has become widespread, I stress the need to contextualize that power, to situate it in relationship to other developments in the economy, and caution in using it to explain Germany and other liberal market economies (LMEs).

In this afterword, I first summarize the argumentation of *PHT* to explore the contrasting shadows: that of the Great Recession of 2008 on the earlier crises, and how the earlier crises frame our views of this one. I then examine the driving forces of this crisis, highlighting the way in which microeconomic regulation in finance enabled the macro forces of the bubble to explode. Finally, I turn to the political factors that enabled this approach to prevail and which guide future developments (Haldane 2011; Shih and Steinberg 2011).

Shadows: Past and Future

Politics in Hard Times explored how countries responded to economic shocks, working on the premise that the universality of the shock would reveal the important differences among national political economies. Although the shock was global, country situations were not, and so comparing country responses to the shock revealed those differences. This comparison proved a useful method. That same approach can applied to the Great Recession of 2008. And yet the world is different both in reality and in our intellectual perspectives. This exploration helps us understand how to adjust our understanding of the past in relation to our views of a new present.

A political explanation of policy must identify whose support makes it possible to resolve disputes among contending policy alternatives. The argumentation of *PHT* presumed that whatever the external pressure on a country, there was some element of choice over the proper response and thus internal disagreement over what to do. The determination of the winner of disagreement led to a search for coalitions, which in turn led to identifying the players and their preferences. Preferences—what groups wanted from the policy process—would shape the deals they cut. In full rejection of unitary actor models, be these realist, constructivist, or neoliberal institutionalist (Katzenstein, Keohane, and Krasner 1998), the search was for domestic foundations for response to international stimuli. In the current crisis, we are aware of the reverse lines of causality: instead of external forces shaping domestic outcomes (the logic of "The Second Image Reversed" [Gourevitch 1978]), we see the two interacting. This point was made by Kahler and Lake (introduction, this volume): the international context of pressure is itself generated by domestic policies shaping global structural imbalances, or fault lines among exporters and importers, lenders and creditors (Rajan 2010).

I am proud to have contributed in some way to the development of open economy politics (OEP) among political scientists, such as Ronald Rogowski's admirable *Commerce and Coalitions* (1989) and the work of Jeffrey Frieden. OEP is a vital approach, fundamental to making sense out of international and comparative political economy. But *PHT* does not fully belong in that camp. It probes the politics of coalition construction, the political sociology of policy choices. In a strict OEP position, there are no mediating aggregation variables, only preferences. Economic situation, or the production profile of groups in the world economy, helps us predict coalitional potential and probabilities. But there are deviations from the prediction: small farmers of Germany could have joined a free trade pattern on the Danish model, rather than the conservative, later fascist one (Gerschenkron 1966). The responsibility for this failure lies in a variety of institutional, organizational, ideological, and leadership choices.

In the first crisis period of the late nineteenth century, the decisive cleavage on economic issues was trade policy. I tried an archaeology of political support: Where in different countries did support come from, and how did coalitions combine to shape outcomes? The similarity of outcomes in Republican France and Imperial Germany undermined my belief in institutionalist explanations, while the sharp change of policy preferences among groups such as the Junkers undermined my confidence in ideology as explanation. At the same time, I did not believe that preferences alone could tell us what happened, as groups could combine in different coalitions, so that other variables were in play.

By the time of the interwar years, the stripped-down interest group model of the first crisis seemed increasingly insufficient. Political space was filling fast. As mass politics emerged with universal suffrage, cities, industrialization, and education, the institutional and ideological space filled. Parties, associations, unions, and business groups rushed in to organize capitalism and structure politics. The Nazi seizure of power in 1933 was not predictable just by knowing the production profile. The Nazis outmaneuvered other groups, to produce quite a different break from orthodoxy than in Sweden and the United States, where roughly similar social groups combined in a very different political framework. For this reason, while institutions, ideology, and leadership skills seem unnecessary in the first period, they play a larger role in subsequent ones. Certainly in the current period, these variables play a more powerful role than they did in the late nineteenth century. Preferences are indeed to be questioned and explained. *PHT* notes this problem in wondering, as Gerschenkron has asked, why small German farmers went along with the high-tariff position of the Junkers, rather than turning imported cereals into ham and cheese as the Danes learned to do. Some groups are cross-pressured in their structural position. Today many writers see all groups and people as cross-pressured. Perhaps they are, but they behave in patterned ways.

Two omissions in *PHT* strike me as particularly interesting in light of the current crisis. One I was aware of when writing: the sociology of preferences approach has an analytic problem concerning power resources. Even if we know perfectly the preference structure, we would still need to know something about the resources available for wielding power to influence the outcome. Although I noted this problem in *PHT*, I did not systematically explore it. By implication rather than direct statement, the book commits the methodological error of circularity by inferring power from the outcome. I take this topic up later in the chapter concerning the role of finance industry in shaping responses to the current crisis.

More intriguing to me in light of the current crisis is the relative neglect in *PHT* of micro-institutions of the economy and structure of finance. The notion of production profile in the book looked at sectors and industries and the terms of trade among them, as new products and new countries changed the rewards and thus the politics. *PHT* focused largely on macropolicies of various kinds: neoclassical policy, trade protection, demand management, and industrial policy. All of them have some microelement to them (antitrust, for example, and patterns of land ownership), but little attention was paid to the institutions of finance, corporate governance, labor, and education.

Yet it is just these variables that seem so important in understanding comparative capitalism (that is, the ways in which market economies differ), and thus how they respond to the financial crisis. The debate over the rise of Japan and East Asia, the revival of Germany, and the hollowing out of the rust belt in the United States proves instructive. The literature of the late 1980s and early 1990s stressed the strong state, the autonomy of the bureaucracy in its ability to "pick winners" in helping key industries to grow (Schoenfield 1965; Katzenstein 1978; Johnson 1982; Haggard 1990; Wade 1990; Amsden 1992; World Bank 1993). As I read through various literatures, the key explanatory driver was not, I concluded, the state "picking winners" or the "strong state" model, but the regulatory model that shaped the tight bonds among patient, or long-term, capital, corporate governance, firm managers, employees, and up- and down-stream networks. The Japanese and German systems contrasted with the arm's-length relationships typical of the United States and the United Kingdom (although not the United States in its early industrialization phase). These ideas have been systematized in the now well-known Hall and Soskice's *Varieties of Capitalism* (2001). What the state did was to sustain the regulations that preserved this system and the logic of the "institutional complementarities" (Milgrom and Roberts 1995) on which it is based. Regulations buffered it from rapid change—not from change altogether but from changes too fast for members to devise modes of adjustment, and so fast as to break the incentive of the long-run commitments the investment strategy required. Corporate governance seemed the linchpin of what held the interdependencies together. We needed a political explanation of what sustained different corporate governance systems.

The Hall and Soskice's (2001) volume brilliantly describes the logic of the equilibrium that sustains countries in one end or the other of the continuum between liberal market economies (LMEs) and coordinated market economies (CMEs). However, it does not explain the choice of poles nor how countries shift from one set of arrangements to another. Over time, countries have switched systems. The United States, today the archetype of the arm's-length model ("LME" in Hall and Soskice's terms), in 1890 in fact resembled Germany. It had main banks (viz JP Morgan), *zaibatsu/keiretsu*, that is, highly integrated systems of supplier chains, and vertical integration. Supervision of managers, the main concern of governance theory, was carried out by having concentrated blockholders with their own agents on the board of directors. Then American politics set to work: it produced antitrust rules, banking regulation, the Securities and Exchange Act of 1934, and numerous other laws and rules. Over time, the system evolved into the current arm's-length, diffuse shareholder model of today (Roe 1994, 2003).

Other countries have gone the other way. Rajan and Zingales' (2003) celebrated "The Great Reversals" showed that before World War I several countries, notably Japan and France, had been moving down a path of high stock market valuations and equity finance but then shifted course toward a blockholding model of centralized control dominated by banks, for which they became famous exemplars. These patterns of reversals shake notions of national capitalism patterns fixed in time and refute the importance given to *long durée* variables like legal family (common versus civil law) found in the well-known literature of La Porta and others (2000; see critiques by Gourevitch 2003; Roe 2003; Gourevitch and Shinn 2005).

The diffuse shareholder model developed a wide range of minority shareholder protections (MSP): no insider trading, clear rules on shareholder ownership and transactions, accounting, compensation, and declaration of ownership patterns. The blockholder countries lacked these rules. Controversy continues over the arrows of causality and the interaction: Did diffusion happen because of strong MSP, or did MSP develop because there were growing numbers of shareholders seeking protection? But the two elements—high MSP and high diffusion—seem correlated. To explain the difference in patterns, we turn to politics, which creates the laws and regulatory posture of enforcement.

In explaining the shift in the United States from a blockholding to a diffuse shareholding model, Roe (2003) focused on populism, symbolized by William Jennings Bryan's "Cross of Gold" speech in 1896. Anger at Eastern money, railroad rate rigging, high prices on industrial goods, and tight money combined into a movement that led to regulation: antitrust, shipping rates, and limits on banking. Roe develops a partisan alignment explanation for corporate governance (the left being against MSP, the right for it). Although stronger as a political argument than as the legal family approach, the left versus right model of cleavage does less well than a cross-class coalitions model (Gourevitch and Shinn 2005; Pagano and Volpin 2005a, b). The "corporatist compromise" began in the 1930s and developed in the postwar years, combining segments of business, labor, and agriculture around regulated markets and high levels of social welfare services. More recently, a different axis has emerged, a "transparency coalition" where labor switches from an opponent of minority shareholder protections to a supporter of MSP because of its interest in pension funds and concern for participation in management (Cioffi and Hoepner 2006; Cioffi 2010; Pinto, Weymouth, and Gourevitch 2010). In recent years, a number of countries have reformed rules and regulations on corporate governance, in response to the pressure of international investors and domestic pressures (Schaede 2008; Culpepper 2010; Woolley and Zeigler 2012).

The globalization of production in recent decades has increased the importance of micro-institutions of comparative capitalism, corporate governance, and the role of finance in the system. It makes management of supply chains a core competence of modern business. The process innovations of Toyota lay in contractor relationships that improved incentives for information sharing, and led to low-defect, low-cost, high-quality manufacturing (Womack, Jones, and Roos 1991). This celebrated "just in time" manufacturing squeezed out the buffering from the high inventory and rework yard characteristic of the American model, but it was itself buffered by corporate governance patterns including cross-shareholding, rotation of managers, main banks that shield the members of the network from hostile takeovers, and short-term economic pressures to fire workers and cut production. It shifted the burden of adjustment to the outer reaches of the network, the low-tier suppliers, to protect the higher-skilled inner core. Japanese and American manufacturers engaged in this system with different structures and strategies (Borrus, Ernst, and Haggard 2000; Zysman and Newman 2006.) Globalization makes for greater efficiency, but also has its fragilities, emphasized dramatically by the Japanese earthquake of 2011.

The intensification of supply chain division of labor into components may contribute to overall financialization of the economy. It encourages the firm to focus on the details of financial management of the system and reduces the importance of manufacturing "lobbies" inside the firm. The engineers of the production system lose influence to the fiscal managers. Relationships that promote production give way to strategies of flexibility and optimization that devalue other skills (Schaede 2008). Politically, the hollowing out in export of jobs weakens the importance of domestic manufacturing, leaving the field to finance. The growth of supply chain outsourcing induces manufacturers to accept strong currency to lower the cost of imports and increase profit margins, linking them with a big-box retail lobby (such as Walmart) and undermining a coalition that might worry about demand and foreign competition (Palley 2012). A massive flood of imports from Pacific Rim countries after 1998 put U.S. manufacturing into recession. The U.S. consumer became a key driver of the world economy, so that emerging market economies at first resistant to globalization came to embrace it.

The evolution of the micro-institutions of capitalism that had evolved over the previous decades in each country set the ground for how an alternative to the more traditional macroeconomic frame for understanding response to crisis. The macro frame focuses on monetary and fiscal policy and the structural imbalances in trade and capital flows. The microeconomic frame stresses institutional structures of the various markets that made up the economy. *PHT* had stressed the former, but my recent work made me more aware of the latter: corporate governance systems interact with banking, stocks, and finance to shape patterns of production but also to influence the politics that shape the policies that then create the patterns of production.

The Trajectory from Crisis Three (1970s) to Crisis Four (2008–?)

PHT's third crisis marked the end, in the 1970s, of the postwar *trentes glorieuses*, the three decades of growth (1945–75). In the 1970s, the rise of commodity prices, notably through the oil shock of OPEC, the inflation caused by the Vietnam War, and the growth of spending from the government interventions all contributed to the breakdown of Bretton Woods and stagflation. In the coordinated market economy countries, the pressures could be managed by corporatist wage bargaining. In the liberal market economies, decentralized labor relations could not contain wage pressures, so governments turned to wage and price controls. These mechanisms did not work well, and publics became disillusioned with government intervention. That set the stage for the Thatcher and Reagan victories and new set of historical experiences that became the "totemic events" that framed political discourse.

The new governments led a process of deregulation: at the international level, the elimination of currency controls, the Single European Act, the Uruguay Round of trade, the adoption of NAFTA, inclusion of China in Most Favored Nation arrangements, and other measures encouraged extensive flows of goods across borders, a shift of low-cost manufacturing overseas, and the movement to services and knowledge industries in Europe and the United States. At the domestic level, deregulation affected transportation, telecommunications, retail, banking, and many other sectors. High dollar valuation encouraged import of consumer goods from the low-wage countries, with lower prices somehow offsetting the loss of jobs and income to foreign producers.

Although the rhetoric of deregulation is associated with Thatcher and Reagan, it was already happening in the United States during the Carter years in the airline, shipping, and other industries. In earlier periods, regulation had been accepted by business as a way of stabilizing markets and had drawn elements of the business community into alliance with labor and agriculture groups seeking the same. But the growth of the world economy and the revival of national economies reduced the stability premium and increased the reward to market opportunities. Business elements pulled out of the stability coalition, with the cooperation of labor and farmers accepting the opportunity for greater growth. Airlines were one example in which the tourist industry allied with aircraft producers to push for deregulation (Richards 2001). Telecommunications was another. As Milner (1988) notes on trade, it is not only the protectionists that organize; free trade and deregulation have interest groups as well (Frieden 1988). In this period, they pushed to unravel the regulatory stability model of the post–World War II compromise.

In so doing, the interest groups were aided by ideological changes. Critics of Keynesian and state regulation gained ground in the academy and think tanks. Although notable in the United States, this change was also true in Europe: Mitterrand stepped back from expansion of state power and moved France at a crucial juncture down a less statist trajectory. The advanced industrial world moved in a neoliberal way (Evans and Sewell, forthcoming). Then the demise of the USSR, the liberalization of China, and the move away from import-substituting state regulatory projects in Latin America all contributed to the growing magnet of world markets.

This liberalization set the stage for emergence of the financial sector. Competition pressed on manufacturing processes, as trade and technology led to intensification of the global division of labor down to components, not just finished products. High-tech components continued to be manufactured in advanced industrial countries, but assembly and many components moved. With the export of jobs, unions and manufacturing weakened within the firm and in the polity (Rajan 2010; Palley 2011). Shareholder primacy emerged in finance theory, the business schools and economics as the prevailing view of the firm, and the securities industry used in turning against conglomerates (Useem 1993, 1996; Lazonick and Sullivan 2000; Fourcade and Khurana 2011).

A number of changes rewarded finance. Banking rules were loosened to break down firewalls among financial institutions, symbolized by the passage of Gramm–Leach–Billey in 1999, which formally repealed Glass–Steagall (already slowly killed in reality through regulatory changes). Financial institutions were now allowed to undertake activities across platforms, to innovate in financial services—such changes were advanced as contributing to efficiency. It allowed these firms to become much bigger, thus "too big to fail." Manufacturing firms engaged heavily in finance as a source of profits (viz GMAC). Pension systems authorized through the Employee Retirement Income Security Act (ERISA) made workers into shareholders. Institutional investors grew substantially. The stock market rose in a dizzying ascent.

Loosening of antitrust regulation encouraged firms to expand, merge, and grow. The world of finance sought opportunities to fund this growth. Financial institutions developed techniques, structures, and institutions to do this. Investment patterns deepened market fluidity; stock market analysts turned away from conglomerates. Managers had liked conglomerates as a way of diversifying firm risk and allowing cross investment across new products and processes. The argument changed in favor of specialization in core competences. Rather than managers making the diversification decisions, profits would go to investors, who would themselves decide on optimal risk hedging.

The change came with the substantial growth of pension and investment funds: the mutual fund industries, ERISA plans (Bonoli 2000). The retirement system in the United States soon became more reliant on private equity holdings than in any other country, which made its citizens concerned with issues of corporate governance and finance. This process greatly expanded public involvement in financial markets and increased the size of institutional investors. The stock market rose to record heights. This created an immense pool of capital, which in turn fueled the economy and considerably increased the importance of the financial sector.

At the same time, finance became ever more important to nonfinancial firms. Nonfinancial firms were getting an increasing share of income from financial activities (GMAC, for example) and financial management became an important part of the firm's strategic concerns.

These changes in market conditions opened the way to changes of power within the firm. The position of chief financial officer (CFO) grew in the hierarchy of the firm's management (Dobbin and Sutton 1998; Hoshi 2001; Schaede 2008). A revealing contrast in the logic of governance between Japan and the United States is that the personnel manager is an important job in the former, but not the latter. This fits the logic of job security, where employees are a fixed asset to be managed carefully. As securities firms rewarded share performance, firms optimize share price.

Executive pay policies such as stock options shifted resources to people at the very top of the firm, away from smaller shareholders and employees. The rationale was to align incentives between managers and shareholders, thus much applauded in the law and finance world as a way of solving the agency problem articulated since Berle and Means ([1932] 1991)—the collective action obstacles that diffuse shareholders face in monitoring managers, and the weakness of boards of directors in achieving this. The perverse effect may well have been to encourage excessive risk-taking, thus widening the gap between high-paid managers and ordinary shareholders. This risk-taking contributed to the financial crisis (Bebchuk and Fried 2004; Bolton, Scheinkman, and Xiong 2006; Bebchuk 2010).

The micro-institutional structure of these funds in the United States allowed the emergence of a conflict of interest between savers and the private owners of the financial institutions that managed them. Financial managers earn fees, which then cut down on earnings. Competition should in theory drive those fees down, but the structure of the industry produces many captives so that fees remain high. The real force behind lowering fees comes from the few "mutually held" funds. Vanguard (Bogle 2005) embraced both the efficient markets view that active investing could not predictably beat the market, thus not worth the fees, with the conflict of interest idea that the shareholders of an investment fund had conflict with the savers over fees charged to the latter for the profit of the former (Monks and Minow 1996; Monks 2007). Fidelity is privately held by the Johnson family, who are thus not obligated to share information about Fidelity with the investors in the funds it manages. The Johnsons were among the leaders in behind-the-scenes lobbying for privatization of Social Security during the Bush administration.

Institutional investors have drawn attention as one of the solutions to the collective action problems in the diffuse shareholder model in U.S. and U.K. corporate governance. As they manage vast sums, it is thought they had reason to take action in monitoring managers. But here, as in bond rating agencies and accounting (Partnoy 2001), conflicts of interest have deadened that incentive: the managers of institutional investors seek the business of chief executive officers (CEOs) to manage a company pension fund (Gourevitch 2008). They have little motive to challenge that manager. Only recently have institutional investors been obligated to divulge how they vote their proxies (Davis and Kim 2006).

As a result, the privately held institutional investors support the policy views of the Business Roundtable, the organization dominated by CEOs of the largest companies, with every incentive high CEO returns, and not the goals of the average shareholder (Monks 2007). In much of Europe, by contrast, employee pension funds are managed with union participation in the process (Bonoli 2000). The public sector and union-based institutional investors behave somewhat differently (Gourevitch 2008).

For the past three decades, in sum, the world economy has grown in a substantially market-oriented way. Deregulation, the opening of world trade, the collapse of the USSR, transition economies, all these led to the opening of markets. At first this stimulated growth and trade. Stock markets boomed and wealth grew. This set the stage for the bubble. The antiregulation forces that turned off the controls of the post–World War II years also prevented prudential regulation during the next thirty years. Politics pushed in the direction of both macro excess and micro passivity. Greenspan's tag lines—"We can manage a bubble if it bursts" and the "counter parties would evaluate and contain risk"—go hand in hand. Blaming Greenspan may be gratifying, but it is not sufficient as an explanation. He could not have pursued these policies without substantial support. What are the political conditions that made possible this regulatory laxity of micro-institutions along with the excesses of macro policy?

Regulatory laxity appeared in Europe as well, as revealed by the Euro crisis of 2011. Banks were allowed to pile up substantial capital requirements with sovereign debt, notably ones in the weaker Global Investment Performance Standards (GIPS) countries of southern Europe. Lending practices in Europe helped pour money into the United States, so that the "culprits," the causal driver of the bubble, can be located there as well as in the United States. What then allowed regulatory laxity in Europe as well as in the United States?

The rise of finance is key to the story, but its growing influence connects to the changing positions of other groups. Finance had allies, "unindicted co-conspirators," or enablers: groups that pushed or supported various measures whose effect was to undermine the groups or lobbies that would have acted as "countervailing force" or balancers. We need to examine both finance and the enablers.

Power Resources

From the stagflation paralysis of the 1970s to the crisis of the 2000s, finance grew in political resources, structural importance, ideological hegemony, and coalitional position, becoming the "pivot point" in the Democratic Party. These variables provide competing or complimentary explanations for the financial sector's ability to influence policymaking so strongly. We confront the problem of mechanisms of influence raised earlier in this afterword and underdeveloped in *PHT*.

We can identify five various mechanisms of power: money, structure, coalitional provision, political institutions, and ideology.

Money

Finance gets its way because of the sheer quantity of money it pours into electoral campaigns. Wall Street buys support via massive contributions to all the political parties. They have a particularly great impact on the Democrats who lack a broad range of corporate donors, relying instead on contributions from entertainment, trial lawyers, and unions. Wall Street's contributions to politics now exceed that of other corporate categories. Campaign contributions of finance pour into the coffers of the leading Democratic congressmen: Senators Schumer, Dodd, and Feinstein, and Representative Barney Frank, who sat on key committees before he retired in 2012. In chastising the Obama administration for not imposing more severe penalties on finance, Simon Johnson (2009), former chief economist at the International Monetary Fund (IMF), writes that the United States reminds him of third-world leaders demanding bailout of their elites who have corrupted their political system. In 2010–11, it appears that Wall Street financial interests pared back their giving to the Democrats, angered by President Barack Obama's criticisms of finance and the Dodd–Frank bill. Indeed, the passage of that bill over Wall Street opposition shows the pressure to gratify an unhappy public and the need to create some impression of fixing the deficiencies that made investors unhappy. This is a familiar pattern for the Democrats: balancing the populist pressures of the general electorate against the goals of specialized interests. In the late nineteenth century, President Grover Cleveland was attacked for giving in to the "Gold Democrats."

Structure

Finance has power because of its vital role in the functioning of the economy. A credit crunch paralyzes all economic activity, as happened when Lehman Brothers went bankrupt and AIG came close to it. Finance is a utility, like water and energy. Without finance, everything stops. Therefore, decision makers have to do whatever it takes to keep funds flowing, keep banks functioning, prevent another collapse, reassure markets, and move the economy along. This provides finance with a functional power. Energy, transportation, and water—a strike in these industries shuts the economy down; the same is true of finance. "I want to return as the bond market" was famously James Carville's comment on hearing Robert Rubin invoke it so often in objecting to spending on social programs during the Clinton administration. In the current crisis, decision makers were inhibited from stricter regulation during the run-up to the bubble, from pricking the bubble when it was happening, and from imposing a "vigorous" haircut in restructuring finance. This power has pushed governments to the severe moral hazard posture of bailing out the very people who led the mess, in the United States, Greece, and Ireland (Krippner 2005, 2011; Eichengreen 2010; Johnson and Kwak 2010; Rogoff 2010).

Structural power cannot be easily measured. This explains its lack of popularity in American political science, which is too positivist to like functionalist arguments of this kind. The Great Recession seems to have brought it renewed attention. When prudent authors like McCarty and others (2010) use phrases like the "regulatory financial complex" and argue that "the money interest dominates the political process except in rare times of populist outrage," when economists and policymakers take seriously ending "too big to fail" as a policy objective, we need to reflect more deeply on the structural drivers of policy outcomes.

The struggle over structural arguments is another familiar echo with earlier crises (Hilferding 1981). Indeed, it may be that in Anglo-American social sciences, it comes back only with economic crises. During the post–World War I years, in European Marxist discussions, this was the Miliband–Poulantzas debate, with the latter as the structuralist. Within the United States, it was Lindblom (1977) among political scientists who articulated it. Sociology was more active in developing these arguments (O'Connor 1973), but they have not come back into the center of political science. The reluctance connects to methodology: it is hard to make this form of power operational. It can be detected by watching capital flows, investments, exchange rates. Policies that inhibit investment or provoke capital flights, labor strikes can all be observed. Simmons (2004) explored the impact of labor strength on French exchange rates in the 1920s. Fisman (2001) looked at how Indonesian markets responded to news of Suharto's health: the closer the corporate link to his favor, the more it was affected by good or bad news. The sheer size and growth of the financial sector is a behavioral indicator of the power of finance, but looking at outcomes to explain cause is circular reasoning.

Some structural analysis focuses on networks: the chain of connections among top officials and decision makers in finance and government. (On the importance of networks, see Hafner-Burton, Kahler, and Montgomery 2009.) The key officials come from the same set of firms, they know each other, share meals, clubs, schools, and as such they protect each other. This is descriptively true, but not clear in its causal mechanisms. The intermingling of the network and the public offices has political impact: having financial leadership coming from Goldman Sachs greatly undermines confidence in the neutrality of policymaking and provokes populist criticism.

Membership in the network and its dominance of key appointments can influence the substance of policymaking. This influence could happen via different causal channels: "group think" making finance healthy as the only route to recovery, excluding other industries or concerns—manufacturing, for example, or labor (Lindblom 1977). Another channel would be personal careerism: the decision makers planning their moves after they leave government, to remain in good standing with the finance firms that hire them. The supposed autonomy of the French and Japanese civil service (well paid, well trained) is presumed to insulate those countries from the in/out pattern in the United States, leading thereby to greater policy autonomy. Doubt about autonomy arises in considering *pantouflage* and *amakaduri* in the two systems: on leaving the civil service, the officials get jobs with the very people they have been regulating (Suleiman 1974; Johnson 1982).

In this way, the networking argument returns to structure. The government needs to reassure markets and investors, and so appoints people who are reassuring to that world, and the finance minister consults them. But this is a description of political reality: the government "needs" the good opinion of that world. Drawing the links is a way of describing a structural reality, rather than a cause of it. It is a way of showing the structural influences, more than an explanation of them. A noneconomic example is Richard Nixon's appointment of Henry Kissinger, a protégé of Nelson Rockefeller, as a signal to the East Coast foreign policy establishment. The network argument blurs with the ideological channel, or structure, or money. In the midst of the great financial crisis of 2008–9, the pressing goal was to reassure markets, not to go off the reservation of conventional wisdom by "breaking with orthodoxy." One can doubt whether the votes were ever there for such a strong break. Appointing Timothy Geithner was reassuring to Wall Street; picking Paul Krugman or Joseph Stiglitz, whom many liberals supported, would have alarmed financial circles.

Coalitional Position: Pivot Politics

Finance in the United States has leverage because of its position in political coalitions. It is a pivot group (Krehbiel 1998), one that could switch sides easily and thus is decisive to the final outcome. Indeed, in a two-dimensional left-right issue space, finance could easily ally with the more pro-business Republican Party. New York financial circles often clashed with manufacturing over issues of trade, international agreements, and foreign policy, which led to bargains with the Democrats. Finance also lacks the large industrial labor force that brought manufacturing into conflict with the labor movement, and it has seen the necessity of some regulation to stabilize the sector.

At the same time, the Democrats need a corporate ally. They cannot succeed solely as a labor party. They need broader sources of support in resources and legitimacy. At major historical moments, these forms of aid came from finance.

This makes the Democrats dependent on a major group, which can veto its moves and can limit the range of progressive programs. The role of finance today evokes the Gold Democrats of the late nineteenth century. These Eastern interests wanted "sound money" and resisted the Populist movement. Some reforms were made: antitrust, the Federal Reserve, but mostly populism was contained until the Great Depression of 1929 opened up the coalitional game again. Finance split into factions, some of which allied with various groups to form the New Deal coalition.

In recent decades the finance-labor alliance has eroded in place of other alignments. The influence of finance has been "enabled" by a series of policy moves led by other groups. Faced with foreign competition, manufacturers developed global supply chains. This undermined labor bargaining power and trade unions. Without domestic production, manufacturers lessened concerns with sustaining demand. Instead of protecting a manufacturing base, trade deficits were accepted as a way of keeping down wages and lowering costs. Instead of keeping the dollar down to fend off imports, big-box retailers like Walmart joined to support a strong dollar as way of lowering their import costs, which was often supported by analysts as aiding consumers and pushing up living standards (despite the loss of jobs). The United States developed strong trade deficits with Pacific Rim countries, as U.S. consumers became the drivers of the global flow of funds (Palley 2011; Streeck 2011). Over time, groups which in earlier periods had provide the core for alternatives to a neoliberal view of economic policy faded from the scene, leaving the terrain open to a free-market, finance, investor model. These developments set the stage for financial hegemony as its goals now came to align with important other sectors in the economy—thus the enablers of finance. No one was left to "take away the punch bowl."

Coalitional analysis opens the issue of how the coalitions are formed. Production profiles identify the players but not necessarily how they combine. If, as I believe, there is some openness, some possibility of alternative outcomes, then leadership can play an important role in shaping the bargains and combinations that prevail. The leaders of each participating group have choices to make on whether to venture or stay out and on what terms. The greatest weakness of the purely structural accounts of outcomes lies here in assuming low agency, the lack of choice of the various players. At times that will be the case: the Junkers did desperately switch to high tariffs. But at other times, the path is less clear and the discretion is greater. The 1930s provide one powerful example of different strategic choices by the major players in Germany, the United States, Sweden, and France (Blyth 2002; Tiberghien 2007).

Although the role of leadership may be striking in each specific case, it becomes harder to see if we find patterns of similar coalitional alliances across countries. Protectionist patterns in the 1873 cut across many situations, strengthening the notion that each interest group faced a similar logic, more powerful in its effects than the particularities of any leader or leader choice, just as it undermines the importance of institutions in producing that outcome. In other periods, there seemed to be more fluidity.

In the current crisis, Obama has been sharply criticized on the left for not imposing a severe haircut on the bondholders, for not making Wall Street pay. We return to the issues of structure. This critique assumes he could have succeeded politically had he done so. Ezra Klein (2011) doubts he could have done so, as do I. Unlike Franklin Delano Roosevelt (FDR), who could let Herbert Hoover and the Grand Old Party (GOP) take full blame for the Depression, which had been under way over three years before he took office, Obama was elected as the crisis got under way and felt immediate pressure to restore confidence. He rapidly became perceived as the incumbent, and as Bartels (2011) notes, incumbents pay a big political price when a crisis erupts. Paul Krugman (2010), a leading liberal economist, pushed Obama to reject the deal with the GOP Congress in December 2010 to extend Bush tax cuts and unemployment benefits: but Krugman does not analyze the political consequences of such a veto. Would this mobilize the liberals, or would it be seen as a move to the left partisanship and conflict that the public dislikes? A structural account would emphasize the potential of destabilizing capital markets to introduce insecurity at a moment of economic weakness as a major force limiting reform.

Political Institutions

Variance in policy output can be linked to variance in political systems. Rogowski and Kayser (2002) find that majoritarian countries favor consumers more than producers (Lijphart 1997). At first inspection, this pattern does not do much to explain the importance of finance in the current crisis. The United States, United Kingdom, Iceland, Spain, Estonia, Greece, and Portugal vary substantially in their political systems, as do Germany, Japan, France, Sweden, Brazil, and China. Financial bubbles and failures have happened in the consensus economies, such as Sweden of thirty years ago. Anyone can be profligate, as any institution could have been protectionist or Keynesian depending on the political circumstances. There is certainly no clear pattern of civil law versus common law as La Porta and others (2000) contend explains corporate governance outcomes. "Countries like Canada, Australia, and New Zealand whose banks were less exposed to mortgage-backed securities, whose banks did not have SIVs [structured investment vehicles] and which did not have under-regulated shadow banking systems largely avoided the recent crisis" (Bordo and Landon-Lane 2010, 31).

And yet there are elements of the crisis that have been influenced by political institutions, via the CME/LME distinction. Strong CME countries like Germany protected jobs more aggressively than the United States by protecting major industries (such as cars); and strong welfare state systems protected purchasing power. If we probe the political foundations of the CME/LME pattern, we find it has some correlation with the majoritarian/consensus distinction (Gourevitch and Shinn 2005; Cusak, Iversen, and Soskice 2007). The varieties of capitalism literature describes an equilibrium whose pieces fit through strong institutional complementarity. Its participants invest heavily in relationships which they then seek to protect. As the CME systems require considerable cross-investment among the parts (labor, education, training, manufacturing techniques), the consensus systems sustain long commitments by protecting against rapid change, or change which does not involve processes of buy-in. Majoritarian systems undermine such commitments because they involve faster policy changes and lower veto point protections from consultation. So, in this way, the political systems do encourage certain patterns of interest group investment in production patterns. Several authors (Thelen 2004; Cusack, Iversen, and Soskice 2007) take these back to older patterns of organization, such as the guilds in Germany, and stress the effects of unintended consequences.

In the CME countries, finance has strong contenders in other forms of business, labor, and the interconnected network of interest groups (Aguilera and Jackson 2010; Aoki 2010). Structures of patient capital retain some ability to limit the more free-wheeling methods of Anglo-American finance. Evidence for this appeared in debates over corporate governance reforms in Germany. A series of measures (Cioffi 2010) were adopted that liberalized some elements of the system (for example, lowering the tax on selling shares, which weakened the cross-shareholding network characteristic of patient capital systems). These measures were opposed by the traditional business groups (the CDU), but attracted both the SPD (concerned with transparency to preserve Mitbestimmung), and the Free Democrats, the classic neoliberal organization in Germany, linked to finance. The SPD felt confident it had the power to prevent these reforms from undermining the CME system as a whole.

In the dramatic crisis over the euro in 2011–12, the divergence between German resistance to having the European Central Bank buy debt from the GIPS countries and U.S. and U.K. support for doing so can be linked to deep structural differences in their economies. The German CME system encourages savings because the highly specific skills that workers have make it harder for them to find jobs if laid off. The export-led growth works best if fiscal policy is restrained: this restraint is the core of German resistance to inflation, not the memory of 1923. Far fewer Germans than Americans own their homes, so that they benefit less from inflation. Unemployment has been lower in Germany than in the United States, thus less political pressure to reflate. The northern European economies thus favor a macro policy that suits their economic model and are willing to impose it on southern and other European economies that would be better off with more reflationary policies, given their economic models.

It is possible to link the structural differences in the political economy of the industrial countries with differences in political institutions, such as electoral laws and legislative-executive relations (Lijphart 1997). Iversen and Soskice (2006, 2009) trace the origins and the persistence of varieties of capitalism (VoC) variables to political roots in political organization, while Thelen (2004) locates these in more social processes.

Ideology

In addition to a general move against regulation, ideological currents (Blyth 2002; Berger 2003) have also shifted to favor finance (Hall 1993b). Business analysis turned against conglomerates (Useem 1993, 1996). Arguments for a stakeholder model of the well-managed firm, for deeper relationships among the various players in a complex system, gave way to the application of principal-agent reasoning that asserted the primacy of shareholders, hence share value and financial management. It traced delegation from shareholder to the board to managers. Only highly skilled managers posed a problem of "agency slack" through the incomplete contract. Recent work has criticized this model, finding many more incomplete contracts in the system, notably with skilled labor (Zingales 2000). Maximizing shareholder return became established as the telos of the firm, the task of the manager, the standard of optimal performance. This emphasis seems obvious in the current ideological climate in the United States, but it is surprisingly recent in being the hegemonic view. Thirty years ago, managers claimed obligation to the firm as a whole, the system, not the shareholders—this perhaps not out of deep obligation to the stakeholders, but as a way of claiming a broader mandate of which they, the managers, were the chief interpreters (Monks 2007). As managing money became supremely important to the firm, the CFO rose to become the most important person after the CEO or president of the firm. In Japan, by contrast, the personnel manager remains quite important in power and prestige as compared to the United States where human resources ranks low; the former ties long-term employment to the inner core, or tier, of workers and makes them an asset whose management is important. In the United States the short-term, arm's-length approach makes employees expendable, hence less important.

The capacity to innovate in finance rose to be the supreme goal. Regulation was judged through this prism. Most regulation of finance became suspect as an inhibition on liquidity. The intellectual firepower behind such arguments was used by the finance industry to undermine regulation. Since the regulators were paid less than finance people, they had to be of lesser quality, and as such could not be expected to understand that the new instruments reduced the level of risk so much as to render older rules obsolete, thereby justifying lower reserve requirements and looser regulation.

This finance "centrism" has received sharp criticism since the crisis. Analysts charge the "real economy" was excessively subordinated to the "money economy" (Solow 2010). This too is a return to an old theme. Analysis of the U.K. economic development in the nineteenth century, its initial surge, then falling behind Germany and the United States, explores the tension between Manchester manufacturing and the City of London, where finance's insistence on low tariffs and a strong currency came at the expense of manufacturing. In contrast, Germany and the United States pursued more aggressive policies to help manufacturers.

If finance is politically so strong, why was it not able to prevent legislation it did not like (Sarbanes–Oxley and Dodd–Frank) and fail in getting something it wanted, the privatization of Social Security? Earlier waves of regulation happened after market collapse and scandal: the Securities Exchange Commission (SEC) after the Pecora hearings of 1933 is the most famous example. The Enron fraud of 2001 was followed by a series of others, leading to the Sarbanes–Oxley Bill of 2002. Five years later, the Lehman failure and AIG bailout of 2008 then led to the Dodd–Frank Bill of 2010.

Why did these pass? The answer lies in the vulnerability of finance to outrage, at least for a time (Culpepper 2010). The scandals and market collapse frightened small investors, especially pension fund owners, an ever-larger share of the population because of U.S. pension systems. They want reassurance, and pragmatists in the business world see the need for reforms to save the system, to bring people back to the market. Then over time, the processes of co-optation and erosion set to work. Already the GOP congressional victory of 2010 means cuts in funding for regulation enforcement and creates obstacles to implementation, such as blocking the appointment of Elizabeth Warren, then of Richard Cordray, to head the new consumer protection agency. This is a classic pattern in reform processes: enough scandal to press forward, then pressure recedes and the industry deflects implantation back toward its preferences.

Most of this discussion has focused on the U.S. case, justified by the importance of the United States in the world economy and the transmission of the crisis from U.S.-developed financial instruments into portfolios around the world. The pressure on the euro in the summer and fall of 2011 revealed that weaknesses in financial regulation were by no means exclusive to the United States. European banks appear to have been a major source of pumping liquidity into the U.S. and world markets (Palley 2011). They were allowed at the same time to accumulate substantial sovereign debt from GIPS countries and to count these as fully secure in their bank reserves. European regulators were therefore also lax. Blame between Europe and the United States thus lies on both sides. Importantly for the future, the policy conflict between stabilizing finance and promoting growth has intensified.

Conclusion

The policy struggle in the current crisis echoes the debates during its forerunners. The dominance of the austerity line in European and American policy circles resurrects the arguments from 1929–31 of the need to restore the conditions for business confidence. The notions of inadequate demand and liquidity trap appear politically weaker today than a half-century ago. In Germany, the memory of the hyperinflation of 1923 seems to push aside the contrasting memory of 1929 deflation and 25 percent unemployment. At present, low unemployment in Germany hides the impact of future deflation. German political economy depends on containing wages and prices.

This fourth crisis in the sequence explored by *PHT* involves the interaction of macro- and micro-policy: large imbalances in government spending and imports and capital inflows create a huge debt overhang, an immense leveraging, a flood of money into the United States producing a bubble which eventually burst (Gourevitch, forthcoming). There is considerable force to this account (see Chinn and Frieden 2011). An alternative perspective looks at micro-institutions: the behaviors of financial structures in generating toxic assets, then spread by loose regulation on mortgages into the world economy. Loose standards of capital adequacy ratios compounded the weakness. The macro-excesses could have been contained by tighter regulation.

However, tighter regulation did not happen because the financial regulatory complex dominated policymaking. The influence of the "Starve the Beast" strategy" (Persson and Svensson 1989; Alesina and Tabellini 1990; Bartlett 2007; Broz, chapter 3, this volume) in the GOP meant that budget deficits would not be addressed, and tax increases on the wealthy were off the table. Seeking to reassure business and finance during the sharpest recession in decades, the Obama administration did not challenge them. Money, structure, ideology, political balance, and institutions favored these influences. Despite differences in all these respects, European regulation was also inadequate.

As of this writing, this current crisis will not mark a sharp challenge to business orthodoxy, as a contrast to the 1930s. There have been only modest changes to the rules of the system, as Dodd–Frank seems modest: no big banks broken up, no major separation of activities, no substantial punishments of financial wrong-doing—no real change in the rules of the game. No major changes are under way that would alter the fault lines of the world economy. Governments in Europe and in the United States seem committed to a plan of austerity, of deflation like Japan in the 1990s and like the industrial world in the early 1930s.

Change seems to require the political will to break the revived fiscal orthodoxy. That political will was hard to find in the early 1930s. It took substantial movement in coalitions and in some cases the collapse of democracy. So far we have seen governments defeated and the rise of nationalist parties and movements, but no great upheaval. This could change if policy continues to punish, particularly unemployment. That will not happen without more suffering or a sharper break with the international system, such as the collapse of trade or finance—or war. The sources of capital may dry up, as it goes elsewhere or becomes absorbed in domestic economies. Changing balances of forces in the world economy could do that, with continued growth of the economies of Brazil, Russia, India, and China (BRICs) and the G-20. The structural imbalances between exporter/creditor and importer/debtor show little sign of change. Barring further collapse in the United States, I do not see any overt challenge to the U.S. pattern of a cheap credit economy, low skills, high flexibility, and low investment in workers. Rather, we are more likely to experience a kind of slow decline à la Japan. Fast change could come from an externally induced crisis more severe than Reinhart and Rogoff's (2009) number 4.

International institutions and treaties cannot solve these problems without strong domestic foundations. The analytic and policy agenda of the coming years will thus be the domestic foundations of international adjustment to the structural weaknesses of the world and domestic economies. Finance is powerful because policy decisions were taken in a range of fields that allowed it to be. Free trade, anti-union sentiment, export of jobs, and outsourcing all reduced rivals, competitors for policy. We cannot thus measure its power by looking only at its resources. We must look also at its position in system and at the absence of countervailing power.

References

Abdelal, Rawi. 2007. *Capital Rules: The Construction of Global Finance.* Cambridge, MA: Harvard University Press.

Abiad, Abdul G., Thierry Tressel, and Enrica Detragiache. 2010. "A New Database of Financial Reforms." *IMF Staff Papers* 57 (2): 281–302.

Abraham, David. 1988. *The Collapse of the Weimar Republic.* Princeton, NJ: Princeton University Press.

Aggarwal, Vinod K., and Min Gyo Koo. 2008. "An Institutional Path: Community Building in Northeast Asia." In *The United States and Northeast Asia*, edited by G. John Ikenberry and Chung-in Moon, 285–307. Lanham, MD: Rowman & Littlefield.

Aguilera, Ruth V., and Gregory Jackson. 2010. "Comparative and International Corporate Governance." *Academy of Management Annals* 4 (1): 485–556.

Aizenman, J., M. Gavin, and R. Hausmann. 2000. "Optimal Tax and Debt Policy with Endogenously Imperfect Creditworthiness." *Journal of International Trade and Economic Development* 9:367–95.

Aizenman, Joshua, and Yothin Jinjarak. 2009. "Current Account Patterns and National Real Estate Markets." *Journal of Urban Economics* 66 (2): 75–89.

Akerlof, George A., and Rachel E. Kranton. 2010. *Identity Economics: How Our Identities Shape Our Work, Wages, and Well-Being.* Princeton, NJ: Princeton University Press.

Alesina, Alberto. 1988. "Credibility and Policy Convergence in a Two-party System with Rational Voters." *American Economic Review* 78 (September): 796–806.

Alesina, Alberto, Reza Baqir, and William Easterly. 1999. "Public Goods and Ethnic Divisions." *Quarterly Journal of Economics* 114 (4): 1243–84.

Alesina, Alberto, Felipe Campante, and Guido Tabellini. 2008. "Why Is Fiscal Policy Often Pro-cyclical?" *Journal of the European Economic Association* 6 (5): 1006–36.

Alesina, Alberto, and Roberto Perotti. 1995. "The Political Economy of Budget Deficits." Staff Working Paper No. 94/85, International Monetary Fund.

Alesina, Alberto, and Guido Tabellini. 1990. "A Positive Theory of Fiscal Deficits and Government Debt." *Review of Economic Studies* 57 (3): 403–14.

Allison, Graham T. 1971. *Essence of Decision: Explaining the Cuban Missile Crisis.* Boston: Little, Brown.

Almond, Gabriel A., Scott C. Flanagan, and Robert J. Mundt, eds. 1973. *Crisis, Choice, and Change: Historical Studies of Political Development.* Boston: Little, Brown.

Almunia, Miguel, Agustín S. Bénétrix, Barry Eichengreen, Kevin H. O'Rourke, and Gisela Rua. 2009. "From Great Depression to Great Credit Crisis: Similarities, Differences and Lessons." Working Paper No. 15524, National Bureau of Economic Research, Cambridge, MA, November.

Alt, James E. 1979. *The Politics of Economic Decline.* New York: Cambridge University Press.

Amable, Bruno. 2003. *The Diversity of Modern Capitalism.* Oxford: Oxford University Press.

Ames, Daniel R. 2004a. "Inside the Mind-Reader's Toolkit: Projection and Stereotyping in Mental State Inference." *Journal of Personality and Social Psychology* 87:340–53.

———. 2004b. "Strategies for Social Inference: A Similarity Contingency Model of Projection and Stereotyping in Attribute Prevalence Estimates." *Journal of Personality and Social Psychology* 87:573–85.

Amsden, Alice. 1992. *Asia's Next Giant: South Korea and Late Industrialization*. London: Oxford University Press.

Anan'ich, B. V., and V. L. Bovykin. 1991. "Foreign Banks and Foreign Investment in Russia." In *International Banking, 1870–1914*, edited by Rondo Cameron and V. I. Bovykin, 253–79. New York: Oxford University Press.

Ancelovici, Marcos. 2002. "Organizing against Globalization: The Case of ATTAC in France." *Politics and Society* 30 (3): 427–63.

———. 2009. "The Unusual Suspects: The French Left and the Construction of Global Finance." *French Politics* 7 (1): 42–45.

———. 2013. "The Origins and Dynamics of Organizational Resilience: A Comparative Study of Two French Labor Organizations." In *Social Resilience in the Neoliberal Era*, edited by P. A. Hall and M. Lamont. Cambridge: Cambridge University Press.

Ansell, Ben W. 2007. "Bubbling Under: Political Preferences during Asset Bubbles." Paper prepared for the 2007 Midwest Political Science Association Annual Conference, Palmer House Hotel, Chicago, April 12.

———. 2009. "The 'Nest Egg' Effect: Housing, the Welfare State, and Political Incentives." Paper prepared for the 2009 Midwest Political Science Association Annual Conference, Palmer House Hotel, Chicago, April 12.

Antràs, Pol, Luis Garicano, and Esteban Rossi-Hansberg. 2006. "Offshoring in a Knowledge Economy." *Quarterly Journal of Economics* 121 (1): 31–77.

Aoki, Masahiko. 2010. *Corporations in Evolving Diversity: Cognition, Governance, and Institutions*. Oxford: Oxford University Press.

Ardanaz, Martin J., Pablo M. Pinto, and Santiago M. Pinto. 2011. "Fiscal Policy in Good Times and Bad Times: Endogenous Time Horizons and Pro-Cyclical Spending in Argentina." Paper delivered at the Annual Meeting of the Midwest Political Science Association, Chicago, March 30–April 3.

Armingeon, Klaus, Sarah Engler, Panajotis Potolidis, Marlène Gerber, and Philipp Leimgruber. 2010. *Comparative Political Data Set 1960–2008*. Berne: Institute of Political Science, University of Berne.

Aslund, Anders. 2010. *The Last Shall Be First: The Eastern European Financial Crisis*. Washington, DC: Peterson Institute for International Economics.

———. 2011. "Lessons from the East European Financial Crisis, 2008–10." Policy Brief No. 11-9, Peterson Institute for International Economics, Washington, DC, June.

Authors, J. 2010. "Why Hoarding Comes Naturally in an Age of Anxiety." *Financial Times*, November 28.

Autor, David, David Dorn, and Gordon Hanson. 2011. "The China Syndrome: Local Labor Market Impacts of Import Competition in the United States." Working paper, School of International Relations and Pacific Studies, University of California, San Diego.

Baccaro, Lucio, and Chris Howell. 2011. "A Common Neoliberal Trajectory: The Transformation of Industrial Relations in Advanced Capitalism." *Politics and Society* 39 (4): 521–63.

Bagwell, Kyle, and Robert W. Staiger. 2009. "Delocation and Trade Agreements in Imperfectly Competitive Markets." Working Paper No. 15444, National Bureau of Economic Research, Cambridge, MA.

Bailey, Andrew, and Cheryl Schonhardt-Bailey. 2005. "Central Bankers and Big Ideas: Independence, Credibility, Uncertainty and Measurement in FOMC Transcripts."

Unpublished manuscript, London School of Economics and Political Science, February 22.

Baker, Andy. 2005. "Who Wants to Globalize? Consumer Tastes and Labor Markets in a Theory of Trade Policy Beliefs." *American Journal of Political Science* 49 (4): 924–38.

———. 2009. *The Market and the Masses in Latin America: Policy Reform and Consumption in Liberalizing Economies*. New York: Cambridge University Press.

Baldwin, Richard. 2009. "Introduction: The Great Trade Collapse: What Caused It and What Does It Mean?" In *The Great Trade Collapse: Causes, Consequences and Prospects*, edited by Richard Baldwin. VoxEU e-book. http://www.voxeu.org/index.php?q=node/4297.

Baldwin, Richard, and Simon Evenett, eds. 2009. *The Collapse of Global Trade, Murky Protectionism, and the Crisis: Recommendations for the G20*. London: Centre for Economic Policy Research.

Baldwin, Robert, Daniel Gros, and Luc Laeven, eds. 2010. *Completing the Eurozone Rescue: What More Needs to Be Done?* London: Centre for Economic Policy Research.

Baldwin, Robert E. 1985. *The Political Economy of U.S. Import Policy*. Cambridge, MA: MIT Press.

Banerjee, Abhijit, Shawn Cole, Esther Duflo, and Leigh Linden. 2007. "Remedying Education: Evidence from Two Randomized Experiments in India." *Quarterly Journal of Economics* 122 (3): 1235–64.

Banerjee, Abhijit, and Esther Duflo. 2008. "The Experimental Approach to Development Economics." Working Paper No. 14467, National Bureau of Economic Research, Cambridge, MA.

Barnes, Lucy, and Peter A. Hall. 2013. "Neo-Liberalism and Social Resilience in the Developed Democracies." In *Social Resilience in the Neo-Liberal Era*, edited by Peter A. Hall and Michèle Lamont. New York: Cambridge University Press.

Barro, Robert. 1979. "On the Determination of the Public Debt." *Journal of Political Economy* 87 (5): 940–71.

Bartels, Larry. 2008. *Unequal Democracy: The Political Economy of the New Gilded Age*. Princeton, NJ: Princeton University Press.

———. 2011. "Ideology and Retrospection in Electoral Responses to the Great Recession." Paper prepared for the Conference on Popular Reactions to the Great Recession, Nuffield College, Oxford, June 24–26.

Bartlett, Bruce. 2007. "'Starve the Beast': Origins and Development of a Budgetary Metaphor." *Independent Review* 12 (1): 5–26.

Bebchuk, Lucien. 2010. "How to Fix Bankers' Pay." *Daedelus* 139 (4): 52–60.

Bebchuk, Lucien, and Jesse Fried. 2004. *Pay without Performance: The Unfulfilled Promise of Executive Compensation*. Cambridge, MA: Harvard University Press.

Beck, Thorsten, George Clarke, Alberto Groff, Philip Keefer, and Patrick Walsh. 2001. "New Tools in Comparative Political Economy: The Database of Political Institutions." *World Bank Economic Review* 15 (1): 165–76.

Beckert, Jens. 2010. "'Gold Will Rise to Two Thousand Dollars': Fictionality in Economic Action." Unpublished manuscript, Max Planck Institute, Cologne, November.

Beer, Samuel H. 1969. *Modern British Politics*. London: Faber.

Berger, Suzanne. 1981. "Lame Ducks and National Champions: Industrial Policy in the Fifth Republic." In *The Fifth Republic at Twenty*, edited by Edward Andrews and Stanley Hoffmann, 292–310. Albany: State University of New York Press.

———. 2003. *Notre première mondialisation: leçons d'un échec oublié*. Paris: Seuil.

———. 2005. *How We Compete*. New York: Broadway Business.

Berger, Suzanne, and Ronald Dore, eds. 1996. *National Diversity and Global Capitalism*. Ithaca, NY: Cornell University Press.

Berle, Adolph, and Gardiner Means. (1932) 1991. *The Modern Corporation and Private Property*. New Brunswick, ME: Transaction Publishers.

Bernard, Andrew B., J. Bradford Jensen, Stephen J. Redding, and Peter K. Schott. 2007. "Firms in International Trade." *Journal of Economic Perspectives* 21 (3): 105–30.

Bernard, Andrew B., J. Bradford Jensen, and Peter K. Schott. 2009. "Importers, Exporters, and Multinationals: A Portrait of Firms in the U.S. That Trade Goods." In *Producer Dynamics: New Evidence from Micro Data*, edited by T. Dunne, J. B. Jensen and M. J. Robert, 513–76. Chicago: University of Chicago Press.

Bernhard, William, and David Leblang. 2008. *Democratic Processes and Financial Markets: Pricing Politics*. New York: Cambridge University Press.

Bhagwati, Jagdish. 2009. *Termites in the Trading System: How Preferential Trade Agreements Undermine Free Trade*. New York: Oxford University Press.

Billings, Robert S., Thomas W. Milburn, and Mary Lou Schaalman. 1980. "A Model of Crisis Perception: A Theoretical and Empirical Analysis." *Administrative Science Quarterly* 2 (2): 300–316.

Binder, Leonard. 1971. *Crises and Sequences in Political Development*. Princeton, NJ: Princeton University Press.

Blattman, Christopher, and Jeannie Annan. 2010. "The Consequences of Child Soldiering." *The Review of Economics and Statistics* 42 (4): 882–98.

Blinder, Alan. 2000. "How the Economy Came to Resemble the Model." *Business Economics* 135 (1): 16–25.

Blinder, Alan, and Ricardo Reis. 2005. "The Greenspan Standard." Paper presented at the Federal Reserve Bank of Kansas City Symposium, Jackson Hole, WY, August 25–27.

Blommestein, H., and A. Gok. 2009. "The Surge in Borrowing Needs of OECD Governments: Revised Estimates for 2009 and 2010 Outlook." *Financial Market Trends* 2009 (2): 177–89.

Blustein, Paul. 2009. *Misadventures of Most Favored Nations*. New York: Public Affairs Press.

Blyth, Mark. 2002. *The Great Transformations*. Cambridge: Cambridge University Press.

———. 2009. "An Approach to Comparative Politics or a Subfield within a Subfield? Political Economy." In *Comparative Politics: Rationality, Culture, Structure*, edited by Mark Irving Lichbach and Alan S. Zuckerman, 193–219. Cambridge: Cambridge University Press.

———. 2012. "This Time It Really Is Different: Europe, the Financial Crisis, and 'Staying on Top' in the 21st Century." In *Can Wealthy Nations Stay Rich?* edited by Dan Breznitz and John Zysman. New York: Oxford University Press.

Bogle, John C. 2005. *The Battle for the Soul of Capitalism*. New Haven CT: Yale University Press.

Bolton, Patrick, Jose Scheinkman, and Wei Xiong. 2006. "Executive Compensation and Short-Term Behavior in Speculative Markets." *Review of Economic Studies* 73:577–611.

Bonoli, Giuliano. 2000. *The Politics of Pension Reform: Institutions and Policy Change in Western Europe*. Cambridge: Cambridge University Press.

Bookstaber, Richard. 2007. *A Demon of Our Own Design: Markets, Hedge Funds, and the Perils of Financial Innovation*. New York: Wiley.

Bordo, Michael D., and John S. Landon-Lane. 2010. "The Global Financial Crisis of 2007–08: Is It Unprecedented?" Working Paper No. 16589, National Bureau of Economic Research, Cambridge, MA. http://www.nber.org/papers/w16589.

Borrus, Michael, D. Ernst, and S. Haggard. 2000. *International Production Networks in Asia: Rivalry or Riches*. London: Routledge.

Bown, Chad P. 2009. "Protectionism Increases and Spreads: Global Use of Trade Remedies Rises by 18.8 Percent in First Quarter 2009." Washington, DC: Brookings Institution.

Boyer, Robert. 1990. *The Regulation School: A Critical Introduction*. New York: Columbia University Press.

———, ed. 2002. *Regulation Theory: The State of the Art*. London: Routledge.

Bradford, Scott C., Paul L. E. Grieco, and Gary C. Hufbauer 2006. "The Payoff to America from Globalization." *World Economy* 29 (7): 893–916.

Brion, Maurice. 1912. *L'exode des capitaux français à l'étranger*. Paris: Arthur Rousseau.

Broda, Christian, Ephraim Leibtag, and David E.Weinstein. 2009. "The Role of Prices in Measuring the Poor's Living Standards." *Journal of Economic Perspectives* 23 (2): 77–97.

Broda, Christian, and David E. Weinstein. 2004. Variety Growth and World Welfare. *The American Economic Review* 94 (2): 139–44.

Broder, Albert. 1997. "La longue stagnation française: panorama général." In *La Longue Stagnation en France*, edited by Yves Breton, Albert Broder, and Michel Lutfalla, 9–58. Paris: Economica.

Bruner, Robert F., and Sean D. Carr. 2007. *The Panic of 1907*. Hoboken, NJ: Wiley.

Budge, Ian, Hans-Dieter Klingemann, Andrea Volkens, Judith Bara, and Eric Tanenbaum. 2001. *Mapping Preferences: Parties, Electors, and Governments, 1945–1998*. London: Oxford University Press.

Bureau of Economic Analysis (BEA). 2010. "International Economic Accounts, Trade in Goods and Services." http://www.bea.gov/international/#trade.

Bureau of Labor Statistics (BLS). 2010. "Union Members Summary." http://www.bls.gov/news.release/union2.nr0.htm.

Cairncross, A. K. 1953. *Home and Foreign Investment, 1870–1913*. Cambridge: Cambridge University Press.

Calandro, Joseph, Jr. 2004. "Reflexivity, Business Cycles, and the New Economy." *Quarterly Journal of Austrian Economics* 7 (3): 45–69.

Calder, Kent. 1988. *Crisis and Compensation: Public Policy and Policy Stability in Japan*. Princeton, NJ: Princeton University Press.

Callon, Michel. 1998. "Introduction: The Embeddedness of Economic Markets in Economics." In *The Laws of the Markets*, edited by Michel Callon, 1–57. Oxford: Blackwell.

Callon, Michel, and Fabian Muniesa. 2005. "Peripheral Vision: Economic Markets as Calculative Collective Devices." *Organization Studies* 26 (8): 1229–50.

Calomiris, Charles. 2009. "Banking Crises and the Rules of the Game." Working Paper No. 15403, National Bureau of Economic Research, Cambridge, MA.

Cameron, David R. 1978. "The Expansion of the Public Economy: A Comparative Analysis." *American Political Science Review* 72:1243–61.

———. 1985. "Does Government Cause Inflation? Taxes, Spending, and Deficits." In *The Politics of Inflation and Economic Stagnation*, edited by Leon N. Lindberg and Charles S. Maier, 224–95.Washington, DC: Brookings Institution.

Cameron, Rondo E. 1961. *France and the Economic Development of Europe, 1800–1914*. Princeton, NJ: Princeton University Press.

Campbell, John A., John A. Hall, and Ove K. Pedersen. 2006. *The State of Denmark*. Montreal: McGill University Press.

Capoccia, Giovanni, and R. Daniel Keleman. 2007. "The Study of Critical Junctures: Theory, Narrative, and Counterfactuals in Historical Institutionalism." *World Politics* 59 (3): 341–69.

Cardenas, Mauricio, and Julia Guerreiro. 2009. "The Limits to Fiscal Stimulus in Latin America and the Caribbean." Washington, DC: Brookings Institution. http://www.brookings.edu/articles/2009/0323_latin_america_cardenas.aspx.

Cardoso, Eliana, and Ann Helwege. 1993. *Latin America's Economy: Diversity, Trends, and Conflicts.* Cambridge, MA: MIT Press.

Carlin, Wendy, and David Soskice. 2009. "German Economic Performance: Disentangling the Role of Supply-Side Reforms, Macroeconomic Policy, and Coordinated Economy Institutions." *Socio-Economic Review* 7 (1): 67–99.

Carmines, Edward G., and Geoffrey C. Layman. 1997. "Value Priorities, Partisanship, and Electoral Choice." *Political Behavior* 19 (4): 283–316.

Carr, Edward Hallett. 1961. *The Twenty Years' Crisis, 1919–1939.* 2nd ed. New York: St. Martin's Press.

Cassidy, John. 2009. *How Markets Fail: The Logic of Economic Calamities.* New York: Farrar, Straus and Giroux.

Caves, Richard. 1976. "Economic Models of Political Choice: Canada's Tariff Structure." *Canadian Journal of Economics* 9 (2): 278–300.

Cecchetti, S. G., M. S. Mohanty, and F. Zamponi. 2010. "The Future of Public Debt: Prospects and Implications." Working Paper No. 300, Bank for International Settlements, Basel. http://www.bis.org/publ/work300.pdf?noframes=1.

Cerra, Valerie, and Sweta Chaman Saxena. 2008. "Growth Dynamics: The Myth of Economic Recovery." *American Economic Review* 98 (1): 439–57.

Chamber of Deputies. *Journal Officiel.* Sessions of February 8, 1907.

Chase, Kerry A. 2008. "Moving Hollywood Abroad: Divided Labor Markets and the New Politics of Trade in Services." *International Organization* 62 (3): 653–87.

Chauvel, Louis. 1998. *Le destin des générations.* Paris: University Presses of France.

Chinn, Menzie D., and Jeffry Frieden. 2009. "Reflections on the Causes and Consequences of the Debt Crisis of 2008." *La Follette Policy Report* 19 (1), Robert M. La Follette School of Public Affairs, University of Wisconsin, Madison.

———. 2011. *Lost Decades: The Making of America's Debt Crisis and the Long Recovery.* New York: W.W. Norton.

Chinn, Menzie D., and Hiro Ito. 2007. "Current Account Balances, Financial Development and Institutions: Assaying the World 'Saving Glut.' " *Journal of International Money and Finance* 26 (4): 546–69.

Chwieroth, Jeffrey. 2008. "Normative Change from Within: The International Monetary Fund's Approach to Capital Account Liberalization." *International Studies Quarterly* 52 (1): 129–58.

Cioffi, John. 2010. *Public Law and Private Power: Corporate Governance Reform in the Age of Financial Capitalism.* Ithaca, NY: Cornell University Press.

Cioffi, John, and Martin Hoepner. 2006. "The Political Paradox of Finance Capitalism: Interests, Preferences, and Center-Left Party Politics in Corporate Governance Reform." *Politics and Society* 34 (4): 463–502.

Claessens, Stijn, Giovanni Dell'Ariccia, Deniz Igan, and Luc Laeven. 2010. "Cross-Country Experiences and Policy Implications from the Global Financial Crisis." *Economic Policy* 25 (62): 267–93.

Clark, Terry Nichols, and Seymour Martin Lipset, eds. 2001. *The Breakdown of Class Politics: A Debate on Post-Industrial Stratification.* Baltimore, MD: Johns Hopkins University Press.

Clift, Ben, and Cornelia Woll. 2012. "Economic Patriotism: Re-Inventing Control over Open Markets." *Journal of European Public Policy* 19 (3): 307–23.

Cohen, Benjamin J. 2007. "The Transatlantic Divide: Why Are American and British IPE So Different?" *Review of International Political Economy* 14 (2): 197–219.

———. 2008a. *International Political Economy: An Intellectual History*. Princeton, NJ: Princeton University Press.

———. 2008b. "The Transatlantic Divide: A Rejoinder." *Review of International Political Economy* 15 (1): 30–34.

———. 2009. "A Grave Case of Myopia." *International Interactions* 35 (4): 436–44.

Collier, Paul. 2006. "Why the WTO Is Deadlocked: And What Can Be Done about It." *World Economy* 29:1423–49.

Cox, G. W., and M. D. McCubbins. 2005. *Setting the Agenda*. New York: Cambridge University Press.

Crafts, Nicholas, and Gianni Toniolo, eds. 1996. *Economic Growth in Europe since 1945*. Cambridge: Cambridge University Press.

Crisp, Olga. 1960. "French Investment in Russian Joint-Stock Companies, 1894–1914." *Business History* 2 (1–2): 75–90.

Crockett, Andrew. 2009. "Rebuilding the Financial Architecture." *Finance and Development* (September): 18–19.

Crouch, Colin. 2009. "Privatized Keynesianism: An Unacknowledged Policy Regime." *British Journal of Politics and International Relations* 11 (3): 382–99.

Crouch, Colin, and Alessandro Pizzorno, eds. 1978. *The Resurgence of Class Conflict in Western Europe*. London: Macmillan.

Crozier, Michel, Samuel P. Huntington, and Joji Watanuki. 1974. *The Crisis of Democracies*. New York: New York University Press.

Crystal, Alec. 1979. *Controversies in British Macroeconomics*. London: Philip Alan.

Culpepper, Pepper. 2010. *Quiet Politics and Business Power: Corporate Control in Europe and Japan*. Cambridge: Cambridge University Press.

Cusack, Thomas R. 1999. "Partisan Politics and Fiscal Policy." *Comparative Political Studies* 32 (4): 464–86.

Cusack, Thomas, and Lutz Englehardt. 2002. *The PGL File Collection: Computer File*. Berlin: Social Science Research Center Berlin.

Cusak, Thomas, Torben Iversen, and David Soskice. 2007. "Economic Interests and the Origins of Electoral Systems." *American Political Science Review* 101 (3): 371–93.

Cuthbertson, Keith. 1979. *Macroeconomic Policy: The New Cambridge, Keynesian and Monetarist Controversies*. London: Macmillan.

Dalton, Russell J., Scott C. Flanagan, and Paul Allen Beck, eds. 1984. *Electoral Change in Advanced Industrial Democracies: Realignment or Dealignment?* Princeton, NJ: Princeton University Press.

Dalton, Russell J., Doh Chull Shin, and Yun-han Chu, eds. 2008. *Party Politics in East Asia: Citizens, Elections, and Democratic Development*. Denver, CO: Lynne Rienner.

Daumard, Adeline. 1977. "La Diffusion et nature des placements à l'étranger dans les patrimonies des français au XIXe siécle." In *La Position internationale de la France*, edited by Maurice Lévy-Leboyer, 427–42. Paris: Editions de l'Ecole des Hautes Etudes en Sciences Sociales.

Davis, Christina, and Jennifer Oh. 2007. "Repeal of the Rice Laws in Japan: The Role of International Pressure to Overcome Vested Interests." *Comparative Politics* 40 (1): 21–40.

Davis, Gerald F., and E. Han Kim. 2006. "Business Ties and Proxy Voting by Mutual Funds." *Journal of Financial Economics* 85 (2): 552–70.

Davis, Lance E., and Robert A. Huttenback. 1982. "The Political Economy of British Imperialism: Measures of Benefits and Support." *Journal of Economic History* 42 (1): 119–30.

De Mel, Suresh, David McKenzie, and Christopher Woodruff. 2008. "Returns to Capital in Microenterprises: Evidence from a Field Experiment." *Quarterly Journal of Economics* 123 (4): 1329–72.

Dequech, David. 2000. "Fundamental Uncertainty and Ambiguity." *Eastern Economic Journal* 26 (1): 41–60.

Derman, Emanuel. 2004. *My Life as a Quant: Reflections on Physics and Finance*. New York: Wiley.

———. 2011. *Models Behaving Badly: Why Confusing Illusion with Reality Can Lead to Disaster, on Wall Street and in Life*. New York: Free Press.

Díaz Alejandro, Carlos F. 1970. "Stop-Go Cycles and Inflation during the Postwar Period." In *Essays on the Economic History of the Argentine Republic*, edited by Carlos F. Díaz Alejandro, pp. 351–90. New Haven, CT: Yale University Press.

Dixit, Avinash, Gene Grossman, and Faruk Gul. 2000. "The Dynamics of Political Compromise." *Journal of Political Economy* 108 (3): 531–68.

Dobbin, Frank. 2004. "Introduction: The Sociology of the Economy." In *The Sociology of the Economy*, edited by Frank Dobbin, 1–25. New York: Russell Sage.

Dobbin, Frank, and John R. Sutton. 2008. "The Strength of a Weak State: The Rights Revolution and the Rise of Human Resources Management Divisions." *American Journal of Sociology* 104 (2): 441–76.

Dooley, Michael P., David Folkerts-Landau, and Peter Garber. 2003. "An Essay on the Revived Bretton Woods System." Working Paper No. 9971, National Bureau of Economic Research, Cambridge, MA.

Dornbusch, Rudiger, and Sebastian Edwards, eds. 1991. *The Macroeconomics of Populism in Latin America*. Chicago: University of Chicago Press.

Dowd, Kevin, and Martin Hutchinson. 2010. *Alchemists of Loss: How Modern Finance and Government Intervention Crashed the Financial System*. Chichester: Wiley.

Drazen, Allan, and Vittorio Grilli. 1993. "The Benefit of Crises for Economic Reforms." *American Economic Review* 83 (3): 598–607.

Drucker, P. 1976. *The Unseen Revolution*. New York: Harper & Row.

Dyson, Kenneth, and Kevin Featherstone. 1997. *The Road to Maastricht: Negotiating Economic and Monetary Union*. Oxford: Oxford University Press.

Edelstein, Michael. 1982. *Overseas Investment in the Age of High Imperialism*. New York: Columbia University Press.

Ehrlich, Sean. 2010. "The Fair Trade Challenge to Embedded Liberalism." *International Studies Quarterly* 54 (4):1013–33.

Eichengreen, Barry. 1996a. *Golden Fetters: The Gold Standard and the Great Depression, 1919–1939*. New York: Oxford University Press.

———. 1996b. "Institutions and Economic Growth: Europe after World War II." In *Economic Growth in Europe since 1945*, edited by Nicholas Crafts and Gianni Toniolo, 38–72. Cambridge: Cambridge University Press.

———. 1997. *European Monetary Unification*. Cambridge, MA: MIT Press.

———. 2002. "Still Fettered after All These Years." Working Paper No. 9276, National Bureau of Economic Research, Cambridge, MA, October.

———. 2003. "Governing Global Financial Markets: International Responses to the Hedge-Fund Problem." In *Governance in a Global Economy*, edited by Miles Kahler and David A. Lake, 168–98. Princeton, NJ: Princeton University Press.

———. 2010. "International Regulation of the Crisis." *Daedelus* (Fall): 107–14.

Eichengreen, Barry, and Douglas A. Irwin. 2009. "The Slide to Protectionism in the Great Depression: Who Succumbed and Why?" Working Paper No. 15142, National Bureau of Economic Research, Cambridge, MA, July.

Eichengreen, Barry, and Kevin H. O'Rourke. 2010. "A Tale of Two Depressions: What Do the New Data Tell Us?" VoxEU.org, March 8. http://voxeu.org/index.php?q=node/3421.

Eichengreen, Barry, and Peter Temin. 1997. "The Gold Standard and the Great Depression." Working Paper No. 6060, National Bureau of Economic Research, Cambridge, MA, June.

Elf, Martin. 2007. "Social Structure and Electoral Behavior in Comparative Perspective: The Decline of Social Cleavages in Western Europe Revisited." *Perspectives in Politics* 5 (2): 277–94.

Erixon, Fredrik. 2008. "From Twin Towers to Fawlty Towers: A Story of the Doha Round." Working paper, European Centre for International Political Economy, July.

Erixon, Fredrik, and Razeen Sally. 2010. "Trade, Globalization and Emerging Protectionism since the Crisis." Working paper, European Centre for International Political Economy, February.

Eslava, Marcela. 2006. "The Political Economy of Fiscal Policy: Survey." Working Paper No. 583, InterAmerican Development Bank, Washington, DC.

Esping-Andersen, Gosta. 1990. *Three Worlds of Welfare Capitalism*. Princeton, NJ: Princeton University Press.

———. 1999. *Social Foundations of Post-Industrial Economies*. Oxford: Oxford University Press.

Estevez-Abe, Margarita, Torben Iversen, and David Soskice. 2001. "Social Protection and Skill Formation: A Reinterpretation of the Welfare State." In *Varieties of Capitalism*, edited by Peter A. Hall and David Soskice, 145–83. Oxford: Oxford University Press.

Evans, Geoffrey. 2000. "The Continued Significance of Class Voting." *Annual Review of Political Science* (3): 401–17.

Evans, Peter, and William Sewell Jr. Forthcoming. "The Neo-Liberal Era: Ideology, Policy and Social Effects." Unpublished manuscript, Program on Successful Societies, Canadian Institute for Advanced Research.

Evenett, Simon. 2009. "Crisis-Era Protectionism One Year after the Washington G20 Meeting." In *The Great Trade Collapse: Causes, Consequences and Prospects*, edited by Richard Baldwin. VoxEU e-book. http://www.voxeu.org/index.php?q=node/4297.

Farber, Daniel A. 2011. "Uncertainty." *Georgetown Law Journal* 99 (April): 1–69.

Federal Open Market Committee (FOMC). 2003. "Transcript of the Meeting of the Federal Open Market Committee on January 28–29, 2003." http://www.federalreserve.gov/monetarypolicy/fomc_historical.htm.

Federal Reserve Board. 2009. "Changes in U.S. Family Finances from 2004 to 2007: Evidence from the Survey of Consumer Finances." http://www.federalreserve.gov/pubs/bulletin/2009/pdf/scf09.pdf.

Feenstra, Robert C., and Gordon Hanson. 2004. "Global Production Sharing and Rising Inequality: A Survey of Trade and Wages." In *Handbook of International Trade,* edited by Kwan Choi and James Harrigan, 146–85. New York: Wiley-Blackwell.

Feis, Herbert. (1930) 1965. *Europe: The World's Banker, 1870–1914*. New York: W.W. Norton.

Ferguson, Niall, Charles S. Maier, Erez Manela, and Daniel J. Sargent, eds. 2010. *The Shock of the Global: The 1970s in Perspective*. Cambridge, MA: Harvard University Press.

Fernandez, Raquel, and Dani Rodrik. 1991. "Resistance to Reform: Status Quo Bias in the Presence of Individual-Specific Uncertainty." *American Economic Review* 81 (5): 1146–55.

Fernandez-Arias, Eduardo, and Peter J. Montiel. 2009. "Crisis Response in Latin America: Is the 'Rainy Day' at Hand?" Working Paper No. 686, Inter-American Development Bank, Washington, DC, June.

Findlay, Ronald, and Stanislaw Wellisz. 1982. "Endogenous Tariffs, the Political Economy of Trade Restrictions, and Welfare." In *Import Competition and Response*, edited by Jagdish Bhagwati, 223–34. Chicago: University of Chicago Press.

Fisman, Raymond. 2001. "Estimating the Value of Political Connections." *American Economic Review* 91 (4): 1095–102.

Flandreau, Marc. 2003. "Caveat Emptor: Coping with Sovereign Risk under the International Gold Standard." In *International Financial History in the Twentieth Century: System and Anarchy*, edited by M. Flandreau, C. L. Holtfrerich and H. James, 17–50. Cambridge: Cambridge University Press.

Fordham, Benjamin. 2008. "Economic Interests and Congressional Voting on Security Issues." *Journal of Conflict Resolution* 52 (5): 623–40.

Fourcade, Marion. 2009. *Economists and Societies: Discipline and Profession in the United States, Britain, and France, 1890s–1990s*. Princeton, NJ: Princeton University Press.

Fourcade, Marion, and Rakesh Khurana. 2011. "From Social Control to Financial Economics: The Linked Ecologies of Economics and Business in Twentieth Century America." Working Paper No. 11-071, Harvard Business School, Harvard University, Cambridge, MA.

Fox, Justin. 2009. *The Myth of the Rational Market: A History of Risk, Reward, and Delusion on Wall Street*. New York: HarperCollins.

Frank, Thomas. 2004. *What's the Matter with Kansas?* New York: Metropolitan Books.

Frieden, J. 1988. "Sectoral Conflict and U.S. Foreign Economic Policy, 1914–1940." *International Organization* 42 (1).

Frieden, Jeffry A., David A. Lake, Michael Nicholson, and Aditya Ranganath. 2011. "Crisis Politics: Uncertainty, Relative Prices and Political Change." Paper presented at the Annual Meeting of the International Political Economy Society, University of Wisconsin, Madison, November 11.

Frieden, Jeffry A., and Ronald Rogowski. 1996. "The Impact of the International Economy on National Policies: An Analytical Overview." In *Internationalization and Domestic Politics*, edited by Robert O. Keohane and Helen V. Milner, 25–47. New York: Cambridge University Press.

Friedman, Benjamin M. 1992. "Learning from the Reagan Deficits." *American Economic Review* 82 (2): 299–304.

Galiani, Sebastian, Daniel Heymann, Carlos Dabus, and Fernando Tohme. 2008. "Land-Rich Economies, Education and Economic Development." *Journal of Development Economics* 86:434–46.

Gamble, Andrew. 1994. *The Free Economy and the Strong State: The Politics of Thatcherism*. 2nd ed. Houndsmills, UK: Palgrave Macmillan.

Garrett, Geoffrey, and Peter Lange. 1991. "Political Responses to Interdependence: What's 'Left' for the Left?" *International Organization* 45 (4): 539–64.

Garrigues, Jean. 1997. *La république des hommes d'affaires (1870–1900)*. Paris: Aubier.

Gavin, Michael, and Roberto Perotti. 1997. "Fiscal Policy in Latin America." *National Bureau of Economic Research (NBER)Macroeconomics Annual* 12:11–72.

Gawande, Kishore, and Bernard Hoekman. 2006. "Lobbying and Agricultural Trade Policy in the United States." *International Organization* 60 (3): 527–61.

Gawande, Kishore, and Pravin Krishna. 2003. "The Political Economy of Trade Policy: Empirical Approaches." In *Handbook of International Trade*, edited by James Harrigan, 214–50. Malden, MA: Blackwell.

Geneva Association. 2009. "The Insurance Industry and Climate Change: Contribution to the Global Debate." *Geneva Reports: Risk and Insurance Research*, July 2. www.genevaassociation.org.
German Bank Inquiry. 1910. *National Monetary Fund Stenographic Reports*. Vols. 1–2. Washington, DC: Government Printing Office.
Gerschenkron, Alexander. 1966. *Bread and Democracy in Germany*. New York: H. Fertig.
Girault, René. 1973. *Emprunts russes et investissements français*. Paris: Armand Colin.
Glyn, Andrew. 2006. *Capitalism Unleashed*. Oxford: Oxford University Press.
Goldsmith, Donald. 1977. *Scientists Confront Velikovsky*. Ithaca, NY: Cornell University Press.
Goldstein, Judith, Yotam Margalit, and Douglas Rivers. 2008. "Producer, Consumer, Family Member: The Relationship between Trade Attitudes and Family Status." Paper prepared for the Conference on Domestic Preferences and Foreign Economic Policy, Princeton University, Princeton, NJ, April 19–20.
Goldstein, Morris, and Daniel Xie. 2009. "The Impact of the Financial Crisis on Emerging Asia." Paper presented at the Asia Economic Policy Conference, Federal Reserve Bank of San Francisco, October 18–20.
Goldthorpe, John H. 1978. "The Current Inflation: Towards a Sociological Account." In *The Political Economy of Inflation*, edited by Fred Hirsch and John H. Goldthorpe, 187–214. London: Martin Robertson.
———, ed. 1984. *Order and Conflict in Contemporary Capitalism*. New York: Oxford University Press.
Goodman, John B., Debora Spar, and David Yoffie. 1996. "Foreign Direct Investment and the Demand for Protection in the United States." *International Organization* 50:565–91.
Goudo, Yoshihisa. 2006. *Nihon no shoku to nou: kiki no honshitsu*. Tokyo: NTT Shuppan.
Gourevitch, Peter A. 1978. "The Second Image Reversed: The International Sources of Domestic Politics." *International Organization* 32 (4): 881–912.
———. 1986. *Politics in Hard Times: Comparative Responses to International Economic Crises*. Ithaca, NY: Cornell University Press.
———. 1999. "The Governance Problem in International Relations." In *Strategic Choice and International Relations*, edited by D. A. Lake and R. Powell, 137–64. Princeton, NJ: Princeton University Press:.
———. 2003. "The Politics of Corporate Governance Regulation." *Yale Law Journal* 112 (7): 11829–80.
———. 2008. "What Do Corporations Owe Citizens? Pensions, Corporate Governance and the Role of Institutional Investors." In *What Do Corporations Owe Citizens? Pensions, Corporate Governance, and the Role of Institutional Investors,* edited by Howard Rosenthal and David Rothman, 45–60. New Brunswick, ME: Transaction Publishers.
———. 2013. "Choice and Constraint in the Great Recession of 2008." In *Back to Basics: Rethinking Power in the Contemporary World: Essays in Honor of Stephen D. Krasner*, edited by Martha Finnemore and Judith Goldstein. New York: Oxford University Press.
Gourevitch, Peter A., and James Shinn. 2005. *Political Power and Corporate Control: The New Global Politics of Corporate Governance*. Princeton, NJ: Princeton University Press.
Government Accounting Office (GAO). 2009. "International Trade: Four Free Trade Agreements GAO Reviewed Have Resulted in Commercial Benefits, but Challenges on Labor and Environment Remain." GAO-09-439, Report to the

Chairman, Committee on Finance, U.S. Senate, Government Accounting Office, Washington, DC.

Green, Donald, and Alan Gerber. 2002. "Reclaiming the Experimental Tradition in Political Science." In *Political Science: State of the Discipline*, edited by Ira Katznelson and Helen Milner, 805–32. New York: W.W. Norton.

Greenhouse, Steven. 2010. "2 Unions' Backing Helps Chances of Trade Pact with South Korea." *New York Times*, December 6, B1.

Greenspan, Alan. 2010. "The Crisis." *Brookings Papers on Economic Activity* (Spring): 201–46.

Griffith-Jones, Stephany, Jose Antonio Ocampo, and Joseph E. Stiglitz, eds. 2010. *Time for a Visible Hand: Lessons from the 2008 World Financial Crisis*. New York: Oxford University Press.

Grossman, Gene M., and Elhanan Helpman. 1994. "Protection for Sale." *American Economic Review* 84 (4): 833–50.

Grossman, Gene, and Esteban Rossi-Hansberg. 2008. "Trading Tasks: A Simple Theory of Offshoring." *American Economic Review* 98 (5): 1978–97.

Group of Twenty (G-20). 2009. "G-20 Finance Ministers' and Central Bank Governors' Communiqué, March 14." http://www.treasury.gov/resource-center/international/g7-g20/Documents/2009_communique_horsham_uk%20March.pdf.

Guilleminault, Gilbert, and Yvonne Singer-Lecocq Guilleminault. 1991. "Le mirage des emprunts russes." In *Le roman vrai de la IIIe et de la IVe république. première partie, 1870–1918*, edited by Gilbert Guilleminault, 1257. Paris: Robert Laffont.

Habyarimana, James, Macartan Humphreys, Daniel Posner, and Jeremy Weinstein. 2007. "Why Does Ethnic Diversity Undermine Public Goods Provision?" *American Political Science Review* 101 (November): 709–25.

Hacker, Jacob. 2004. "Privatizing Risk without Privatizing the Welfare State: The Hidden Politics of Social Policy Retrenchment in the United States." *American Political Science Review* 98 (2): 243–60.

Hacker, Jacob, and Paul Pierson. 2010. *Winner Take All Politics*. New York: Simon and Schuster.

Hafner-Burton, Emilie. 2005. "Trading Human Rights: How Preferential Trade Agreements Influence Government Repression." *International Organization* 59 (2): 593–629.

Hafner-Burton, Emilie M., Miles Kahler, and Alexander H. Montgomery. 2009. "Network Analysis for International Relations." *International Organization* 63:559–92.

Haggard, Stephan. 1990. *Pathways from the Periphery: The Politics of Growth in the Newly Industrializing Countries*. Ithaca, NY: Cornell University Press.

———. 2000. *The Political Economy of the Asian Financial Crisis*. Washington, DC: Institute for International Economics.

Haggard, Stephan, and Robert R. Kaufman. 2008. *Development, Democracy and Welfare States: Latin America, East Asia, and Eastern Europe*. Princeton, NJ: Princeton University Press.

Hainmueller, Jens, and Michael J. Hiscox. 2006. "Learning to Love Globalization: The Effects of Education on Individual Attitudes towards International Trade." *International Organization* 60 (2): 469–98.

Haldane, Andrew. 2011. "Control Rights (and Wrongs)." Wincott Annual Memorial Lecture. Bank of England, October 24. http://www.google.com/search?sourceid=navclient&ie=UTF-8&rlz=1T4GGHP_enUS457US457&q=Wincott+Annual+Memorial+Lecture.

Hall, Peter A. 1982. "The Political Dimensions of Macroeconomic Management." PhD dissertation Harvard University, Cambridge, MA.

———. 1986. *Governing the Economy*. Oxford: Polity Press.
———, ed. 1989. *The Political Power of Economic Ideas*. Princeton, NJ: Princeton University Press.
———. 1993. "Policy Paradigms, Social Learning, and the State: The Case of Economic Policy-Making in Britain." *Comparative Politics* (April): 275–96.
———. 2006. "The Politics of Social Change in France." In *Changing France: The Politics That Markets Make*, edited by Pepper Culpepper, Peter A. Hall, and Bruno Palier, 1–26. London: Palgrave Macmillan.
Hall, Peter A., and Daniel W. Gingerich. 2009. "Varieties of Capitalism and Institutional Complementarities in the Political Economy." *British Journal of Political Science* 39:449–82.
Hall, Peter A., and David Soskice, eds. 2001. *Varieties of Capitalism: The Institutional Foundations of Comparative Advantage*. Oxford: Oxford University Press.
Hansen, Berndt. 1968. *Fiscal Policy in Seven Countries 1955–1965*. Paris: Organisation for Economic Co-operation and Development.
Hansen, Lars Peter, and Thomas Sargent. 2010. "Wanting Robustness in Macroeconomics." Unpublished paper, Department of Economics, New York University. http://homepages.nyu.edu/~ts43/research/Elements_robustness_tom_5.pdf.
Hara, Junnosuke, ed. 1999. *Shakai kaiso: yutakasa no naka no fubyodo* (Social Stratification: Inequality in Wealthy Society). Tokyo: University of Tokyo Press.
Harris-Lacewell, Melissa, Kosuke Imai, and Teppei Yamamoto. 2007. "Racial Gaps in the Responses to Hurricane Katrina: An Experimental Study." Unpublished paper, Princeton University, Princeton, NJ.
Harvey, William H. (1894) 1963. *Coin's Financial School*. Edited by Richard Hofstadter. Cambridge, MA: Belknap Press of Harvard University Press.
Hau, Harald, and Marcel Thum. 2009. "Subprime Crisis and Board (In-)competence: Private versus Public Banks in Germany." *Economic Policy* (October): 701–52.
Helleiner, Eric. 2010a. "Understanding the 2007–2008 Global Financial Crisis: Lessons for Scholars of International Political Economy." *Annual Review of Political Science* (December): 67–87.
———. 2010b. "What Role for the New Kid in Town? The Financial Stability Board and International Standards." Memo prepared for the workshop on New Foundations for Global Governance, Princeton University, Princeton, NJ, January 8–9.
Hellwig, Martin F. 2009. "Systemic Risk in the Financial Sector: An Analysis of the Subprime-Mortgage Financial Crisis." *De Economist* 157:129–207.
Helper, Susan, Timothy Krueger, and Howard Wial. 2012. "Why Does Manufacturing Matter? Which Manufacturing Matters? A Policy Framework." Working Paper, Metropolitan Policy Program, Brookings Institution, Washington, DC.
Henning, C. Randall. Forthcoming. "Economic Crises and Regional Institutions." *In Integrating Regions: Asia in Comparative Context*, edited by Miles Kahler and Andrew MacIntyre. Stanford, CA: Stanford University Press.
Hermann, Charles F. 1963. "Some Consequences of Crisis Which Limit the Viability of Organizations." *Administrative Science Quarterly* 8:61–82.
Hibbs, Douglas A. 1977. "Political Parties and Macroeconomic Policy." *American Political Science Review* 71 (4): 1467–87.
Hilferding, Rudolf. 1981. *Finance Capital: A Study of the Latest Phase of Capitalist Development*. London: Routledge and Kegan Paul.
Hiscox, Michael J. 2006. "Through a Glass and Darkly: Framing Effects and Individuals' Attitudes towards International Trade." *International Organization* 60 (3): 755–80.

Hiscox, Michael J., and Nick Smyth. 2009. "Is There Consumer Demand for Improved Labor Standards? Evidence from Field Experiments in Social Labeling." Unpublished manuscript, Harvard University, Cambridge, MA.

Hjertaker, Ingrid. 2011. "Regulating Risk: A Study of Basle II and the Copernican Turn to Financial Regulation." MA thesis, University of Oslo.

Hobson, J. A. (1902, 1905) 1965. *Imperialism.* Ann Arbor: University of Michigan Press.

Holmes, Douglas. 2009. "Economy of Words." *Cultural Anthropology* 24 (3): 381–419.

———. 2010. "Currency of Confidence." Unpublished manuscript, Department of Anthropology, Binghamton University, Binghamton, NY.

Honkapohja, Seppo. 2009. "The 1990s Financial Crises in Nordic Countries." Research Discussion Paper No. 5/2009, Bank of Finland, Helsinki.

Hopner, M. 2003. "European Corporate Governance Reform and the German Party Paradox." Paper presented at the Fifteenth Annual Conference of the Society for the Advancement of Socio-Economics (SASE), Aix-en-Provence, France, June 26–28. http://www.sase.org/oldsite/conf2003/papers/hoepner_martin.pdf.

Hoshi, Takeo. 2001. "What Happened to Japanese Banks?" *Monetary and Economic Studies* 2:1–30.

Howell, Chris. 1992. *Regulating Labor: The State and Industrial Relations Reform in Post-War France.* Princeton, NJ: Princeton University Press.

———. 2005. *Trade Unions and the State: The Construction of Industrial Relations Institutions in Britain 1890–2000.* Princeton, NJ: Princeton University Press.

Hüfner, Felix. 2010. "The German Banking System: Lessons from the Financial Crisis." Working Paper No. 788, Economics Department, Organisation for Economic Co-operation and Development.

Humphreys, Macartan, and Jeremy Weinstein. 2009. "Field Experiments and the Political Economy of Development." *Annual Review of Political Science* 12:367–78.

Hyde, Susan. 2007. "The Observer Effect in International Politics: Evidence from a Natural Experiment." *World Politics* 60 (October): 37–63.

Inglehart, Ronald. 1990. *Culture Shift.* Princeton, NJ: Princeton University Press.

Inter-American Development Bank (IADB). 2008. *All That Glitters May Not Be Gold: Assessing Latin America's Recent Macroeconomic Performance.* Washington, DC: Inter-American Development Bank.

International Monetary Fund (IMF). 2011. "Fiscal Monitor: Addressing Fiscal Challenges to Reduce Economic Risk." Washington, DC: International Monetary Fund, September.

Irwin, Douglas A. 2005. "Trade and Globalization." In *Globalization: What's New?* edited by Michael M. Weinstein, 19–35. New York: Columbia University Press.

Iversen, Torben. 1999. *Contested Economic Institutions.* New York: Cambridge University Press.

———. 2006. "Class Politics Is Dead! Long Live Class Politics! A Political Economy Perspective on the New Partisan Politics." *American Political Science Association–Comparative Politics (APSA-CP) Newsletter* 17 (20): 1–6.

Iversen, Torben, and Thomas Cusack. 2000. "The Causes of Welfare State Expansion: Deindustrialization or Globalization." *World Politics* 52:313–49.

Iversen, Torben, and David Soskice. 2006. "Electoral Institutions and the Politics of Coalitions: Why Some Democracies Redistribute More Than Others." *American Political Science Review* 100 (2): 165–81.

———. 2009. "Distribution and Redistribution: The Shadow of the Nineteenth Century." *World Politics* 61:438–86.

Iversen, Torben, and Anne Wren. 1998. "Equality, Employment and Budgetary Restraint." *World Politics* 50 (July): 507–46.

Iyengar, Shanto, and Donald R. Kinder. 1987. *News That Matters: Television and American Opinion.* Chicago: University of Chicago Press.

Japanese Statistics Office. 2008. *Nougyo kouzou doutai chosa houkokusho* (Report on the Survey of Structural Dynamics of Agriculture). http://www.e-stat.go.jp/SG1/estat/List.do?lid=000001058425.

Jha, Veena. 2009. "The Effects of Fiscal Stimulus Packages on Employment." Working Paper No. 34, Employment Sector, International Labor Organization, Geneva.

Johnson, Chalmers. 1982. *MITI and the Japanese Miracle: The Growth of Industrial Policy, 1925–1975.* Stanford, CA: Stanford University Press.

Johnson, Peter A. 1998. *The Government of Money: Monetarism in Germany and the United States.* Ithaca, NY: Cornell University Press.

Johnson, Simon. 2009. "The Quiet Coup." *Atlantic Monthly* (May). http://www.theatlantic.com/magazine/archive/2009/05/the-quiet-coup/7364/.

Johnson, Simon, and James Kwak. 2010. *Thirteen Bankers: The Wall Street Takeover and the Next Financial Meltdown.* New York: Pantheon.

Jonsson, Asgeir. 2009. *Why Iceland? How One of the World's Smallest Countries Became the Meltdown's Greatest Casualty.* New York: McGraw Hill.

Jordà, Òscar, Moritz Schularick, and Alan M. Taylor. 2010. "Financial Crises, Credit Booms, and External Imbalances: 140 Years of Lessons." Working Paper No. 16567, National Bureau of Economic Research, Cambridge, MA, December.

Kabashima, Ikuo. 1984. "Supportive Participation with Economic Growth: The Case of Japan." *World Politics* 36 (3): 309–38.

Kahler, Miles. 1991. "Old Game or New Order: Theory and the Interpretation of International Change." Paper presented at the Conference on Facing the Challenges of the Twenty-First Century: International Relations Studies in China, Beijing, June 17–19.

———. 2009. "Global Governance Redefined." In *The Challenges of Globalization*, edited by Andrew C. Sobel, 174–98. New York: Routledge.

Kahler, Miles, and David A. Lake. 2009. "Economic Integration and Global Governance: Why So Little Supranationalism?" In *Explaining Regulatory Change in the Global Economy*, edited by Walter Mattli and Ngaire Woods, 242–75. Princeton, NJ: Princeton University Press.

Kaminsky, Graciela L., and Carmen M. Reinhart. 1999. "The Twin Crises: The Causes of Banking and Balance-of-Payments Problems." *American Economic Review* 89 (3): 473–500.

Kaminsky, G., C. Reinhart, and C. Vegh. 2004. "When It Rains, It Pours: Pro-cyclical Capital Flows and Macroeconomic Policies." Working Paper No. 10780, National Bureau of Economic Research, Cambridge, MA.

Karol, David. 2000. "Divided Government and U.S. Trade Policy: Much Ado about Nothing?" *International Organization* 54 (4): 825–44.

Katzenstein, Peter J. 1978. *Between Power and Plenty: Foreign Economic Policies of Advanced Industrial States.* Madison: University of Wisconsin Press.

———. 1985. *Small States in World Markets: Industrial Policy in Europe.* Ithaca, NY: Cornell University Press.

Katzenstein, Peter J., Robert Keohane, and Steven Krasner. 1998. "*International Organization* and the Study of World Politics." *International Organization* 52 (4) (1998): 645–85.

Kaufman, Robert R. 2011. "The Political Left, the Export Boom, and the Populist Temptation." In *The Resurgence of the Latin American Left*, edited by Steven Levitsky and Kenneth Roberts, 93–117. Baltimore, MD: Johns Hopkins University Press.

Kemmerling, Achim, and Oliver Bruttel. 2006. "New Politics in German Labor Market Policy? Implications of the Recent Hartz Reforms for the German Welfare State." *West European Politics* 29 (1): 90–112.

Kennan, George G. 1984. *The Fateful Alliance.* Manchester: Manchester University Press.

Kenworthy, Lane, and Jonas Pontusson. 2005. "Rising Inequality and the Politics of Redistribution in Affluent Countries." *Perspectives on Politics* 3 (3): 449–71.

Keohane, Robert O. 1984. *After Hegemony.* Princeton, NJ: Princeton University Press.

Keohane, Robert, and Helen Milner, eds. 1996. *Internationalization and Domestic Politics.* New York: Cambridge University Press.

Key, V. O. 1955. "A Theory of Critical Elections." *Journal of Politics* 17 (1): 3–16.

Keynes, John Maynard. (1921) 1948. *Treatise on Probability.* New York: MacMillan.

———. 1924. "Foreign Investment and National Advantage." *The Nation and the Athenaeum* 35 (August 9): 584–87.

———. 1937. "The General Theory of Employment." *Quarterly Journal of Economics* 51:209–23.

Kindleberger, Charles P. 1978. *Manias, Panics, and Crashes: A History of Financial Crises.* New York: Basic Books.

Kindleberger, Charles P., and Robert Z. Aliber. (1978) 2005. *Manias, Panics, and Crashes.* Hoboken, NJ: Wiley.

King, Gary, Robert O. Keohane, and Sidney Verba. 1994. *Designing Social Inquiry: Scientific Inference in Qualitative Research.* Princeton, NJ: Princeton University Press.

King, Gary, Christopher J. L. Murray, Joshua A. Salomon, and Ajay Tandon. 2004. "Enhancing the Validity and Cross-cultural Comparability of Survey Research." *American Political Science Review* 98 (1): 191–207.

Kingdon, John W. 1995. *Agendas, Alternatives and Public Policies.* 2nd ed. Boston: Little, Brown.

Kitschelt, Herbert. 1997. *The Radical Right in Western Europe.* Ann Arbor: University of Michigan Press.

Klein, Ezra. 2011. "Obama's Flunking Economy: The Real Cause." *New York Review of Books*, November 24. http://www.nybooks.com/articles/archives/2011/nov/24/obamas-flunking-economy-real-cause/?pagination=false.

Knight, Frank. 1921. *Risk, Uncertainty, and Profit.* New York: Houghton Mifflin.

Kono, Daniel Y. 2006. "Optimal Obfuscation: Democracy and Trade Policy Transparency." *American Political Science Review* 100:369–84.

Kontopoulos, Y., and R. Perotti. 1999. "Government Fragmentation and Fiscal Policy Outcomes: Evidence from OECD Countries." In *Fiscal Institutions and Fiscal Per- formance*, edited by James Poterba and Jurgen von Hagen, 81–102. Chicago: University of Chicago Press.

Koremenos, Barbara, Charles Lipson, and Duncan Snidal. 2001. "The Rational Design of International Institutions." *International Organization* 55 (3): 761–99.

Kotz, David M., Terrence McDonough, and Michael Reich, eds. 1994. *Social Structures of Accumulation: The Political Economy of Growth and Crisis.* New York: Cambridge University Press.

Krehbiel, Keith. 1998. *Pivotal Politics: A Theory of U.S. Lawmaking.* Chicago: University of Chicago Press.

Krieger, Joel. 1986. *Reagan, Thatcher, and the Politics of Decline.* New York: Oxford University Press.

Kriesi, Hans-Peter, Edgar Grande, Romain Lachat, Martin Dolezal, Simon Bornschier, and Timotheos Frey, eds. 2008. *West European Politics in the Age of Globalization.* Cambridge: Cambridge University Press.

Krippner, Greta. 2005. "The Financialization of the American Economy." *Socio-Economic Review* 3:173–208.
———. 2007. "The Making of U.S. Monetary Policy: Central Bank Transparency and the Neoliberal Dilemma." *Theory and Society* 36:477–513.
———. 2011. *Capitalizing on Crisis: The Political Origins of the Rise of Finance.* Cambridge, MA: Harvard University Press.
Krugman, Paul R. 1980. "Scale Economies, Product Differentiation, and the Pattern of Trade." *American Economic Review* 70:950–59.
———. 2000. *The Return of Depression Economics.* New York: W.W. Norton.
———. 2010. "Appeasing the Bond Gods." *New York Times,* August 19.
Krugman, Paul, and Robin Wells. 2010. "The Slump Goes On: Why?" *New York Review of Books,* September 30. http://www.nybooks.com/articles/archives/2010/sep/30/slump-goes-why/?pagination=false.
Kume, Ikuo. 1998. *Disparaged Success: Labor Politics in Post-War Japan.* Ithaca, NY: Cornell University Press.
———. 2005. *Roudou seiji: rekishi no naka no roudou kumiai.* Tokyo: Chuko Shinsho.
La Porta, Rafael, Florencio Lopez-de-Silanes, Andrei Shleifer, and Robert Vishny. 2000. "Investor Protection and Corporate Governance." *Journal of Financial Economics* 58: 3–27.
———. 2002. "Investor Protection and Corporate Valuation." *Journal of Finance* 57 (2): 1147–70.
Ladewig, Jeffrey W. 2006. "Domestic Influences on International Trade Policy: Factor Mobility in the United States, 1963 to 1992." *International Organization* 60 (1): 69–103.
Laeven, Luc, and Fabian Valencia. 2010. "Resolution of Banking Crises: The Good, the Bad, and the Ugly." IMF Working Paper 10/146, June, 1–35.
Lake, David A. 2006. "International Political Economy: A Maturing Interdiscipline." In *The Oxford Handbook of Political Economy,* edited by Barry R. Weingast and Donald A. Wittman, 757–77. Oxford: Oxford University Press.
———. 2009a. "Open Economy Politics: A Critical Review." *Review of International Organizations* 4 (3): 219–44.
———. 2009b. "Trips across the Atlantic: Theory and Epistemology in IPE." *Review of International Political Economy* 16 (1): 47–57.
Lake, David A., and Jeffry A. Frieden. 1989. "Crisis Politics: The Effects of Uncertainty and Shocks on Material Interests and Political Institutions." Unpublished paper, Department of Political Science, University of California, San Diego.
Lallement, Michel. 2007. *Le travail: une sociologie contemporaine.* Paris: Gallimard.
Latsis, John, Guillemette de Larquier, and Franck Bessis. 2010. "Are Conventions Solutions to Uncertainty? Contrasting Visions of Social Coordination." *Journal of Post Keynesian Economics* 32 (4): 535–58.
Laves, Walter H. C. 1927. "German Governmental Influence on Foreign Investments, 1871–1914." PhD dissertation, University of Chicago.
Lawson, Tony. 1985. "Uncertainty and Economic Analysis." *Economic Journal* 95 (December): 909–27.
Lazonick, William, and Mary O'Sullivan. 2000. "Maximizing Shareholder Value: A New Ideology for Corporate Governance." *Economy and Society* 29, pt. 1, 13–35.
Leamer, Edward. 1996. "Wage Inequality from International Competition and Technological Change: Theory and Country Experience." *American Economic Review* 86 (2): 309–14.
Leroy-Beaulieu, Paul. 1905. *L'art de placer et gérer sa fortune.* Paris: Librairie Ch. Delagrave.

Levitsky, Steven, and Kenneth Roberts, eds. 2011. *The Resurgence of the Latin American Left*. Baltimore, MD: Johns Hopkins University Press.

Levy, Jonah. 2005. "Redeploying the State: Liberalization and Social Policy in France." In *Beyond Continuity,* edited by Wolfgang Streeck and Katherine Thelen, 103–26. Oxford: Oxford University Press.

Lévy-Leboyer, Maurice. 1977a. "La balance des paiements et l'exportation des capitaux français." In *La position internationale de la France*, edited by M. Lévy-Leboyer, 75–143. Paris: Editions de l'Ecole des Hautes Etudes en Sciences Sociales.

———. 1977b. "La Capacité financière de la France au début du XXe Siècle." In *La position internationale de la France*, edited by Maurice Lévy-Leboyer, 7–33. Paris: Editions de l'Ecole des Hautes Etudes en Sciences Sociales.

Lévy-Leboyer, Maurice, and François Bourguignon. 1985. *L'Economie française au XIXe siècle: analyse macro-économique*. Paris: Economica.

Lewis, Michael. 2010. *The Big Short: Inside the Doomsday Machine*. New York: W.W. Norton.

———, ed. 2008. *The Real Price of Everything: Rediscovering the Six Classics of Economics*. New York: Sterling.

Lijphart, Arend. 1997. *Patterns of Democracy*. New Haven, CT: Yale University Press.

Lindblom, Charles. 1977. *Politics and Markets*. New York: Basic Books

Linden, Greg, Kenneth L. Kraemer, and Jason Dedrick. 2007. "Who Captures Value in a Global Innovation System? The Case of Apple's iPod." Personal Computing Industry Center, University of California, Irvine, June.

Lindert, Peter. 2004. *Growing Public: Social Spending and Economic Growth since the Eighteenth Century*. Cambridge: Cambridge University Press.

Lipset, Seymour Martin. 1964. "The Changing Class Structure and Contemporary European Politics." *Daedalus* 93 (1): 271–303.

Lohmann, Larry. 2010. "Uncertainty Markets and Carbon Markets: Variations on Polanyian Themes." *New Political Economy* 15 (2): 225–54.

Lombardi, Domenico. 2009. "After the Fall: Re-asserting the International Monetary Fund in the Face of Global Crisis." Washington, DC: Brookings Institution, September 14.

Lu, Xiaobo, Kenneth F. Scheve, and Mathew Slaughter. 2012. "Inequity Aversion and the International Distribution of Trade Protection." *American Journal of Political Science* 56 (3): 638–65.4

Lysis. 1912. *Contre l'oligarchie financière en France*. Paris: Albin Michel.

MacIntyre, Andrew. 2001. "Institutions and Investors: The Politics of Economic Crisis in Southeast Asia." *International Organization* 55 (1): 81–122.

MacKenzie, Donald. 2006. *An Engine, Not a Camera: How Financial Models Shape Markets*. Cambridge, MA: MIT Press.

MacKenzie, Donald, Fabian Muniesa, and Lucia Siu. 2007. "Introduction." In *Do Economists Make Markets? On the Performativity of Economics*, edited by Donald MacKernzie, Fabian Muniesa, and Lucia Siu, 1–19. Princeton, NJ: Princeton University Press.

Maclachlan, Patricia L. 2001. *Consumer Politics in Postwar Japan: The Institutional Boundaries of Citizen Activism*. New York: Columbia University Press.

Magee, Christopher. 2010. "Would NAFTA Have Been Approved by the House of Representatives under President Bush? Presidents, Parties, and Trade Policy." *Review of International Economics* 18 (2): 382–95.

Magee, Stephen P., William M. Brock, and Leslie Young. 1989. *Black Hole Tariffs and Endogenous Policy Theory*. Cambridge: Cambridge University Press.

Maier, Charles C. 1981. "The Two Postwar Eras and the Conditions for Stability in Twentieth-Century Europe." *American Historical Review* 84 (2): 327–52.
Mankiw, N. Gregory. 2007. "How to Avoid Recession? Let the Fed Work." *New York Times*, December 23. http://www.nytimes.com/2007/12/23/business/23view.html?ex=1356066000&en=3337604c870871 0a&ei=5090&partner=rssuserland&emc=rss.
Manow, Philip. 2001. *Social Protection, Capitalist Protection: The Bismarckian Welfare State and the German Political System*. Habilitation thesis, University of Konstanz.
Mansfield, Edward D., and Diana C. Mutz. 2009. "Support for Free Trade: Self-Interest, Sociotropic Politics, and Out-Group Anxiety." *International Organization* 63 (Summer): 425–57.
Mansfield, Edward D., and Eric Reinhardt. 2003. "Multilateral Determinants of Regionalism: The Effects of GATT/WTO on the Formation of Preferential Trade Agreements." *International Organization* 57 (4): 829–62.
Manuel Committee (Committee on IMF Governance Reform). 2009. Final Report, March 24. http://www.imf.org/external/np/omd/2009/govref/032409.pdf.
Manufacturing Institute. 2009. *The Facts about Modern Manufacturing*. 8th ed. Washington, DC: Manufacturing Institute.
Manza, Jeff, Michael Hout, and Clem Brooks. 1995. "Class Voting in Capitalist Democracies since World War II: Dealignment, Realignment, or Trendless Fluctuation?" *Annual Review of Sociology* 21:137–62.
Martin, Andrew. 1979. "The Dynamics of Change in a Keynesian Political Economy: The Swedish Case and Its Implications." In *State and Economy in Contemporary Capitalism*, edited by Colin Crouch, 88–121. London: Croom Helm.
Martinelli, Cesar, and Mariano Tommasi. 1997. "Sequencing of Economic Reforms in the Presence of Political Constraints." *Economics and Politics* 9 (2): 115–31.
Martinez-Alier, Juan. 2003. *The Environmentalism of the Poor: A Study of Ecological Conflicts and Valuation*. London: Edward Elgar.
Martynova, M., and L. Renneboog. 2010. "A Corporate Governance Index: Convergence and Diversity of National Corporate Governance Regulations." CentER Discussion Paper Series No. 2010–17, Department of Finance, Tilburg University.
McCarty, Nolan, Keith T. Poole, Thomas Romer, and Howard Rosenthal. 2010. "Political Fortunes: On Finance and its Regulation." *Daedalus* 139 (4): 61–73.
McCracken, Michael. 2010. "Disagreement at the FOMC: The Dissenting Votes Are Just Part of the Story." *Regional Economist* (October): 11–16.
McNamara, Kathleen. 1998. *The Currency of Ideas*. Ithaca, NY: Cornell University Press.
Megginson, William L. 2010. "Privatization and Finance." Working paper, Social Science Research Network, January 30. doi: 10.2139/ssrn.1544889.
Mian, Atif, Amir Sufi, and Francesco Trebbi. 2010a. "The Political Economy of the Subprime Mortgage Credit Expansion." Working Paper No. 16107. National Bureau of Economic Research, Cambridge, MA.
———. 2010b. "The Political Economy of the U.S. Mortgage Default Crisis." *American Economic Review* 100 (5): 1967–98.
Michalet, Charles-Albert. 1968. *Les Placements des épargnants français de 1815 à nos jours*. Paris: University Presses of France.
Milgrom, Paul, and John Roberts. 1995. "Complementarities and Fit: Strategy, Structure and Organizational Change in Manufacturing." *Journal of Accounting and Economics* 19:179–208.
Milner, Helen V. 1988. *Resisting Protectionism: Global Industries and the Politics of International Trade*. Princeton, NJ: Princeton University Press.
———. 1997. *Interests, Institutions, and Information*. Princeton, NJ: Princeton University Press.

Milner, Helen, and Keiko Kubota. 2005. "Why the Move to Free Trade? Democracy and Trade Policy in the Developing Countries." *International Organization* 59 (1): 107–43.

Milner, Helen, and B. Peter Rosendorff. 1997a. "Appendix." In *Interests, Institutions and Information: Domestic Politics and International Relations*, edited by Helen Milner, 263–74. Princeton, NJ: Princeton University Press.

———. 1997b. "Democratic Politics and International Trade Negotiations: Elections and Divided Government as Constraints on Trade Liberalization." *Journal of Conflict Resolution* 41 (1): 117–47.

Minsky, Hyman P. 1975. *John Maynard Keynes*. New York: Columbia University Press.

———. 1982. *Can "It" Happen Again?* New York: M. E. Sharpe.

Miyazaki, Hirokazu. 2007. "Between Arbitrage and Speculation: An Economy of Belief and Doubt." *Economy and Society* 36 (3): 396–415.

Moen, Ellis W., and Jon R. Tallman. 1990. "Lessons from the Panic of 1907." *Federal Reserve Bank of Atlanta Economic Review* 75 (3): 2–13.

Monks, Robert A. G. 2007. *Corpocracy*. New York: Wiley.

Monks, Robert A. G., and Nell Minow. 1996. *Watching the Watchers*. Oxford: Blackwell.

Montebourg, Arnaud. 2011. *Votez pour la démondialisation*. Paris: Flammarion.

Moriguchi, Chiaki, and Emmanuel Saez. 2008. "The Evolution of Income Concentration in Japan, 1886–2005: Evidence from Income Tax Statistics." *Review of Economics and Statistics* 90 (4): 713–34.

Munich Re Group. 2004a. "Occupational Diseases: Are They Insurable?" Discussion paper prepared by the Worker's Compensation Center of Competence, Munich Re Group, December.

———. 2004b. "Underground Transportation Systems: Chances and Risks from the Reinsurer's Point of View." Munich Re Group.

———. 2009. "Insurance-linked Securities (ILS)." Market Update Q2 2009. Risk Trading Unit, Munich Re Group, July.

———. 2010. "Managing for Value in an Uncertain Economic and Regulatory Environment." Paper presented at the Morgan Stanley European Financials Conference, London, March 24.

———. 2011. "Caught between Low Interest Rates and the Risk of Inflation." Topics Online 1/2011. Munich Re Group, January.

Murillo, Maria Victoria, Virginia Oliveros, and Milan Vaishnav. 2011. "Economic Constraints and Presidential Agency." In *The Resurgence of the Latin American Left*, edited by Steven Levitsky and Kenneth Roberts, 52–70. Baltimore, MD: Johns Hopkins University Press.

Musgrave, Richard A. 1959. *The Theory of Public Finance: A Study in Public Economy*. New York: McGraw-Hill.

Nakagawa, Shinobu, and Yosuke Yasui. 2009. "A Note on Japanese Household Debt: International Comparison and Implications for Financial Stability." Paper No. 46, Bank for International Settlements, Basel.

Naoi, Atsushi. 1979. "Shokugyoteki Chiishakudo no Kosei (The Construction of the Occupational Status Scale)." In *Nihon no Kaiso Kozo*, edited by Ken'ichi Tominaga. Tokyo: Tokyodaigakushuppankai.

Naoi, Megumi, and Ikuo Kume. 2011. "Explaining Mass Support for Agricultural Protectionism: Evidence from a Survey Experiment during the Global Recession." *International Organization* 65 (4): 771–95.

Nardulli, Peter F. 1995. "The Concept of Critical Realignment, Electoral Behavior, and Political Change." *American Political Science Review* 89 (1): 10–22.

Nelson, Joan M. 1990. *Economic Crisis and Policy Choice: The Politics of Adjustment in the Third World.* Princeton, NJ: Princeton University Press.

Nelson, Stephen, and Peter J. Katzenstein. 2011. "Uncertainty, Risk and the Crisis of 2008." Unpublished paper, Political Science Department, Northwestern University, Evanston, IL.

Noel, Alain.1987. "Accumulation, Regulations, and Social Change: An Essay on French Political Economy." *International Organization* 41 (2): 303–33.

Noyes, Alexander D. 1909. "A Year after the Panic of 1907." *Quarterly Journal of Economics* 23 (2): 185–212.

Oatley, Thomas. 2011. "The Reductionist Gamble: Open Economy Politics in the Global Economy." *International Organization* 65 (Spring): 311–41.

O'Connor, James. 1973. *The Fiscal Crisis of the State.* New York: St. Martin's Press.

Oesch, Daniel. 2008. "The Changing Shape of Class Voting: An Individual-Level Analysis of Party Support in Britain, Germany and Switzerland." *European Societies* 10 (3): 329–55.

Offe, Claus. 1983. "Competitive Party Democracy and the Keynesian Welfare State: Factors of Stability and Disorganization." *Policy Sciences* 15:225–46.

———. 1985. *Disorganized Capitalism.* Cambridge, MA: MIT Press.

Olson, Mancur. 1965. *The Logic of Collective Action: Public Goods and the Theory of Groups.* Cambridge, MA: Harvard University Press.

Organisation for Economic Cooperation and Development (OECD). 2009a. *Agricultural Policies in OECD Countries: Monitoring and Evaluation.* Geneva: OECD.

———. 2009b. *OECD Economic Outlook 85.* Paris: OECD.

Organisation for Economic Cooperation and Development, World Trade Organization, United Nations Conference on Trade and Development (OECD-WTO-UNCTAD). 2009. "Report on G20 Trade and Investment Measures." September.

———. 2010. "Report on G20 Trade and Investment Measures." March.

O'Rourke, Kevin, and Richard Sinnott. 2002. "The Determinants of Individual Trade Policy Preferences." In *Brookings Trade Forum*, edited by Susan M. Collins and Dani Rodrik, 157–206. Washington, DC: Brookings Institution.

Pagano, Marco, and Paolo F. Volpin. 2005a. "Managers, Workers, and Corporate Control." *Journal of Finance* 60 (2): 841–68.

———. 2005b. "The Political Economy of Corporate Governance." *American Economic Review* 95 (4): 1005–30.

Pahre, Robert. 2006. "Divided Government and International Cooperation: An Overview." In *Democratic Foreign Policy Making: Problems of Divided Government and International Cooperation*, edited by Robert Pahre, 1–20. New York: Palgrave Macmillan.

Palier, Bruno, and Kathleen Thelen. 2010. "Institutionalizing Dualism: Complementarities and Change in France and Germany." *Politics and Society* 38 (1): 119–48.

Palley, Thomas. 2011. "Explaining Global Financial Imbalances: A Critique of the Savings Glut and Reserve Currency Hypotheses." Working Paper 13/2011, Macro Economic Policy Institute.

———. 2012. "The Economic and Geo-Political Implications of China-Centric Globalization." New America Foundation, Washington, DC, February.

Park, Jong Hee, and Nate Jensen. 2007. "Electoral Competition and Agricultural Support for OECD Countries." *American Journal of Political Science* 51 (2): 314–29.

Parti Socialiste. 2011. "Projet 2012." http://www.parti-socialiste.fr/static/11069/les-30-propositions-le-4-pages-110384.pdf?issuusl=ignore.

Partnoy, Frank. 2001. "Barbarians at the Gatekeepers? A Proposal for a Modified Strict Liability Regime." *Washington University Law Quarterly* 79. http://dx.doi.org/10.2139/ssrn.281360.

Paulson, H. M., Jr. 2010. *On the Brink: Inside the Race to Stop the Collapse of the Global Financial System.* New York: Business Plus.

Persson, Torsten, and Lars E. O. Svensson. 1989. "Why a Stubborn Conservative Would Run a Deficit: Policy with Time-Inconsistent Preferences." *Quarterly Review of Economics* 104 (2): 324–45.

Pettersson-Lidbom, Per. 2001. "An Empirical Investigation of the Strategic Use of Debt." *Journal of Political Economy* 109 (3): 570–83.

Phillips, Nicola, and Catherine E. Weaver, eds. 2010. *International Political Economy: Debating the Past, Present, and Future.* New York: Routledge.

Phillips, Warren, and Richard Rimkunas. 1978. "The Concept of Crisis in International Politics." *Journal of Peace Research* 15 (3): 259–72.

Pierson, Paul. 1996. "The New Politics of the Welfare State." *World Politics* 48 (2): 143–79.

———, ed. 2001. *The New Politics of the Welfare State.* New York: Oxford University Press.

Pinto, Pablo, and Santiago M. Pinto. 2008. "The Politics of Investment: Partisanship and the Sectoral Allocation of Foreign Direct Investment." *Economics and Politics* 20 (2): 216–54.

Pinto, Pablo, Stephen Weymouth, and Peter Gourevitch. 2010. "The Politics of Stock Market Development." *Review of International Political Economy* 17 (2): 378–409.

Piore, Michael, and Charles Sabel. 1984. *The Second Industrial Divide.* New York: Basic Books.

Pizzorno, Alessandro. 1978. "Political Exchange and Collective Identity in Industrial Conflict." In *The Resurgence of Class Conflict in Western Europe since 1968*, edited by Colin Crouch and Alessandro Pizzorno, 277–98. London: Macmillan.

Pollard, Sidney. 1985. "Capital Exports, 1870–1914: Harmful or Beneficial?" *Economic History Review* 38 (4): 489–514.

Pontusson, Jonas, and Peter Swenson. 1996. "Labor Markets, Production Strategies, and Wage Bargaining Institutions: The Swedish Employer Offensive in Comparative Perspective." *Comparative Political Studies* 29 (April): 223–50.

Prasad, Eswar, and M. Ayhan Kose. 2010. *Emerging Markets: Resilience and Growth amid Global Turmoil.* Washington, DC: Brookings Institution.

Prato, Giuseppe. 1912. *Le protectionnisme ouvrier.* Paris: Marcel Riviere.

Proissl, Wolfgang. 2010. *Why Germany Fell Out of Love with Europe.* Bruegel Essay and Lecture Series. Brussels: Bruegel.

Przeworski, Adam, and Michael Wallerstein. 1982. "The Structure of Class Conflict in Democratic Capitalist Societies." *American Political Science Review* 76:215–38.

Putnam, Robert D. 1988. "Diplomacy and Domestic Politics: The Logic of Two-Level Games." *International Organization* 42 (3): 427–60.

Raffalovitch, Arthur. 1931. "L'abominable vénalité de la presse." D'Après les Documents des Archives Russes (1897–1917). Paris: Librairie du Travail.

Rajan, Raghuram G. 2010. *Fault Lines: How Hidden Fractures Still Threaten the World Economy.* Princeton, NJ: Princeton University Press.

Rajan, Raghuram G., and Luigi Zingales. 2003. "The Great Reversals: The Politics of Financial Development in the Twentieth Century." *Journal of Financial Economics* 69 (1): 5–50.

Reinhart, Carmen M., and Vincent R. Reinhart. 2009. "Capital Flow Bonanzas: An Encompassing View of the Past and Present." In the *National Bureau of Economic*

Research (NBER) International Seminar in Macroeconomics 2008, edited by Jeffrey Frankel and Francesco Giavazzi, 1–54. Chicago: Chicago University Press.
Reinhart, Carmen M., and Kenneth Rogoff. 2009. *This Time Is Different: Eight Centuries of Financial Folly*. Princeton, NJ: Princeton University Press.
Ribière, Roger. 1913. *De l'admission à la cote dans les bourses françaises de valeurs*. Paris: A. Pedone.
Richards, John E. 2001. "Institutions for Flying: How States Built a Market in International Aviation Services." *International Organization* 55:993–1017.
Riles, Annelise. 2011. *Collateral Knowledge: Legal Reasoning in Global Financial Markets*. Chicago: University of Chicago Press.
Rodrik, Dani. 1995. "Political Economy of Trade Policy." In *Handbook of International Economics*, edited by Gene M. Grossman and Kenneth Rogoff, vol. 3, 1457–94. Amsterdam: Elsevier B.V.
———. 1998. "Why Do More Open Economies Have Bigger Governments." *Journal of Political Economy* 106 (5): 997–1032.
Roe, Mark J. 1994. *Strong Managers, Weak Owners*. Princeton, NJ: Princeton University Press.
———. 2003. *Political Determinants of Corporate Governance*. Oxford: Oxford University Press.
Rogoff, Kenneth. 2010. "No Need for a Panicked Fiscal Surge." *Wall Street Journal*, July 20.
Rogowski, Ronald. 1987. "Political Cleavages and Changing Exposure to Trade." *American Political Science Review* 81 (4): 1121–37.
———. 1989. *Commerce and Coalitions*. Princeton, NJ: Princeton University Press.
Rogowski, Ronald, and Mark A. Kayser. 2002. "Majoritarian Electoral Systems and Consumer Power: Price-Level Evidence from OECD." *American Journal of Political Science* 46 (3): 526–39.
Romer, Christina D., and David H. Romer. 2008. "The FOMC versus the Staff: Where Can Policymakers Add Value?" *American Economic Review* 98 (2): 230–35.
Romer, David H. 2010. "A New Data Set on Monetary Policy: The Economic Forecasts of Individual Members of the FOMC." *Journal of Money, Credit, and Banking* 42 (5): 951–57.
Romer, Paul M. 1990. "Endogenous Technological Change." *The Journal of Political Economy* 98 (5): S71–S102
Roubini, Nouriel, and Stephen Mihm. 2010. *Crisis Economics: A Crash Course in the Future of Finance*. New York: Penguin Press.
Rueda, David. 2005. "Insider-Outsider Politics in Industrialized Democracies: The Challenge to Social Democratic Parties." *American Political Science Review* 99:61–74.
Ruggie, Gerald. 1982. "International Regimes, Transactions, and Change: Embedded Liberalism in the Postwar Economic Order." *International Organization* 36 (2): 379–415.
Rust, Michael Jared. 1973. "Business and Politics in the Third Republic: The Comité des Forges and the French Steel Industry, 1896–1914." PhD dissertation, Princeton University, Princeton, NJ.
Sally, Razeen. 2007. "The Social Market and Liberal Order: Theory and Policy Implications." *Government and Opposition* 29 (4): 461–76.
Sandbrook, Dominic. 2010. *State of Emergency: The Way We Were. Britain. 1970–1974*. London: Allen Lane.
Schaede, Ulrike. 2008. *Choose and Focus: Japan's Business Strategies for the 21st Century*. Ithaca, NY: Cornell University Press.
Scharpf, Fritz, and Vivien Schmidt. 2000. *Welfare and Work in the Open Economy: From Vulnerability to Competitiveness*. Oxford: Oxford University Press.

Schelkle, Waltraud. 2010. "Consumer Protection—Social Policy in Disguise or on Display? Attempts at Regulating Mortgage Credit in the EU and the U.S." Paper presented at the conference on the Social Policy Dimension of Regulatory Crisis Management in the EU and the US, Social Science Research Center (WZB), Berlin, November 19.

Scheufele, Dietram. 2000. "Agenda-Setting, Priming, and Framing Revisited: Another Look at Cognitive Effects of Political Communication." *Mass Communication and Society* 3 (2–3): 297–316.

Schlesinger, Arthur M., Jr. 1957. *The Crisis of the Old Order, 1919–1933*. Boston: Houghton Mifflin.

Schmitter, Philippe, and Gerhard Lehmbruch, eds. 1979. *Trends toward Corporatist Intermediation*. Beverly Hills, CA: Sage.

Schoenfield, Andrew. 1965. *Modern Capitalism*. London: Oxford University Press.

Schumpeter, Joseph A. 1939. *Business Cycles: A Theoretical, Historical, and Statistical Analysis of the Capitalist Process*. New York: McGraw-Hill.

———. 1961. *The Theory of Economic Development: An Inquiry into Profits, Capital, Credit, Interest, and the Business Cycle*. Translated by Redvers Opie. New York: Oxford University Press.

Schwartz, Herman. 2009. *Subprime Nation: American Power, Global Finance, and the Housing Bubble*. Ithaca, NY: Cornell University Press.

———. 2012. "Finance and the State in the Housing Bubble." In *Subprime Cities: The Political Economy of Mortgage Markets*, edited by Manuel Aalbers, 53–73. New York: Wiley-Blackwell.

Schwartz, Herman, and Leonard Seabrook, eds. 2009. *The Politics of Housing Booms and Busts*. Basingstoke, UK: Palgrave Macmillan.

Sewell, William H. 1996. "Three Temporalities: Toward an Eventful Sociology." In *The Historic Turn in the Human Sciences*, edited by Terrence J. McDonald, 245–80. Ann Arbor: University of Michigan Press.

Shih, Victor, and David Steinberg. 2011. "Interest Group Influence in Authoritarian States: The Political Determinants of Chinese Exchange Rate Policy." Unpublished manuscript, University of Oregon, Eugene.

Shin, Hyun Song. 2011. "The Global Banking Glut and Loan Risk Premium." Paper presented at the 12th Jacques Polak Annual Research Conference, International Monetary Fund, Washington, DC, November 10–11.

Shinn, James. 2011a. "Future Shocks." *Institutional Investor* (July): 52–60.

———. 2011b. "Political Diligence Is the Key to Successful Trading." *Institutional Investor*, March 14. http://www.iimagazine.com/banking_capital_markets/Articles/2785731/Political-Diligence-is-the-Key-to-Successful-Trading.html.

Shonfield, Andrew. 1969. *Modern Capitalism*. Oxford: Oxford University Press.

Sil, Rudra, and Peter J. Katzenstein. 2010. *Beyond Paradigms: Analytic Eclecticism in the Study of World Politics*. New York: Palgrave.

Simmons, Beth. 2004. *Who Adjusts? Domestic Sources of Foreign Economic Policy*. Princeton, NJ: Princeton University Press.

Sinclair, Timothy J. 2009. "Let's Get It Right This Time! Why Regulation Will Not Solve or Prevent Global Financial Crises," *International Political Sociology* 3 (4): 450–53.

Sinn, Hans-Werner. 1999. *The German State Banks: Global Players in the International Financial Markets*. Cheltenham, UK: Edward Elgar.

Skocpol, Theda, and Vanessa Williamson. 2011. *The Tea Party and the Remaking of American Conservatism*. New York: Oxford University Press.

Slaughter, Matthew, and Kenneth F. Scheve. 2004. "Economic Insecurity and the Globalization of Production." *American Journal of Political Science* 48 (4): 662–74.

Sniderman, Paul M. 2000. "Taking Sides: A Fixed Choice Theory of Political Reasoning." In *Elements of Reason: Cognition, Choice, and the Bounds of Rationality*, edited by Arthur Lupia, Mathew D. McCubbins, and Samuel L. Popkin, 67–84. New York: Cambridge University Press.

Solow, Robert. 1999. "The Amateur: Making Billions and Misunderstanding the Market." *New Republic*, February 8.

———. 2010. "The Bigger They Are. . . ." *Daedalus* 139 (4): 22–30.

Soros, George. 1987. *The Alchemy of Finance*. Hoboken, NJ: Wiley.

———. 1998. *The Crisis of Global Capitalism: Open Society Endangered*. New York: Public Affairs.

———. 2008. *The New Paradigm for Financial Markets: The Credit Crisis of 2008 and What It Means*. New York: Public Affairs.

———. 2009. "The Soros Lectures." *Financial Times*, October 26–30. http://www.ft.com/indepth/soros-lectures.

Soskice, David. 1990. "Wage Determination: The Changing Role of Institutions in Advanced Industrialized Countries." *Oxford Review of Economic Policy* 6 (4): 36–61.

Soskice, David, and Torben Iversen. 2000. "The Non-Neutrality of Monetary Policy with Large Price or Wage Setters." *Quarterly Journal of Economics* 115 (1): 265–84.

Spiller, Pablo T., and Mariano Tommasi. 2007. *The Institutional Foundations of Public Policy in Argentina: A Transactions Cost Approach*. New York: Cambridge University Press.

Stein, Arthur. 1991. *Why Nations Cooperate*. Ithaca, NY: Cornell University Press.

Stevens, Albert C. 1894. "Analysis of the Phenomena of the Panic in the United States in 1893." *Quarterly Journal of Economics* 8 (2): 117–98.

Stiglitz, Joseph. 2003. *The Roaring Nineties*. New York: W.W. Norton.

Stolper, W., and P. Samuelson. 1941. "Protection and Real Wages." *Review of Economic Studies* 9 (1): 58–73.

Story, Louise, and Graham Bowley. 2011. "Market Swings Are Becoming New Standard." *New York Times*, September 11. http://www.nytimes.com/2011/09/12/business/economy/stock-markets-sharp-swings-grow-more-frequent.html?_r=2andhp.

Streeck, Wolfgang. 1991. "On the Institutional Conditions for Diversified Quality Production." In *Beyond Keynesianism*, edited by Egon Matzner and Wolfgang Streeck, 21–61. Aldershot, UK: Edward Elgar.

———. 2011. "The Crises of Democratic Capitalism." *New Left Review* 71 (September–October): 5–29.

Streeck, Wolfgang, and Christine Trampusch. 2005. "Economic Reform and the Political Economy of the German Welfare State." *German Politics* 14 (2): 174–95.

Streeck, Wolfgang, and Kozo Yamamura, eds. 2001. *The Origins of Non-Liberal Capitalism: Germany and Japan in Comparison*. Ithaca, NY: Cornell University Press.

Subramanian, Arvind. 2011. "The Crisis and the Two Globalization Fetishes." In *New Ideas on Development after the Financial Crisis*, edited by Nancy Birdsall and Francis Fukuyama, 68–84. Baltimore, MD: Johns Hopkins University Press.

Suleiman, Ezra N. 1974. *Politics, Power, and Bureaucracy in France: The Administrative Elite*. Princeton, NJ: Princeton University Press.

Suominen, Kati. 2009. "A New Age of Protectionism: The Economic Crisis and Transatlantic Trade." Brussels Forum Paper Series, German Marshall Fund of the United States, Washington, DC. http://209.200.80.89//doc/Suominen%20final.pdf.

Svedberg, Peter. 1978. "The Portfolio-Direct Composition of Private Foreign Investment in 1914 Revisited." *Economic Journal* 88 (December): 763–77.

Swedberg, Richard. 2004. "On Legal Institutions and Their Role in the Economy." In *The Sociology of the Economy*, edited by Frank Dobbin, 74–92. New York: Russell Sage.

Talvi, Eduardo, and C. Vegh. 2005. "Tax Base Variability and Pro-cyclical Fiscal Policy in Developing Countries." *Journal of Development Economics* 78 (1): 156–90.

Taylor, John B. 2009. *Getting Off Track: How Government Actions and Interventions Caused, Prolonged, and Worsened the Financial Crisis*. Palo Alto, CA: Hoover Institution Press.

Testis. 1907. *Le rôle des Etablissements de Crédit en France. La vérité sur les propos de Lysis.* Paris: Aux Bureaux de la Revue Politique & Parlementaire.

Thatcher, Mark. 2004. "Winners and Losers in Europeanization: Reforming the National Regulation of Telecommunications." *West European Politics* 27 (2): 102–27.

Thelen, Kathleen. 2004. *How Institutions Evolve: The Political Economy of Skills in Germany, Britain, the United States, and Japan*. New York: Cambridge University Press.

Thelen, Kathleen, and Ikuo Kume. 1999. "The Effects of Globalization on Labor Revisited: Lessons from Germany and Japan." *Politics and Society* 27 (December): 477–505.

Tiberghien, Yves. 2007. *Entrepreneurial States: Reforming Corporate Governance in France, Japan, and Korea*. Ithaca, NY: Cornell University Press.

Tilly, Richard. 1991. "International Aspects of the Development of German Banking." In *International Banking*, edited by Rondo Cameron and V. I. Bovykin, 90–112. Oxford: Oxford University Press.

Tokarick, Stephen. 2008. "Dispelling Some Misconceptions about Agricultural Trade Liberalization." *Journal of Economic Perspectives* 22 (1): 199–216.

Tomz, Michael. 2007. *Reputation and International Cooperation*. Princeton NJ: Princeton University Press.

Tornell, A. 1995. "Are Economic Crises Necessary for Trade Liberalization and Fiscal Reform? The Mexican Experience" In *Reform, Recovery, and Growth*, edited by Rudiger Dornbusch and Sebastian Edwards, 51–75. Chicago: University of Chicago Press.

Trentmann, Frank. 1998. "Political Culture and Political Economy: Interest, Ideology, and Free Trade." *Review of International Political Economy* 5 (2): 217–51.

———. 2008. *Free Trade Nation*. Oxford: Oxford University Press.

Truman, Edwin M. 2008. "Asia's Interests in IMF Reform." Remarks at the High-Level Dialogue on Asian Perspectives on the Future Role of the International Monetary Fund, Singapore, January 18. http://www.iie.com/publications/papers/paper.cfm?ResearchID=869.

Trumbull, Gunnar. 2012. *Consumer Credit in Postwar America and France*. New York: Cambridge University Press.

Tsebelis, George, and Eric C. C. Chang. 2004. "Veto Players and the Structure of Budgets in Advanced Industrialized Countries." *European Journal of Political Research* 43 (3): 449–76.

Tuckett, David. 2011. *Minding the Markets: An Emotional Finance View of Financial Instability*. New York: Palgrave Macmillan.

Tyson, Laura. 2009. "A Progressive Agenda for Competitiveness and Trade." In *Change for America: A Progressive Blueprint for the 44th President*, edited by Mark Green and Michele Jolin, 78–89. New York: Basic Books.

Useem, Michael. 1993. *Executive Defense: Shareholder Power and Corporate Reorganization*. Cambridge, MA: Harvard University Press.

———. 1996. *Investor Capitalism: How Money Managers Are Changing the Face of America*. New York: Harper Collins.

U.S. International Trade Commission (USITC). 2010. *Small and Medium-Sized Enterprises: Characteristics and Performance.* USITC Publication 4189. Washington, DC: USITC.

Van Kersbergen, Kees, and Philip Manow, eds. 2009. *Religion, Class Coalitions, and Welfare States.* New York: Cambridge University Press.

Velasco, Andres. 1999. "A Model of Endogenous Fiscal Deficits and Delayed Fiscal Reforms." In *Fiscal Institutions and Fiscal Performance,* edited by James M. Poterba and Jürgen von Hagen, 37–58. Chicago: University of Chicago Press.

Velikovsky, Immanuel. 1950. *Worlds in Collision.* Garden City, NY: Doubleday.

Visser, Jelle, and Anton Hemerijck. 1997. *A Dutch Miracle?* Amsterdam: Amsterdam University Press.

Vogel, Steven. 1998. *Freer Markets, More Rules: Regulatory Reform in Advanced Industrial Countries.* Ithaca, NY: Cornell University Press.

———. 1999. "When Interests Are Not Preferences: The Cautionary Tale of Japanese Consumers." *Comparative Politics* 31 (2): 187–207.

Wade, Robert 1990. *Governing the Market: Economic Theory and the Role of Government in East Asian Industrialization.* Princeton, NJ: Princeton University Press.

Wantchekon, Leonard. 2003. "Clientelism and Voting Behavior: Evidence from a Field Experiment in Benin." *World Politics* 55 (3): 399–422.

Warsh, David. 2006. *Knowledge and the Wealth of Nations.* New York: W. W. Norton.

Waseda University. 2009. Global Center of Excellence Program. Summary of Waseda CASI-PAPI 2009, conducted with Yomiuri Shimbun. http://www.globalcoe-glope2.jp/wcasi/summary09.pdf.

Weller, Nicholas. 2009. "Trading Policy: Constituents and Party in U.S. Trade Policy." *Public Choice* 141:87–101.

Wessel, David. 2009. *In Fed We Trust: Ben Bernanke's War on the Great Panic.* New York: Crown Business.

White, Harry D. 1933. *The French International Accounts, 1880–1913.* Cambridge, MA: Harvard University Press.

Wibbels, Erik. 2006. "Dependency Revisited: International Markets, Business Cycles, and Social Spending in the Developing World." *International Organization* 60 (2): 433–68.

Wibbels, Erik, and Moises Arce. 2003. "Globalization, Taxation, and Burden-Shifting in Latin America." *International Organization* 57:111–36.

Widmaier, Wesley W., Mark Blyth, and Leonard Seabrooke. 2007. "Exogenous Shocks or Endogenous Constructions? The Meanings of Wars and Crises." *International Studies Quarterly* 51:747–59.

Williamson, John, ed. 1990. *Latin American Adjustment: How Much Has Happened?* Washington, DC: Institute for International Economics.

Womack, James, Daniel T. Jones, and Daniel Roos.1991. *The Machine That Changed the World.* New York: Harper Perennial.

Wong, Joseph. 2011. *Betting on Biotech: Innovation and the Limits of Asia's Developmental State.* Ithaca, NY: Cornell University Press.

Wood, Adrian. 1994. *North-South Trade, Employment and Inequality: Changing Fortunes in a Skill-Driven World.* Oxford: Oxford University Press.

Woolley, John T., and J. Nicholas Ziegler. 2012. "The Two-Tiered Politics of Financial Reform in the United States." In *Crisis and Control: Institutional Change in Financial Market Regulation,* edited by Renate Mayntz, 29–65. Frankfurt: Campus.

World Bank. 1993. *East Asian Economic Miracle: Economic Growth and Public Policy.* London: Oxford University Press.

———. 2009. *Economic Policies Supporting Recovery in East Asia.* Washington, DC: World Bank.

———. 2011. World Development Indicators. http://data.worldbank.org/indicator/BN.CAB.XOKA.GD.ZS.

World Trade Organization (WTO). 2011. "Report on G20 Trade Measures (May to mid-October 2011)." WTO, Geneva, October 25.

Yi, Kei-Mu. 2009. "The Collapse of Global Trade: The Role of Vertical Specialization." In *The Collapse of Global Trade, Murky Protectionism, and the Crisis: Recommendations for the G20*, edited by Richard Baldwin and Simon Evenett, 45–48. London: Centre for Economic Policy Research.

Zhang, Yanchun, Nina Thelen, and Aparna Rao. 2010. "Social Protection in Fiscal Stimulus Packages: Some Evidence." Working paper, Development Program, United Nations.

Zimmermann, Eduardo. 1995. *Los liberales reformistas.* Buenos Aires: Editorial Sudamericana.

Zingales, Luigi. 2000. "In Search of New Foundations." *Journal of Finance* 55:1623–53.

Zysman, John, and Abraham Newman, eds. 2006. *How Revolutionary Was the Digital Revolution? National Responses, Market Transitions, and Global Technology.* Stanford, CA: Stanford University Press.

About the Contributors

Suzanne Berger is Raphael Dorman and Helen Starbuck Professor of Political Science at the Massachusetts Institute of Technology. Her previous writing on the politics of globalization includes *How We Compete* (2005) and *National Diversity and Global Capitalism* (with Ronald Dore, 1996). She currently leads an MIT research project on the future of manufacturing (Production in the Innovation Economy Commission).

J. Lawrence Broz is associate professor of Political Science at the University of California, San Diego. Broz has held faculty appointments at Harvard University and New York University and received his PhD from the University of California, Los Angeles, in 1993. He is the author of *International Origins of the Federal Reserve System* (1997), and his recent articles have appeared in a number of top journals, including the *American Journal of Political Science* and *International Organization*. His research focuses on the institutions of monetary and financial policymaking—central banks and international financial institutions.

Peter Cowhey is dean and Qualcomm Professor at the School of International Relations and Pacific Studies at the University of California, San Diego. In 2008–9, he co-chaired the presidential transition team on trade policy and then served as senior counselor to Ambassador Kirk in the Office of the U.S. Trade Representative, where he advised on the agenda for trade policy and supervised multiple USTR offices. Cowhey serves on the binational experts group appointed by the U.S. and Chinese governments on innovation policy. He served in the Clinton administration as the head of international policy for the Federal Communications Commission. His most recent book is *Transforming Global Information and Communications Markets: The Political Economy of Change* (MIT Press, 2009).

Peter A. Gourevitch is Distinguished Professor of Political Science at the School of International Relations and Pacific Studies, University of California, San Diego, of which he is also the founding dean. His book *Politics in Hard Times: Comparative Responses to International Crises* (Cornell, 1986) has been published in Spanish, Italian, and Chinese. *Political Power and Corporate Control: The New Global Politics of Corporate Control* (with James Shinn, Princeton, 2005) just appeared in Japanese. His most recent book, *Credibility and Non-Governmental Organizations in a Globalizing World* (co-edited with David Lake and Janice Stein) was published in 2012 by Cambridge University Press. Other publications focus on U.S.-Japan relations after the Cold War, international economic relations, and an essay on corporate governance published in the *Yale Law Journal* (2003). From 1996 to 2001, he co-edited, with David Lake, *International Organization*, a leading scholarly journal on international relations.

From 1991 to 2009, Gourevitch chaired the Council on Foreign Relations' International Area Fellows Program Selection Committee. In 1996, he was elected to the prestigious American Academy of Arts and Sciences. He taught at Harvard University from

1969 to 1974, at McGill University from 1974 to 1979, and joined UC San Diego's Political Science Department in 1979. Gourevitch received a PhD in political science from Harvard University in 1969 and his BA in government with high honors from Oberlin College in 1963.

Stephan Haggard is Krause Distinguished Professor at the Graduate School of International Relations and Pacific Studies, University of California, San Diego. His publications include *Pathways from the Periphery: the Political Economy of Growth in the Newly Industrializing Countries* (1990), and with Robert Kaufman, *The Political Economy of Democratic Transitions* (1995) and *Development, Democracy, and Welfare States: Latin America, East Asia and Eastern Europe* (2008). His work on financial crises includes *The Political Economy of the Asian Financial Crisis* (2000).

Peter A. Hall is Krupp Foundation Professor of European Studies in the Department of Government and a Faculty Associate of the Minda de Gunzburg Center for European Studies at Harvard University. He is the author of *Governing the Economy* (Oxford, 1986) and many articles on comparative political economy, and editor or co-editor of *The Political of Economic Ideas*, *Varieties of Capitalism* (with D. Soskice), *Changing France* (with B. Palier and P. Culpepper), as well as *Successful Societies* and *Social Resilience in the Neo-Liberal Era* (with M. Lamont). His current research focuses on institutional change in the developed political economies, the crisis of the Economic and Monetary Union, and social inequalities in health.

Miles Kahler is Rohr Professor of Pacific International Relations and Distinguished Professor of Political Science in the School of International Relations and Pacific Studies and the Political Science Department, University of California, San Diego. He was founding director of the Institute for International, Comparative, and Area Studies at UC San Diego. He has been a Fellow at the Center for Advanced Study in the Behavioral Sciences at Stanford University and a Senior Fellow at the Council on Foreign Relations.

Peter J. Katzenstein is Walter S. Carpenter Jr. Professor of International Studies at Cornell University. His current research interests focus on the politics of civilizational states; on questions of public diplomacy, law, religion, and popular culture; the role of anti-imperial sentiments, including anti-Americanism; regionalism in world politics; and German politics. Recent books include *Beyond Paradigms: Analytic Eclecticism in World Politics* (Palgrave, 2010), with Rudra Sil; *Civilizations in World Politics: Plural and Pluralist Perspectives* (Routledge, 2010); and *European Identity* (Cambridge University Press, 2009), co-edited with Jeffrey T. Checkel.

Ikuo Kume is a professor of political science at the School of Political Science and Economics, Waseda University, Tokyo. His publications include *Disparaged Success: Labor Politics in Postwar Japan* and "Coordination as a Political Problem in Coordinated Market Economies" in *Governance* 12 (1) (co-authored with Kathleen Thelen).

David A. Lake is Jerri-Ann and Gary E. Jacobs Professor of Social Sciences and Distinguished Professor of Political Science at the University of California, San Diego. He is the author of four books, co-editor of ten volumes, and author or co-author of more than 80 articles and book chapters on international relations, international political economy, and American foreign policy. Lake is the founding chair of the International Political

Economy Society and past president of the International Studies Association. The recipient of the Chancellor's Associates Award for Excellence in Graduate Education, he was elected to the American Academy of Arts and Sciences in 2006.

Megumi Naoi is an assistant professor of political science at the University of California, San Diego. She received her PhD from Columbia University in 2006. Her area of specialty is international and comparative political economy with a focus on the politics of globalization, especially trade, in East Asia. Her current projects include large-scale survey and experimental research on the responses of Japanese consumers, firms, and legislators to globalization and financial crisis, funded by the Japanese government's Grant-in-Aid for Scientific Research, and a survey experiment on American voters' attitudes toward financial crisis and bailout.

Stephen C. Nelson is an assistant professor of political science at Northwestern University. He received his PhD from Cornell University. His research interests span comparative and international political economy, the behavior of international organizations, and how economic agents and policymakers cope with risk and uncertainty. He was the 2010 recipient of the American Political Science Association's Helen Dwight Reid Award for the best dissertation in the field of international relations, law, and politics.

Pablo M. Pinto is an associate professor of political science at Columbia University. His areas of expertise are international and comparative political economy. His main research analyzes the causes and consequences of foreign investment. He is the author of *Partisan Investment in the Global Economy* (Cambridge University Press) and co-author of *Politics and FDI* (Michigan University Press). His research has been published or is forthcoming in *Economics and Politics, Comparative Political Studies, International Organization*, and the *Review of International Political Economy*, among other journals. Pinto received an MA from Aoyama Gakuin University in Japan and a PhD from the University of California, San Diego. He also received a law degree from Universidad Nacional de La Plata in Argentina.

James Shinn is a lecturer at Princeton University's School of Engineering and Applied Science. His research interests include risk management, corporate governance, and technical innovation. After careers on Wall Street and Silicon Valley, he served in the U.S. departments of State and Defense, as well as the Central Intelligence Agency. He has a BA from Princeton University, an MBA from Harvard University, and a PhD from Princeton University.

Index

Note: tables and figures are in italics.